RED BAIT!

RED BAIT!

Struggles of a Mine Mill Local

AL KING

with Kate Braid

RED BAIT: Struggles of a Mine Mill Local

CANADIAN CATALOGUING IN PUBLICATION DATA

King, Al, 1915-
  Red Bait!

  ISBN No. 0-9683768-0-0

  1. King, Al, 1915- 2. International Union of Mine, Mill and Smelter Workers. Local 480—Biography. 3. Trade- unions—British Columbia—Officals and employees—Biography. 4. Trade- unions—Miners—British Columbia—History. I. Braid, Kate. II. Title.
HD6525.K56A3 1998   331.88'122'092   c98- 910467-2

Front cover illustration:
Consolidated Mining and Smelting, Zinc Roaster crew, Trail BC, 1938 (photographer unknown). From left to right: Bianco (janitor), Bob Lyle, Tony Dibiassio (squatting), Fred Stoushnow, Frank Ash, Jim McDicken, Buck Jones and Al King. Back: Mowat Gowans and Bill Fowler. Trail, British Columbia, circa 1930s. Photo courtesy of Vancouver Public Library, Special Collections Photo #9401.

Editor: Linda Field
Cover design: Jim Brennan
Typesetting: Patty Osborne, Vancouver Desktop Publishing Centre
Printed in Canada by Transcontinental

Permission to reprint "Joe Hill" words and music by Alfred Hayes and Earl Robinson on page 167, from MCA Music Publishing. A Division of MCA Inc., 1755 Broadway, New York, NY 10019.

Kingbird Publishing
8096 Elliott Street
Vancouver, British Columbia, Canada
V5S2P2

*This book is dedicated to my family and to the people
of the Rossland-Trail District, British Columbia.*

CONTENTS

Foreword: Vince Ready

In 1963, several of us—contract miners working at the South Seas Mine in Ashcroft—went on a wildcat strike to shut the mine down over poor safety and working conditions. We weren't unionized at the time and we knew enough to shut it down but then what? And that's how I met Al King.

Contract miners—the ones who open up a new mine—are a wild bunch and Mine Mill was the only union that would take on organizing us. When Al came up, I was impressed at how carefully the man listened. He had all the patience in the world, explaining issues, teaching us, helping us work things out. He was a good trainer and leader, especially for young hotheads. He had great energy and knew how to mobilize people. He was—and is—a "go-for-it" kind of guy, so he wasn't hard to follow.

As he tells in this book, several of us in that strike ended up being hired by Al King as organizers for the International Union of Mine, Mill and Smelter Workers and I had the pleasure of working with him over the next several years. I was twenty years old at the time—the youngest organizer hired by Mine Mill. Under Al, we formed Local 1037 of the Shaft and Development Workers' Union. Mine Mill leadership went out of their way to maintain close ties with their members and there was a great sense of camaraderie in that union. No matter where you went in North America, you always felt like you were home. I spent many a pleasant afternoon in a Mine Mill office in some new town, visiting with local miners and exchanging news and stories.

In those days, as Al's book makes clear, being a union activist was pretty swashbuckling stuff. If you got into trouble there was no unfair labour practice law to bail you out, so you had to know how to survive a fight once it started. You had yourself and your fellow workers and not much law to back you up, and Al King is a fine example of that kind of creative leadership. He was also completely dedicated to the union movement—still is—one of the men who'll never turn his back on you, never let you down.

He is a very honest guy—you could take his word to the bank—and perhaps this was part of the reason for his tremendous ability to keep people's confidence, to hold them together and keep them in support of a cause through struggles and hard times.

He is an enormously compassionate man which is perhaps why he has been such a pioneer in the areas of occupational health and safety and Worker's Compensation. The widows of BC and across Canada owe him a lot. In his work for the families of men who died because of disease and illness due to their work, Al was noteworthy for taking up and challenging impossible claims. He would find some lead, do the appropriate research and take the claim forward to win it. He always knew whose chain to tweak at the WCB. That was his personality.

Don't get me wrong—Al King is not a saint. He can be short in the fuse and he'll never leave you in any doubt as to what he's thinking, but he was always very clear on his priorities, on his commitment to working people. As Al says, he always knew "which side he was on" and he fought, and continues to fight, for people who are treated unjustly. His dedication and compassion have no equal.

Al King had a tremendous influence on me in my early years in the labour movement. I learned from him the skills of leadership, organizing, negotiating, and working out honourable compromise. He showed me that there's always a way through the most difficult problems. I'm proud to still call him a friend.

Today it's important that stories like this one be recorded, not just so that we can honour the way the frontiers of the labour movement have been moved forward by pioneers like Al King, but also as a guiding light for direction for the future. Trade unionists like Al King have made a major contribution to society and to the current success and strength of the labour movement. His story, and that of others like him, need to be told—to all of us.

Vincent L. Ready
Labour Arbitrator and Mediator
Vancouver, BC
April 1998

Foreword: Kate Braid

first met Al King in 1992 when, as the new Director of Simon Fraser University's Labour Program, I interviewed him for a history of the BC Federation of Labour's Health and Safety Committee. The history was in honour of Marianne Gilbert, the first woman to chair the committee, and I was struck by the fact that the gracious and still-dynamic eighty year old man I was interviewing had not only suggested her as the chair, but had stepped aside himself to make room for her.

A year later I got a phone call from Al King. He wondered if I'd mind taking a look at a manuscript. The manuscript was tantalizing, provoking many questions. It named names and hinted at vital events in BC labour history, but with only fifty pages, it gave too few details.

I suggested Al find a writer to help him flesh out the story, recommended several and wished him luck. But Al kept phoning me back. In hindsight I think that, like any good trade unionist, he knew what he wanted and he was going to get it: he wanted me to help him write his book.

No. I was too busy. I'm a poet. I've never done this before. But in his gentle way, Al wouldn't take no for an answer and before I knew it I was agreeing to "just a few interviews." The result, you now hold in your hands. I guess you could say Al won. To my surprise, I won too.

Working with Albert Lorenzo King has been a delight, an honour and an education. We started with a few taped conversations that I later found embarassing. How could I have asked such stupid questions? Didn't I know anything about Mine Mill? The answer is no. All of it I learned from Al, and soon Lil, as we spent hour after hour at their kitchen table with me asking my poor questions while Lillian helped correct when a date or name went wrong and Al answered my questions with infinite patience.

Well, almost infinite. Occasionally, like when I asked yet again what it was like to be labelled a Communist in the '50s, his still-strong hand would smack down on the kitchen table top and he would say loudly, "Don't you get it?" I'd shake my head, Lillian would fill the teapot, and we'd start again.

The hardest things we talked about were his experience of being labelled a Communist in the '50s and his decision to support the merger into the Steelworker's union. The facts are here in Al's words, as he told it. What is not, and the reason I often yearned for radio more than a poor dumb pencil, was the power of his silence. Particularly on the day when I pushed him: "What was it like for you, personally, to give up the fight you'd fought all your life against Steel, and agree to merge?" At first I thought he hadn't heard me. I repeated the question and he muttered something.

"What?"

He was holding the teacup to his mouth so I almost couldn't hear the answer. His voice was thick as he said, "You're turning the knife in me." And I realized how painful some decisions had been.

The rest of the time, Al was an articulate chronicler with an astonishing memory. Once, trying to get straight who was who in the early days of organizing in Trail, I casually asked who was on his first crew (the crew pictured on the cover of this book). He proceeded to list the first and last names of some dozen men plus the names of the shift boss and foreman he had worked with, briefly, some sixty years earlier. When I expressed astonishment at such regular feats of memory, Al was always impatient. "Well, of course," he would say.

Somehow, this memory seems to me symptomatic of Al King. Apart from having a good memory, he simply cared enough about each individual he worked with to learn their names and their wive's and children's names, and often, where they came from and where they ended up. This seems symptomatic to me, of a man—a trade unionist—who cares passionately for ordinary working people. "It wasn't right!" he would exclaim, smacking the table over yet another injustice, another widow denied her husband's WCB pension. To this day, in his mid-eighties, Al King continues to pursue—and to win—appeals for workers at the BC Workers' Compensation Board.

This book is entirely the memories of Al King, in his own words. I have helped elicit the stories and organized them, encouraging Al to give details and background that would help explain, to those of us who weren't there, what was going on, what it was like to live during the tumultuous times in BC and Canada in which he played a key part. He and I have not agreed on everything, but where we disagreed, Al's voice is the one printed here.

I would like to thank the many people who helped me in my share of this book, especially Lynne Bowen at the University of British Columbia. Also sincere thanks to Olive Anderson, Emil Bjarnason, Bud DeVito, Jack Diamond, Jack MacDonald and Vince Ready , who helped with detail; Susan Meurer who cheered; Don Crane for legal relief; Linda Field for my sanity; George Brandak and the staff at the UBC Archives for digging out old files; and my partner, John Steeves, who kept the home fires burning. A special thanks to Ken Neumann and Andy King of the United Steelworkers of America for believing in the importance of this story.

But most of all, thank you Al and Lillian King, for taking me into your kitchen, your hearts and your family. It has been a great pleasure. I hope the story we have saved here will become part of a growing body of the stories of the amazing, "ordinary" people who built this country.

Introduction: Al King

When I first decided ten years ago to record my experiences in the International Union of Mine, Mill and Smelter Workers, I was motivated not to write a history as such (because I think that is the business of historians), but mainly to tell the story as I experienced it and to attempt to correct some of the incorrect and at times vindictive attacks on some of my colleagues in the labour movement who are no longer here to defend themselves.

This is the story of a young, ordinary worker's life in heavy industry in Trail BC, from the 1930s on. Beginning in 1938 with my commitment to the Mine Mill union, I became deeply involved in the tangle of union-employer relations that was in its second infancy in Canada at the time. The greatest part of these memoirs covers my many years of organizing and then defending Mine Mill from other unions and the years of my loyalty to the ideals of the Communist party and the terrible 'red scare' of the '40s, '50s and into the '60s that caused enormous anguish, not just in the labour movement, but in virtually every aspect of North American society.

My greatest satisfaction is that there is still a Local 480 union in Trail and that this is due to the efforts and struggles of the working people of all creeds and 'isms of Trail and District. It is to all these people, the workers and their families, and to my own family, that I respectfully dedicate this book.

The King family in Vancouver, BC. From left to right: Geri, Sherrill, Lorraine, Mavis, Al, Lillian, Wayne.

Acknowledgements: Al King

I wish to name and deeply thank the following individuals who have influenced my life: my mother and my father, my sisters, Nancy Burge, Patsy Isnor, Olive Anderson and Gwenny Gianfrancesco and my brothers Jack King, Ray King and William King. In Pincher Creek, Alberta I would like to thank the Birds, the Cooleys, the Schoenings and the Chiesas.

In BC I would like to thank the Rev. Robert Stott, Harry Drake, Bill and Marian Bagg, Alf and Maggie Jenkins, Remo and Ilda Morandini, Nancy Green, Martin and Marie Walsh, Pearl Chytuk, Nels and Marie Thibault, Joyce and Bill Muir, Dulcie and Al Warrington and Sheila, George Gagne, Gar Grant, Kay and Dan Dosen, Tillie and Gar Belanger, Ed Benson and Gordon Martin, Jack Walton, the Bjarnasons, Bruce York, Carl Liden, Mr and Mrs. Mel Brown, Homer Stevens, Rosaleen Ross, Lil and Lorne Robson, Flo Mays, Mr. and Mrs. Dusty Greenwell and the Sid Sheards, the Nelmes and the Flobergs, George and Lillian Gee and son Jim, Geri Da Rosa and Bobby Kromm, Jim Kinnaird and Cliff Worthington, the McIntyres, the Maileys and Ab Cronie, the Banatynes, Doug Cameron and Tom Berger, Monica and Pete Stiles, the Alec McCormick Family, Shirley and Jim Forsythe, Neil and June McLeod, Eric and Leonora Inglis and Leslie Koziel.

Also Peter Steen, Pat Gillick, Doug Gold, Kay and Ken Smith, Jim Clifford and Tina and Jack Diamond. Harvey Parliament, Jack Merrett and Sam Elias, Don and Elspeth Munro, John Baigent, Harry Rankin, Peter Gzowski, Ray Gardner, Penrod Baskin, Jim and Elaine Duval, Connie Munroe and Paul Petrie, Elmer Pontius, Bob and Linda Baird, Clem Thompson, Neil Munro, John Baigent, Andy Dembicki, Bill Copeland and many, many others. Finally I would like to acknowledge all the silicosis widows—too many to be named, but they know who they are. God bless 'em.

My thanks also to the following who assisted with the actual manuscript: Olive Anderson, Bud DeVito, Jack Diamond, Mavis Floberg, Rosa Jordan, Lil King, Jack MacDonald, Joe Mukanik, Vince Ready, Ann and Howie Smith and Geri Thompson. Also John Mansbridge and Bill Sloan of Selkirk College.

A special thanks to the Local 480 Executive and to Ken Neumann of the USWA and finally, to my friend, editor and vulgarity expunger, Kate Braid.

GUIDE TO ABBREVIATIONS

AFL American Federation of Labour

CCF Co-operative Commonwealth Federation, later the New Democratic Party.

CCL Canadian Congress of Labour, later the CLC.

CCU Canadian Congress of Unions, later the CLC.

CIO Committee of Industrial Organization, later Congress of Industrial Organizations

CLC Canadian Labour Congress

CM&S Consolidated Mining and Smelting Company; later (as of 1966) Cominco. Owner and operator of the smelter in Trail, B.C.

Cominco current name by which the Consolidated Mining and Smelting Company is known

IWW Industrial Workers of the World, commonly known as Wobblies.

IUMMSW International Union of Mine Mill and Smelter Workers, commonly abbreviated to Mine Mill.

LPP The Labour Progressive Party, the political arm of the Communist Party in Canada.

NDP New Democratic Party

OBU One Big Union.

SWOC Steel Workers Organizing Committee.

TLC Trades and Labour Congress, precursor of the Canadian Labour Congress.

UAW United Auto Workers (now CAW or Canadian Auto Workers in Canada).

UE United Electrical, Radio and Machine Workers.

UMWA United Mine Workers of America (primarily a coal miner's union).

WFM Western Federation of Miners, later IUMMSW.

WUL Workers' Unity League, the Communist labour organizing arm in the 1930s.

PART I

Getting To Trail

I was born and raised in Manchester, England, in the small parish of St. Anthony, a Catholic enclave surrounded by an ocean of Protestants. There were eight kids in our family—four boys and four girls, four red heads and four brunettes—and once they started, they came pretty steady. After Jack, the eldest, in 1911, there was Nancy in 1913; myself, at that time called just Albert, on March 3, 1915; Patsy in 1919; Olive in 1921, who would later be secretary and assistant to Harvey Murphy of Mine Mill; Gwennie in 1923; and Ray in 1925. The youngest, William, was born in 1930 after we moved to Saskatchewan. As Bill King, he would one day be the Minister of Labour under Dave Barrett and British Columbia's first New Democratic government.

There were four Communists in our family of ten—my mother, my sisters Olive and Patsy, and myself. Mother joined the Party later in life, when she came out to BC. Long before that, she married my father, Patrick, in Manchester, England in 1909.

Mother's name was Evans, Minnie Agnes Evans: same name as Art Evans who later helped us organize the Trail smelter. Mother was a good-looking woman, tall and slim with beautiful, curly black hair. She was Welsh, a suffragette and a fighter. I'm not sure where she got the fighting streak because her folks were not left-wing, though her grandfather, my great-grandfather, was a Welsh coal miner. My grandfather and his wife, my grandmother Annie Evans, thought the sun rose and set in British Prime Minister David Lloyd George's asshole, because he was Welsh. My mother never did support Lloyd George, a Liberal, but she hated the Tories worse than poison. I recall as a young kid listening to my mum argue with her mother, her stepfather and her two brothers. She always took the point of view of the underdog. She was also an organizer, doing things like organizing a "book club." She got all the local women to give one shilling a week each to the club. Then each took turns getting the total of that week's collection so she could buy something large, like winter clothes or shoes for the kids.

She also loved writing poetry. At any moment during the day she might think of something, pick up a scrap of paper and scribble a poem on it. Her

The King family.
Back row: Gwennie,
Albert, Jack, Raymond.
Front row: Patricia,
Patrick, William, Minnie,
Olive

poems used to lie all around the house and for years after she died, we kept finding them inside recipe books, tucked into apron pockets and in odd corners.

She married an Irish man, Patrick Joseph King, who wasn't particularly progressive, though he did join the CCF when he became a farmer in Canada. His father was a farmer and a wheelwright back in Eire.

My father was just short of six feet tall and was a very tough, physical man known for his fighting abilities. He fought in both World Wars. He had a dark brown, curly head of hair and whiskers red as a fox's arse, but when he came out of World War I, after three years and nine months in the trenches, his hair was white as snow. He was in the Irish Fusiliers and in the first retreat from Mons where he won the Mons Star, but when he came back, he was all buggered up and drank too much.

Dad was a hard-working man. He was big, well-muscled and solidly built, and a good farmer because he'd grown up on a farm in Ireland. In his family there were ten children—a boy and a girl, a boy and a girl, five times over. When he was still a youth, he emigrated to England after his father died. My family were devout Catholics—still are. When I went over to visit them in Ireland years later, my uncle gave me a rosary and took me to church before I could go to Moonie's bar.

The Protestants of Manchester didn't treat our family kindly. We were considered, well, "different," and kids being kids, they never let us forget it.

Stone throwing and pitched battles were not unusual and more than once I had to run very fast and dodge my way home. Pretty early on, I learned how to fight—not from my dad but from a friend of his, an old Welsh boxer named Charlie Parry. Charlie taught me the right way—clean and honest, not just street fighting—and I used everything he taught me, not only as a kid but later, during some of the darker days of union raids.

After the first war, my dad worked for the Ford Motor Company in Manchester, but when the Depression came in 1926, he lost his job. Mother knew how to write letters—she had a beautiful hand—so she started writing to get us the hell out of the Manchester smog and depression, but Dad didn't want to leave. He had his sisters and his family and all his cronies in the Legion, but once Mother made up her mind, there was no stopping her. She was turned down by Australia, so she wrote to New Zealand and then Canada. They all turned her down. You see, if you emigrated, you were supposed to have your health, and one of my sisters, Gwennie, had asthma, and Olive had a heart murmur. Mum just kept writing. Damned if I know how she did it, but after a mess of letters, she finally got us the okay to immigrate to Canada, to northern Saskatchewan, under the Soldier's Settlement Board.

After we got permission, we found out it excluded Gwennie, the two-year-old, because of her weak heart. Mother went in and argued that if she left her daughter in Manchester, the child would surely die, and that only the clean Canadian air could make her better. My sister was allowed to come.

Then Immigration told us that for reasons of weight, we couldn't bring any furniture, including Mother's sewing machine. Mum sewed clothes for the entire family and there was sure no money to buy them—she had to have that sewing machine. So she quietly dismantled it, hid the bits and pieces all through the baggage and put it back together again when we were in Canada.

We arrived in Canada in the spring of 1928. One month, I was in a big Manchester Council School with forty-six boys in my class, and a few months later I was pulling a cow's teats! I turned thirteen on the boat on the way over.

Within a year we were in the depths of the Great Depression. Mostly I remember hardship. We'd come out of a huge, industrial English city and landed in the wilderness of northern Saskatchewan where we didn't know anybody and where we were looked upon as greenhorns who might just as well go back where we came from. The Canadian government wouldn't provide us land until we proved we could survive. There were lots of people, born Canadians, in the same boat as us, with no money and no land of their own. It was tough.

After one term of school I had to drop out and work. We all had to, to earn money. I was only thirteen, but I worked for a while as the flunky on a harvest crew. My sister Nancy, brother Jack and my dad all went out to work for farmers and my mum got a job nursing our neighbour, Mr. Jackson, because she was pretty good at looking after people. I don't remember how long she worked—it seemed a long time to us kids because we relied on her more than our father. Even though she was nursing plus raising seven and then eight kids, she still found the time to go out and raise money for various causes.

Growing up in the Depression was a struggle, but it was no worse for us as newcomers to Canada than it was for tens of thousands of others in that period. At least we didn't have the terrible Dust Bowl situation of farmers south of us whose topsoil all blew away in the dryness and winds of those years. We were in the Carrot River Valley where we were frozen out in the winters but never dried out and we always had crops. Mixed farming thrived and there was lots of game, moose and deer. All the boys hunted; we used to get grouse and rabbits just with our slingshots. We never went hungry, and with everyone working, we survived. After two years, under the provisions of my father's Soldier Settlement grant, the government gave us a mortgage on a farm near Tisdale in northeast Saskatchewan.

Some people were friendly. I remember one day some of the local ladies came to teach my mum how to cook, but she could already cook rings around them. Our closest neighbours were some dozen or so families of French Canadian, Roman Catholic origin. They kept to themselves, maybe partly because some of the Anglo people who lived around us were very backward people, very bigoted. They despised French Canadians and natives and they could be very abusive. "Frog" and "Swamp Singer" as descriptions of fellow human beings were new to us. My mum couldn't stand that kind of injustice.

It felt odd, after years of being persecuted because we were Catholic, that here in Canada the Protestant Anglos accepted us more readily than they did their fellow French Canadians—perhaps because we spoke only English, whereas our French Canadian neighbours were bilingual. In England, we'd come from a place where we'd been abused too, so we were sympathetic and the French, especially, were friendly to us because we, too, were Catholic.

One day a local Native hunter rode by on his horse and my mum asked him in for tea. Bob Nippie was his name, though I'm not sure how to spell it. He was a leader of the Dogrib tribe and a courteous old guy. When he came by, he'd sometimes bring us a nice piece of venison. All the old ladies around looked down their noses and thought it was just terrible that that new Mrs. King took an Indian into her house. That got Mum mad and every time she saw Bob Nippie after that, she went out of her way to invite him in for tea. That's the way my mum was.

My dad and mum soon paid all the debts for bringing us out—we didn't cost the government a penny. But it was rough, coming from a large, close community to suddenly find ourselves in a remote shack in rural Saskatchewan with absolutely no means of communication with anyone. There was no radio or telephone; virtually no communication with our family back home. We'd had a radio in England, but we couldn't afford one over here. We didn't even have a horse. We had to walk several miles just to get to somebody who had a telephone.

Some of the after-dark hours were pretty long, especially in the northern Saskatchewan winters, but we helped to pass them by singing. Our father couldn't carry a tune in a bucket, but mother had a sweet Welsh voice and she taught us all the old Celtic and Cambrian ballads. We had a lot of songs but no instruments, not even a mouth organ. When I was fifteen, my brother Jack, who wanted to become a carpenter and was very clever at making things, made me a fiddle. I learned to play the fiddle and later, guitar and harmonica. Later on, my familiarity with music served me well in representing workers in isolated northern mining camps.

In the mid-'30s, thousands were roaming the country, going anywhere there might be work. In 1935, my brother Jack and I left Tisdale to go further west, looking for farm work and maybe a little adventure along the way. I was twenty years old at the time and Jack was twenty-four. We were supposed to head to Saskatoon where my married sister, Nancy, had in-laws who wanted us to stay with them, but we were too proud. Instead, we went out of town and slept in a haystack—but it was cold! This was April and we figured we'd head to BC to look for work because it was bound to be warmer there, and anybody who'd ever been to the coast talked about how great things were there.

We headed down the Goose Lake Line, the main rail line from Saskatoon to Calgary. That was the first time I saw the Rocky Mountains, a sight I'll never forget. In Calgary we asked if we could stay at the Salvation Army Hostel because it was freezing cold, but they turned us down. Jack and I didn't sleep anywhere that night—we were afraid we'd freeze to death. We didn't want to go any further by rail because the railroad was clearly headed toward Kicking Horse Pass, which was in the mountains and even colder. So the next morning we headed south—walked out to the highway and caught a ride as far as High River where we were given a bed and hot breakfast in the hoosegow.

Then we reached southwestern Alberta. The funny thing about it was that it wasn't planted in grain. In those days on the Prairies, if they grew anything at all after several years of drought, they grew oats, barley or wheat; those were the main money crops. But when we got to Pincher Creek, the crop was timothy. The previous year, they'd sold six million dollars worth of timothy seed from that area alone. Timothy is a hay that grows wild and is quite common, but when it's cultivated, the seed is bagged and sold all over the world. The other grain-growing parts of the province were just dust bowl, so here in Pincher Creek, for the first time since we left home, we had a real possibility of finding paying work.

Jack and I went into town and inquired around. Everyone said, "Go see Harwood. If there's any farmer who needs help, Harwood will know about it." Harwood was an insurance salesman, very cultured and quite friendly. We were in his office when a guy sticks his head in the door and Harwood says, "Reg, you know anybody needs help?"

Reg says, "Yup. Fred needs someone and I think his brother needs someone, too."

The guy who put his head in the door was Reg Bird, my future wife's dad. Jack and I decided by the flip of a coin that I would work for the brother whose farm adjoined Reg Bird's place and he would go to the other. Otherwise Lil might have married my brother.

In those days you made your own fun, so all the neighbours saw each other regularly at ball games and parties and so on. Once, on a trail ride, we were all sitting in a ring having our lunch and Alice Schultz threw a tomato sandwich at Lil's brother, but she missed him and hit me. When I threw it back, she ducked and it hit the girl behind her. That's how I met Lil.

In the fall of 1936, Bob Stott, a friend who worked in the Trail Smelter, told us that good paying work was available there. Neither Jack nor I even knew what a smelter was but we weren't going to say no. And although we both had money saved from harvesting at Pincher Creek, we weren't about to spend it on travel. Neither of us owned a car, so we took the transportation of the day—we hopped a freight train. When it got to the BC-Alberta border, the RCMP chased everybody off and disallowed entry to anyone except BC citizens or any others they deemed acceptable according to some standard known only to themselves.

That eliminated my brother and me, but this setback was soon overcome. On the advice of a sage old-timer, the two of us retreated to Blairmore, Alberta, where we bought a ticket apiece to Fernie, BC, and rode the cushions through the Crow's Nest Pass, unmolested by the minions of the law. From there we made our way to Trail in somewhat less comfortable conditions, to apply for a job. At the time, the main train went through Castlegar, twenty miles away from Trail, so if you wanted to get to Trail you either hitched a ride or walked. We walked.

Somewhere between leaving home and getting to Trail, we came across a dark, tall, skinny kid who attached himself to us. Although we had no extra money, we took him along. I forget what language he spoke, but he could only say a few words in English. Jack christened him "Fanakapan." I don't know where he got the name, but we took Fanakapan with us—fed him and protected him. We saw that he didn't get beat up, that he got food and drink. We didn't have much, but if we had a beer, he had a beer. He couldn't sing, he couldn't dance, he couldn't talk, but the kid had sad eyes. We looked after him for miles and miles, riding the rods. I think he came all the way to Trail with us and finally disappeared. I often wonder what happened to him.

It would be difficult to estimate the number of unemployed men in the 1930s who, hearing rumours about work, converged on the small town of Trail in south-eastern British Columbia. There must have been many thousands, because work was terribly scarce in those days. And of course, the majority of us who poured in, mostly on foot, were broke.

The people of Trail were tolerant, but they just couldn't feed all of those who came looking for work. Guys like us would bum a meal or eat the apples off the trees or get a few days work in the local dairies or on the railroad. But even working from three or four a.m., for ten and twelve hours a day, we didn't get paid enough to live on. It was the smelter jobs we all had our eyes on.

THE "PROMISED" LAND

The city of Trail lies in the Columbia River Valley in the interior of BC, a few miles north of the US border at Waneta, in a rocky basin closely surrounded by hills. It originally got its name from a nearby trail called the Dewdney Trail. The Dewdney Trail ran from Hope to the East Kootenay and was a key transportation and trade route from the coast to the southern Interior of the province.

The city of Trail was originally built on the west side of the Columbia River, below and down-wind of the smelter. When a bridge was built across the river in 1912, the residential part of the town spread to the east side of the river and was referred to as "East Trail." Across from it, on a raised, triangular-shaped mesa of several hundred acres, 200 feet above the river, was the village of Tadanac. Here were the smelter and subsidiary plants and buildings including a large general office. The western part of the mesa consisted of company-owned residences.

In the early 1920s, over the opposition of Trail taxpayers, the company had formed the Municipality of Tadanac as a separate municipality with a reeve and councilors. It was entirely company-owned and the people who lived there were the upper echelons of management plus private professional people. Workers called it Knob Hill. It was no coincidence that Tadanac was up-wind of the fumes from the smelter and at the very top end of it, furthest away from the smoke, was the luxurious home of Selwyn G. Blaylock, the plant's general manager.

The new Warfield chemical and fertilizer complex was another mile southwest of Tadanac and some 400 feet higher still in elevation. Since there were no buses in Trail at the time, those of us who had no car or a friend with one, had to walk to work uphill to the smelter and sometimes further on, to Warfield. It was a long hike and a hell of a lot further at the end of a tiring shift over roads pot-holed and dusty in the summer and covered with snow in the winter.

Eventually, when I got a car, I drove in my stocking feet so I could get a better grip. My friend Harry Drake taught me this. If you were driving the steep roads around Trail or Rossland in the winter and you started slipping, you'd never make it. The trick was to get your speed up and if you had to shift down, make sure the wheels never started to spin. Also, you never gave it too much gas. The more sensitive your touch on the gas pedal, the more control you had—hence the stocking feet. Later, young guys like Vince Ready who hadn't been raised in the mountains used to laugh at me, but of course, by the time they got there, the cars were automatic and roads were a lot better.

In the early '30s, the smelter complex in Trail had begun a vast extension to its operations with the addition of a chemical and fertilizer division. Smoke stack emissions drifting south of the border cost the company huge amounts of money every year in reparations paid to Washington State farmers so the addition of chemical and fertilizer plants served a dual purpose—it saved the company reparation costs to the Americans, and it created a profitable new line of products.

In 1936, the Trail atmosphere was still dominated by a thick smoke from the smelter that lay like a pall over everything. It was well known that at night they sometimes opened the baffles in the smoke treaters and let big batches of smoke escape. We'd know it in the morning because overnight the leaves on trees and bushes would turn black at the edges. The prevailing wind was downriver and Trail was downriver from the smelter, so there was always smoke.

Sometimes it was black and sometimes blue or yellow, but it was always stinky. The colour and odour of it changed depending on which furnace or flue was opened. We never paid much attention except when the yellow smoke came. The yellow was sulphur and if you got a good gutful, you'd almost choke to death. On bad days, it burned your mouth. It was the yellow smoke that killed most of the plant life in Trail and the surrounding valleys. Some people said the place looked like hell—literally.

There's no doubt the smoke was hell on all life. At the turn of the century, the valleys around the town were full of orchards, but by the '30s, the few leaves that struggled to show themselves would turn black and fall before their time. In those days, Trail looked like Sudbury, Ontario, another smelting town. There were no trees, no plants, no greenery on the surrounding hills, and in downtown Trail it was impossible to keep a garden or even a lawn. There were no pets and hardly any insects—no flies or mosquitoes, no rats or mice. The smoke killed almost every form of life, it seemed, except humans—and later I got to wonder about the humans.

The company isn't paying penalties for the air now, but for a long time they were paying for polluting the Columbia River, and no wonder—the black shit we used to throw into that river! It was a steady black waterfall, plus all the sewage—and we sent the whole shiteroo down to the Yanks!

In spite of all this, a job at the smelter was considered one of the finest plums around, and Jack and I handed in our names and lined up with hundreds of others for our chance at a job with Consolidated Mining and Smelting (CM&S).

Picture this—a small wooden building with gray drop siding on an alley off Victoria Street in downtown Trail in southeastern British Columbia. Steep brown hills, stripped of all vegetation, rise all around. Every weekday morning, those who want to apply for work congregate by the hundreds on this street, sometimes pouring over into the surrounding alleys. They all wait for one thing—the front door of Consolidated's employment office to open. When it does, a CM&S staff man steps outside to call a few names. On some days he calls many names. On others, the door remains closed all day.

Not all of the unemployed who waited nervously outside the offices of CM&S were young, single men like Jack and me. Many of them were married with children and wives to support, and along with the rest of us, they squatted hour after hour and day after day waiting for a job, any job, so their families could survive. There was no unemployment insurance or social welfare in those days and poverty was everywhere.

When Jack and I applied for a job with Consolidated, we were healthy, strong young men. Jack stood six foot two and one half inches in his stocking feet and weighed 185 pounds. I was a little shorter and about the same weight. It was considered a real advantage that both of us could read and write. My brother had high school graduation and some courses toward becoming a cabinet maker and I had about grade eight.

Finally, one day the staff man in the company office called my name. I went in and talked to a man named Jack Hoyle who was from the UK like me. Management at the smelter were very fond of sturdy young farmers who were used to hard work. Hoyle told me to report for work at seven a.m. the next day. That was March 17, St. Patrick's Day, 1937, the same day—in 1943—that I later landed overseas in World War II. Jack was hired two weeks later.

On May 12 of that year, I went back to Pincher Creek to marry Lillian Bird. We moved to Trail where we lived in a little apartment for three months before we bought an acre of land from our friends, the Drakes, and Jack and I built a shack on it.

COMMUNITY

The history of the Trail smelter as I knew it really started in 1898 when the Canadian Pacific Railway purchased the original smelter from an American mining engineer named Heinze. They did this mainly in order to buy out his railway franchise which posed a potential threat to CP Rail business in southern BC. In 1906, CPR combined all its Kootenay holdings into the Consolidated Mining and Smelting Company of Canada Limited. This included several mines, the Rossland Power and Light Company, and the Trail smelter. The smelter originally smelted mostly copper and gold, but in 1909 when they started mining ore from the Sullivan zinc, lead and iron mine in nearby Kimberley, it changed the focus of production. By 1936 when I arrived, Trail was primarily a lead and zinc smelter that also handled a small amount of copper.

The new company almost immediately began producing profits. In 1937, it was Trail's primary employer with an hourly workforce of some 6500. Like most Canadian mining companies in the 1930s, it relied for most of its skilled work force on experienced workers from the rest of the world. The town's population was therefore a broad ethnic mix that was typical in most small mining towns of the day. There were few, if any, Aboriginal peoples but there were plenty of Scots and a large settlement of Italians. Many of the Italians in Trail had immigrated before the turn of the century to help push the first Canadian Pacific Railway right-of-way through the mountains, and as stone masons, carpenters and craftsmen they could not be excelled.

Many of the Scottish workers came from Lewis, one of the Hebrides Islands. They were inter-related, clannish, rough and ready, and were clearly preferred by the company higher-ups as petty straw bosses and shift bosses. It was almost as if a Hudson Bay Company "factor" syndrome influenced the company in its choice of junior disciplinarians. The Scots were tough on everyone but their own. If you wanted to, or could stomach it, you could ingratiate yourself with the Sommerville's and the Murray's by attending the Presbyterian Church or by buying a beer for the Murdo McKay's and the Bill MacLeod's.

There were also a few English, Welsh, Irish and Scandinavians. When union organizing activity began later, the Welsh and the Danes in particular were outstanding for their union militancy.

Perhaps it was only natural that those who came from places far away from this little mountain town would help each other make a community out of it. In 1937 in Trail, radio was just beginning and television had not arrived. In comparison to working class people elsewhere in Canada, those of us working at the smelter were well-off, but we were by no means affluent. Most of us didn't own a car and there were no paid vacations so we had to look after each other. Both the Catholic and the Protestant churches were well attended. Italians, Scots and those of us from the Canadian prairie found jobs for each other, socialized together and created our own fun. We were a community.

There was lots of music—concerts, festivals, brass bands and the Trail Ladies Choir. There was even a gang of us who formed an orchestra shortly after Lillian and I married and we used to play at house parties. I played guitar and harmonica and Lil sang. Sometimes the men would go practice and party a bit in an old mine shaft we called The Tunnel—we went there for the sound. The Tunnel went into a hill a couple of hundred feet and I guess we would have been entombed there if it had ever caved in. Nobody would have found us.

In 1928 the company had created a Trail Community Chest which in 1946 became the Trail District Patriotic and Welfare Society. We called it the Recreational Projects Society and it organized picnics and dances or whatever for kids and grown-ups both. We paid one dollar a month that was matched by a company dollar and it helped pay for excellent sport and recreational facilities.

CM&S also had a policy of sponsoring and providing jobs for top-flight amateur athletes, especially in hockey and lacrosse. In 1936 and 1938 the Kimberley Dynamiters and then the Trail Smokeaters won the Allan Cup Championship for amateur hockey. The company was a little touchy about the name 'Smokeaters.' Especially after they won the Allan Cup, they kept trying to get it changed—it hit a little too close to home, I guess—but nobody was going to change the name of a winning team, so CM&S had to simmer down and live with it.

In the summer we had box lacrosse and baseball of a semi-pro calibre, and in the winter we curled. Many famous and popular athletes in hockey, lacrosse and other sports honed their skills in Trail during these years. Some of them, including Gerry Thompson, Jimmy Morris and Pete McIntyre worked in the Personnel Department of CM&S.

The social and night life of Trail was also pretty exciting. Maybe because there were a lot of young people there, the beer parlours, gambling joints, pool and dance halls did a roaring trade. It was a wild little town. The local police force under Chief John Laurie in Trail and Chief Campbell in Tadanac were kept busy handling drunks, fights and petty theft, but there was almost nothing in the way of major crime. All in all, Trail was a good place to raise kids. Lil and I still keep in touch with the friends we made in those days.

With the employment of hundreds of young men on shift work, many of them married, there was always lots of gossip as to fidelity—or lack of it—when a young wife had to sleep without a bed mate for fifteen nights. There were many accusations and ribald speculations that this or that boss had assigned a man to shift work because he had designs on his wife, but in retrospect, although there were a few incidents, there were probably far less than were speculated on. Trail, Rossland, Fruitvale, Castlegar and environs were peopled by a work force conservative in more ways than one.

I can only recall one specific case where domestic tranquillity was disturbed. One day, one of my work mates on afternoon shift received word his wife had crashed their car into a beer parlour on Rossland Avenue in what was then familiarly known as 'The Gulch.' The problem was that my pal didn't own a car. The story was that when the car came to rest on the main floor of the hotel, the bartender just said, "Yes, ma'am, what will it be?" Luckily, no one was hurt, at least not physically.

All the cultural and recreational benefits, plus the secure employment many of us enjoyed at CM&S, worked toward making people forget the bleak physical environment and dangerous, difficult working conditions we endured at the smelter. That was true for me too. At first.

Getting hired by the company was like securing entry to a whole new world. In 1937, a job at the Trail smelter instantly elevated your status from deprivation to one of relative economic security, provided you were willing to work. One of the bonuses that came with a job on the 'Hill,' as we referred to the smelter, was that the business people of Trail and the surrounding district granted easy credit terms to smelter employees, and it was not unusual for an employee to purchase a new car within a few weeks of being hired.

CM&S itself had a long tradition of extensive corporate paternalism. Standard employee benefits included a company share grant that by 1940 rose to a high of five shares after three years of service, a subsidized coal purchase system, a garden allotment system, a subsidized recreation program, a company-paid pension plan and a medical and family health plan. All the doctors in town were company doctors working at the C.S. Williams Clinic, the only medical facility in Trail at the time. Later, there was also a flourishing sick benefit plan administered by an independent Benevolent Society that looked after you in case of non-occupational illness, disease or accident.

In this plan, individual contributions of one dollar per month were matched by CM&S. And there was a company dairy set up in Warfield to supply dairy products to Trail at moderate prices.

In addition to sponsoring sports and providing employment to leading athletes, CM&S also provided more traditional benefits a turkey every Christmas, a Christmas bonus and an annual company-sponsored picnic to Lakeside Park in Nelson that was really a big drunk.

All this was not done for strictly benevolent reasons. Their intention, of course, was to maintain labour peace and hold on to experienced workers at minimum cost to themselves. Back in the post-World War I years, a lot of new people coming to BC were finding jobs away from Trail, and Selwyn Blaylock, the plant manager, decided that if he wanted to keep a stable labour

ANGELO

By far the majority of supervisors on the Hill were staunch Presbyterians who surrounded themselves with an array of largely Scottish subordinates who had many things in common—they loved Scotch whiskey, haggis, and the company, and they hated unions and anyone from the inferior (ie. non-British) races. Angelo had the bad luck to be born several hundred miles south of Glasgow, in Italy. He had the further bad luck to be one of only two non-Anglo supervisors on the Hill and one of the youngest strawbosses, assigned to the afternoon-evening shift.

There was only one small lunch room for the crew on this shift, and it was *not* for the use of the labourers, but for the Fire Department, Security Department and the labour gang strawboss (in this case, Angelo). One evening after lunch, the bosses were sitting around smoking as Angelo nonchalantly put a CM&S light bulb into his empty lunch bucket. This was common practice. Every house in Trail with a CM&S employee living there was lighted this way, but that night on his way off shift, Angelo was stopped by security and told to open his lunch bucket. He was fired on the spot for theft.

Now it was a well-known fact that CM&S provided light bulbs to all their employees. Through their subsidiary, West Kootenay Power and Light, they held the local monopoly on electricity. It was also common knowledge they provided a heck of a lot more than light bulbs to middle and upper management, but that's another story. The president and general manager of the company, Selwyn Blaylock, once described with great hilarity how, when marooned on a trip to Saskatchewan, he went into a farmer's house in the middle of the Priairie and saw a CM&S light bulb brightening the place. It was funny then, but he didn't think it funny when poor old Angelo openly took one home. The firing of Angelo for a lousy light bulb was a huge joke to the bosses—but not for him and his family.

CM&S rehired Angelo after a year or two of unemployed misery, when the only thing he had left was his pride. They relieved him of that too, when they made him a janitor and put a Scot in his old place as straw boss.

force and particularly his skilled tradespeople, he was going to have to keep them happy. And it worked, starting with the company pension plan in 1926, fully paid by CM&S.

Blaylock had studied at McGill about the time that William Lyon Mackenzie King was developing his liberal industrial relations policies, bringing forward the idea that if management gave a little, workers would be less militant. I don't know if that was any influence on Blaylock, but I do know he was a smart old bastard.

Nonetheless, if you dug a little at Consolidated Mining and Smelting, all was not as great as it at first looked. For example, the coal purchase system was only for those, mostly the wealthy, who could afford a coal heating system. The rest of us still had to collect and burn our own wood. The garden allotment that gave plots of land upwind of the smelter wasn't for everybody either, and the dairy (of prized Ayrshire cattle) was intended to demonstrate—over people's complaints about the smoke, that it was possible to raise prize herds next to a smelter.

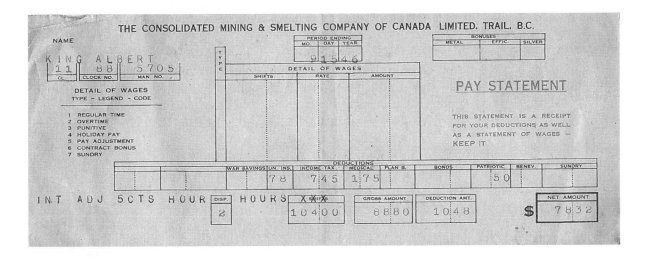

THE CONSOLIDATED MINING & SMELTING COMPANY OF CANADA LIMITED, TRAIL, B.C.

NAME

KING ALBERT
11 88 5705

PAY STATEMENT

THIS STATEMENT IS A RECEIPT FOR YOUR DEDUCTIONS AS WELL AS A STATEMENT OF WAGES — KEEP IT.

Blaylock was clever. Many of these benefits cost the company little or nothing but they were an important part of the comfort and security of the thousands who worked for CM&S. For example, the pension plan was fully funded by the company, but the money they put into it was deductible from their federal taxes, so it didn't cost as much as it might seem. Also, if you left the company employ or were fired for any reason, your pension stayed with CM&S and you just walked away, no matter how many years of service you'd put in. Likewise, the company mortgage plan apparently cost them little or no money because it operated without a loss by using pension funds.

Perhaps one of the largest benefits to CM&S was the fact that it paid no municipal taxes to Trail for the entire municipality of Tadanac, where the chemical and fertilizer plants and company houses were located. Not until Bud DeVito was elected mayor of Trail in 1967, was the Social Credit government of the day finally pressured to enact a bill that forced companies like CM&S to fulfill their tax commitments to surrounding towns. Until then, Tadanac people had paid little if any of their fair share of taxes to Trail.

When I started on the Hill as a labourer, there were three shifts of eight hours each on a rotating schedule of fifteen and five—fifteen days on and five days off. Wages were comparatively high—and based on such a bewildering confusion of contracts and bonuses that no one understood it—or had any idea how much their next paycheque would be. On your regular pay statement were listed such items as lead bonus, silver bonus, efficiency, extra effort and even a war bonus. A war bonus in 1937? It was weird—nothing was ever filled in in those bonus boxes on our paycheques, but the fact that the pay bounced up and down was always explained, if anyone bothered to ask, by the changes in the bonus. And because it was extra pay, no one questioned it.

There's no doubt that, by the standards of the day, we were well paid. The base rate for a labourer was $3.35 a day, but most labourers were on a bonus and the bonus could be as much as the wage. In a month I might make $80,

In 1946, we still had the mysterious and fluctuating bonuses listed on our paycheques.

which was great money in those days. On the Prairie I'd worked for a dollar a day, hard too, sixteen hours a day.

So in spite of not knowing what your pay would be from week to week, people didn't complain too much because there were always six guys waiting to replace you. These relatively good wages and the financial security of working at CM&S would later make union organizing a real challenge.

New workers in the smelter, including Jack and I, usually spent a break-in period on various labour gangs. As a labourer, I did a variety of jobs, including loading fertilizer, 100 and 400 pound bags of it. On the big bags it took four guys to stack them up in the boxcars that took them to Asia. That was a contract job. We'd load so many cars—as per our contract—and then go home. There were quite a few contract jobs in the plants, and we usually worked our butts off so we could finish them and go home after five or six hours.

I remember early one morning soon after Jack started work, the foreman of the lead smelter labour gang, Joe Filipelli, was assigning work crews. He turned to Jack who was fair-complexioned with red hair and prominent blue eyes and said, pointing at me, "Tell me, King, how come you're so fair but your brother is so fucking black?" The gang roared with laughter. In my family I'd always been 'Darkie' but from that day on in Trail, I was 'Blackie' King.

My straw boss on that labour gang was a gangling, inarticulate Scotsman from the northern isles named MacLeod. He was barely literate, the butt of many jokes, and kept track of his gang with great difficulty. MacLeod took sniggering delight in assigning me to graveyard shift the day I reported back to work from my honeymoon in May of 1937. Little did either of us know then that years later, as president of Local 480 of the International Union of Mine, Mill and Smelter Workers, I would successfully push through a Workmen's Compensation Board widow's pension for Alice MacLeod, his wife. None of us knew then that MacLeod was already suffering from silicosis as a result of his mining work in the Connaught Tunnel of the CPR, east of Revelstoke, BC.

PART II

Local 480

A smelter is a big oven that uses heat and chemicals to melt rock so the component metals can be separated out and sold. In Trail, all the rock, or ores, came from different mines, the biggest being the Sullivan Mine in nearby Kimberley, but we had ore from as far away as the Yukon, from the Big Missouri mine and from Echo Bay in the Northwest Territories.

All these unprocessed ores came in to the D&Ls, the primary lead furnaces of the smelter, where they were stored in a long row of huge bins. The D&Ls, named for Darryl and Lloyd, the two engineers who invented the process, were also called sintering plants because, in order to be broken down in the furnaces, the ore first had to be made into a porous material called sinter. This was done by operators who regulated the flow of rock from the bins, adding lime, silica and other ingredients, mixing it like a big sponge cake, and feeding the whole thing onto a belt that carried it into the sintering machines.

There were several of these—long chains of metal pallets on which the ore was run under an extremely hot flame to bake the cake and cause it to form into porous sinter slabs. These in turn were fed into the blast furnaces where, along with other components, they melted and the base metals sank to various levels while the useless part of the rock, called slag, floated to the top. Depending on its weight, each metal was then drained off, or tapped, at a different level. The first tap was the slag, the second was copper and so on. In those days there were about a dozen metals in the ore including gold, silver, cadmium, bismuth, antimony and tin—and a whole lot of zinc and lead. As it was tapped, each metal was sent to the refineries to be purified and all the by-products were put back into a secondary system so nothing was lost.

THE EARLY DAYS

One of my first jobs was barring down in the lead blast furnaces. After they'd operated for several days, the furnaces would crust up around the edges and a gang of labourers with long bars and double jacks had to go in to bar down

---

Tapping from the main furnace to go to the drossing plant (by crane).

the crust from the sides. The furnaces wouldn't be operating at the time, but they were still full of heat, gasses and dust, while we balanced some twenty feet above them, on two or three planks about a foot wide. We worked that way, keeping our balance on the planks while we pried away at the crust on the sides, with gasses and crap coming up from below. For safety, we attached a rope to a leather belt that went around our waist, with the other end of the rope tied to a ring that slid along a pipe through the top part of the furnace.

If you fell, well, I guess you'd dangle on the end of the rope. One guy, Scotty Aitken, did fall. He fainted, fell down through the planks and dangled on the rope until we yarded him out and an ambulance took him away.

There were about a dozen minerals in the furnace feed and it smelled like ammonia in there, a lot of acrid smoke and gasses from the different metals. It was sure hot, especially in July. Hotter than hell! We wore shirts, denims and heavy Stanfields underwear because we figured it absorbed the heat. The more the heat, the heavier the underwear.

We had big long bars to work with. One guy held the bar and the other guy hit it with a double jack—that's a big sledge hammer that weighs about twelve pounds. I once took the end off Elisio Maniago's thumb with one of those things. I went down with the double jack just as he put his thumb over the end of the bar.

To protect our lungs, they gave us a little pad to breathe through. It was a piece of cheesecloth, doubled, with cotton wool in between, is all it was. We tied them on our heads with elastics and breathed through these pads until they got plugged up and then we changed them—it sure was hard on the wind! It was also thirsty work. We used to throw a few handfuls of oatmeal in a bucket of water and we'd drink from that. I don't know why the oatmeal—maybe it was more thirst quenching.

Of course we couldn't stay in the furnaces very long. If we started feeling sick, we could get out—there was nobody there with a lash or anything. If anybody felt sick, which we did periodically, especially if we'd knocked a big chunk down because that's when the gasses came up—that's when we'd have to get out.

Some guys refused to go in the furnaces at all, but guys like me from the Prairies were used to hard work and rotten conditions. We were farmers, so we just grinned and bore it. Plus the money was good and on the bonus system, as soon as we finished, they'd let us go home early. We cleaned the furnaces maybe twice a month and depending on how crusty it was, there might be only four hours work on that day.

There were excellent wash facilities at the smelter. We wore our street clothes to work and changed into heavy work clothes there. There were showers and soap for cleaning up, but we always took our clothes home for the women to wash and of course, that meant our wives and families got exposed to the same health hazards as the men, except for the gasses, though they picked some of those up too, just breathing the air in Trail.

But in those days we never thought about what effect any of this was having on our health. When you're twenty-two years old, big and strong and

THE MYSTERY OF NEWTON'S HOLE

Chapter One

This is the way it all started. Mr. Newton, furnace superintendent at the time, chanced one day to be crossing a walkway below the blower room that linked the coal dryer to the coal mill. There on the floor below was a great pyramid of fine coal with no apparent reason for its being there at all, since it was precisely in between both coal plants which were some twenty yards or so distant. This was an untidy affair decided the methodical-minded Mr. Newton, but how did it get there in the first place?

Chancing to look up above his head he spied a pipe about four inches in diameter traversing the walkway. Standing on tip-toe and reaching up, he ran his finger along the top of the pipe, found a small hole therein and, upon inserting his index finger, promptly had it removed by the rotating steel screw that was pushing the coal from one plant to the other. Thus simply, began the story of Newton's Hole.

Chapter Two

News of the amputation of Newton's pinky spread like wildfire throughout the plants and through the telling, the importance of the loss of the superintendent's most valuable digit was completely overshadowed by the mysterious manner of its dismemberment. After a period of excitement and speculation, however, the tumult subsided and little was heard for a period of some weeks until one day the weird story of Newton's Hole was again repeated with painful similarities when the same ominous pyramid of coal was explored by a CM&S employee of lesser station than Mr. Newton, but whose inquiring forefinger was alas none the less vulnerable.

Again, meetings were held into the long, long hours by groups of serious-faced men in whose hands the company had placed the responsibility for the safety of all employees. Orders and counter-orders were given and rescinded. Superintendents were rebuked like office boys and the same uproar of rumour and speculation spread through the plants until it seemed that the subject on everyone's lips was the whereabouts and facts of the insidious threat named Newton's Hole.

The head man of engineering and maintenance was summoned to Montreal and there the board of directors issued an ultimatum: eliminate Newton's Hole, or else! Upon his return, the whole engineering staff was called in for consultation to devise a method of overcoming the terrible hazard and it was at this time that one of the bright young men of engineering suggested the pipe be threaded and a 'T' screwed in so no further exploratory digits would be amputated.

Chapter Three

In the simplicity of the suggestion, however, lay the seeds of a third catastrophe and the dismemberment of still another innocent victim of Newton's Hole. A simple work order was issued to the plumber shop, merely for a plumber to go to Newton's Hole, thread it and insert a 'T.' Thus it was that Joe Pipefitter, ambling along in search of his assignment, discovered the same ominous black pyramid of coal dust and, wishing to know if this was indeed the place where the job was required, reached up, found the hole and repeated the process in all its gory details to make himself the third victim of the dreaded Newton's Hole.

All hell broke loose! The head of engineering and maintenance was transferred to Tulsequah as a straw boss, and the company, fearful of an alarmed mass exodus of its employees, initiated a strong course of action that resulted in the directors of head office in Montreal, the whole engineering staff and supervision of the smelter area, under armed guard, escorting the senior superintendent of the plumbing department to the site of Newton's Hole, watching him thread the hole, screw in the 'T' pipe and thus remove forever the misadventure that had befallen the curious forefingers of three valuable employees. Alas, their fondest hopes were soon to be shattered.

Chapter Four

The fears of the workmen were thus allayed and the terrific fuss subsided until later when the CM&S joint safety committee underwent changes in personnel and, in the discussions of past practices, and as an example of the terrific hazards that existed in the plants, the almost unbelievable story of Newton's Hole was related to the newcomers. Again the company was to face the deepest humiliation, for they had not taken into account the curiosity bump on the educated heads of their safety and hygiene personnel. The newly appointed representative in the area just simply had to see for himself the actual surroundings where the grisly fantastic story of Newton's Hole had unfolded, and thus he became the final victim of that strange compulsion to which each of its victims had succumbed.

The same sad story unfolded—the employee explored and found the self-same pyramid of coal which now escaped via the inserted 'T' pipe. Not being able to see the 'T' pipe from where he stood, he raised his arm, felt along the top of the pipe, found the 'T' pipe, gently unscrewed it, found the hole and thus victoriously became the final victim of the dreaded Newton's Hole.

This was IT! If all hell had broken loose before, it was nothing compared with the fury and spleen that was evoked from all strata of company management. The Workmen's Compensation Board was rocked to its foundations, governments teetered on the edge of dissolution and blasts of criticism reached out from every section of supervision in every department in the Consolidated empire. The problem was submitted to the engineering faculties of all the leading universities in the country and during all this fuss, unbeknownst to anyone except himself, a young welder of no great prominence but of great discernment, had gone to Newton's Hole by himself and welded on an adjunct pipe that, while allowing the necessary escape of air and overflow from the transmission of coal, forever solved the problem of the hazard.

Papers which were written on the subject from the great men of the engineering world arrived and were carefully perused by the engineering fraternity of Consolidated and when the decision was made to implement one or the other of these, the great men found that the problem of Newton's Hole had been solved in a manner as mysterious as its existence, and to this day the same apparatus is still in existence which has served, no one knows how many valuable fingers that they may be utilized to some more profitable endeavour to the company than quick and summary amputation by investigating Newton's Hole.

Thus ends the saga of the dread Newton's Hole, which has waited many years for the telling, for its discoverer will feel no humiliation now, and let it not be said that this account be written in a spirit of disrespect for the dead, for those that knew Walter Newton and worked for him will always respect him.

Other companies, however, should take heed that similar occurrences may never happen in their operations, which caused such severe disquiet and humiliation as did the whole story of Newton's Hole to the great Consolidated Mining and Smelting Company of Canada Limited.

Pouring molten metal from the furnaces, circa 1940. Note the absence of protective equipment.

making a good dollar after being out of work for a while, you don't think about your health at all. This was the mid-'30s, right?

The biggest danger in the lead furnaces was getting what we called leaded. Lead was one of the main components of the feed and 'leading' was the term used to describe lead poisoning. Most people got leaded if they were in the furnaces and the D&LS long enough. After working as a labourer, I spent some time as an operator and my brother Jack worked as a tapper on the furnaces, but he managed to never get leaded. I wasn't so lucky.

There were various ways you knew if you were leaded. I ached and was very tired. Some guys said it affected your sex drive, but I didn't ever hear of anybody with that symptom. They used to test for it with blood tests—taking stipple counts. A sample of your blood was put on the field to see how many of those red things—corpuscles—weren't red any more. That was lead poisoning. Of course, the company never called it lead poisoning. They called it stippling. "You're stippled," they'd say, "so there's a danger of your becoming lead poisoned." And then they'd ship you out to a cleaner plant outside the lead area of the smelter.

In the meantime, to offset the lead poisoning, they handed out free milk

Lead anodes being loaded

to those working in the lead areas. Milk was supposed to overcome the lead in our bones, but we only found out much, much later that it actually made it worse because all the cows were leaded too.

Partly to prove how safe the environment was around the smelter, CM&S kept their own dairies, but for years, the smoke and gasses from the plant had been poisoning everything, including the grass the cows grazed on. Years later, I talked to a Creston doctor who had conducted a post mortem on a retired Trail smelter man who worked all his life in the furnaces. The man's bones were black—pure black. The doctor wondered if the guy had ever worked in the coal mines, but it wasn't coal at all, it was lead. That guy drank a lot of milk and I figure that's what carried the lead very efficiently to his bones.

In my case, when I got 'stippled,' they shipped me to the zinc roasters. They were even dirtier than the lead plant.

The zinc plant where the company recovered zinc from the ore had one of the greatest concentrations of workers on the Hill. It was made up of three separate tank rooms, each with two hundred guys pulling zinc out of about

Foundry workers pouring iron moulds by hand circa 1940.

fifty tanks in each room. The process had been introduced in 1930 and involved large anodes or plates that hung in tanks filled with an acid in which the zinc was suspended. Every day, new electrolyte was fed into the tanks and when an electric current was run through them, the reaction caused the zinc to adhere to the plates, like batteries. The plates then had to be stripped.

Since the tanks were hip high, the men had to lean over to pull out the plates, or cathodes, on which the zinc had collected. They used a long-handled shovel-like tool they kept sharpened to pull the cathodes out, one at a time. Then they'd chip the zinc off each side and load it into a little buggy that, as soon as it was filled, was wheeled away.

On that job, winter and summer, guys wore tall rubber boots with steel toes and long, black rubber gloves. They also wore heavy, grey Stanfields underwear and a rubber apron that protected them from the acid in the tanks because that acid would eat through denim like nothing. All the company provided was the apron, boots and gloves, and the same cotton batten masks we used in the lead furnaces.

The tank rooms were well-lit, but there was always a mist in there because

Zinc Melting Room.
Pouring zinc ingots by hand.

the tanks were electrically charged and the liquid was hot from the chemical process. That steam had acid and chemicals in it that rotted a guy's teeth. You'd know the men who had worked in there because after a while, their teeth would go in an arc from the front where they'd be almost down to the gum, to the back where they'd maybe still have full teeth. Much later, a guy told me that at one point, when an employee started work in the zinc tank rooms, they took a picture of his mouth because they knew his teeth would rot from the acid and the company only wanted to pay for the teeth he had when he started working there.

It was pretty bad in the zinc plant. The septum in your nose could disintegrate too, and zinc poisoning was just as bad as lead poisoning, but it was more subtle and took longer to manifest itself. Guys used to break out in boils and skin eruptions and very, very bad diseases.

But the men accepted all this in exchange for extra money. A bonus was paid according to the number of pounds of zinc you weighed out. On a good day you could make almost double your base pay, maybe seven, eight dollars a day. That was very good money in the 1930s. Plus, if you managed to get the zinc stripped in only four or five hours, you could go home right after. If a guy really

MY OWN ASBESTOSIS

After I worked with Frank Tickle knocking down the silver bag house, the dust from that job sat in my chest for fifty years until 1990, and then we wondered why I kept getting what they thought was pleurisy. When the internal specialist couldn't figure out the crackling noise in my chest, I went to see my old friends at the University of British Columbia's Occupational Health Clinic. Dr. David Ostrow there said, "Al, you've got asbestosis."

I said, "Bullshit!"

He said, "Where'd you work in an asbestos mine?"

I said, "I never worked in an asbestos mine in my life," though as a union rep in later years, I'd occasionally serviced the Cassiar asbestos mine in northern BC. But Ostrow kept after me. For months he grilled me, "What dusty jobs were you on?" Finally I remembered the bag house.

He said, "What were the walls made of?"

"It was called gunite." I don't know how I remembered it.

"You know what gunite is?"

"Yeah, it's cement."

"It's cement with one addition; it used to have asbestos in it."

didn't want to work there, they would give him a transfer to another plant, but most guys wanted to because of the bonus. I started to work in the zinc tank rooms, but thank Christ there was a lay-off so it didn't last very long!

From there I went on to various jobs, including helping the plumbers install miles of overhead heating pipes in the newly constructed ammonium sulphate plant and smoke recovery units. There were about seven plants in all at the smelter, so it was a huge undertaking to put in that smoke recovery system.

All the pipes were heavily wrapped in a white cloth that was fire-proofed, I realized much later, with asbestos fibres. That was where I got my first sniff of asbestos. Bob Laface used to empty big bags of short asbestos fibre into a cement mixer and this mix was used as a sort of glue to hold the cloth around the pipes. When he emptied those bags, asbestos fibres floated in the air like flour dust, but we didn't know there was any danger. This was in 1937.

If I didn't get my asbestosis there, I got it later, when I had a job with Frank Tickle knocking down the existing bag house to build a new one. The bag house was a tall building where the fumes from the silver refinery were forced through a series of filters to capture the residue for its high metal values. In 1940, the company decided to remodel the silver refinery. Using an air gun, Frank and I were told to knock down the bag house walls.

Frank came from a coal mining family in Nanaimo and got married at the same time I did; we were good friends. We started at the top, on ladders, two or three of them roped together, and moved down, breaking up the walls as we went, taking turns with a pneumatic drill. It wasn't a heavy job because the walls were only thin stuff. I can't remember how long I worked there, though it must have been several weeks. Frank worked longer in that environment than I did because when I got there he had one side of it already down and he was still working on it when they sent me to another job.

Years later, after I found out there was asbestos in that dust, I went back to try and find Frank. I knew who he'd married, but after I came back from overseas, I'd never seen him again. I phoned around and found out he'd died, though he was younger than me. Eventually I tracked down his wife. She had remarried to a guy called Alex Bremner, a carpenter in the zinc plant,

and gone to Washington state. She told me how, when Frank got sick, they sent him to Tranquille Sanitarium in Kamloops, BC, where he died in 1945, she said, of tuberculosis. Tuberculosis, my foot. In those days, if you had anything wrong with your chest, they called it tuberculosis.

I asked her, "Did you get any Worker's Compensation?" Hell no, she didn't get anything, and here was a guy who got dusted—must have been full of asbestos because he died within five years—a good-looking, healthy young guy. I tried to get her interested in filing a claim after all those years, but she wasn't interested.

In those early days in the smelter, safety was the last consideration. There were hazards everywhere. In addition to the ones I've mentioned, there were hot metal burns and abrasions caused by furnace eruptions, and smoke and fumes from the furnaces that caused asthma and chest diseases. Each plant had different kinds of hazards and nothing seemed to be done about any one of them. The number of accidents was high, but there was no such thing as a Safety Committee. Occupational health and safety rules and regulations like the ones we have today were completely unknown, but people didn't

Zinc Leaching Plant. Brown sludge as a by-product of the zinc plant returns for re-treatment in the furnaces.

THE DECAPITATION OF ROBERT Q. L.

It's the late, dirty thirties and a fairly typical Saturday night crew on graveyard shift in the CM&S zinc roasters in Trail. One or several of the boys have been into the "O be joyful" juice and it isn't unusual for anyone mooching through one of the empty buildings at three a.m. to stumble over the foreman, Ole R., recumbent in his favourite wheelbarrow, sleeping off a snootful of gin or, as he tenderly called it, his "yin."

Now this is not a putdown of this shift, which happened to be one of the more productive and accident-free crews in the zinc plant. There was a good spirit among the boys on Ole's shift and little or no resentment if someone occasionally showed up a little the worse for wear. The culprit was usually laid out full-length on a hard piece of cardboard, pushed out of sight under a row of lockers, and revived in the morning in time to shower and go home. His work, in the meantime, was willingly shared out among the rest of the crew. However, when Bob L. embarked on a fairly steady schedule of 'Whoopee,' the rest of the crew came up with a plan that we thought would teach him a lesson. Did I mention there was some feeling among the crew that Bob exercised a little less than vigour in his duties because he happened to be married to the sister of Trail's Chief of Police?

On this night we simply stood old drunken Bob L. up in a furnace hopper (yes, the furnace was down for repairs) and ran feed (zinc concentrate) around him until just his head showed on the surface of the hopper. Then we shut the belt down and scooted across to the cyclone floor and hid.

Right on schedule, along ambles the straw boss, Dan Davies, looking for someone to straw boss. Then he sees poor old Bob's severed head with eyes rolling in it on top of the hopper and Dan does three things: he screams, he shits and he runs. He descended four floors to get to the phone in record time.

Dan's fanny had barely dusted out of sight before five husky shovelers dug Bob out and while two of us hid him under the lockers, the other three filled in the hole, levelled the hopper and were unconcernedly running feed to the other furnaces when Dan, Ole, the Fire Department, Safety Department, Police Department, the superintendent of the zinc roaster, superintendent of the zinc plant and others too numerous to mention, all beseiged Number 8 Furnace Hopper on the top floor of the zinc roasters, looking for a body. A headless one. Thirty pallid white faces, sixty bulging eye-balls, afraid of what they'd see.

Ralph 'Meow Meow' Young was the senior on our crew. He'd been around a bit and could be voluble at times, but he could also be most laconic. He had a furrowed brow like a half-extended accordian, a needle nose and the slitted cold gray eyes of a good poker player. On this evening, Meow Meow was at his best. "What head?" asked Meow Meow. "Where's the blood?"

His performance, for which he should have received an Oscar, was too much for old Dan. It was one confused Dan who was sent home for the night, and a silent, uneasy assembly of staff people who left the zinc roaster in all their shiny brass buttons with their deathly paraphernalia. When Bob L. arrived on shift the next night, he couldn't figure out why Dan the straw boss stared and stared at his neck.

complain much because you could be fired at the boss's whim and there were too many people willing to replace you. If somebody got hurt it was just, "So? Too bad."

When Nick 'Alley Oop' Ceremelli accidentally dropped a slab of boiler-plate metal on my right leg and broke it, I had no income. I didn't know anything about Worker's Compensation, never made out any forms. I don't think anybody else ever heard about it either. Instead, I borrowed one hundred dollars off my best friend, Harry Drake. Later, I limped up Sayward Creek in deep snow and shot a nice, fat, white-tailed doe that kept food on the table. That accident happened in the fall and I didn't get back to work until after Christmas. When I went back, someone told me about Compensation and when I filled in the forms, they eventually sent me a cheque, from which I repaid Harry.

THE WORKMEN'S CO-OPERATIVE COMMITTEE

The only token protection that existed for the safety of workers was a company-sponsored group that called itself the Workmen's Co-operative Committee. This was a cozy fellowship set up by the General Manager, Selwyn Blaylock, after the company broke a strike by the Western Federation of Miners in 1917. Under the labour laws of those days, companies weren't obliged to recognize unions and many of them set up the in-house equivalent of a union as a means of controlling their workers. They were called 'company unions' by legitimate union organizers because they were closely controlled by management.

In 1937, a Mr. Hankin was the Committee chairman on the Hill, but he was replaced by Tim Buscombe. The committee had about forty representatives at any one time, elected by the workers to represent every department. The D & LS, for example, had two representatives, the zinc tank room and the labour gang, possibly more. But although representatives were elected from each department, they were mostly people who were in good with the boss. The Workmen's Co-operative Committee was supposed to bargain for the men and represent our interests to the company, but since they went along with pretty much anything the company suggested, we didn't even have a Grievance Committee because the Workmen's Committee was too scared to say boo. The idea of pursuing grievances or improving wages or working conditions were matters as alien to their minds as unionism itself. And although a plant worker was secretary, Selwyn Blaylock sat as the chairman and he called and ran every committee meeting.

The appointment of Blaylock was apparently divine in nature; he was never elected. His Committee met maybe once a month and Blaylock decided the agenda. He sat at the head of the table with a gavel and when that gavel came down, the decision was made—period. Sometimes the men (they were all men in those days) would try and pass their own motions, but Blaylock just ignored them. He was king of all he surveyed. From time to time, some guy would get a little upset about the arrangement, but by and large, they all accepted the status quo.

When we later came to organize a legitimate union, there was vehement opposition from the Workmen's Co-operative Committee because its members were not only willing, they actually competed strenuously among themselves to serve on the Committee—or more exactly, to serve on a sub-committee. Being appointed to a sub-committee such as the Coal Committee, the Garden or Welfare or Picnic Committee, was considered a plum, mostly because of the special benefits attached. These were real sinecures, so for example, if you were on the Picnic Committee, you could invent a bunch of 'picnic' business and run around the plant, not working, while you received full pay.

It's only natural that human barnacles like these would fight like hell to protect their little kingdoms. The characters who sat on the Workmen's Committee such as Louis Demore, Jock Lilley, Jerry Thomson, Dave Kenneway, Johnny Graham and others, were willing tools of CM&S's determination to resist any challenge to its absolute power by an upstart union.

BORING FROM WITHIN

I never heard any talk of 'union' in those first months in Trail except that I knew there wasn't one. By the fall, though, I started hearing of a union they called Mine Mill-CIO, but it was terribly hushed because of the dangers of getting fired. I suspected my best friend, Harry Drake, was tied up in it, but we didn't discuss it at the time.

I was always a reader and in those days there was a lot of stuff coming out in newspapers and magazines like *The Nation* about what was going on around the world, especially in Russia, and it seemed at that time, from what I read, that what was going on there was pretty good. I thought there was too big a contrast between the way things were there, where the workers seemed to be in control, and here, where we were the lowest of the low. And there were so many injustices. Like, on the prairie you couldn't afford to buy your kid an apple, while here in BC they were lying on the ground, rotting under the trees because farmers couldn't afford to ship them. It didn't take much sense to figure that was a crazy economic system, though it's no better now. The money lenders are still in the temples.

The longer I worked at CM&S, the more injustice I saw. Apart from the well-known health hazards, there was a lot of chauvinism. The company was highly organized into a 'pecking order' that delivered blatant discrimination at its lower end. If you had good connections, or were WASP (White Anglo-Saxon Protestant), you had an edge. On the other hand, the workers who got some of the dirtiest, crappiest jobs, were the Italians. They called them 'wops.' There were others who were also treated badly.

In those days, if you were related to one of the bosses, you didn't have to work—other guys got to do it for you. The secretary of the Workmen's Committee automatically got a steady bonus on top of his wages and didn't do a tap of work the whole time because the guys loading metal loaded extra tons to cover him.

Besides this undercurrent of favouritism, the lack of any system of seniority, promotion or demotion provided fertile ground for a variety of dirty, nasty practices dependent entirely on a boss's whim. For example, one hot day after work, Ed Stott, myself and a few others stopped for a beer. A couple of bosses, Murdo McKay and Bill McLeod, were sitting at the table next to us. and one of them leaned over and said, "Okay, King. It's your turn to buy a round of beer for our table."

"Fuck you," says I, without thinking much about it. "You make more money than I do. Buy your own beer."

When you are twenty-two, your judgement is perhaps not always acute. In any event, until the day I left that crew, I was the recipient of every dirty job that could be dredged up by the fertile and vengeful minds of those sons of Caledonia.

There were no paid holidays. When asked, Blaylock said, "Sure you can have holidays, but you won't get any pay while you're on 'em! Take all the holidays you want!" It was also Blaylock who, in 1926 when there wasn't the demand for base metals there had been during the first war, arbitrarily put all the single men on half time and the married ones on three-quarter time. That was a good example of his paternalism and the kind of absolute control he exercised.

I knew there was something lacking in the workplace. We were relatively well paid, but anybody with an ounce of common sense could see there was no consistency or seniority, wage-wise or shift-wise. There was this fluctuating 'Maggie's drawers' bonus system over which workers had no control, and there was no fixed wage schedule, like today, where you get so much per hour. Instead, from the time I started work at CM&S until after the war, we had a system of pay that was all over the map. Wages started at a base rate of $3.35 an hour, which in the 1930s was pretty good, and on top of that, the rest of your pay was made up of 'bonuses' and which weren't really a "bonus" at all—they were something the company used for their own convenience. So on every pay stub there was a space for the Efficiency Bonus, the Metal Bonus, the Silver Bonus, a Christmas bonus for married men and/or a War Bonus. Why a War Bonus in 1937? I don't know why! And I don't think anybody else knew either, but we weren't about to say no. As an employee, you just did as you were told and kept your goddamned mouth shut.

The bonus system meant that on every paycheque, the figures moved up and down at the will of the company. For example, when the price of metal went down on international markets, we got a pay cut. Funnily enough, though, when the price of metal went up, we didn't get an increase. Later, in the union, we were always pointing these things out. The company lowered our bonus when the world price went down, sure, but they didn't *sell* their metal when the price was down—they hoarded it until the price went up again. Yet all those years when the price was low, our wages were deflated. At the same time, we were very productive and the shareholders were receiving terrific dividends.

HARRY DRAKE

Harry Drake signed me into the union and the Communist Party

I had met Harry Drake during my service in the D&LS. He and I became close friends at work and shortly after Lil and I married, his mother sold me an acre in Columbia Gardens on one of the benches above the valley. That made the Drake family our neighbours.

Columbia Gardens was a small farming and orchard community between Trail and the international boundary at Waneta. I say "farming and orchard," but that was what they were before the smoke and industrial effluent of the smelter had poisoned the atmosphere so badly that most of the growth stunted and died. The company had bought up all the land in the area in order to eliminate damage suits by farmers, and Harry's father, Harry Sr., worked for CM&S keeping an eye on the property, though they didn't use it for anything except an airport.

Harry wasn't yet married and still lived with his mum and dad. Drake Sr. and his wife, Ada, were typical old-country English people—decent, generous, religious and hard-working, but as stubbornly reactionary as two British Imperialists could be. They couldn't understand why their son was a radical, so sometimes, just to get away for a while, Harry would take off. Often he'd come to our place and his mum would come looking for him there. She'd drive into our yard—"Yoo hoo! Is Harry there?"—and then ask me to turn the car around. She had a whole acre in which to maneuver, but she asked me to do it for her because she was always nervous about that car. It's funny—before I enlisted, Mrs. Drake was a real, big 'C' Conservative. She was the agent for one of the Conservative candidates, came up to me with a Bible and all when I went overseas. But she changed. I don't know what happened, but by the time I got back, she was as red as a fox's arse and supported her son, Harry, all the way in his politics.

Harry was a bit kicked out of shape physically. He wasn't big—about 140 pounds—and he had a disproportionately large head. He wasn't well educated in a book sense, either, but he was very smart and a skilled mechanic. Anything mechanical, Harry Drake was good at.

I knew vaguely about Communists, but not much. In those days of terrible hard times, a lot of thinking people figured the Communist model in the Soviet Union made a lot of sense, so when Harry asked me to join the Party, I said, "I'll think about it." It soon became clear that joining could be a prelude to membership in the new union.

I'd never worked anywhere where there was a union and I didn't know anything about labour or labour history. I came from a northern Saskatchewan farm and before that, from the UK, and I knew absolutely nothing about the struggle of workers in BC or anywhere else. I didn't even know that BC was where the first eight hour day—with portal-to-portal pay for time spent travelling to and from work underground—was established out of the Rossland local of the Western Federation of Miners back in 1899. But the idea of a union, of someone who would stick up for working people and their families—well, that made a whole lot of sense to me.

Harry lent me some literature: the *Communist Manifesto* and *Das Kapital*. I'm a good reader, but still it took me a while to get used to the Godless part and I had some trouble with those long-fangled economic theories of Marx and Engels. I asked Harry, "You really think you're going to sell this 'dialectical materialism' thing to the masses?" but he just laughed. Shortly after I read the stuff Harry gave me, I joined the Communist Party of Canada.

There were two reasons. One was that I believed in the Party and what it was doing in the Soviet Union and what it aimed to do for working people here. Second was that I wanted to join the union, but union organizers had to be very careful they didn't sign up people who were informants, and there were lots of those in the smelter, believe me. The organizers figured that if a guy was a Party member, he wasn't likely to be an informant, so the fact that I joined the Party first made it easier to join the union. That was in 1938 when I was twenty-three years old—the youngest guy in the union.

When I joined the International Union of Mine, Mill and Smelter Workers, my card number was 64. I was the sixty-fourth guy to join the union in Trail.

As far as Communists go, I doubt if we ever had twenty Party members in the local, total, but the ones we had were good people. Most of them are dead now, and a lot of them didn't work there very long anyway. They either got fired or quit, guys like Garfield 'Gar' Belanger, George DeGroff, Harry McTague and Harry Drake. Later, the fact that some of us in the union were also members of the Communist Party became a crucial issue—or a big red herring—depending on which way you looked at it.

THOSE GODLESS COMMUNISTS

One day Harry Drake and I were driving home from work when he said to me, "Blackie, do you believe in God?"

"Of course!" says I. "Everybody believes in God, don't they?"

He says, "No. We don't."

"Who's we?"

"Us Communists."

"Oh, shit."

That was quite a shock to me, raised a good Irish Catholic. I'd never been an altar boy but I could vave been—I can still recite the credo—and I'd never heard of good people not believing in God!

BEGINNINGS

In western Canada, Mine Mill had had its beginnings in the militant Western Federation of Miners (WFM) which formed in 1893 in Butte, Montana to represent North American hard rock miners. It almost immediately began organizing in British Columbia and miners established the first Canadian Local 38 of the WFM at Rossland in 1895. (See Appendix, *The Struggle: A Brief History of Local Labour Movements and the Rossland Miners' Union Hall*.) At first, all the rest of BC was a single local, 289, but quite soon the different mines and smelters were given their own locals. Later still, Trail would be part of District 7 of the International Mine Mill union that extended from the Mexican border north to the pole, and west from the Continental Divide to the Pacific.

In 1916, the WFM changed its name to the International Union of Mine, Mill and Smelter Workers (IUMMSW). There were several famous union people associated with the WFM, or Mine Mill, including 'Big Bill' Haywood, Eugene Debs and the organizer and musician, Joe Hill.

From the beginning, Mine Mill was a union very proud of its rank and file democracy. The shop steward's manual declared that, "No worker in Mine Mill's jurisdiction is barred from full-fledged membership on the basis of the colour of his skin, the church he attends, the political party he votes for, or the fact that he or his ancestors came from a certain country. Women members are guaranteed equal rights. There are penalties provided for anyone who violates this basic principle of the Union. Does he support the Union and its Constitution? This is the main condition of membership."

But the union soon had a series of internal problems over whether it was the One Big Union (OBU) or the Industrial Workers of the World (IWW), both of which it helped to found. There was also political dissension in the top ranks between, among others, Big Bill Haywood who headed the IWW (of which the Western Federation of Miners had been for a time, the mining department), and Charles Moyer of the WFM. All this created divisions that made the union more vulnerable.

Some of the early organizing by the Western Federation of Miners in Trail had been done by a well-known organizer and union martyr, Ginger Goodwin, who was later shot in the back on Vancouver Island. At that time the Trail union president and the secretary-treasurer, Jack McKinnon and Monty Davidson, were offered management jobs, probably by Blaylock, which they took. They were still working for CM&S when I started in 1937.

There had been a strike in 1917 and Blaylock warned the organizers, "Wait until my boys come home from overseas. They'll look after you bastards!" and they did, too. He refused to rehire about four hundred of the strikers, and he persuaded returning soldiers to abandon the Western Federation of Miners and instead adopt his Workmen's Co-operative Committee—the company union. Blaylock appointed himself chairman of the committee and gave himself powers that he quickly showed he would not be loathe to exercise.

So an independent union disappeared from the Trail smelter after World War I and after that, if management ever found or even suspected someone of being a union man, they fired him.

The 1930s, however, saw major changes happening in the Canadian and US workforce, including rapidly growing numbers of industrial workers, especially in the auto and steel industries. Up until this time, the only national labour organization in the US was the American Federation of Labour (AFL). The AFL was made up of several independent craft unions, that is, unions of skilled tradespeople like carpenters, plumbers and electricians—hence the term, 'trade' union. Its equivalent in Canada was the Trades and Labour Congress (TLC). The AFL, which called itself 'international' because it also had many locals in Canada, saw the rapidly growing numbers of unorganized industrial workers in North America not as potential union members, but as threats to its existing members' skilled jobs. It was very uneasy about what it considered militant ideas by a new breed of union organizers about the importance of educating and organizing *all* workers, regardless of their so-called 'skill.'

In 1930, a Communist International directive out of the Soviet Union instructed all Communists to sever their ties with 'reformist' organizations such as the AFL and the TLC. In the US and Canada, the result was the formation of a revolutionary union central called the Workers' Unity League (WUL) made up mostly of Communist-led unions in mining, logging and the garment industry. These unions quickly became noted for aggressive organizing. But in 1935, Soviet policy again changed and international Communists were instructed to again join existing unions. This was primarily so the unions could help form a 'united front' against fascism and the brewing possibility of war.

This development released a large number of militant union organizers into the general workforce at the same time as there was a large-scale drive for industrial organization in the United States. Many of these people crossed the border and began organizing unions in Canada. In 1935, the AFL couldn't take these upstart radical ideas any more and expelled several of the newly formed industrial unions, who promptly got together under the leadership of John L. Lewis to form the Committee for Industrial Organization, later renamed the Congress of Industrial Organizations, or CIO. Mine Mill was one of the eight founding unions of the CIO. I guess the powerful interests that were hostile to labour—the National Manufacturer's Association and so on—were delighted when the biggest US labour central divided in two. By 1938, the CIO clearly represented the left-wing of the labour movement.

Most of the time, this dispute between craft and industrial unions, the AFL and CIO, appeared vague to BC workers because it was mostly taking place far away, in the eastern US and Canada, but over the long run it would have an increasing impact through groups like the Steel Workers Organizing

Committee (swoc). When swoc came together with the specific aim of organizing the North American steel industry (including big corporations like Bethlehem and US Steel), the head organizer was a Communist named William Z. Foster, from the CIO. There were, I think, six unions who provided the money to fund swoc whose work eventually led to the formation of a large new union called the United Steelworkers of America. These funding organizations included Mine Mill (IUMMSW), the United Mine Workers (UMW), the United Electrical Workers (UE), the Meatpackers, United Auto Workers (UAW), International Ladies Garment Worker's Union (ILGWU) and the Fur & Leather and Needle trades unions, all of them very left-wing at this time and very active in organizing other, primarily industrial, workers. The Steelworkers Union they helped organize eventually became a mighty force in the CIO, and was later very helpful in getting Mine Mill and some of the others expelled from the same CIO on the grounds of 'red' domination. But that came later. In the beginning, in the 1930s, swoc waged a magnificent struggle based on support—cash and organizers—from these other unions.

THE DRIVE TO ORGANIZE

By the time I came along in 1937, the International Union of Mine, Mill and Smelter Workers (IUMMSW) generally went by the name Mine Mill, but it was also simply called CIO. It was easier when organizing to say CIO than International Union of Mine, Mill and Smelter Workers, and to many people, the two were synonymous anyway, so we went by the name CIO as easy as Mine Mill, and were proud of it.

One of the first organizers I remember in Trail was Ora L. Wilson from the International Mine Mill office in Spokane. Wilson didn't have a hair on his head—he was bald as a bladder of lard. I remember once when we produced an organizing bulletin, he advised us to use the headline: "Workers, don't be fooled!" Today, nobody ever mentions him, but he was a good man.

There was another one when we first started organizing, whose name was George Price. I don't know where he came from, because I never met him but he was in the Vancouver office very early on, where he helped to organize two foundries under Local 289.

But the man most people remember is Slim Evans. Arthur H. 'Slim' Evans was a highly respected organizer who came out of the Mineworkers and the Carpenters unions. He was a Communist who joined the Party in 1926 and made no bones about it. Among other things, he was key in the WUL-inspired "On to Ottawa Trek" by unemployed Canadians in 1935. He arrived in Trail in 1938 to help organize for Mine Mill.

Evans received shameful treatment at the hands of CM&S and the *Trail Daily Times*. Apart from fulminations from the company and the media about ungrateful workers, the terrible CIO and the dangers to democracy of giving uneducated men a voice, the worst incident was the burning of Slim Evans' car. The newspapers said it was some sort of secret, but there was no secret about it—everybody knew because it happened in broad daylight. Two well-known supporters of the Workmen's Committee hauled Evans' car away with a truck, towed it up past the guard house of the CM&S plant, set fire to it and pushed it over the bank a couple of miles down the road at Stoney Creek. Both men were employed on the Hill at the time and they boasted openly about dumping Evans' car over the bank—and why not? They were heros to most of the population of Trail who were largely against the idea of a legitimate union, at that time.

I never actually met Arthur Evans and often wondered how I missed him. I'd like to have met him because my mum was an Evans. He wasn't holding that many meetings because he was simultaneously organizing in Rossland and the other mines in the District. When he was in Trail he was mostly around the union office and when he held the big organizing meeting at Butler Park, I was on afternoon shift. For the rest of the time, I guess I missed him because I lived out of town and only went into Trail to go to work. Anyway, I never laid eyes on the man. I think that when Evans was in Trail, our local was still the original Local 289 of Mine Mill and it was only after he left that the union agreed to give us our own charter.

It took a lot of courage to damn the tyrant to his teeth, but in 1938, fifteen Trail smelter workers applied for and received a charter for Local 480 of the International Union of Mine, Mill and Smelter Workers. Of these, fewer than half were members of the Communist Party.

You can tell by the number of our union, when it was organized. The unions in Ontario were organized around the same time as Local 289 because their numbers were 240 and 241. Local 651 in Kimberley came six years after we were chartered. The guys in Kimberley were very solid union people because miners are different. Their attitude toward the union was always much healthier than that of the smelter workers and with good reason. First was the natural mutual reliance that exists in the more dangerous underground mining industry. Miners have always known how important it is to protect each other, to look after each other. And second, the barrage of anti-union poison that was being spread by the smelting company could not be matched by the smaller mining companies.

After Slim Evans left, he was followed as a union organizer by John McPeake, a worker from the lead refinery in Trail. At considerable sacrifice, John quit the company in order to work full-time for the union.

Some of those who joined us in the union in Trail had been Socialists in England. Bill Cunningham was one of them. When he first came to Canada he had joined the Co-operative Commonwealth Federation, the CCF (the forerunner of the NDP). In those days, the CCF was known as a Socialist organization. Around 1938, Bill Cunningham was called into the office by Blaylock who demanded he quit the CCF. Bill was less than five feet tall, but

LOCAL 480, IUMM&SW: CHARTER MEMBERS

Garfield 'Gar' Belanger*
William Coulter
Cedric Cox
William 'Bill' Cunningham
George DeGroff*
Dan Dosen*
Harry Drake*
Dick Gopp*
R. Lloyd
Dave Logan
Gordon Martin*
James McMow
John McPeake*
Leo Nimsick
Alva Rennika

*Member of the Communist Party

he stood up to Blaylock who was almost six feet, and told him to go to hell. And Blaylock didn't fire him, probably because Cunningham was a topnotch machinist. He still held his membership in the Amalgamated Engineering Union in Britain, and after he joined Local 480 of Mine Mill as a Charter member, he paid dues to both unions for the rest of his life. He was full of principle, Billy Cunningham. The fact that he stood up to Blaylock and didn't get fired gave the rest of us heart that we could get a little more audacious.

In 1938 we didn't have certification—we weren't yet legally eligible to represent the members to management— and we didn't go to any conventions or other union affairs because we couldn't afford to. We certainly never thought of striking or taking job action. We were just trying to build up a union so that someday we could get in a position to take the company on. I don't even think most of us had any deep understanding of what we were trying to do. Maybe some of the people who had the bigger picture, people who came in from the international like Slim Evans or later, Harvey Murphy, had a sense of where we were going, but for the rest of us, the CIO had been established to organize mass industry workers and this was a mass industry, so we were going to organize it. Most of us wouldn't have known in those days what to put forward as a 'platform', wage-wise or shift-wise, or anything about bargaining. We figured we'd get the place organized—we would become the certified bargaining agent for the Trail smelterworkers—and after we got organized, we'd decide what our policies would be.

The same struggle was going on to organize northern Ontario mines under Mine Mill. The fight in those days, all over Canada and the US, was for this basic union recognition.

In Local 480, although such good men as Leo 'Squeaky' Nimsick, Bill Cunningham, Cedric Cox and others were charter members, they were never in the forefront of organizing. Leadership fell to a core of about five Charter members who, along with others, did a lot of the original organizing work. Active Charter members included Dan Dosen, Harry Drake, George DeGroff, Dick Gopp and Gar Belanger, who was president when I joined. John McPeake was also very active and later became the union's full time organizer. All these men were Communist Party members. Then there were guys like Mike Lypchuk, Louis d'Andrea, Joe 'Sig' Colautti, Fred Heintz, myself—the baby of the group—and a few others who tried to organize and went to union meetings. Other activists at that time included Sammy Sivorot in the refinery, Sammy Muirhead, Fred Hostetter and Alex Gripich from Castlegar, and my brother, Jack. These men formed the guts of the drive for Mine Mill in Trail.

There weren't too many Italians interested in the union at first, although from the beginning we were aware they were an important constituency that we somehow had to reach. Sig Colautti was one of the first who signed up. Another was Louis d'Andrea, who was a very progressive guy, but eventually Louis quit because he couldn't stand the smelter and he could make better money in the mines. There was never an Italian organizer until the Steelworkers brought one in when they raided us after the war, and that's when we hired Remo Morandini on the Mine Mill staff.

THE GRASSROOTS

To become certified as a union, we had to get over fifty per cent of the men to sign union cards. (The smelter was all men until the labour shortages of World War II forced the company to hire women.) When we had more than fifty per cent signed up, we could apply for certification to become the official bargaining agent for the smelter and if we then won the vote, we could begin to negotiate a first contract.

It was an uphill battle. The men who worked for CM&S were top-of-the-walk materially—and we knew it. We lived in a little oasis in the middle of a world-wide depression. Little Trail was booming. It was booming!

Which is why in 1938 when we began to form a union, most of the guys in the smelter thought we were, to put it mildly, a bit ungrateful. They laughed at us, sneered at us and derided us: "Are you nuts?" Even guys who supported us thought we were crazy. Everyone, even some of us at times, figured it was hopeless; we were just an idiot group of malcontents who dared to challenge the mighty company.

Throughout 1938 and early 1939, the enrollment of new members into the union was slow and little if any signing up was done. One of the most effective methods CM&S used to frustrate our efforts to organize was fear. They threatened all kinds of disaster if our efforts should ever succeed and a union be certified, including the threat that a union strike would force the permanent closure of the smelter. Their favourite example was Anyox, a BC copper mine. They blamed the closure of the Anyox mine and mill on the fact that workers there had joined the Mine Mill union and gone on strike. But it wasn't the union at all. Years later we found out that Anyox went belly up because the ore body had run out. There was nothing left to mine, but the company used the strike to blame the union for the closure.

It's not hard, in retrospect, to understand the dislike and fear with which our efforts to form a union were received by our peers at the smelter.

Mostly, the company encouraged people to fear Mine Mill by painting the CIO as a radical, Communist-led, and therefore dangerous organization that would destroy the well-being of the people. In this they had the support and entrenched resources of most of the local fraternal organizations, all of the churches and a vicious local paper, *The Trail Times*, under the editorship of a reactionary Bill Curran. They also had the loyalty of an army of stooges on the job including most members of the Workmen's Committee—men who told tales in return for company favours. And remember, unions were still barely legal. There was no Labour Code to protect organizers or to discourage employers from harassing union organizers. If you got caught, you were fired—like Alva.

Alva Rennika was a union member, a cigar-smoking Finn who had played professional hockey with the New York Americans hockey club and was now working graveyard shift in the lead furnaces. Somehow, company people got wind that Alva was organizing for Mine Mill. They came in the middle of the night, broke into his locker and found his union cards. They took him right off the job and straight to Rossland and by the next morning, he and his family were gone, never to be seen again, though I heard later that he ended up helping to organize a lime quarry west of Calgary.

Alva's firing had a sobering effect and a few changed their minds and took back their union cards. The rest of us were even more careful. We began to carry application cards in the soles of our boots, but though it was dangerous, we continued signing men up at work. We had to. We'd catch a guy to sign in the washroom or the lunchroom because Trail, even the smelter itself, was widely scattered and most of us didn't have cars. If I lived in Fruitvale and the guy I wanted to sign up lived in Castlegar, the only way I could get to him was on the job.

We had to be so careful. Even guys who were signed up as members were afraid to go to meetings. Leo Nimsick, for one, never came to a meeting, not one that I was at, anyway. I didn't even know he was a union member until a long time afterward. I used to ride with him in the truck on the job when he was in the union and I wasn't. After I joined and found out he was a member and never tried to sign me up, I would have chewed his ass off but, by coincidence, I never got to ride with him again.

We were so few that when we had our annual meeting to elect the union's officers, it was pretty much musical chairs. As the youngest member, I wasn't yet capable of handling senior duties, but I was a fast learner and at one point, Howard Forbes and I competed for the office of Conductor. I beat him by one vote.

Later, Claire Billingsley, who was once President of Local 480, told an interviewer that Forbes was a Communist, but Howard was no Communist, he was simply a man with a strong sense of justice. That's why he was one of the first guys to join the union. Later I heard he'd become a United Church minister, God bless 'im.

For our Communist Party meetings there was no way we could have a meeting in town, even if someone had agreed to rent us space, so usually we all climbed into Belanger's car and took off into the bush somewhere. It was mostly six of us because that was all we could fit. We'd drive to Bear Creek or Columbia Gardens or along Merry's Flats and just sit in the car and talk. The handiest place was Merry's Flats just east of Trail, owned by the D.B. Merry Lumber Company. It was a big chunk of flatland covered with brush and trails, above the river. Nobody could see us there.

We never drank at these meetings; we couldn't afford the beer! We just smoked and plotted how to fan the flames of discontent. We discussed, among other things, who to ask to sign up in the union. The number of signed-up members was going up and down as things happened. The company would do something, there'd be a lot of criticism and we'd get a few more guys to join the union. Something would happen in the plant and we'd get a few more. We used to watch for people who were prime to be organized, people who were pissed off at the company. But people could also change their minds and take back their cards, so it was a constant effort.

I want to make it very clear that we never tried to sign anybody up in the Communist Party through the union. We might have done it privately, outside the local if we had some idea of a guy's attitude, but mostly, if a guy wanted to join the Party, he'd make himself available. I don't know if I ever did sign anybody up in the party the whole time I was there. We were busy trying to build a union, and if you wanted to join the Party—fine. It said even more about your commitment. But the priority was always the union.

As I remember it, all during the organizing period, which lasted about six years, we received fifty dollars a month from union headquarters in Denver, Colorado. Fifty dollars went a long way in those days. Together with our dues, it was enough to help pay Gordon Martin early on, as a financial secretary, although he had to eke out his existence with an additional part-time job.

Martin was a Communist who moved to Trail from Vancouver to work for the union. He didn't work on the Hill so I think he must have had a subsidy from the Party to live on, plus we paid him a little which he supplemented with a job at the Crown Point Hotel in Trail as a bellboy. Later, around 1940 when things were heating up, he got fired from the hotel for his union work and we hired a Vancouver lawyer, John Stanton, to defend him. Even in those days there was a statute that prohibited firing a guy because of his union affiliation, so we took it up and won. Old John Kerr, the manager, had to reinstate him and give him back pay. The next day when Gordon went back to the hotel to pick up his cheque, he said to Kerr, "I wouldn't work for you for all the money in the world!" and he never did go back to work there. But the case was important for Mine Mill because for the first time we established that a worker does have some rights. The union publicized this win up, down and all over, that the company can't just fire you at their whim.

The other important thing we used the fifty dollars from headquarters for was to publish a union newspaper. It was called *The Commentator* and was printed by the *Trail-Ad* news, one of the only printers in town who would work for the union. The owner, Elmer Hall, had been blacklisted earlier by CM&S for union organizing, so he was willing to help us out.

But it was difficult to find volunteers to help with newspaper distribution. Besides the inconvenience and loss of time for family and other pursuits, those who gave the paper out at the company gates had to deal with the ever-present fear of reprisals. This job therefore fell primarily to Communist Party members, the inner circle of the union. We also got help from miners from the surrounding Salmo and Erie mines in distributing several special organizing editions to every home in Trail. Miners, including John Anderberg and Jim Stuart—both of whom later died of silicosis—would go house to house all night long until the job was finished.

FRYING PAN INTO THE FIRE

At a Party meeting sometime in 1939, a decision was made to seek redress for some of our complaints through the Workmen's Co-operative Committee. Harry Drake had just been elected to the Committee from the oxide leaching plant. And there was Gil Handley, a hell of a good guy, who was already a member of the committee and favourable to the union. He was quite active and well respected and I think he stepped aside to let Harry run, but I'm not sure. At any rate, at Harry's very first meeting he put up his hand and made a motion that the entire Workmen's Co-operative Committee disband and join Local 480 of the Mine, Mill and Smelter Workers Union.

There was dead silence. They were all so terrified, with Blaylock sitting there at the head of the table waving his gavel, that nobody would even second it! Then Blaylock kicked Drake not only out of the room, but off the Workmen's Committee. No one said a word; they just let Blaylock eject an elected guy.

Back went Harry Drake to the oxide leaching plant and up went the nomination papers for his replacement. We all worked hard to convince the guys to let only Harry's name stand again, and sure enough, at the end of the month, only one name appeared on any of the forms for Harry Drake's replacement: Harry Drake. So back to the committee goes Harry. When he appeared, Blaylock didn't say a damned word—but Harry didn't make the same motion again, either. We told him not to.

This was not just a sign of how popular Harry Drake was—in fact, as soon as the union was certified, he was one of the first ones kicked off the executive—but it was the sign of a slowly growing belligerence against the company. Blaylock had suffered one of his first defeats and small though it was, it represented for us a clear bell tolling the ultimate fate of the company union.

After that, we decided to deliberately infiltrate the Workmen's Committee to try and derail the thing. We began an active campaign to elect people who would be more loyal to the interests of workers and seek better working conditions. Basically, our goal was to win a majority on the Workmen's Committee so we could then vote it out of existence and vote the union in. In fact, we did get a few guys in there in addition to Harry Drake, but not enough to do much damage. The previous representatives on the committee from my part of the plant, the D&L's, had been Jack Powell and Joe 'Glo Coat' Hardy. Hardy was re-elected, but the other man elected was a unionist and a Party member, Dan Dosen. Other union members elected were Mike Lypchuk (from the lead furnaces), Sammy Sivorot (lead refinery) and a couple more from the zinc department. Dave McMartin from lead furnaces was either elected at this time or later. Membership in Local 480 picked up slightly after this.

In this whole organizing period there was very little violence. There was the 1938 incident when Slim Evans' car was burned, and once someone picked a fight with old Bill Coulter in the oxide plant, attacking him with the handle of a pick and damn near killing the guy. Coulter was an old man half his assailant's size, but a well-known unionist. In spite of very strict company rules about violence on the job, the assailant was never even rebuked for this.

WORLD WAR II

When Canada declared war in 1939 a dramatic change took place overnight in the company's attitude to Local 480. Since smelter workers were now declared an essential industry and could neither quit nor be fired, the old dread of being out of work was effectively removed. Suddenly jobs were breaking out all over and it became a little easier to organize. The company couldn't fire anybody and they could hardly get new employees, so they didn't have the absolute power they used to have.

Organizing immediately became easier and people began to talk about unionism more openly, but we weren't in the clear yet. Many of the new employees who replaced the enlisted men had come from the Prairies, like us, and after years of poverty they were grateful for any work. They weren't particularly eager to sign up in a union. Also, for those only recently arrived in Trail, the idea of long-term stability or workplace gains wasn't crucial.

When the war broke out we had maybe a hundred members in the union, a few of us also members of the Communist Party—this was out of some 6000 people in the plants, hourly and staff. Some secrecy was still vital, so we decided that a continuing core of the most trustworthy types would continue to meet regularly, but the union itself could relax a little.

Union success at the Tadanac plant was still spotty. At the lead furnaces where my brother Jack worked, many men joined the union. Dave McMartin (Cliff's father) and Mike Lypchuk were early supporters, as were Alva Rennika, Chuck Kelley and Louis D'Andrea.

Thanks to Harry Drake, the union was strong in the oxide leaching plant where he worked. Jake 'King' Kelly was non-committal, although he later became a strong supporter, but George Fertich, Sam 'the Turk' Fame, Bill Coulter, Dave Bissett, Gil Handley and many others were supportive.

The shift in the D&Ls in which I worked was one hundred per cent signed up in the union by Dan Dosen and I. Dan was a well-liked senior member of C-shift as well as a Communist and a card-carrying member of Local 480. In fact, Dan held card number one as the first charter member of Local 480. Every worker in the D&Ls was in the union, but only Dan and I were active. Because it was still quite secret, the others all paid dues, but they paid them directly to Dan and I and they didn't attend union meetings.

Of course, we didn't sign up the shift boss in the D&Ls, Ewart Crispin. Crispin knew damn well that Dosen and I were organizing but we weren't stupid enough to be caught. I used to get into the damndest arguments with him. He liked arguing about everything, but especially about the union and about politics in general.

The lead refinery, despite being an unhealthy and undesirable place to work, was not as quick to respond. Claire Billingsley, who worked there and who would later be president of the union at a crucial time, was conspicuous by his absence in the roll of new union members, despite his brother Jack being a member from the labour gang. However, after many years I have concluded that the reasons for Billingsley and others in the lead refinery holding aloof from the struggle to organize went deeper than we then realized and had a lot to do with personal loyalties. When the union was destroyed in the post World War I period and several union leaders defected to the company, one of them was Jack McKinnon, the union secretary, who was rewarded with a boss's job in the zinc melting room. All of his daughters married salaried company supervisors, one of whom was Pete McIntyre, superintendent in the lead refineries and later a big cheese in personnel.

Now Pete McIntyre, newly returned from World War I and in possession of an Engineer's degree from Queen's University, was a most affable, decent and attractive individual. He played a good, bruising hockey game, excelled at curling and was later a left-handed golfer of no mean ability. Pete personally commanded almost unanimous admiration and respect from refining department workers. Looking back, I don't think many of them wanted to upset him by joining Local 480.

Later, two other senior company executives also served at the refineries on their way to the top. One was W.S. Kirkpatrick and the other, Ralph Perry. Both of them exercised an iron hand in an oh-so-velvet glove. There, too, for personal reasons, the troops were loath to publicly upset their employer by joining a union.

For a long time the only hall in town that had been open to the union for public meetings was the Elks Lodge, which we rented through Brother Fred Heintz. But after the declaration of war in 1939, we rented an office in a building known as the Doukhobor Block on Bay Avenue and were soon having fairly regular union meetings there. The pressure was off. Guys were no longer afraid of losing their jobs for being seen at a union meeting.

Depending on what was happening on the Hill, the attendance at these meetings varied quite a bit. At one of them, we nearly got ourselves an accidental president.

It was a very hot day. We were preparing for the election of a new executive, as we did every year, and as usual we'd left the front doors open for air when a little guy wandered in late and sat down at the back. Somebody nominated him for president. There were several more nominations, but all through them this guy kept jumping up trying to say something and the president kept telling him to sit down because it wasn't his turn to speak. Finally, when it was his turn, the president asked, "Do you accept the nomination for president?"

The guy says, "I'm not even a member! I thought this was a public meeting so I just dropped in to get out of the heat!"

That's how loose some things were—or else it proves how desperate we were for members!

About this time, someone on the Workmen's Committee had the idea of sabotaging worker's faith in unity by starting a co-operative, one they could control and that would perhaps fail. I can only imagine their thinking was that in this way they could encourage people's cynicism about trusting each other and therefore belittle the union and lessen it's attraction. This is how the Butcher's Co-op in Trail started. The Co-op was ill-conceived, poorly run and serviced and not even the company union people bought their meat there. It wasn't originated by the people who would use it and that's why it died an early death.

As the war progressed into 1940, production of lead and zinc reached new highs at the smelter. Although prices for those two metals were fixed, the company was making good profits on other, unregulated, metals. By the end of the war, in spite of severe labour shortages, CM&S would have supplied the British Empire with fifty percent of all its lead and zinc needs, not to mention many other metals, huge amounts of fertilizer to grow more food, as well as pumps and top notch marine engines from the Tadanac shops for use in Canadian war vessels.

Sometime in 1940 as the war was deepening, the hours of work at the smelter increased due to the demand for metals. This was achieved by Mr. Blaylock simply declaring it to be so and the Workmen's Committee duly agreeing. Day shift increased from a routine of five days on and two days off, to a regime of six days on and one day off, which further reduced time spent with the family. Shift work went to fourteen days on and two days off (all at straight time) which was exhausting, especially for those on night shift, but there wasn't loud objection from any quarter because of support for the war effort. In fact, in many of the jurisdictions where Mine Mill was organizing, including Trail, a resolution was passed that if we did become the bargaining agent during the war, there would be a no-strike policy for the duration. This was in line with a policy advocated by the Communist Party at the time, but opposed by many left-wing members of the CCF.

We in the union did not object to the new smelter hours. We did object, however, to worsening conditions of work and we maintained the request we'd put forward consistently in the *Commentator*, asking for a one dollar per day increase in pay. That had been, and continued to be, our clarion cry. It was on all our bulletins: "A dollar a day increase in pay."

AT HOME

The domestic bliss of the young King family was uneasy during this period. Two children, Wayne in 1938 and Geraldine in 1940, added major responsibilities that Lillian felt, quite rightly, were not being adequately shouldered on my part. Lil raised the kids, I didn't. It was hard on her with two, and later five, young kids who needed their dad around, but it was also hard because I think she thought that what I was doing was all so futile. Why shouldn't she? She was raised on a farm in southwestern Alberta where she'd never heard of unions. More, she hadn't experienced the injustices that I had on the Hill and she heard the talk around town that we were off the wall if we thought we were going to get a union out of all this.

Endless, and to me vital meetings were held daily and at all hours (due to shift work) in order to keep the union afloat. Being a Party member meant even more meetings. This is the same dedicated 'volunteer' union work ethic that continues to bedevil union families. Today, at least, much of it is paid for. In those days, it was not. In fact, when the two dollar per month dues, the one dollar per month organizing assessment and the one dollar per month to the Party were added up, we were actually paying for the doubtful privilege of putting our jobs and livelihood in jeopardy.

What made it worse for Lil was that there were almost no other women she could talk to. Before the war, I was the only union activist with a young wife and family so it was tough for her. She was nineteen years old with two young kids, living in a strange town away from her family, stuck out in the country in a two-room shack by the railroad track. One night while I was at work, somebody came and flashed a light in the window after Lil and the kids were in bed. Another time, somebody drove into the yard in the middle of the night, loud as could be, and banged on the door. All this was especially scarey because at the time, there were a lot of homeless people roaming around looking for work, and women left alone felt vulnerable. Lil now tells me stories that make me wince, like the time Geri was born. When Lil was pregnant this second time, we were living at Columbia Gardens. I went off to night shift and, instead of going home to check on my very pregnant wife, I went straight to a meeting. Lil got the milkman to deliver her to the hospital. I didn't even know she'd gone and had a baby.

I missed another one of the kids, too. I'd be quite surprised to go home and see another little bundle! Really, I was a bit of an asshole and after the war when I got involved in the Legion, it got worse; I was away twice as much, for most evenings and many days. The resulting pressures, both time and money-wise, were a terrible strain and very nearly wrecked our marriage.

At least I can say I always came home with a paycheque—I never stopped at a gambling joint and lost half of it. So it could have been worse, but it could have been a lot better, too. It's a very easy thing to do, to be so committed to a union cause that you sacrifice your family. A lot of union marriages have broken up over it. I owe Lil a very large thanks for sticking with me.

OFF TO WAR

Because the smelter was considered an essential service for the duration of the war, there was no pressure on us to sign up for military service. In fact, CM&S management were desperate to keep whatever experienced workers they could, so I could have stayed on at the smelter like a lot did, but I wouldn't have felt right. I didn't sign up for strictly patriotic reasons. I hated the Germans for what they'd done in Spain, and we were sending funds to help the Mackenzie-Papineau Batallion. I was very conscious of minority rights and since the time I first went on a union payroll, I've contributed to the NAACP. As far as the war went, I still had relatives getting the shit bombed out of them in Manchester and maybe that's why I eventually felt honour-bound to go. Lil agreed and said she would wait for me. I enlisted in the Canadian Air Force in 1941, and in 1942 I was called up to go overseas.

At about the same time, Lillian left Trail. Her folks wanted her back home, so she spent the remaining war years with her family and the kids, then three and five, in Pincher Creek, Alberta.

During the war, as in industry, there weren't enough men left on prairie farms, so the women had to take over. Lil worked like hell. She later told me how she and her sister would walk a mile and a half every morning to work in the fields, work all day at heavy labour including stooking the sheaves at harvest time, then walk back. Her mum was alive then and she kept the kids at home during the day.

Later, Lil took a job housekeeping for her mum's cousins, four single men in a big house, so she could have the kids with her. She did all the housework: washing, cooking, cleaning, mending, everything to keep a household of four hard-working men on a large farm, plus the extra hired men at harvest and thrashing times. Thrashing, especially, was rough. Lil would cook six times a day starting with breakfast, then carry a lunch out to the men in the field for their morning break. They would all come in for dinner and she'd send another lunch out for afternoon break, then they were in for supper and out again after. She'd feed them for the last time in the day when they came back in for the night, often at eleven p.m. because they'd work as late as the light would let them. Then she'd get up at dawn and start all over.

It was a huge job, especially with the two little kids, though the men were good to her and the kids. Then her mum got ill and died. It was very rough.

Meanwhile, from the time I went overseas, Drake, Belanger and the others continued to work, building the union.

THE SEA BISCUIT

Some people have said Trail was turned into an 'armed camp' during WWII because the smelter was vital for war production, but if so, it wasn't much of an armed camp. They'd have had to have had a regiment to cover all those plants. What they did was station a few of the home guard—the older guys and kids—at the bridges and on the outskirts of town. And it's not like they were heavily armed. When the war broke out, I bought the last rifle available in Trail for $52.50, just in case. I've still got it.

One year, Blaylock said in his Annual Report that the company brought in an armoured tank to protect the smelter, but that was bullshit. The guys told me later that what he did was put a bunch of steel plate on an ordinary car. For some reason it was called the Sea Biscuit, and Blaylock boasted about how it carried "four machine guns and six rifles ready for action at any moment," but the townspeople all laughed at it. It was heavily plated all around, but because of its ordinary rubber tires, one nail would have wiped out Blaylock's entire armoured division.

PC1003

By 1944, Prime Minister William Lyon Mackenzie King recognized that, in carrying out Canada's successful war effort, his government had asked for, and got, the support of Canadian working people. But now the war was almost over and labour unrest was high—taxes were increasing, work weeks were long and most wages had been frozen or held down by the National War-Time Prices Board. One of the signs of unrest had been a major Mine Mill strike at Kirkland Lake in 1941-42. King would soon have to call a national election and he was afraid, both of losing working people's support and of the growing popularity of a new Socialist party, the Co-operative Commonwealth Federation (CCF).

In the US, President Roosevelt had passed the Wagner Act in 1935 declaring company unionism and open discrimination against trade unions illegal, and I guess Mackenzie King figured that progressive laws and labour policies might kill two birds for him at once—gain labour's support and short-cut the CCF.

In 1944 under the Canadian War Measures Act, the Liberal government of Mackenzie King passed federal Order in Council, PC 1003. During the war, the War Measures Act had given the federal government wide powers to pass laws that superceded provincial and local laws. Some of the regulations passed under it were oppressive, such as the order for the disgraceful internment of Japanese Canadians in 1942, but PC1003 was of a far more benevolent nature. It required employers for the first time to bargain collectively whenever a majority of people in a bargaining unit voted to belong to a union. Until then, unions were legal, but there was no obligation for the employer to respond.

When PC1003 was incorporated into provincial labour laws, employers were forced to bargain with legitimate unions. The bill provided provincial Labour Boards with the power to certify any union that had the majority in a bargaining unit, and it required the employer to negotiate.

Until the advent of PC1003, the proportion of workers signed up in Local 480 in Trail remained pitifully low and in the Kimberley mine, nil. Given how naturally militant the Kimberley miners were, this might seem odd at first, but it made sense when you looked more closely. Miners don't need bosses. There is more brotherhood, more safety awareness and a keener sense of discipline in miners—especially underground miners—than in most other workers. The dangers of the job make it that way, so a good boss trusts his miners to produce. The worst thing an underground boss could ever do was turn off his light so he could spy on his crew, because he'd be beaten up. Miners know what's needed and what the conditions require without anybody watching over their shoulder. The Workmen's Committee in the Kimberley mine showed discipline—they never sucked up to the company. Perhaps it also made a difference that the working conditions were better than in the smelter and the company was more respectful of grievances. Whatever the reason, the Kimberley miners were a spunky lot who didn't bend their knee to anyone. Perhaps, also, the lack of a union had something to do with the fact there were no Communist Party members to spearhead the organizing.

But when PC1003 got passed, the Kimberley Workmen's Committee promptly voted to disband and form the Mine, Mill and Smelter Workers Union Local 651, and that was that. It wasn't nearly that straight-forward in Trail, but in either case, PC1003 made all the difference. It energized the trade union movement partly because it legitimized it in the eyes of the public. We were no longer just a bunch of malcontents—we now had the government on our side at last, saying unions had to be taken seriously.

PC1003 was an important turning point for Canadian labour. It outlawed company unions like the Workmen's Co-operative Committee and helped force CM&S to recognize Mine Mill as the legitimate, democratic choice of the workers. It opened the way for Local 480 to step up our organizing drive, but by itself, it still didn't accomplish the organization of the smelter. Organizers still had to get fifty-one per cent of all the day pay (or hourly) employees in the smelter to sign union cards.

Of course, I was overseas at the time. All I knew was that, one day in 1944, I was called in and told I had a wire from Canada. I immediately figured it was from Lil and something terrible had happened to one of our kids. But it was from Harry Drake. It said only, "Local 480 is certified." That meant fifty-one per cent of the employees were signed up in Mine Mill. It took six years from the time we started, but the boys (and by that time, the girls, too) had finally done it.

It didn't mean a thing to anybody else in the squadron, but I went out that night and got pie-eyed. I went on the goddamnedest drunk I could afford. I had heard that word "never" so many times while we were organizing: " No, boy, you'll never . . . . This company will never . . . . You'll never, never, never . . . ." and still we got our union certified!

Certification of the union in Trail was a reflection of two things: a sharply changed federal attitude toward unions plus a new confidence among workers because they now had no fear of losing their jobs. These two things dramatically changed the political and labour landscape and created a receptive climate when Mine Mill organizers asked men to sign union cards after January 1944. And Trail wasn't the only place such changes were happening—similar developments were taking place in major industries right across Canada. By the end of the war, union membership in Canada had almost doubled, from 359,000 to 711,000.

PC1003 ended an inglorious era in the operations of the Consolidated Mining and Smelting Company during which (from 1919 to 1944), the company could boast that not a day, not an hour, not a minute's production had been lost. Yet during this time, many honest men who simply disagreed with the status quo paid the price of instant dismissal, black listing from future smelting jobs and terrible personal loss.

THE INSTANT PRESIDENT

In about 1940, a union member in the sulphur dioxide plant brought forward a serious question that had to be dealt with initially by a Party decision. A fairly prominent worker with several brothers and a wide circle of friends, he proposed that he would join the union with all his brothers and use his influence to attract everyone he could to do likewise, on one condition—that as soon as he was sworn in as a member, he would be immediately installed as president of the local union.

The colossal nerve of the man! But Fred Henne, a heavy-set man with sharp green eyes, was known to be a crafty, careful individual. He was also a leader in the recreational and sporting life of the community and the union was in serious need of the popular acceptance he was offering to bring with him.

Party people debated pro and con for hours and, to make a longer story short, we did it. And that's how Fred Henne became the instant president of Local 480. He served in that capacity for several years. Fred was not the best president Local 480 ever had but he wasn't the worst, either. In many ways this development signaled another important change in the growth of the union in Trail and the Kootenay area. It was one more sign that the powerful hold of CM&S was at last showing signs of slipping.

Not only had the union changed its public image, it had begun to seriously challenge the traditional relationships between workers and their supervisors. Petty tyrants were having to face a new reality. The elitism the company had nourished for over a quarter century had come to a crashing halt and the element of fear and uncertainty that had pervaded both the industrial and the domestic atmospheres, was no more. The dignity of labour had arrived at last in the Kootenays.

It was a lot of good guys working together who helped to make the union happen. When we started, most workers on the Hill weren't eager to join a union. We were treated with disdain because they didn't think we'd succeed, and feared we were going to upset the job applecart. Some people simply disagreed with us. So it was pretty tough. I would say the change in the law was vital; we probably would never have succeeded without it. In the end, however, the Trail smelter workers decided to have a union, so they got one.

Around this time, my brother Jack cried enough and quit the company forever. Jack was a great guy and a progressive one. He joined the union, but he didn't have as much faith in the working class as I did and he never joined the Party. He was too busy being a hustler and a carpenter. He left the smelter because of his lungs—he had a bad case of pneumonia so he had to find a job in the fresh air. Despite this, he only lived another twelve years. He died of cancer of the lungs, from lead dust exposure and smoking. He was forty-two years old.

THE MAPLE LEAFERS

What I didn't know, and what Harry Drake didn't bother to tell me in his telegram telling me Local 480 was certified, was that the struggle for the union was far from over, even after the federal government passed Bill PC1003.

As soon as it was passed in 1944, the miners on the Workmen's Committee in Kimberley disbanded and joined Mine Mill *en masse*, but the response in Trail was very different. There, several members of the old Workmen's Co-operative Committee, with company approval, hastily formed what they called the Independent Smelter Workers Union, to continue opposition to Local 480. Most members of the Workmen's Committee plus many others faithful to CM&S obediently joined. Anything, my God, but Mine Mill Local 480 and the hated CIO!

This time, the ploy used to dislodge Local 480 was patriotism. The group chose as their logo a small red maple leaf that they wore as a pin on their lapels so that everyone was soon calling them the 'Maple Leafers'. In fact, scratch the surface and the Maple Leafers were the same old Workmen's Co-operative Committee but with a new name. They sniped and they criticized and they sulked and they wouldn't join the union and in general they behaved like kids—or like a bunch of stooges whose secure little sinecure had been wiped out. I should make it clear that some one-time members of the Workmen's Committee, notably Kitchener 'Kitch' Bannatyne and George Patrick LeFort, later joined Mine Mill and became valuable members and officers of the legitimate union movement. But men like these were a minority and the bulk of the Maple Leafers never ceased their opposition.

There was little doubt that CM&S was sympathetic. Selwyn Blaylock, chairman of CM&S and the power behind the old Workmen's Committee, died in 1945, but his successors were clearly as dedicated as he had been to stamping out the Mine Mill union, or at least to keeping its progress as limited as possible. Company and pseudo-union now both attacked Local 480 as being part of an international, US-associated union, a pawn of the CIO that was still busy organizing industrial plants all through the US and Canada. It was an unsubtle attempt to call up people's feelings of loyalty to

a Canadian organization (even if it was completely controlled by the boss) instead of the Mine Mill union with its international connections in the US.

In fact, one of the vital differences between Mine Mill and most other international unions is that most of our members didn't recognize the international boundary for purposes of work. Among miners, especially western miners, one week they'd be working in Kellogg, Idaho and the next in Kimberley, BC. Miners were migrants—still are—who go where the work is. This is something others don't understand when they draw hard lines in the so-called history of Mine Mill. They don't recognize that the members of the Western Federation of Miners and later the International Union of Mine, Mill and Smelter Workers wandered up and down the entire north-west side of North America. The Canada-US boundary was nothing to a miner. That's why being an international union was important to us, because we were truly international and that was a strength. If you don't understand that, you don't understand Mine Mill.

I think our eastern brothers in Mine Mill didn't have the same feeling for the International and maybe this is why. In eastern Canada, particularly Ontario, they didn't have the almost-daily cross-border contact that we did with US mines and miners, particularly with the Sunshine Mine just across the border in Kellogg, Idaho. When there was a terrible underground fire there in about 1970, we sent two mine rescue crews down immediately. Plus, as administrator of the union's Death Benefit Plan and without waiting for approval from the members, I okayed a donation of $5,000 from our Death

Signing the 1st collective agreement in 1944. Standing (l to r): Miller Mason, William Guillame, Peter McIntyre, Ed Campbell (all CM&S staff), Fred Henne, Rene Morin, Leo Nimsick, Hubert O'Dell (all union barganing committee members). Seated (l to r): W.S. Kirkpatrick, Ralph Diamond, Harvey Murphy (bargaining committee spokesperson and BC union director).

Benefit Plan to go to the widows and families. Then I asked the locals for their approval and only one—Kitimat—refused.

So, unlike the attitude of many craft union members to their international offices, the feeling of most Mine Mill members to their international—certainly here on the west coast—was always very friendly. This was especially so after Chase Powers, an American, became the District 7 board member in 1944-45.

Chase was my favourite international officer, maybe because he had the Irish in him. Before he was a union rep, Powers was a sand hogger, pushing tunnels under rivers and through bad ground. He was a great guy and a very handsome man. For a while, his girlfriend was Jo Stafford, a well-known singer, but when he finally married, it was to a miner's daughter from Butte, Montana.

I later heard it wasn't hard to sign up the veterans returning from World War II into the union and so help foil the company's hopes for the Maple Leaf union. Despite Blaylock's fond expectations, veterans did not join in a conspiracy against the legitimate Mine Mill union as the McKinnons and Davisons and others had done in 1919. On the contrary, the veterans' response to joining Local 480 was just about unanimously positive. There were several reasons for this, one of the main ones being that Harvey Murphy, who had become BC District Director of Mine Mill, was a very shrewd negotiator.

Before he came to BC for Mine Mill, Murphy worked for the Worker's Unity League, the Communist labour organizing central, against the United Mine Workers (UMW) in Alberta. At some point he was Secretary of the Town Council in Blairmore and maybe that's why, until recently, there was a boulevard down the main street of Blairmore called Tim Buck Boulevard. Tim Buck was leader of the Canadian Communist Party for years. I don't know if Murphy was a part of it, but I suspect so, because he was more a Communist than any of us. I think it was Jack Scott who said Murphy called himself "the reddest rose in the garden." At first Murphy was appointed by the International, but later, when the Canadian Mine Mill gained its independence, he was elected as one of Mine Mill's most competent and effective leaders for many years.

It was Murphy who, along with Chase Powers, was the union's spokesman in the first negotiated agreement between Mine Mill and CM&S that took place in 1944. Murphy insisted on a seniority clause that counted all time served in the armed forces as time worked for the company for the purposes of calculating seniority and pension benefits. This clause applied not only to all those returning to employment at CM&S, but also to those who had never worked for the company at all prior to joining the armed services.

All a man had to do to get seniority on the Hill was apply or re-apply for work with CM&S within three months of discharge. So for example, Bob Keiver, who never worked in the plant until after the war, ended up with just a few months less seniority than me who had joined CM&S in 1937 because he'd been in the services since 1939. Harvey Murphy got that for them.

That first Agreement also accepted all veterans into membership in Local 480 without having to pay initiation fees or the first month's dues. This was very helpful to those of us organizing new members, but I must say, it didn't help me. Because I was already a member of the union, I had to pay reinstatement. I had to pay to get back in! I was probably the only damned guy in the local who had to pay, but I was sure glad to see all those new young union members.

As I understand it, that first contract offered just the bare bones of union protection, things like union recognition and the right of the union to bargain on behalf of its members. I think there was a total of four pages to that first agreement, then year by year we worked to improve it.

Some people say that after years of fighting the union, having to actually sit and bargain with Mine Mill was what finally killed Selwyn Blaylock. Of course, the fact that he was getting older and had just come through a major war effort probably had something to do with it too, but it sure hurt him to acknowledge the hated Mine Mill. The story goes that on the very first day union and management began to bargain, Blaylock sat at the head of the table, banged his gavel and said, "They told me I had to recognize the union. Hello, union."

Then he turned his chair around to the window and refused to have anything else to do with the whole thing. He must have been very impressed with Chase Powers nonetheless, because when the whole thing was finished, Blaylock tried to hire him. I guess he didn't know Chase was a Communist.

THE LEGACY

The top floor meeting hall of Branch 11 of the Canadian Legion in Trail was packed. A mixture of greed, curiosity and honest interest had brought the veterans of WWII of Trail together for a special meeting called to deal with a single item of business. Before he died in 1945, the then-President and Managing Director of CM&S, Selwyn G. Blaylock, had left a sealed envelope addressed to the returning warriors to be opened after his death, when all the veterans had returned.

President Stanley T. Dawson, magistrate and businessman, called the special meeting to order. The envelope was opened with a flourish and in the dead silence that followed, President Dawson read out in a choked voice Mr. Blaylock's legacy: "One, fifty dollar war bond."

The shocked silence was punctuated by a nervous giggle. Then the meeting erupted in screams of laughter, rage and frustration, depending on the outlook of each member.

At the next election of officers of Branch 11, Royal Canadian Legion in Trail, there was a transfer of power from the old forces to the new and nobody ever mentioned Mr. Blaylock's Legacy again.

UNION SISTERS

I found out later that although there were no women working in the plant before the war, management had to hire many of them during World War II because of a lack of labour power, and these women were better than the men for supporting the union. The company's newspaper later said the women's work had been "most satisfactory." I was overseas at the time so I didn't see it, but I also heard that the women were paid eighty per cent of the wages men were paid to do the same job—some things are very slow to change.

I think women are naturally more militant than men. Mine Mill was unique in the labour movement in that it recognized this. From very early on, we took the position that wives work for the company too, keeping the

Ladies' Auxiliary, at the Mine Mill convention, mid 1950s. Left to right, Julia Rigby, Imelda Brown, Margaret Bystrom, Ann Walton, Rose Patterson, Betty Donaldson (Director, Western Ladies Auxiliary), Margaret Canothan, Verona Christianson, Dot Radcliffe.

guys scrubbed and clean and fed and raising the kids. Really, the women are unpaid employees of the goddamned company, and a lot of them look at it that way, too. Harvey Murphy always said that organizations lose touch with their membership at their own peril, and by 'membership' he didn't mean just the men who were drawing pay and paying dues. He meant the whole family—wives and kids worked for the union too.

Mine Mill was one of the first unions to recognize the important role of women—the wives, widows, mothers, daughters and sisters of union members—by setting up Ladies Auxiliaries that were independently affiliated with the union. Their purpose, as set out in our Constitution, was to see to "the education and training of women in the labour movement and to assist their Local Unions in time of need and labour disputes, to support the Union in its legislative efforts and to provide educational and cultural activities for our members and their children." By our Constitution, wives were always welcome—and some did come—to local union meetings. They didn't have voice or vote but they could find out first hand what was going on and who was saying what, and each Auxiliary was entitled to one vote at the International union convention.

Later, when we were being raided by the Steelworkers union, one of the vital elements in the support for Mine Mill was the participation of Local 131 of the Ladies Auxiliary of Trail and Rossland. Led by people like Tilly Belanger (Gar's wife and a senior nurse in the Trail Tadanac Hospital), several women and sisters including Inis Gattrell, Ilda Morandini, Betty Donaldson, Kay Dosen, Bernie Laarz, Dulcie Warrington, Dot Radcliff, Hilda Scott, Marg Bystrom, Emma Penson, Marie Walsh, Evelyn Lewis, Joyce Muir, Joan McIntyre and dozens of others, including my wife, Lil, pitched in to assist their men folk. At all hours of the day and night, in every weather and with little or no notice, they distributed bulletins, conducted voting, catered to socials, broadcast on radio station CJAT and all in all, provided a depth of support that neither the company nor the raiding Steelworkers could effectively counter.

In times of labour trouble, women walked Mine Mill picket lines and passed out leaflets, did radio broadcasts—whatever was necessary to help the brothers on the job. Any union that doesn't recognize the importance of women in the working lives of their men—let alone the importance of women as active union members in their own right—is, like the song says, fighting with one hand tied behind its back.

When the war was over, though, and the veterans came back to work at the Trail smelter, the women had to leave. They went willingly, I think, because they knew when they took the jobs that they were just taking our places while we were away.

COMING HOME

I returned from overseas in July 1945, not to Trail but to a hospital in Edmonton for problems with my ankle. Lillian and the kids came back when I was finally sent home to Trail in January 1946.

The first thing we had to do was find a place to live. Before the war we'd lived in the little shack I'd built out in the country, but that was no longer big enough. Lil had saved all her money during the war so with that and the money from our acre of land, we went house hunting. But with all the veterans returning, there was literally nothing to rent in Trail and only one house left to buy, at 1445 Second Avenue. We bought it and moved in.

There were a lot of changes. Most of our old friends were still in town and there were new ones because many of the veterans came back with European wives, but when guys have been away at war that long, they've got a lot of adjusting to do. All of us had to get used to losing family and friends. Two of my closest pals were killed in Italy and on Lillian's side of the family there were three killed.

Apart from the general scramble to get re-established, it's also just plain hard for soldiers to readjust to civilian life. The guys who'd been away but not actively fighting found it easier than the ones who were overseas. A lot of the ex-soldiers were emotionally distraught and showed it in different ways, like drinking too much, or acting violently around town or with their families. Some never did adjust properly—they'd seen too many horrors. One or two veterans committed suicide.

It was hard for families, too. My daughter, Jeri, didn't know who I was, a stranger coming into her house after four years away. Our kids were five and seven when I got back.

And of course, we were going back to work. There had been major changes in the union I'd known when I left. In the first elections after we were certified, some of the same people who'd worked so hard for years to build the union were turfed out through the efforts of people who were much more company-oriented. Now that it was safe to belong to a union, a group of opportunists under the leadership of Claire Billingsley became active. In addition to Billingsley, this group included Lloyd Bailey, Bill Melvin, Ralph Fletcher, James Quinn, George Bishop, 'Loyal' Laurie Hamilton and others.

On the other side, many young veterans and new union members supported Local 480, including Bill Godber, Fred Pearson, Martin Walsh, Al Warrington, Bill Gattrell, the brothers Bill and George Eastcott and George and Joe Mukanik, John McWilliams, Maurice McWatters, Art Ahrens, Harry Nicol, Dave Schapanski, Elton Ozust, Jack Scott, Gerry Bertrand, Jack Cox, George LeFort, Colin Donalson, Nels Bystrom, Kitch Bannatyne, Tiny Noakes, Pat Kennedy, Art Kelly, Arne Engfelt, Soren Kilt, Frank Barnes, Teddy Hall, Les bogie and many more. Although a few of the old gang remained, including Dan Dosen, Gar Belanger, Dick Gopp, Sig Colautti, Chuck Kenny, Sam Muirhead, Mike Lypchuk, Doug Murdoch, Dave McMartin, John Page, Bill Cunningham, Leo Nimsick and a few others, many equally good union builders such as Harry Drake, John McPeake, George DeGroff, Howard Forbes, Sam Sivorot and Harry McTague had disappeared—either quit or were fired or voted out of office. Gordon Martin enrolled at the University of British Columbia law school.

Harry Drake was one of those who was promptly voted out of office. It didn't seem right to me—this man who had worked for years, who did more to build the union than any ten of the rest of us, was replaced by a bunch who were far more company minded. My wife thinks I spent a lot of time on union business, but that guy Drake spent far more time and more money. If the union was ever short of funds, Harry was always the one who came up with the necessary cash.

When Harry was defeated, he no longer had even the meager allowance of union secretary, so he approached CM&S for his old job on the Hill. They no doubt remembered his various challenges to Mr. Blaylock in the old Workmen's Committee days, and refused. They did more than just refuse him a job—they blacklisted him for life. Harry had to leave Trail because he couldn't get any work in town. He drove taxi for a while, then went to Nakusp where he got a job as a faller in the forest industry and helped organize IWA locals up and down the Kootenays. But some of the IWA reps gave him a hard time because Harry was a Communist, so he quit that and went hardrock mining. We always kept in touch. He eventually married and after his death, we tried—unsucessfully—to contact his children. The workers in Trail owe Harry Drake a lot for what he did to form their union.

The Billingsley group were quick to see that they were protected from a fate like Harry's by soon getting a clause in the agreement that gave them continued seniority at work if they went on a leave of absence for union work.

WORKING HARD FOR MY MONEY

When I first came back from overseas, I wasn't able to return to my old job of full manual work because of my disability. Instead, I was assigned to the milkhouse in the zinc plant at an hourly rate of ninety-seven cents an hour. That was labour pay, the lowest pay in the smelter, but it was still decent money for the time.

Remember, in those days, the company gave a daily pint of milk to every man working in lead or mine dust to prevent lead poisoning. As the milk-man, it was my responsibility to issue the free milk to those entitled to it, sell it to those not entitled, and to keep financial records for all the other milk consumed.

My foreman was Manny Triggs, an old Cornishman who worried about the 'books' partly because he couldn't write anything except his own name. So Manny and I made a deal. I would do his books for him, tell him the time and give him a free bottle of milk every day, on condition that he bring every new man hired into the zinc plant labour gang to me in the milkhouse. There I'd sign them up in the union and give them a free bottle of milk—compliments of CM&S. I must say it was difficult at times to explain to Chief Clerk Gus McDonald in the office why there were so many 'breakages.'

All good things must end, however, and two years later, in about 1948, my leg had healed sufficiently for me to be transferred to a better job as an operator in the seven man cadmium plant where I became Shop Steward. The transfer to the cadmium plant was welcome for several reasons. Since Lillian and I now had a third child (Sherrill, in addition to Wayne and Geri), the increase in pay was important. The fact that it meant no more afternoon shift on a twelve-four schedule of twelve days on, four days off, was even better. It was in this plant that I worked until 1950.

The first summer I worked in the cadmium plant, I suffered an attack of

THE MILK HOUSE

One day, Manny arrived with two flat cars with twelve men on each car.

"Jesus, Manny," says I, "I can't sign them all up here. Take this case of milk to the Salvage Yard and I'll follow you." By the time I closed the Milk House, walked to the Salvage Yard and signed them all up, the day was over.

I went to my cross-shift counterpart and said, "Look, I broke a case of bottles today and you broke another one, right?" and he said, "I did? Okay, right!" and we got away with it. Of course, Gus was suspicious as hell because I'm sure he thought I was selling the milk and keeping the proceeds. If they'd ever found out why union organizing was flourishing in the zinc plant, all hell would have broken loose—I'd have been fired, Triggs would have been fired, and probably so would Gus MacDonald.

But that was not a bad day's work considering a clause in the 1944 Collective Bargaining Agreement (CBA) that prohibited union organizing on the job.

appendicitis immediately after finishing my shift, on the first of my four rest days. The day after the operation when my superintendent, Stuart Smillie visited me in hospital, I was up and walking around. Smillie jokingly suggested I return to work on my usual day, but temporarily return to the lighter work of the milkhouse where a holiday vacancy had come up. So with the promise that help would be given to lift the heavy milk cases, I returned to work—probably the first case of a patient being operated on for appendicitis without missing a shift.

THE 1946 AGREEMENT

In Trail one of the earliest goals in bargaining was to get rid of the fluctuating bonus system, but it took six years of bargaining, until 1950, before we finally achieved an hourly rate of pay. All this time we were also busy bargaining to get vacations with pay, overtime pay, statutory holiday pay, and various medical and hospital provisions. After that we formed a Job Evaluation Committee that went around evaluating jobs and setting rates. It was easy to evaluate the craft jobs, the so-called 'skilled' trades like carpenters and plumbers. But for what were called the 'semi-' or 'unskilled' or operating staff—many of whom had enormous skill and expertise—it took several years to evaluate the jobs and set appropriate rates.

Negotiations took place between the union and the company in '44 and '45, but the first collective agreement in which I was involved was the one in 1946, after I came back from overseas.

It was pretty important to Harvey Murphy at that time that the agreement he'd negotiated be approved by the members because it included some crucial changes. The union had agreed, for the first time, on a national plan for bargaining that he was convinced would make this one of the best industrial agreements in Canada. He figured that the time was right. The world economy was booming and with all the rebuilding and prosperity, the demand for metals was very high, so the proposals included demands for a forty hour work week, paid vacation and holidays, shift differential and guaranteed annual work or wage.

What we got in the 1946 negotiations in both Trail and Kimberley, of course, was somewhat less than what we'd originally asked for. It was an excellent agreement in many ways, except that some of us felt there was not enough of a money increase. So Fred Pearson, Martin Walsh, Al Warrington, Jack Scott, some other Party people and I, all of us just out of the services, got together and decided we were going to oppose it.

I guess Murphy figured the politics of getting the thing voted in in Trail was in the capable hands of Don Guise, the Party organizer. Guise didn't work in the smelter and he wasn't a veteran, but he was a good guy, a coal miner and a Party member. I think Guise sympathized with us because he didn't do a lot to dissuade us from our decision.

Don, who was the International rep for a while, came from the Lethbridge coal mines. Later he moved to Vancouver where he and Jack Phillips, the

HARVEY MURPHY

In some circles there's been a lot of spiteful talk about Harvey Murphy. Murphy was a vital part of Mine Mill and he's an important part of the reason we survived as long and as well as we did in Trail. He certainly was a strange and complex web of a man, and he was a brilliant strategist. It would take a book to fully describe Harvey Murphy.

Murphy wasn't anything to look at—a fat, rotund little chap who couldn't sing and couldn't dance, with a big, raucous voice you could hear a mile away. Like a lot of the rest of us, he was an immigrant. I think his original name was Polish, and early on—back in eastern Canada—he'd served time in jail as a 'subversive' for being an active organizer with the Communist Party of Canada (CPC).

Murphy was a very clever, accomplished and cagey operator, a great public speaker and a superb strategist on behalf of workers and their families. But he could also on occasion be an unscrupulous bastard and once he made up his mind, absolutely nothing stopped him from pursuing it. He was completely single minded—it was work and politics for Harvey Murphy, period. He was hopeless at sports.

After going to a single hockey game with him, none of us ever wanted to go with him again because he wouldn't stop talking the whole time. You'd get into some really tight moment in the game—and Harvey wouldn't shut up about the union or politics.

Murphy's singular focus stemmed from his enormous compassion for the underdog. One small example of this is the time citizens in Vancouver were trying to rally support against a planned increase in bus fares. A lot of ordinary people opposed it, but none of the candidates then running for mayor was paying any attention. It was Murphy's idea to run Effie Jones, a very plain-spoken housewife, as a candidate for mayor, opposed to any increase in bus fares. Effie didn't get elected, but the bus fares didn't go up either, thanks to the interest raised by her campaign.

It was his sense of humour that made Murphy bearable. He was quick-witted and used to get some pretty good one-liners off. He also liked to play cards; he couldn't play worth a shit, but he was always jovial about losing. You either loved Harvey Murphy or you hated him.

Little Corporal, formed the first Vancouver municipal workers' union, the Vancouver City Outside Workers, Local 28 (now CUPE). It was a good, independent union. Phillips was a doctrinaire Communist—a pain in the ass at times— but a great little guy.

In the Kootenays, Murphy scheduled both meetings to ratify the '46 Agreement on the same night, one in Kimberley and one in Trail. Because he had a pretty good little cell of Party members in Trail, he wasn't worried about the vote passing there, but he thought he might have trouble selling it in Kimberley. So he went to that meeting and left the handling of the one in Trail to Don Guise.

I was just one of several guys who voted it down in Trail.

When Murphy came back, was he ever pissed off! He said, "I figured it was a cinch to get this passed in Trail. I went to what I thought was the difficult place and here it was the easy place that sunk the thing!" He had to go back to the company and dig a little more out of them, which he did. That was the first time I met Harvey Murphy.

Although all the other Mine Mill locals in BC had to go on strike to reach a settlement that year, the Trail and Kimberley locals remained at work since the union and CM&S had an agreement. The strike elsewhere was settled favourably to the unions shortly afterward, and BC miners and smelter workers emerged as the highest paid in North America. However, the Company rigidly maintained its opposition to strengthening the union security or 'check-off' provisions of the collective agreement.

CHECK-OFF

In those days, the crucial time when any union was the most vulnerable was when annual negotiations were pending. Two months prior to the termination of our annual agreement was the only time another union could legally 'raid' and challenge the union for the right to represent its members. Under the terms of the Provincial Industrial Conciliation Act, if another union could convince fifty-per-cent-plus-one of our members to sign their own union cards, they would then take over the legal right to represent those workers.

Traditionally, unions discourage raiding because it divides workers and depletes limited resources. Most union centrals have rules against it, but the odd union breaks the rules and takes the consequences. And if a union is not a member of the same central, then it's open season. Of course, the Mine, Mill and Smelter Workers' Union had been tossed out of almost every central it had ever belonged to, from the AFL to the CIO in the US, and in Canada, the Canadian Congress of Unions, because it was too radical. By that I mean too focussed on actually improving the lives and working conditions of its grassroots membership.

Under provincial labour law, the acknowledged form of proving the size of your membership—and therefore your right to be the certified bargaining agent—was by the monthly payment of dues, but the volume of dues waxed and waned for a variety of reasons.

Today, there is a legal requirement for what is called 'dues check-off,' by which employers automatically deduct union dues from a worker's paycheque. But in those days, all dues were paid in cash on a monthly basis and the collection of dues at the workplace was not permitted by the company. It was therefore a week-to-week, month-to-month, member-to-member 'by Jimmy Higgins' struggle for the union to survive. Shop stewards and officers devoted enormous time and effort to collecting dues.

There were an infinite number of reasons why members might not pay their monthly dues: if there was no active job steward, or no steward at all in that part of the smelter; if the member was short on cash and chose to spend his money elsewhere; or if he was angry at the union for something done or not done; or if he simply felt less support that month for the union and its activities, then he might not pay.

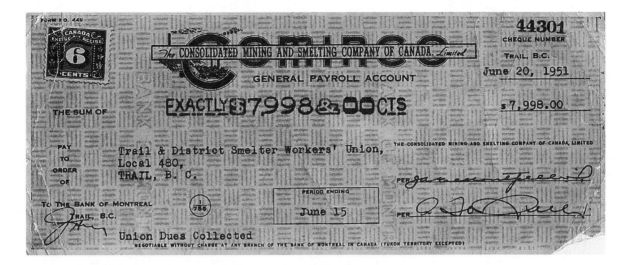

Comnco

44301
CHEQUE NUMBER

The CONSOLIDATED MINING AND SMELTING COMPANY OF CANADA, *Limited*

TRAIL, B.C.

GENERAL PAYROLL ACCOUNT

June 20, 1951

CANADA EXCISE ACCISE 6 CENTS

THE SUM OF   EXACTLY $7998&00CTS $ 7,998.00

THE CONSOLIDATED MINING AND SMELTING COMPANY OF CANADA, LIMITED

PAY TO ORDER OF   Trail & District Smelter Workers' Union,
Local 480,
TRAIL, B. C.

PER

TO THE BANK OF MONTREAL
TRAIL, B.C.   PERIOD ENDING   June 15   PER

Union Dues Collected

NEGOTIABLE WITHOUT CHARGE AT ANY BRANCH OF THE BANK OF MONTREAL IN CANADA (YUKON TERRITORY EXCEPTED)

At times we fell way below the fifty per-cent-plus-one number and we knew it, especially in the first years after we became the bargaining agent when we were politically opposed both inside and outside the union. But for a long time we weren't challenged for our right to represent the members because we always managed to fall below the fifty per cent mark during the period when we couldn't be decertified. And when we started bargaining, guys got interested in the union again and we'd get our membership back up. But it was always very fragile.

At that time there was a long union tradition of wearing insignia in the form of buttons. This now became important to the identity and strength of our union. Monthly dues were three dollars. As each man paid, he was given a small metal button with the Mine Mill insignia on it to wear on his lapel or on his cap. The colour changed from month to month. These buttons were useful because they identified union brother to union brother and also identified non-members as potential candidates for membership. There were also always some timid souls who paid their dues but refused to wear a button. These were soon recognized and left alone.

With a partial check-off agreement, the 1946 contract agreement provided some resolution to the problem of dues collection. From 1947 on, some form of check-off was included in each successive collective bargaining agreement until the Sloan Formula in 1951 (the Rand Formula, elsewhere) granted us the right to collect non-salaried employees' dues through company paycheques, whether people were union members or not, because the union was obliged to represent them anyway, and they benefitted from its work. The decision was challenged by CM&S until finally Judge Eric Dawson in Nelson confirmed that if all employees are protected by the union, they should all pay dues to the union. The only exception allowed would be on religious grounds, but to the best of my knowledge, no one ever requested such deferment. So from 1947 onward, shop stewards were relieved of the necessity of collecting cash dues on a one-on-one basis.

This resolution did, however, require concessions from the union that boded ill for the future. Prior to 1947, the financial position of the union was

First company payment of mandatory check-off of dues to Local 480 Mine Mill by order of Chief Justice Sloan. This was the end of voluntary revocable check-off. It forced all anti-union workers to start paying dues.

always unknown to the company. After check-off was initiated and the company deducted monthly dues from employee paycheques, CM&S knew exactly the financial status of the local.

Oddly enough, we did sign a check-off once, earlier—in about 1940. Two guys, Ace 'Bugalug' Haddrell and Alex Shaak, came to Trail to collect money for a big sit-down strike that was going on in the Pioneer Mine at Bralorne. Our local organized a campaign that persuaded the company to honour requests by employees for a check-off of five dollars each in aid of the Bralorne strikers. We shamed the company into doing it. But at that time, signing up to contribute money wasn't like saying you were a union member because there were guys who weren't in the union, lots of them, who felt the Bralorne miners deserved our support. The Bralorne miners also got support from the Kimberley miners and from Ma Murray, the feisty editor of the Lillooet newspaper.

CM&S checked the money off our paycheques but guess what they did with it? They couldn't bear to send it to a union, so instead they sent it to the Catholic Chuch in Lillooet! The church might have been fair about it, but we never knew—maybe the union rebels didn't get any, but the devout Catholics probably did. Anyway, the miners won their strike.

In retrospect I'd say we had no alternative to obtaining the check-off. Not only were our energies being seriously drained by having to collect current monthly dues, but check-off was becoming the norm in the BC labour movement. However, we paid a terrible price, and in some ways, getting a check-off agreement was one of the worst things we ever did. Our jobs as shop stewards got much easier, but it was conducive to what we now call 'business unionism,' where the union executive conducts the business of the union and the members stay uninvolved. When we got dues check-off, we lost the sinews of trade unionism, the man-to-man, worker-to-worker contact we'd had on a monthly basis, the sense of communication and responsibility to each other that regular contact created.

It's very difficult to say what would have been the best thing to do. At the time, we thought check-off was the answer. We needed it to survive because politically we were a relatively immature working class group, new to unionism. Perhaps it would be different today, with working people more educated, more exposed to trade union principles and objectives. But it's a very bad thing to let the company know what your strength is, how much money you have in the bank.

Then again, perhaps it's too easy to say it would be different today. Trade unions have problems now that we didn't have to face then. In the 1940s there was only one enemy and that was the boss. Today there's a pervasive media and a more dedicated, organized and subversive political opposition. The press was our enemy then too, but it wasn't as pervasive as it is now. The CBC only started in Canada in 1936, but it was a while before we could pick up their signal in Trail. When Lillian and I eventually got a battery radio, all we received were the US stations and we didn't get our first radio station in Trail—Station CJAT—until 1940. Until then, there was only one newspaper and lots of leaflets and one-on-one talk.

COMMUNITY

After my return from overseas I continued to work as a shop steward for Local 480, but I also joined Branch 11 of the Royal Canadian Legion, mainly because my dad had been a staunch member following his demobilization after World War I. It was through my Legion membership that I met most of the 'comrades', as we called them in the Legion, who were to become lifelong friends: Bud DeVito, Fred Pearson, Al Warrington, Jack Scott, Martin Walsh, George LeFort and many others.

In 1926 the people of Trail had built a three storey building in downtown Trail as a memorial to the veterans of WWI. There was a gym, bowling alley, swimming pool, library and a space rented to the Canadian Legion Branch 11. During wwii, the Trail Patriotic Society collected funds for the use of returning veterans and their families and at the end of the war, the Society turned the building and its large bank account over to the Legion to show the citizens' appreciation for the sacrifices of their sons and daughters. The existing Legion executive decided to spend all the money—$87,000—on renovating the building. They hired a firm and when it turned out $87,000 wasn't enough, we had to raise another $30,000 for the over-run. Some of us thought this was a scandal so we got together to turf the whole executive out and elect Bud DeVito the new president and me, vice-president, of Branch 11 in Trail.

It's funny—there's a clause in the Legion constitution that bars Communists from membership and office in the Legion, but at the time I joined, I was not only generally known as a Communist, but also as the chairman of the Labour Progressive Party (LPP) which was the party of Marxist-Leninist philosophy in Canada. It didn't seem to matter to the people who elected me. Jack Scott and Al Warrington were two other well-known Communists who weren't barred from Legion membership.

I continued to go to union meetings, but with Billingsley and his cohorts in office I'd regularly get into disagreements, so instead, I spent most of my time in the Legion. I once commented that at that time I was able to get more progressive motions through Branch 11 of the Canadian Legion than I could get through Local 480 of Mine Mill. That was largely a sign of the growing hostility of management and of some in the union to anyone designated as a 'red' in the period after the war.

Lillian and I had been able to buy a house in Trail after I returned from overseas, but in so doing, we were more fortunate than scores of others in Trail or practically anywhere else in Canada. The late '40s were a landlord's hey-day. Under the pressure of thousands of veterans returning home, getting married and starting families, rental rates were sky-high and some of the hovels people had to live in were unfit for pigs. Government aid for new housing was sketchy and required yards of red tape. The Central Mortgage and Housing Corporation (CMHC) could build houses okay, but there was no money with which to acquire land or services, so the first issue Bud DeVito and I tackled was the lack of decent housing at reasonable rates for veterans. We set up a Housing Committee with me as the Chair. Then

BUD DEVITO

Frances E. 'Bud' DeVito was the eldest son of a highly regarded Italian-Canadian family who ran a shoe repair business in Trail. During the war he served as a radar technician for the RCAF overseas where he met and married his wife, Betty. Later he would serve briefly as the International rep for Mine Mill in the 1950 executive. He was never a Communist. Buddy ran for CCF MLA in 1958 and later served as alderman and then mayor of the town of Trail. He was always a thoughtful man, always reading, always searching for answers to the problems he saw around him, not just in Trail but in the world.

There's a funny story about how Buddy got to be president of the Legion. When we were trying to get him elected, we had a meeting of our little Legion Ginger group where Buddy announced, "I'll run for president, but I won't vote for myself. I'll vote for the other guy."

I said, "If you vote for the other guy, I'm not going to vote for you! If you won't vote for yourself, fuck you!" And the guys all agreed with me. Buddy won that election by one vote and with him as president and me as vice-president, we promptly embarked on a program of action that shook up a lot of people.

we secured the co-operation of Bill Curran, the Editor of the *Trail Daily Times*. He didn't share our politics—he was as far right as you could get—but he was a veteran of World War I and he had a streak of decency in his makeup, particularly with respect to veterans, so he became a valuable ally.

Bill went to bat for us by loaning us one of his staff to photograph some of the shacks. Then he printed the pictures in the *Times* along with a list of the exorbitant rents that vets were being charged, and he put editorials and pictures on the front pages. We editorialized and criticized the provincial and federal governments (through the CMHC), the municipality, the landlords and last but not least, the lordly Consolidated Mining and Smelting Company of Canada Ltd., and ended up shaming the company into giving us 175 lots for one dollar each, lots I suspect the company acquired because of the smelter's pollution. We were on our way.

The City of Trail provided free servicing, free water, power and sewer, and CMHC provided the money for the houses, though not for basements. We built 175 beautiful veteran's homes up-river from the smelter, out of the smoke, in a place called Sunningdale that used to be an old sheep ranch owned by Robert Somerville Sr. Of course, there were more than 175 vets in Trail who needed housing, so we decided who should get the new housing on the basis of credits: so many points for the size of your family, so many points for years of service, and so on. Returning vets didn't have a bunkerful of money for the down payment, so houses were distributed on a rental basis. Rental was lease-to-purchase and the interest rate was five per cent. There might have been a token down payment of $100, I can't remember, but if there was a down payment, it was minimal and nobody paid more than $100 a month rent.

A lot of guys never did buy their houses outright. If they'd had to borrow the money to buy them, the interest would have been a heck of a lot more than five per cent. They were amortized over twenty-five years so at the end of paying rent for twenty-five years, you owned your house.

It was a proud day for Bud DeVito and Al King when in 1947, within a year of beginning the campaign, we held a presentation for the opening of the first house built to house veterans and their families. I must say, I got into some trouble with the people who owned the original hovels because they saw me as causing them to lose rental income.

Anyway, veteran's housing was one windmill Buddy and I tilted at and won. We weren't always so successful—including on the home front. We were spending a great deal of time on our joint endeavours and eventually our wives, Betty and Lil, were quite put out at the amount of time we spent on Legion business. In addition to housing, our other activities included projects like the erection of a decent cenotaph in Trail. We got all the labour donated by veterans, the City of Trail furnished the lot and the masonry work, and Consolidated Mining and Smelting provided the metal castings, in memory of local young people killed in the wars.

After the war many veterans, including myself, had become disenchanted with the lack of efforts toward preserving world peace, and had joined or rejoined progressive political parties. Many joined the CCF—predecessor of the NDP—but some, like myself, joined the Labour Progressive Party. I was the Chair in Trail until I resigned in 1950; most of our efforts there were directed toward the peace movement. In this early post-war era there was naturally a strong desire for peace, particularly among returned veterans, and veterans in particular supported the Stockholm Peace Initiative that aimed to secure world-wide endorsation by getting thousands of signed petitions. Another avid supporter of the Peace Initiative was Jim Endicott, a local doctor who along with his children, Bill and Mary Louise, collected hundreds of signatures for peace.

John Foster Dulles, Churchill and others characterized it as another Russian gimmick, but it wasn't. It was the result of an international meeting held in Stockholm in 1945 or '46 to denounce all wars. It called for the resumption of discussions and the abandonment of territorial aggression by any nation. Those of us who supported it were called 'reds' and 'dupes' of the Soviets, but had it been followed, the wars in Vietnam and Korea wouldn't have happened. It was seen as a signal by many of us who'd gone through the war that another one wasn't to be endured, ever, by anybody.

RED HYSTERIA

Increasingly, the reason so many people were in such a hurry to get rid of Mine Mill was a lurid fear of Communism.

Prior to World War II, the company, the Workmen's Committee, the press and the pulpit had all preached against Local 480's connection with the CIO.

At that time, the issue was that of being a radical, grass roots organization of so-called 'unskilled or semi-skilled' workers, and the fact that many of the leaders of CIO unions were also Communists was hardly a factor. But after WWII the degree of perceived threat posed by the CIO and Communism underwent a substantial change.

The major western powers, especially the US, had been worried about the potential power of the Soviet Union even before the war, and they formed an uneasy alliance during it. As soon as the war was over, the gloves came off. In 1946, Winston Churchill came to the US and made a speech in Fulton, Missouri about how the Russians were now our enemies. In it he used the

THE AUGUST JUDGE

Most of us who supported the Stockholm Petition solicited signatures everywhere, so early in the '50s when we took the train to a union convention in Vancouver, several of my fellow unionists naturally spent some of their time walking through the train securing signatures.

I was sitting in the smoker car with Les Walker, Secretary of Local 480, when a well-dressed individual entered, sat down and proceeded to belch large clouds of smoke from an expensive-looking cigar. Les leaned over to me and said, "Oh, Christ. I hope none of the boys ask him to sign the petition."

"Why?" says I.

"Because that's Judge J.V. Clyne, returning from court in Nelson or Cranbrook. He is one reactionary old bastard."

The words were scarcely out of his mouth when in bounced Sarge Walsh, Al Warrington and Jack Scott, sassy and smiling, and made a beeline for Judge Clyne.

"Sir," says Walsh, "would you like to sign the Stockholm Peace Petition?"

Poor Walsh. The august judge unloaded on him with a blast that denounced the open-mouthed Walsh and all the rest of us as dupes of the 'reds.' In short, Judge Clyne declined to sign. Then he threw his cigar down and stomped out.

The spectacle of this crusty old curmudgeon—who had never heard a shot fired in anger—lecturing men like Sarge Walsh who'd been blown out of a tank at the Falaise Gap, and Jack Scott who'd been decorated with the Croix de Guerre by the French, and Al Warrington who'd fought with the Seaforths for more than six years in Italy and northern Europe—was so outrageous that it didn't really register until later. Here were men who'd seen up to seven years of battle now returned home to ask people to sign a peace petition, having abuse thrown at them by someone who hadn't even been there.

Clyne's attitude to us as veterans of WWII seemed consistent with his later self-confessed involvement as a scab against the veterans of WWI. When the First War ended in 1918, the powers that be tried to interfere with the Russian revolution of 1917 by sending troops to support the White Russians against Lenin. But the European troops rebelled; they wouldn't go. I know this because my dad was one of them. Longshoremen in the UK went on strike and the stevedores and workers on the Tilbury Docks in London refused to load and prepare ships.

It was a small revolution, but in his memoirs, Clyne talks about being upset about all this. He joined the militia and worked for the London Dock Authorities, riding around on horseback and kicking the shit out of working people. It figures.

expression, "an iron curtain has descended over Europe" and that was the sign for the beginning of the cold war and the manufactured paranoia about Communism. Unfortunately, most people had extremely short memories and they went for it hook, line and sinker. In my opinion, what it was really about was American fear of losing potential world influence.

The Soviet state with its Communist ideals as opposed to the American capitalist ones, was the single greatest threat to US world hegemony and the US fought back with a propaganda campaign of fear. It worked, too.

For labour unions, the legislation that largely initiated this campaign was the Taft-Hartley Act. Passed by the United States government in 1947, it was a pernicious piece of poison that, among other things, required all US labour unions to forbid members of the Communist Party from holding leadership positions. Defiance of this measure would result in the Labour Relations Board refusing vital services to the union. The only international union that ever successfully defied Taft-Hartley was the United Mine Workers Union (UMW) led by that quixotic old fighter, John L. Lewis. The rest, sooner or later and with more or less enthusiasm, complied. This, of course, had major implications for progressive international unions like Mine Mill.

The atmosphere of accusation and fear was fed in the US by media-hyped events such as the espionage trial and execution of Julius and Ethel Rosenberg, the witch-hunts of the US House Un-American Activities Committee and the infamous McCarthy hearings. Harvey Matusow, who was one of the chief witnesses at the McCarthy trials, later published a book called *False Witness* in which he admitted he'd lied about most of the people he accused, people who never worked again, whose reputations and lives he ruined.

In Texas they considered passing legislation that would condemn all Communists to death, executing people on the basis of their political belief!

"Pernicious" is a terrible word. Funk and Wagnalls describes it as "the strongest word. Implying the power to kill or destroy utterly." So was the period following the passage of Taft-Hartley a pernicious one in which legislators and unionists began to purge from the labour movement (and government and the film industry and so on) not only Communists but anyone who sympathized with them and, eventually, any progressive person at all who could be dubbed 'left.'

In this atmosphere of hostility to anything progressive, Mine Mill suffered terrible losses. In the US our union was expelled from the CIO based on the report of a kangaroo court that 'tried' us on charges of being dominated by Communists. This was after we had just won significant gains for our membership in bargaining and a highly successful wage drive. Mine Mill was charged with being dominated by foreign interests, yet we were always known as one of the most democratic unions in North America. All our officers were elected. Every policy, every program, every important action taken by our members was decided by a secret vote of the entire membership. Our Ladies Auxiliaries were unmatched by any other union. But while we were concentrating our energies on improving the working standards of our members, others were busy with phony trials of militant unions like Mine Mill.

Sure, a few of us were Communists. It was the Communists who played a vital role in creating some of the same unions who were now pointing fingers. It was the Communists who revitalized the union movement of the 1930s and '40s. But we weren't organizing for Mother Russia, as some people insisted. We were organizing because we believed in the dignity of workers and their right, our right, to a fair deal. What was so UnAmerican—or unCanadian—about that? But maybe, in hindsight, the answer to that question is clear.

Mere accusations of 'red domination' were enough to set off landslides. Members left Mine Mill in droves, especially in the US where the hysteria was greatest. The District Director of the Brass Valley Connecticut metal & machine industry, including all the fabricating shops in the whole Connecticut Valley and the state of New Jersey, led his members *en masse* over to the United Steelworkers of America (USWA), the union that emerged from the old Steelworkers Organizing Committee that Mine Mill once helped establish. Mine Mill lost a quarter of its entire dues-paying membership at one blow. After that we lost the Tri-state area over the same Communist issue. We had had very strong locals in Joplin, Missouri and the whole Tri-state area, a huge base metal district. And we lost the whole shiteree, just like that. There were struggles in Arizona, New Mexico and Texas, terrible struggles where many men ended up going to jail unjustly. The International executive were under terrible pressure. Among many others, Asbury Howard, the vice-president, was thrown in jail and there were endless legal battles.

In the early 1950s we had a big strike in the States at our Local 890 in Bayard, New Mexico, and it got recorded in the film *Salt of the Earth*. It spoke favourably about Mine Mill and its attitude toward the wives of members. When the courts wouldn't let the men picket, the Ladies Auxiliary took over and were soon thrown in jail, kids and all. There's a great scene in the movie where it's driving the sheriff crazy, what with the kids crying and the women yelling for baby bottles—"We want the formula! We want the formula!"—while they rattle their tin cups across the bars! All Mexican-American women—they were great! They raised so much hell that the company finally had to settle.

A Mexican actress played the lead female role, but almost everybody else in the film was a real miner or from a miner's family. The male star was Louis Chacon, the actual president of the local.

The Mine Mill organizer both in the film and in real life was Clinton Jencks, a friend of mine. His hair was so blonde it was almost white. The New Mexicans had never seen anything like it so they called him "El Palomino." He was an air force gunner in the Pacific during the war, but after the movie was made, he ended up in jail as a Communist for a time because of the testimony of the FBI informer, Harvey Matusow. Matusow later recanted in his book *False Witness*, but Clint and his wife Ruth never received an apology.

Because of anti-red hysteria, a lot of people didn't want a pro-union movie like *Salt of the Earth* to be made. They had to finish filming it in Mexico after they got kicked out of the US Miners, actors, the director—nearly everyone worked for nothing. In the end the film had to be smuggled across the border in short lengths mixed in with other films, to get it developed at US labs. Unions and others in both Canada and the US who tried to show the finished picture found their leases suddenly terminated, or their theatre windows broken as they sat and watched it.

This deadly brew of anti-Communist fear and propaganda flowing from the United States in the '40s and '50s flooded over the border and affected virtually every life in Canada in the post-war years.

It affected the church. Most churches ignored the agony to which many of their supporters were exposed during this lengthy period of emotional travail, but in Sudbury, Ontario where the largest local of Mine Mill in North America was located, Laurentian University ran courses in union busting conducted by a priest, Father Boudreau. Across Canada, many church-goers were labeled as sympathizers to left-wing causes if they simply agreed with humanitarian principles. I heard about someone who said that, in 1949 when she was four years old, she was taught to finish her prayers with, "And please protect us from the Communists." This was in Prince Albert, Saskatchewan, for God's sake! She didn't even know what Communism meant—she figured it was some kind of disease.

Newspapers, magazines and radio stations all regularly quoted "solid citizens" and heads of corporations calling for the 'purging' of 'reds.' It was a witch hunt. Anything off the absolutely straight and narrow was suspect. There were even accusations that that new music—rock and roll—was the work of those devilish Communists, created to lead our children astray! It was crazy—terrible and crazy.

The poison injected by Taft-Hartley was nourished by some of the international unions, notably under the very Catholic president of the United Steelworkers of America, Phillip Murray. It quickly spread into Canada and affected several of the more progressive and left-wing International unions including the Canadian Seamen's Union on the Great Lakes. In Ottawa, the Minister of Immigration, Mr. Harris, overruled an immigration panel's rejection of the infamous Hal Banks' immigrant status. Banks was thus let into Canada to do his dirty work in destroying the dynamic—and left-wing—Canadian Seamen's Union. The poison also set to work in the United Electrical Workers, the IWA and last but not least, the Mine, Mill and Smelter Workers Union.

Late in 1947 or early '48, Senator Taft of Taft-Hartley stood up in the US Senate and said that northern Ontario in Canada was being "invaded" by Communists running away from the Taft-Hartley Act in the US Immediately after, the government of Mackenzie King announced they would not renew the entry permits of any US citizen who was working as an organizer for the UMMSW in Canada. At the time—and by no small coincidence—Mine Mill was in the middle of an aggressive organizing drive in the gold fields of northern Ontario and Quebec. Reid Robinson, International Vice-President of the union, was arrested on charges of subversive activity and held incommunicado for a few days before he and several others, including Rudy Hanson, Henry Horovitz and Harlo Wildman, were deported. The government's action left the northern gold fields open for the only other significant hard rock union in Canada—the Steelworkers. (In 1907, before the Steelworkers Union existed, an agreement between Mine Mill's predecessor, the Western Federation of Miners, and the UMW, had amicably divided the North American mining jurisdiction—hard rock and coal mining—between the two.)

Robinson was deported from Canada "on suspicion that he was a Communist or one who advocates the overthrow of the government by force." This was pure malarky, of course. What Reid Robinson and his organizing drive in northern Canada were advocating was not the overthrow of government. They were trying to put a limit at last to the huge profit employers had been making on the backs—and off the dead bodies—of hard rock miners, and to do it in the name of Mine Mill. But the charge of being a Communist, or even a 'suspected' Communist, worked.

There were other problems, too, with our international executive board. At one point we elected a new secretary named Al Pezatti from the New Jersey area and under the anti-red pressure, he faded away—he stopped performing as the secretary. I guess he couldn't stand the pressure so he simply stopped coming in to work.

Another guy named Alton Lawrence was an ordinary executive board member from, I think, the mid-west. Lawrence wasn't a Communist, but when he was forced to go before a committee charging him with being a Communist and violating Taft-Hartley, he pleaded *nolo contendere,* meaning he did not contest the charge. That was the end of him. Everyone accepted *nolo contendere* as his being guilty and he soon resigned his position in the union.

Paranoia and fear infected everyone. In Trail, some of the guys on the Hill honestly believed that we, the more left-leaning members of Mine Mill, were dangerous to them.

Under the impact of Taft-Hartley, unions split every which way—internally, one from the other, the CIO from the AFL and then within the CIO—all over the question of whether or not the leadership were 'red.' Unions billing themselves as "anti-Communist" felt free to raid and destroy sister unions on the basis of their having a 'red' leadership, which is what happened to Mine Mill. It ended up devastating the labour movement on both sides of the border for decades. Certainly in the US, they've never recovered.

TURNING UP THE HEAT

In 1946, Fred Henne, the president of 480, became a staff representative servicing the Northwest Territory locals of Mine Mill. In July of that year, Harvey Murphy had got the rest of the guys to agree to ask Don Berry, one of Trail's most decorated RCAF veterans, to run as vice-president of the local so when Henne left, Berry automatically became president.

This helped give credence to the union and strengthen it in the eyes of the public—here's this war hero as president of the new union. It was a good move to make, in my opinion, but Don didn't stay long. His dad, old Bob Berry, had had a business at Shawnigan Lake on Vancouver Island and when he suddenly died, Don quit the union to take over the business. This left an opening that was soon filled by Claire Billingsley.

Early on, Murphy had encouraged Claire Billingsley's participation in the local. Claire's brother Jack had been very gung-ho about the union and one of its earliest members but he'd left Trail to become president of the Blubber Bay local of Mine Mill on Texada Island. I guess Murphy thought Claire must be okay because he's Jack's brother, so for a short time in 1946, he appointed Billingsley as a part-time International representative working for him in Trail. This turned out to be a good example of Murphy's poor judgement of character.

One of the assignments Murphy gave Billingsley was to organize the outside mines. But instead of forming a distinct local as Ken Smith and Bill Muir did later on with Local 901, Billingsley catalogued them a, b, c, and d of Local 480, which didn't work. They never were organized until Smith came along in about 1951 and formed the Nelson and District Miner's Union.

Billingsley claims to have joined Local 480 without being asked, but we'd been inviting him to join since the union started in 1938. By July of 1947, he was elected a business agent for the local and by October he was elected president and continued a campaign to actively subvert the union from within as leader of a group of unionists eager to leave Mine Mill for the Steelworkers Union.

By 1947 when Claire Billingsley was first elected president of the local, many of us were very suspicious of him. He and his supporters were seemingly well infected with the popular anti-'red' phobia. For example, soon Billingsley and company wouldn't let John Gordon, the Mine Mill staff representative, into executive union meetings. Billingsley was also developing strange friends. By this time we knew that the Steelworkers Union were preparing to openly raid Mine Mill and we knew that Billingsley had met with Bill Mahoney, the head of the Steelworkers. We knew they were planning something and they weren't very subtle about doing it.

Union meetings at this time were pretty raucus. The two sides were outspoken in voicing their opinions. Anything detrimental to the union, the Billingsley side would support. Anything in favour of the union, they'd oppose and we'd have to go up against them. Sometimes even our allies were pretty haywire, and that's when a lot of fights broke out. Once, Mahoney even came to a Local 480 meeting. Billingsley invited him to talk about how good the Steelworkers Union was—it was that open. There were Billingsley and his bunch of githorns sitting at the front, and us who opposed him sitting at the back, despising him.

When we came out of the meeting, Billingsley and his gang headed into the Bluebird Cafe with Mahoney—I guess he had an open cheque book—and one of the men with them was George LeFort who was a vet. I hollered across the street, "Right in there, eh, George?" He stopped and

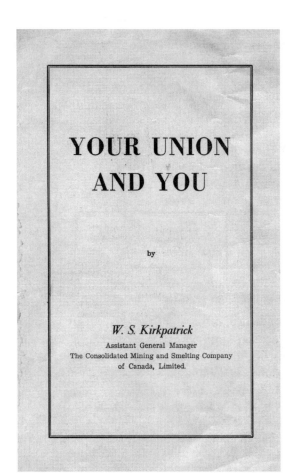

**YOUR UNION
AND YOU**

by

W. S. Kirkpatrick
Assistant General Manager
The Consolidated Mining and Smelting Company
of Canada, Limited.

looked at me and then he walked away from them and came with us. He always stayed with us in the battles afterward, but he had been tempted.

There's no doubt, alcohol was a big part of the union way of life. After meetings you'd go to the Legion to have a beer and discuss how the last meeting had gone and plan the next one. We all drank. Harvey Murphy was one of the heavy drinkers, but I never saw him drunk at work, while he was bargaining or whatever. He'd only drink after. Drinking was a way of life. Metro Nazarchuk, who was an organizer with us in the '60s, walked up the aisle to his wedding waving a bottle of Canadian Club.

Miners never drink on the job because it's dangerous work and they know their life—and the life of the guy next to them—depends on everyone having a clear head. But they're often heavy drinkers afterward, because of the stress. A miner never knows if he'll come out on a slab or on the man-train so he drinks—or at least used to—to relax.

I think that attitude is changing and it's a good thing, not just in the labour movement but through society. It might have been an easy way to get together when unions were mostly made up of men in mining camps, in industry and fishing, but it hurt a lot of innocent people. A lot of the organizing situation, a lot of the work force, has changed since then, starting with the presence of a lot more women who have to get home to the kids. Come to think of it, a lot of the men have to get home to the kids these days, too. Maybe we are getting a little bit smarter.

The hostility to Mine Mill culminated in '49 when Billingsley and company wouldn't even let Murphy, District President of the union, be the union spokesman in bargaining. They were marginal trade unionists, injecting a spirit of division inside the union, encouraging it to decapitate itself.

From 1944 to 1950—and after—Local 480 was being continuously harassed. The Maple Leafers harassed us mostly from the outside, but some of them joined the union to tackle us from the inside, as well. The forces against us were a combination of Maple Leafers, other unions (starting with the Steelworkers), the company and the Billingsley group—all united in trying to defeat the progressive elements who had founded Local 480 and who were still fighting for a dynamic union. All these forces (with the exception of the company, who tacitly welcomed Steel) would join the Steelworkers when they raided us in 1950. You can see what a damned devil's brew we had to contend with!

Meanwhile, the company was getting bolder in its opposition to Mine Mill and began to give its implicit support to the Steelworkers Union as presumably easier for management to deal with. On February 11, 1948, W.S.

Kirkpatrick, Assistant General Manager of CM&S in Trail, and later, President of the Canadian Chamber of Commerce, broadcast an address over radio station CJAT called *Your Union and You* that, in the guise of pleading for union democracy, was a blatant management attempt to urge union members to get rid of any suspected Communists in their union. It was gross interference in internal union business and in union democracy, but that didn't stop the company printing it up as a pamphlet and distributing thousands of copies to their employees in Trail and District.

In his address and later the pamphlet, Kirkpatrick said (the bold highlights being his own): **"Very skillful and highly organized efforts are being made to ... bring your locals under communistic domination. My main objective in talking to you at this time is to make sure you are aware of this fact,"** and "there is in Canada a highly organized group of people, who have embraced the philosophy of Soviet Communism—a system that is completely repugnant, both morally and politically, to our democratic way of life. These people are working vigorously and continuously to destroy our freedom. They would take away our right to choose our own way of life, and our own government."(p. 2)

He carries on to say, **"Communists propose to abolish our Canadian way of life. If they succeed, your freedom to bargain collectively will be at an end."**(p. 3)

One of his most offensive statements was when he said that Communists, **"will stay, if necessary, to the very end of the meeting. If matters are not going to their taste, they will keep the meeting going until after the majority has become fed up and left. Then they will force through their motions."**(p. 4) This idea must have come from one of our members. The union Ritual accepting new members specifically states that it is a member's duty to "if possible, stay until the end of the meeting, although it may often be against your inclination." This was specifically to make sure union business was properly carried out by everyone, not just a few who stayed. The union's Constitution also provides an agenda for all union meetings; the last item is Good and Welfare. Motions are inadmissible under Good and Welfare. So whoever the labour spy was who relayed the information to Kirkpatrick was bullshitting when he said we stayed to the end merely to "force our motions through." Those of us active in Mine Mill were dedicated union men and if the Constitution told you to stay until the end, you tried to do so, even when it went against your inclination to get home early.

Kirkpatrick had the nerve to finish by saying, **"The Company is not opposed to a strong union that truly represents the will of all those for whom it holds the collective bargaining rights."** (p. 5) In 1952 when Mine Mill definitively won the support of a majority of the Trail and Kimberley workers, we didn't hear any more about how "the company was not opposed to a strong union."

On the local scene, the red scare business continued on all fronts, supported by the press. Both the *Trail Daily Times* and the *Nelson Daily News* were owned by Howard Green from Kaslo, a Cabinet Minister and prominent member of the Conservative party. Personally, I sort of liked Green

MINE MILL CONSTITUTION

Mine Mill's Constitution, relatively unchanged from that of its predecessor, the Western Federation of Miners, embodies the union's commitment to democracy and fair dealing Although the language is dated as to gender, it is courtly and eloquent in intention. Every new member took the obligation: "Do you solemnly pledge.... that you will practise the principals of fraternity by giving support as you may be able to your brothers in time of trouble or affliction; that you will uphold and at all times aid in securing the rights of the working man; that you will not unlawfully receive or misappropriate any of the funds of any union of the International; that you will keep secret all business of the International and will endeavour in your efforts to advance true labour reform. And in pursuance of the pledge you have taken, do you as a faithful and loyal member of this union, further pledge that whether you remain a member of this organisation or not, the obligations you have taken shall be preserved inviolate. So help you God."

The philosophical heartbeat of the union follows. "My brothers, as members of a labour organization, whose objects are to better the conditions and make happier the lives of the labouring class who are the wealth producers of the world, it is your duty to take an active part in the affairs of your Union; attend the meetings regularly, and, if possible, stay until the end of the meeting although it may often be against your inclinations. Practise the spirit of fraternity at all times by lending your assistance to your fellows in a time of need; speak kindly one to another and be careful to not unjustly criticize any member, nor attribute to him unworthy motives simply because he may differ with you. It is by honest difference of opinion that we arrive at sound conclusions and correct judgments." Candidates were then introduced to the assembled meeting and were seated.

because he was a member of the 54th Battalion in WWI and he always stuck up for veterans. He was the one who helped up get housing for veterans through the Legion.

But through the years, Green's paper was on the far right, supporting the company and the company union on every labour issue. It produced scathing editorials about "Big Union Bosses" when Art Evans first came to town to organize, and generally it tried to inflame people against the very idea of 'little guys' challenging the mighty citadel up the Hill. We referred to it as the "Trail Tory Times" and later, "The Trail Daily Diefenpaper." To show you how conservative it was, on its masthead was a quote from Winston Churchill to the effect that, "We must beware of building a society where thrift has no privilege and enterprise no reward"—real bottom line, capitalist dogma.

When Ed Costello left the editorship in the early '50s, his position was filled by a talented writer named Dennis Williams who took to the Trail scene like a duck to water. Differing somewhat from the blatant anti-union pro-employer fulminations of past *Trail Times* writers, Williams brought a more sophisticated and, we believed, a more dangerous editorial expertise toward combating organized labour in Trail and District. Whenever Local 480's monthly paper, *The Commentator*, took a contentious position, Dennis would tear into it and of course, since he edited a daily newspaper that was widely distributed and whose stories were picked up by other newspapers outside the district, his journalistic clout was far greater than ours, except in the smelter itself.

Another effect of extensive red baiting was that members of Mine Mill and other progressive organizations began to find less and less justice. One example of this was the case of Garfield Belanger. In 1938, Gar was the first president of the new local that inherited the legacy of organizers like Ginger Goodwin and Art 'Slim' Evans. Oddly enough, it was a written record of the murder of Ginger Goodwin by Special Constable Campbell, and Blaylock's part therein, that brought the full vengeance of the company down on Gar Belanger's head, along with those of three co-workers.

Mr. Blaylock had died in 1945, so in 1947 or '48 Belanger and three friends, Ernie Weed, Lloyd Noakes and Jack Scott, decided no harm could befall anyone if they copied an article written for the *Tribune*, the Party newspaper, by a Party member named Bruce Mickleburgh (whose son, Rod, is now a journalist). The four of them passed out copies to their fellow workers on the Hill as an important piece of union history. Among other things, it said that Blaylock's insistence that the ashthmatic Goodwin was fit for military service had opened Goodwin to the charge of desertion, which helped justify the later search and murder of Goodwin near Comox Lake on Vancouver Island. Although the four men were careful to remain off company property and on their own time when they distributed the pamphlet, all four were promptly fired.

As they all belonged to Local 480, several of us members immediately pressed the president, Claire Billingsley, to take action on the grounds that the company was infringing on the basic rights of free speech of the four workers. A grievance was carried to arbitration under the chairmanship of Judge Eric Dawson of Nelson, BC. Ralph Perry (Billingsley's old boss from the lead refinery) and Miller Mason acted for the company. The union representative was Harvey Murphy. Buddy and I went to it, me as vice-president of the Legion, Buddy as president, to represent the veterans because three of the four were veterans. Perry, the company rep, objected to us being present. He said the Legion had no damn business there. They discussed it and the judge said that as a member of the union and an employee, I had a right to stay but DeVito had no status, so they ruled him out. Then I said, "I'm here as vice-president of the Legion and if the president can't stay, I'm not staying either," and I left too. I don't know if it would have made any difference if I'd stayed or not.

When the decision came down, the majority upheld the action of the company, citing as precedent an 1860 English court case that held the company's name had been "injured." It appears that in 1860, a butcher boy had worked effectively for his master during his working hours but on his own free time maligned the butcher by telling his customers his boss's meat was bad. He had been discharged by the butcher.

Murphy filed a minority report. Judge Dawson had enough of a spark of decency to attach a strong recommendation to his decision favouring the company. He mentioned the fact that dismissal meant different things to different people. Scott, Weed and Noakes were relatively new employees of two and three years compared to Belanger, who had about twenty years service with the company. Therefore, he recommended a suspension of limited time so that Belanger's substantial pension credits would not be lost.

Perhaps if he had known Belanger's long history as a union organizer and the depths of the company's hatred of him, Dawson would have insisted on exempting Belanger from his decision altogether. But he didn't, and Gar Belanger's firing stood. To the best of my knowledge, no legal action was ever taken against Bruce Mickleburgh, the author of the article.

Belanger didn't complain. From then on, he was blacklisted by CM&S and never worked for any of their operations again. Instead, he went back to the mines where he had begun in the 1920s and for the rest of his working life, worked underground in various mines in the Kootenays where he was a leader in union struggles there.

Leaders of the Co-operative Commonwealth Federation (CCF) were caught up in the red-scare business as well. In fact, they were up to their necks in the raid against Mine Mill, not only in Trail but across the country. Jimmy Quinn, who was one of the Billingsley crowd, had earlier been an elected MLA for the CCF in Trail and District, but he only served one year before being defeated in the 1949 election. Herbert 'Bert' Gargrave, who had also been defeated as an MLA for the CCF, was hired by the Steelworkers and sent to Trail to run their campaign against Mine Mill (along with a cohort named Shakey Robinson).

One of our Local 480 allies, however, was John Gordon, another CCF'er and the International Mine Mill representative. In 1950 when the CCF had a provincial convention in the Okanagan, the Trail CCF Club sent two delegates: John Gordon, who was not only a prominent CCF'er and Mine Miller but also the ex-mayor of Rossland, and Les Walker, the Secretary of the Local, to denounce the position of the CCF in the raid in Trail. They were not even allowed to speak.

Workers in Trail were split by the interference of the CCF in the union situation. In a heavily industrial town like ours, a lot of the working guys were, like me, strongly left-wing. Maybe they wouldn't go so far as to join the Communist Party, but a lot of strong trade unionists were also CCF supporters.

That's why, in the 1951 election, a lot of people who would otherwise have voted CCF didn't, and the CCF were defeated in Trail. This was an important election. It was the first time the Social Credit Party ran in BC and that's how the Socreds under W.A.C. Bennett got into power; they won nineteen seats and the CCF won eighteen. If the CCF had won Trail, the outcome would have been reversed. Instead, Bennett formed his first government and six months later when he ran again, he became strongly entrenched. But the first time, he only had a plurality of one over the CCF.

It was brother against brother in Trail in the '40s and '50s—a very, very unhappy time. All the preachers were preaching, "Keep your men out of that Godless Mine Mill because they're nothing but a bunch of Communists," and everyday the paper was flailing away at us and the company was putting out garbage like *Your Union and You*, warning people to beware the evil Communists. And from 1947 on, there was growing pressure by Billingsley and company as well as by the CCF and the Canadian Congress of Labour (the central labour body), to exclude all active Mine Miller's including Harvey Murphy and Don Guise, from all union business.

But it was the Communists who built the goddamned union.

RED HOT

I found out much later that Billingsley was not only telling people that Local 480 was run by Communists, but that all the miners in the province were paying Communists too. The way he knew was that the miners were all assessing themselves one dollar per paycheque to go into a strike fund and they were also paying into the union's Death Benefit Plan. This was a plan initiated by the Western Federation of Miners whereby if a man was killed, money was available for their families. Billingsley wasn't the first who refused to allow Local 480 to pay into either the Strike Fund or the Death Benefit Plan, but he gave as his reason the 'fact' that all the money was going directly to the Communist Party.

Though I was mostly involved in the Legion at this time, I was still a shop steward and actively commited to the union. In 1948, Harvey Murphy came to Trail and called a meeting to choose a staff representative, an appointed position working directly for the International office under Murphy. There were three guys at that meeting: me, Kitch Bannatyne and John Gordon. I was the only Communist of the three.

I could tell Murphy wanted me to take the job, but I didn't want it for a number of reasons. Number one was I didn't think I could get along with him. Number two was that I thought John Gordon, being older than me by some twenty years, would be more suitable. And number three, I wasn't prepared to stop the work I was doing for the Housing Committee at the Legion.

So John Gordon was appointed Staff Rep. Because of the Communist paranoia, his work focused entirely around our local instead of the whole District, as it would have under ordinary circumstances. But these were no ordinary circumstances and our local was where all the fun was. After Murphy appointed Gordon, the Billingsley group barred Gordon from all executive meetings—I guess they didn't want him there while they plotted! I never knew that at the time or if I did I've forgotten, because I don't think they'd have gotten away with that if I had been the Staff Rep instead of John Gordon. One thing I had over Gordon and the other guys was that I had my union whiskers. I was in the union before the war, long before any of those guys thought of joining, so I probably would have had more influence, especially with the vets. But who's to know that. As it turned out, if I'd taken the job, I probably wouldn't have been eligible for the position of president when it suddenly came up in 1950.

TRANSFUSION

Mr. Hurlburt Senior was one of those who supported the belief shared by many in Trail in the 1950s, that anyone who didn't go along with the Steelworkers' raid was a Communist or worse.

Early in 1952, Dr. Jack Harrigan phoned me at the Mine Mill union office and asked if I could give an emergency blood transfusion to a seventeen-year-old boy suffering from haemophilia. I had been giving blood ever since I'd been overseas, and I hurried directly from the union office to the Trail Tadanac hospital.

When I walked into the waiting room wearing my Local 480 jacket, who should be sitting there but the very sad-looking parents of the sick boy, Mr. and Mrs. Hurlburt. I'll never forget the look on old Hurlburt's face when he realized his son would soon be using some of Al King's Communistic corpuscles! Maybe he was afraid his kid would turn 'red.' The boy soon rallied and I wasn't too suprised that I never received a word of thanks from his family.

RAIDING

The major Canadian labour central, the Canadian Congress of Labour, was no ally of Mine Mill. In fact, they now sanctioned the raiding of Mine Mill by the Steelworkers Union. They signed the cheques for Bert Gargrave who led the raid in Trail.

Since they couldn't justify raiding a sister union, we had to somehow be suspended from the CCL. They accomplished this in 1948 when Murphy was ejected from a CCL convention in Victoria for publicly attacking Aaron Mosher, the president. Harvey was furious at the direction of some of Mosher's policies. He stood up at the mike and told the full meeting that if Mosher was going to kiss the boss's ass, he better be sure to pull his pants down first. Murphy could be pretty direct.

The CCL expelled Mine Mill a year later. Some say that was the reason other unions, starting with Steel, raided Mine Mill, but the real reason had nothing to do with that. Besides, Murphy was right. Everybody knew Mosher was up the boss's githorn. The real reason we were finally expelled from the CCL in 1949 was because a majority (not all) of those unions were out to destroy the most progressive ones, the ones they called 'red'.

The fact that we were no longer affiliated to the Canadian labour central meant it was open season for raiding by other unions. By what they called coincidence, at the same time as we were expelled, the Steelworkers paid the CCL $50,000 for some very vague reason. Murphy always charged that Mine Mill was sold to the Steelworkers for $50,000 —that that's what it cost for the CCL to sanction the raid on Mine Mill. The CCL never denied it. But let's be clear, when they evicted Murphy from the CCL, they weren't only gunning for Murphy. They were gunning for anybody who was left-wing in the labour movement.

By law, our union was vulnerable to raiding by other unions every spring before the anniversary of certification came up. In those days it was unknown for labour contracts to run longer than one year and those annual contracts were one of the things that saved us. The time when we were open to raids—the last sixty days of the collective agreement—was also when the union got all its bargaining programs prepared, so in that time we were really appealing to the dollars and 'sense' of the members—if you want more money, you'll get behind this program. We also worked to get members more involved, especially after 1950, to set up programs we knew would be enticing.

We were fighting for our lives. That's why, in the 1949 union elections, I ran for president against Claire Billingsley. Several others also ran, friends of mine, mostly veterans. In that election, Billingsley and company campaigned on the basis of being anti-Communists. They typed up a list of who not to vote for and distributed it in all the plants, on the grounds that we were all 'reds'. I headed the list.

It's ironic that I was defeated. I was acceptable as vice-president of the Legion, but was considered too far left for my union.

We, the lefties, were a very small group in the union and that was reflected in the vote. Billingsley beat me by about three to one, and that's about the way he and the others who supported Steel viewed the division in Local 480. Although at the time the 1949 election results seemed unfair to some of us, it isn't hard to see the reasons. We knew there was a large body of workers on the Hill who were very unhappy with the union getting in at all. These included the suckholes in the Workmen's Committee and the Maple Leafers. Until they were eventually forced by the Sloan Formula and the collective agreement of 1952, they never paid dues or supported the union in any way whatsoever. There were hundreds of men like that!

After the election, Billingsley got bolder and decided to do his own bargaining. He and his crew completely cut Harvey Murphy out of the bargaining process. They wouldn't let John Gordon, the International staff rep, in either. Those were the only Trail negotiations of which Harvey Murphy wasn't a part, and it was the worst agreement the union ever signed.

At the January 1950 union membership meeting chaired by President Claire Billingslely, we had just found out about Mine Mill's expulsion from the CCL and CIO. Jack MacDonald therefore moved that local 480 move to defend its jurisdiction by condemning the CCL and endorsing Mine Mill. I seconded the motion and there was some discussion until we voted to table it and vote on it at the next meeting. That probably helped precipitate what happened next.

THEY MAKE THEIR MOVE

On February 9, 1950, we got the evening *Trail-Times* and there was a full page ad announcing that the entire local executive of Mine, Mill, including all the chief shop stewards except Dan Dosen and most of the shop stewards led by Billingsley, had just 'resigned' and walked over to the Steelworkers union *en masse*. The text began, "A motion introduced at the last regular meeting of Local 480 . . . asked the local Trail membership to condemn the Canadian Congress of Labor and endorse the policies of Mine, Mill . . . . If the membership of Local 480 vote for this resolution they will . . . refuse to accept the labour movement's invitation to remain with them by joining the United Steelworkers of America (CIO-CCL) . . . . On the other hand, if the local votes against the resolution, it will be guilty of violating the constitution of Mine, Mill and every officer and member voting against Mine, Mill will be liable for expulsion."

This was a cowardly rationalization of the fact that they were already fully

UNION MEMBERS OF TRAIL . . .

WE'RE STAYING WITH CIO·CCL

A motion introduced at the last regular meeting of Local 480, International Union of Mine, Mill & Smelter Workers, asked the local Trail membership to condemn the Canadian Congress of Labor and endorse the policies of Mine, Mill. The membership voted to table the motion at that time but it must be voted upon at the next meeting.

If the membership of Local 480 vote for this resolution they will cut themselves off from the rest of the Canadian labor movement. They will refuse to accept the labor movement's invitation to remain with them by joining the United Steelworkers of America (CIO-CCL). Since Mine, Mill is now on trial by a special C.I.O. Committee on charges which they cannot hope to disprove, the local will also cut itself off from the C.I.O.

On the other hand, if the local votes against the resolution, it will be guilty of violating the constitution of Mine, Mill and every officer and member voting against Mine, Mill will be liable for expulsion.

Believing that the Trail membership must remain united locally and also believing that the union members in Trail, if given a free choice, want to stay united with the C.I.O. and the C.C.L., the undersigned have signed the statement reproduced below on this page.

The undersigned members of Local 480, International Union of Mine, Mill & Smelter Workers (including elected officers and a majority of the stewards and elected committeemen) welcome the recent recommendation of the Canadian Congress of Labor that metal miners and smeltermen unite with iron ore miners, basic steel workers and other metal workers in the United Steelworkers of America (CIO-CCL). We are resigning as members of the Mine, Mill & Smelter Workers and are making application for membership in the United Steelworkers of America. We call upon our fellow members to take similar action as quickly as possible.

Trail Union Members Want Unity

We believe that the vast majority of Trail union members want to remain united with their fellow workers in the Canadian Congress of Labor and the C.I.O. We want an international union with strong financial resources, a record of successful organization, adequate research, educational and publicity services, regular Canadian policy conferences, the ability to organize the thousands of metal miners and smeltermen now unorganized and the respect of its members, other unions and the community.

Mine, Mill Has Failed

Long and bitter experience has proved that none of these things are possible to us within the Mine, Mill & Smelter Workers. The fine principles which produced our union and brought it early success have been warped and distorted by a top leadership completely dominated by outside political influences. Its money has been wasted, its membership has been cut in half, it has failed to unite those who still remain within its ranks. It has no unified Canadian policy for its Canadian members, it has lost the respect of its membership, it has lost the support of other unions and the community. It has already been expelled from the Canadian Congress of Labor. We are convinced it will shortly be expelled from the C.I.O. It is becoming a weak, independent union.

We Can't Vote to Stay C.I.O.-C.C.L.

We cannot change the Mine, Mill & Smelter Workers. Overwhelming election results are tossed aside on flimsy technicalities. The opinions of the membership are ignored. Under the constitution we cannot even hold a vote to stay with CIO-CCL. The only way we can stay with CIO-CCL is by signing cards in the United Steelworkers.

The Steelworkers Have What We Need

On the other hand the United Steelworkers of America is one of the largest unions in the world. Its international president is Philip Murray, President of the C.I.O. Under its elected Canadian leaders, the Canadian section of the Steelworkers has grown steadily until it is now the largest union in the Dominion. It has organized locals in every province where there are plants under its jurisdiction, it has won standard wages in the base metal section of the steel industry, it has raised wages in low-wage areas as well as in high-wage areas. It is prepared to use its money and experience to help us organize, it has the competent research, educational and publicity services we need. It has the respect of its own members, the respect of other unions and the respect of the community.

Unite Canada's Metal Workers in One Union

We have made gains here in Trail. But we have made those gains because of our united organization here in Trail. We have never been able to count on effective financial and other backing from the international Mine, Mill & Smelter leadership. Their policies have often hindered us and discredited us. United with other metal workers in the United Steelworkers of America we can further improve our position here in Trail, and, just as important, we can pull up the standards in other mining and smelting areas.

Our Agreement Remains in Effect

The undersigned recommend that you join the United Steelworkers of America now. The labor laws of B.C. protect our agreement and it remains in effect until termination date and a new bargaining agency has been formally certified as a result of your choice. Let us reunite with organized labor. Let's stay with the CIO and the CCL. We urge you to sign an application card in the United Steelworkers of America NOW!

MEMBERS OF LOCAL EXECUTIVE	COMMITTEE MEMBERS (Not Listed Above)	Tank Rooms	Warehouse	First Aid	Warfield Plants	Sulphate	Electric
R. C. Billingsley—President	Gordon McLaren	Ted Eggertson	Larry Goetz	Frank Warne		R. A. McPeek	Doug Janson
Laurie Hamilton—Vice-President	Ken Ridgers	Don Philips	W. H. Craig	Machine Shop	Ammonia	Nitric Acid	Plumbers
Lloyd R. Bailey—Financial Sec.	Sam Stewart	R. B. Gourlay		Frank Woodrow	George Metcalfe	Denis Miller	Malcolm Hodson
James Cameron—Warden	Leo Lawlis	Melting Room	Lead Refinery	Doug Jerome	Roger Campbell	Nitrate Plant	Steam Plant
Arnold Saunders—Conductor	E. C. Ackerman	Rudolph Weishaupt	Bob Richardson	Tramming	Graham Ferguson	L. L. Prough	Dan Alton
Joe Haley—Trustee	Bud Benedict	Gordon Brennan	A. Pighin	F. McIntyre	Charlie Stevenson	F. F. Shrieves	
George Bishop—Trustee	Henry Haynes	George Graham	C. Kisby	R. Lehus	Phosphate	F. L. Olsen	
Les Greenwood—Castlegar B.M.	H. J. Moor	John A. Granstrom	G. Marrocco	J. S. Scott	Jim Tebo	Meter Shop	
Jack Findlay—Fruitvale B.M.			M. O'Donaughy	Electric Shop	Ed. Zarowny	Bruce McAulay	
Jack Speirs—Rossland B.M.	STEWARDS AND OTHERS (Not Listed Above)	Smelter	A. K. Rijkstahl	F. B. Cunci	Joe Owen	Machine Shop	
CHIEF STEWARDS (Not Listed Above)		G. F. Kelley	Luigi Tognotti	Plumbers	John Davidson	R. E. Mulvihill	
James Quinn—Miscellaneous Dept.	Todanac Plants	Johnny Draper	M. Baldassi	Ralph Fletcher	Harry Hanson	Bill Cameron	
Charlie McLean—Tramming	Zinc Roasters	Steam Plant	M. Murrison	Boiler Shop	Ted Elliott	Lead Burners	
Ernie McLaren—Zinc Dept.	Reino Tavorell	Bert Johnson	J. Fornelli	H. I. Huitema	Clarence Curragh	G. E. McMillan	
R. Bartola—Refinery	Zinc Machinists	Acid Plants	Jule Lewis	D. V. Thompson	Storage	Boiler Shop	
	A. F. Dafoe	A. J. "Red" Warner	Walter Rognas	Instrument Shop	N. Sanderson	James Bate	
			Oilers	Reg. German	J. C. Doig		
			Bill Melvin				

Stay United With C.I.O. and C.C.L. by Joining

THE UNITED STEELWORKERS OF AMERICA

For further information LISTEN IN Station CJAT at 9 TONIGHT

planning to join Steelworkers, these men who had, every one of them, taken an oath to be "faithful and loyal" to Mine Mill even after their membership ended, when their promise "shall be preserved inviolate."

In the ad, all shop stewards were advised to quit the union without notice. The ad, published by the United Steelworkers of America, stated, "We're staying with CIO-CCL." It's another irony that the once dreaded CIO was now on the side of the angels.

The next day, a raiding party of Billingsley supporters and Steel organizers moved into all the plants, telling people that Mine Mill was no longer in existence and signing men up into the Steelworkers Union. They told them there was no union, that Local 480 was finished. Everyone had seen the newspaper ad saying the entire executive and most of the stewards had gone over to Steel, so when Steel asked the members, "Do you want a union?" and the members said "Yes," they just said, "Sign here." It was easy. Hundreds of guys immediately signed the blue cards (Mine Mill's cards were cream colour) in the genuine belief that what Billingsley and the others told them was true, that Local 480 no longer existed.

When Billingsley and the Steel raiders signed up our members, they asked them to sign two things: one was to the company, revoking their dues checkoff to Local 480. At the time, the union security clause in the collective agreement gave us what was called "revocable check-off," the most minimal form of union security, so this automatically cancelled their membership in 480 and cut off most of our income.

The second thing our members were asked to sign was a Steel membership card—but no money changed hands. The law required that a minimum one dollar be paid whenever anyone signed an application card as a union member, but the Steelworkers neglected this requirement. That was a mistake. They also never administered an oath of membership. You don't have to take an oath when you sign up these days, but you had to then. These errors gave us grounds for delay and argument later on in front of the BC Labour Relations Board in Victoria.

The company seemed to be in full support of the Steel raiders. Working guys suddenly sprouted briefcases and wandered freely around the plants having long discussions with the men about why they should abandon Mine Mill and signing people up into the Steelworkers Union during working hours. The Billingsleys and McLarens signed guys up in the plants like this, day after day after day, day shift and night shift! Mine Millers had been canned and blacklisted for trying that.

THE SHITHOUSE EXECUTIVE

We had known they were planning to do something but this was astounding. Following the raiding actions, John Gordon was immediately appointed administrator of the local because it was left without any officers, and he called a big meeting in the Legion Hall to decide what to do. When I left to go to the meeting Lillian said to me, "Please be careful." She knew feelings

"BLITZ" EXECUTIVE

TRAIL & DISTRICT SMELTERWORKERS UNION

LOCAL 480 — I.U.M.M. & S.W.

— 1950-51 —

J.A. MacDONALD
FIN. SEC.

A. KING
PRES.

E.L. WALKER
VICE. PRES.

C.B. McMARTIN
REC. SEC.

D. DOSEN
CONDUCTOR

J.E. GORDON
ADMINISTRATOR INTER. REP.

G. CARTER
WARDEN

M. WALSH
TRUSTEE

H.N. SMITH
TRUSTEE

F.A. PEARSON
TRUSTEE

F.E. DeVITO
INTER. REP.

were running high and she was worried about fist fights.

The usual turnout for a union meeting was twenty or thirty men but that night 600 showed up, many of them young veterans. There were so many, they couldn't all fit in the hall. They filled up the building and overflowed outside, down the steps and into the street. When we saw these numbers, we knew we had a chance.

Murphy was there. John Gordon chaired the meeting. The two of them explained what had happened and said that, contrary to what Billingsley and the Steelworkers were saying, the union had not, in fact, gone out of existence. They explained that we had to organize and elect new officers, right here, right now, on a temporary basis until we could have full elections. Then Gordon called for nominations for president. Right away there were about eighteen nominations. All evening it went like that. For every position, there were many guys wanting to take part in the battle and defend the union.

Jack Scott later said he nominated me for president, but all I can remember is a chorus of voices. Then John Gordon said, "We haven't got time to conduct a ballot, so for each position, I'm going to send you down to the back." There was a big washroom back there, the only other large room in the place. So Gordon says, "You eighteen go back into the toilet and when you come out of there, whoever you decide on among yourselves will be the new president."

Most of those who were nominated didn't want the position. I didn't really want the job either. I wasn't ambitious. I always figured I'd work in the smelter until I retired, but most of these guys hadn't done much work for the union, whereas I was well-known, both from union work and as vice-president of the Legion and chairman of the Housing Committee. Also, I was a veteran and the guys who'd been overseas supported me.

I guess they trusted me; they unanimously agreed I would be the president. When we came out, everybody said "Okay. Next bunch," and in went the candidates for vice-president. There wasn't time for any niceties or long speeches. The vice-president's group came out with Les Walker and so on, until, out of all the pandemonium of that meeting, we had a full slate of officers. Some people called us the 'Blitz' Executive after the German

TURNING POINT IN THE TANK ROOMS

Very soon after the raid in 1950, one of our guys, Bob Keiver, spotted Ernie McLaren, one of the Billingsley group, sitting in the lunch room of the zinc tank rooms with his briefcase, signing tank pullers into the Steelworkers Union. Ernie McLaren was from coal mining stock in Nanaimo. Some of those old coal miners would have turned over in their graves if they'd seen what their sons were doing.

Keiver came racing over to the cadmium plant where I was working to ask me to intervene. I went and sat down at the table and debated with McLaren about what had happened and the rotten way the Billingsley people went about it, while all these zinc tank pullers, maybe two hundred guys, stood around listening. One of them, Dave Shaw, was a big, good-looking guy, very popular. I didn't know him that well, but he'd been away at the time of the raid and this was only his first shift back. Dave was sitting at the opposite end of the table from me with a bottle of milk in his hand

when all of a sudden he slammed it down on the table and shouted, "No!" and again, "No!" just as loud as he could. We hadn't been that strong there, but when Dave Shaw came out for the union, it was the turning point in the tank rooms. We had him on the bargaining committee not long afterward.

That was a microcosm of what was going on all through the plants. Guys like 'Loyal' Laurie Hamilton and Ernie McLaren, traitors to their union, were going around holding these bloody meetings on company time and the company was allowing them to do it, where just a few short years before, if they'd seen a Mine Miller even looking like we were going to sign somebody up, we would have been fired! Yet these guys were openly signing people up, encouraging them to revoke their membership and bankrupt Local 480.

But Dave Shaw rebelled. He shouted, "No!" and by the living Jesus, we held onto the tank rooms.

Blitzkrieg attacks, but the guys who were there called us the Shithouse Executive.

The Steel raid on Local 480 was by no means endorsed by the entire labour movement, nor even by all the members of the CCL. On April 14, 1950, 300 members of the CCL and AFL met at a 'labour unity' conference in Vancouver to condemn the officials of the United Steelworkers for their raid against Mine Mill. Jack Stevenson, president of the Vancouver and District Trades and Labour Council, referred to the raiders as "pseudo-unionists who, through despicable raiding methods, seek to destroy an established and militant union." Even the Secretary of Local 3302 of the Steelworkers, Fred Horton, courageously took the platform and said it was not the members raiding Trail but the top leaders and called for unity in the trade union movement. The fact that the conference unanimously endorsed a resolution "strongly condemning" the raid, was very encouraging to us in Trail.

As a new Executive, we were pretty audacious. After what we'd been through in the war, we said "What the hell," you know—this wasn't as bad as being shot at. And we had nowhere to go but up. We immediately put out a bulletin to try and reassure all our members. It ended: "Men trusted by the rank and file have assumed the duties as your local officers. Relations with the company have been reestablished. New shop stewards are taking over the job left by the quitters. Grievances will be rapidly processed. It will take some time to overcome this disruption, but we will bring this union back to good working shape and it will be stronger, as a result, than it has been in the last few years in the hands of these deserters."

Here was the dilemma: in addition to our concerns about raiding, there was a requirement under the Industrial Conciliation Act that you had to maintain a majority of the members right up to the time of bargaining. If it was proved you didn't have a majority sixty days before you started bargaining, you were automatically redundant. The company could then apply for decertification on the grounds that the union no longer represented a majority in the bargaining unit. This was February. We were still the bargaining agents for CM&S and they couldn't kick us out until the current collective agreement expired in June. Our fear was that a successful application for decertification by the company would result in the union continuing to represent employees only until the existing contract expired in June, and then being unable to bargain for the new one. The options were that employees could either reject both unions and the company could lead the men back to company unionism, or that a rejection of Mine Mill would support the Steelworker's application for certification.

As soon as we were elected, Les Walker and I went to the Local 480 Mine Mill offices to check the books. There was nothing there—not a penny. The old executive under Billingsley had emptied the bank account by paying each other full wages, severance pay, holiday pay and so on until there was nothing left. That left us broke, but we still held certified bargaining agent's rights. The union paper, the *BC District News*, published a picture of the pay stubs.

There were around four thousand guys working on the Hill at this time, not all of whom were members of Mine Mill. On February 13, 1950, when 1,284 revocations of check-off were handed into CM&S, the union was left in serious financial straits. Certainly there was no money for salaries, and none with which to defend the union. We immediately sent off appeals to every local and every miner in BC, the Northwest Territories and the Yukon, to come to our immediate aid. They gave us enough money to keep our union intact and punching a little longer.

The period immediately following the Steelworkers' raid was critical. The process in a situation like this was that as soon as they thought they had a majority signed up, the Steelworkers would call in the Labour Relations Board (LRB) to confirm their application. The LRB would then verify that the cards workers had signed, were legitimate. If so, we would proceed to a vote as to whether Steel or Mine Mill should represent them.

As the new officers, we knew we faced enormous problems in winning back majority support for Mine Mill. Apart from a lack of funds, it seemed the entire world including the church, the press, the company, the leadership of the CCF and too many other unions all wanted to see the end of Mine Mill. Clearly, the defecting executive expected a swift and complete elimination of Local 480, so they wanted to hurry up the legal process, while we as the new executive fought for time, using anything to delay so we could gather support and fight back.

The local initiated a civil suit against ex-President Billingsley, ex-Vice-President Hamilton and ex-Financial secretary Bailey for breaking their oaths and deserting their posts to Steel while receiving salaries and expenses from Mine Mill. Mine Mill lawyer John Stanton did a lot of the legal wrangling for us, holding them off in the courts.

The Steelworkers, meanwhile, were up to their own tricks. One of the first gimmicks they used was to choose a misleading name and number. The name of our union, the one they were raiding, was the "Trail and District Smelterworker's Union Local 480." In an effort to confuse our members, the Steelworkers now applied for certification for what they called the "Trail and District Smelterworker's Union Local 4281." The two names were identical, as were two digits of the Local number. Mine Mill therefore took legal action to restrain the raiders from using that designation. What a hope!

The judge we were assigned was BC Supreme Court Justice Alex Manson. I wasn't there at the time, but I was later told that Judge Manson threw out our application. He said the Steelworkers could call their new local anything they liked, regardless of confusing the workers. Then he added a comic-opera flavour when he spotted a man he thought was Harvey Murphy at the back of the court room and proceeded to deliver a personal attack on Murphy, Mine Mill and all their various evil works. But the man he was speaking to wasn't Murphy at all—it was Les Walker, so the old guy blew a fuse for nothing.

Those first few months, even the first year or two, weren't very smooth, I'll tell you. There was nobody to show us or tell us anything because our predecessors had all run out and now wished us the worst. The only training I had was through my work in the Legion. I had learned how to chair a meeting and I was good at it, but we had some personnel problems in the office. Finally we got a good, competent woman named Gerry de Rosa who was top-notch in every way. She, and later Remo Morandini, made that office hum.

I wasn't the only one with no experience. Les Walker, who soon became Financial Secretary, knew nothing about managing money. All of us were learning as we went. In the short period left in the current collective agreement, we gathered our resources. We had a new and militant slate of elected officers and shop stewards and financial help from all our fellow Mine Mill locals with the exception of Bralorne, who sent a message of support to the Steelworkers. Now we needed time to build our strength, win back the members we had lost, and do things in a way that would encourage the public to support us.

To get members on our side, we focussed on getting the word out to all the workers on the Hill as to what was really going on. So, for example, we initiated a series of reports in union newspapers, the local *Bulletin* and the *BC District News*, as well as paid ads and letters asking for financial and other support and alerting trade unionists and the public across the country as to what was going on. Smeltermen including Al Warrington, Bill Muir, Arnold Laarz, Percy Berry, Joe Mukanik, Harry 'Major' Treneman and others, wrote columns and bulletins. One of our regular columnists was Chuck Kenny who went under the moniker, 'The Cheerful Cynic.' We also began daily radio broadcasts on local radio station CJAT. Guys like Dave Shaw, Les Walker, Bill Cunningham, Chuck Kenny, Cliff McMartin, Kitch Bannatyne, Al Warrington, Major Treneman and others broadcast about bread and butter union issues, and twice a week the Ladies Auxiliary of Trail and Rossland took over the program with excellent broadcasts. The Peace River Dam, the discontinuation of the CPR line through the Kettle Valley to the coast, and the Stockholm Peace Plan, in addition to union activities, were all discussed and commented on.

The efforts of the new Local 480 soon attracted the interest and support of other union supporters outside the smelter. An invitation to attend a Local 480 shop steward school was responded to by civic and forestry as well as various trades workers. Spear-headed by Aubrey Burton, the Trail civic employees began to organize as well.

Internally, we had to make people see why they needed to keep Mine Mill as their union. For this, we worked on a number of fronts at once, mostly in the area of contracts, health and safety (or as we called it then, safety and health), and pensions.

Some people have said that the Communist Party became dominant in Trail in Mine Mill after 1950—in other words, when I became president—but they're wrong. They're right about the organizing phase of the union—we were in the leadership of it. But from then on, we were a minority. On the Shithouse executive, there were maybe four Communists: Dosen, Walsh, Pearson and me. The vast mojority of the people I've always associated with were not Communist. And as I said before, we never tried to sign anybody up in the Communist Party through the union. Of the executive of the International in the US, there were only three of maybe ten or twelve who were Communists—the secretary, Maurice Travis, was a Communist, but John Clarke, the president, was never remotely Communist. Nor was Reid Robinson, an earlier president, though he was evicted from Canada on the assumption that he was.

On the Canadian national side, it was Harvey Murphy, Ken Smith, Bill Longridge and I, but none of the executive in Ontario that I know of, were Communist. Maybe that's why they later went down the tube. And John Gordon, our staff representative when the Steel raids broke out, who reported directly to the Western District President, Harvey Murphy—was a died-in-the-wool CCF'er.

CULTURE

Mine Mill saw its members as whole human beings and tried to address that as well, so Local 480 sponsored cultural events as well as political ones. In some of the northern Ontario towns such as Sudbury, Mine Mill built theatres and opera houses and routinely sponsored ballet and opera and Saturday morning movies for the kids. Weir Reid did a lot of that work as full-time recreational and cultural director for the Local. The Sudbury local was even big enough to have a full-time teacher who taught dance to workers and their families.

In Trail, in 1952 when the Recreational Projects Society built a new arena, the Local sponsored a circus as the first event. We invited every kid in the District to come for free—boss's kids as well as workers' kids—everyone. There were elephants and tigers and acrobats for the kids, and a theatre agent from Spokane brought in the well-known singer, Lou Rawls, for the grown-ups. I think every soul in Trail was there that night—the place was jammed. It was great.

FIGHTING BACK

Soon after we took office in 1950, it was time to bargain the next agreement. When Murphy came to Trail from Vancouver to carry it out, he had a pretty green crew. In fact, none of us had never bargained before in our lives.

In those days, the way we bargained was that only a single rep from each side spoke. If anybody else wanted to say something during negotiations, he asked for a recess and we went outside to talk. So before going up to the company offices on the first morning, the Trail and Kimberley guys met very early in the union hall to make sure all our points were covered for Murphy, our spokesman.

Suddenly the phone rang.

"Al, this is Pete McIntyre." Pete was head of Personnel. He said, "You men better come up now, Al, but I just wanted to tell you we can't bargain with you as long as Harvey Murphy is your spokesman."

"Why not?"

"Well, he's a Communist and it's against the company's policy to deal with Communists."

I said, "Okay, we'll see about that," and hung up.

Of course, everybody immediately wanted to hit the bricks, including me. Let's throw a picket line up right now! Walk out on them! We didn't know what else to do—we had to keep meeting with the company, but none of us except Murphy had any experience. What the hell did I or John Gordon know about negotiations?

COCONUT DAY

From 1950 on, Local 480 sponsored an annual celebration on February 8, the anniversary of the day when Claire Billingsley and the others deserted to Steel. We wanted to remember the day that saw the rebirth of a fighting union. We called it Coconut Day because at our first Shithouse Executive meeting, Bobby Eccleston from Kimberley sang us the Coconut Song with the words slightly changed to suit the occasion.

Down in Mahoney's lair
One evening I was there.
This is what I heard him shout
While sitting in his chair.
CHORUS:
I've got a loverly bunch of coconuts
There they are a-standing in a row,
There's Billingsley and Bailey, Saunders and Spiers
Hamilton and Bishop, at who the workers sneer!

Should I roll a bowl or throw them in the ditch,
roll a bowl or throw them in the ditch?
Roll a bowl or throw, roll a bowl or throw,
Should I roll a bowl or throw them in the ditch (son of a bitch!)

and so on. Every February 8 after that we'd have a big meeting, invite the national executive to come speak, make presentations to activists, honour retirees and finish with a big dance in the Legion Hall.

Mine Mill Barganing Committee, 1950. Standing (left to right): John Gordon, Dan Dosen, Joe Rollhiser, Jack MacDonald, P.C. Berry, Bobby Eccleston, Doug Gold, Lloyd Dowell, Kitch Bannatyne, Sam Muirhead. Seated (left to right): Jack Smith, Clem Thomson, Harvey Murphy (Chair), Al King, Les Walker. Brother Dowell, President of the Mine Mill local at CM&S Alberta Nitrogen, attended negotiations as a guest of Mine Mill. This was the first time Calgary employees of CM&S were involved in co-union bargaining.

Murphy just laughed at us. "Go on up there," he said, "and meet with them. Present your proposals, then come back down here. And every time they say anything important, break off, come down here and we'll meet again."

It was another example of Murphey's strategic sense. He knew immediately that if we made him the issue, the Steelworkers would win. There was no way Mine Mill had enough support yet in the plants, and if we'd tried to get the guys to walk out over Harvey Murphy, the well-known Communist, bargaining for us, we would have been beheaded.

Murphy's plan worked perfectly. It took about two days before the company got tired of all the delays and said, "Okay. Bring him up here!" Those were the negotiations where, for the first time, we established a basic wage and once and for all got rid of the last vestiges of the old bonus system. That was my first inkling of Harvey Murphy's keen ability to sort the wheat from the chaff.

In 1949 Billingsley and company had excluded Murphy from any negotiations and that collective agreement was a sorry affair. With Murphy back at the helm, annual negotiations now took a decided turn for the better as far as the workers were concerned, and the company negotiators, Perry and McIntyre, were no match for Harvey Murphy. This changed in 1952 with the appearance of a new head negotiator for CM&S, named Benson. The son of a miner in the Sullivan Mines in Kimberley, Benson was a good match for Murphy, and he raised the quality of the company's bargaining. But he was probably more highly regarded as a fair and decent human being by the union than by his employer, and when he was not adequately rewarded, he soon quit CM&S for greener pastures elsewhere. Before he left, he indirectly admitted the success of our pamphlet and publicity campaign when he told the union that, "The company was always a step behind the union in its published reaction to any and all developments in the plants. They exercised a degree of mobility which we were completely incapable of matching."

MURPHY'S CHARMS

In 1950 when we were being raided by the Steelworkers, after the guys were off shift we all used to go down to the union office to talk about the raid. Harry Nicol reported that we had a strong guy in one of the plant shops, a real leader and he hated the Steelworkers. Harvey said, "Sign him up."

The next day Harvey asked if he'd signed him up yet.

"No," says Nicol, "he hasn't signed yet but this guy sure hates the company."

"Put a little more pressure on him," says Harvey. "Maybe you'll sign him up tomorrow." The next day, in comes Nicol with a long face.

"Did you sign him up?" Harvey asks.

"Jesus, no," says Nicol. "He hates you, too, Harvey."

Some bargaining situations were a lot different from others. Later in the '50s, when Rudychuk and I were bargaining at Duncan Lake, a new mine north of Kaslo, we were sitting across from Al Martin and the mine manager, Jack McKay, who was an old miner himself. At one point Martin got so mad at McKay for agreeing too much with the union that he yelled, "Why don't you just go across the table and sit with them!" McKay stood up on his bandy legs and did just that—came round and sat down beside us union guys and grinned back at Martin.

Even in the worst of times, there was always a place for humour. Years later, Bill Mahoney told how, when he was busy raiding Mine Mill, a bunch of Steelworkers were on the train riding from Toronto to Ottawa, sitting around playing poker, when all of a sudden the door opens and a big red face looks in on them and Harvey Murphy bellows, "Hello, fellow travellers!" 'Fellow traveller' was the euphemism for someone who supported the Party. It broke them up.

CONTRACTS

There was a longstanding injustice on the Hill on the issue of pay for contractors. For years, the company had cheated the hundreds of men who worked on contract by deducting general wage increases from their contract earnings.

You only tried to get contract work if you were big and husky because, even though it meant you worked harder, you got more pay. The 'contractor'

I remember one issue that was raised at a policy committee meeting by the secretary of the Kimberley local, a guy named Jim Patterson. Patterson came up with the outlandish and then-unheard-of idea that the union should take up the problem of the pollution that was happening to our environment. This was in the 1950's! It didn't get to first base with the Bargaining Committee because all we were desperately trying to do was increase our union security and fringe benefits. We didn't want to know about this pollution business—I was one of the guys who opposed it. I've been kicking myself ever since. We poisoned a lot of air and water and land around that area.

Patterson was twenty years ahead of his time on that one, but he was off base on others. Another time, we were trying to get better insurance and social benefits for our families and Patterson opposed it. He said, "Do you think I'm going to work my guts out, then have a slab of loose rock come down and wipe me out and leave a bunch of money for my widow so some long-cocked farmer from Saskatchewan can come along and claim all my insurance money?" His point of view didn't prevail, and in fact we doubled the death benefit, but every time I see Jim now, I remind him of the L.C.F. of S!

got so much money per ton or per job. It was piecework—payment by the piece—and when you completed the alloted work you could go home, sometimes in as little as four or five hours.

Anything over the basic unit of pay was called a bonus and for years the company had been fiddling it so that every time there was a general wage increase, that amount was deducted from the contract earnings so the contractors never got the benefit of wage increases and continued to work for the same take-home pay. Billingsley had worked in the middle of all this in one of the worst places it was going on, in the lead refinery, and did nothing about it. We got onto it immediately.

The issue of fair pay for the contractors was settled early in Trail but it took longer in Kimberley. In the summer of 1952 or '53, they couldn't agree on rates, and finally the contractors called a meeting and instructed their union reps, Frank Malone and Ken Wocknitz, to cut off all the contracts so that every miner went on straight pay. It was a work-to-rule and we called it on the basis of safety. The miners were told, "So long as you keep moving, they can't fire you. Don't sit down, don't provoke anything, don't swear at the boss but especially, don't go at your usual productive rate of speed. Remember, it's safety first!"

So guys would pick up their lamps, fuses, assignments and the peg that showed who was underground, then take the man-train to where the heading was and spend all day getting maybe a quarter of a round drilled or half a pile mucked out. Then they rode back. They kept working, kept moving, but all of it very slowly and very, very safely! The ore was just trickling out of the mine.

Up until now there had been one full train-load of ore delivered from Kimberley to Trail every single night, seven nights a week, every week, all year round, since 1906. But there was no ore train every night for those few weeks, I can tell you, and after a couple of months we were getting awfully thin for muck over in Trail!

The company was pissed right off. They tried everything, including pressuring the weakest guys to work faster. We told the miners, "If they fire you, or if you start to go hungry, the union will keep you and your family fed and when we settle the thing, you'll get your money back." But we were protected by the fact that no one was ever compelled to work by the bonus system. From the beginning it had always been done by oral agreement and the company had refused to write it down because so far, it had always worked in their favour. But now, the union turned that around.

We kept that thing going, with the guys taking their pay cheques—straight miner's pay, no bonus—every two weeks for two or three months. They never fired anybody in Kimberley as a result of that job action. When tonnages went down, the smelter in Trail started to lay off people but it didn't bother us because by then the union was pretty solid and we made sure the laid-off guys were looked after. Finally the company caved in. We got good rates and conditions established firmly and consistently—in writing. We made them pay retroactivity as well.

All over the Hill—in the storage plant where they were loading cars, in the metal sheds where they were loading bulk—we re-wrote the contracts so contractors got the full benefit when the rest of us got an increase, and we formed Contract Committees to police them. We also got the company to check off two percent of all the bonus earnings from then on in order to pay for two union contract reps to work underground full time, to keep the contracts fair. Frank Malone and Ken Wocknitz were the first of a series of underground Contract Committee men.

It was a struggle, but in some places we had

THE RULES OF ORDER

Union meetings by this time had settled down quite a bit and everything was done by Robert's Rules of Order, but once during a meeting I particularly remember, one guy was abusive. I told him that as long as I was president, there could be any amount of criticism, but nobody was allowed to abuse the chair like that. If we were demanding that workers no longer be abused by the boss, then we couldn't abuse each other. I took it seriously that the Mine Mill Ritual says: "Speak kindly one to another and be careful to not unjustly criticize any member, nor attribute to him unworthy motives simply because he may differ with you. It is by honest difference of opinion that we arrive at sound conclusions and correct judgments."

So when this guy still wouldn't stop, I adjourned the meeting for ten minutes so I could take him out and educate him. Nobody in the room stirred—they knew what was going to happen. I took him out back, took his glasses off and whacked him one. Then I put his glasses back on, left him lying there and went back into the meeting. I knew he'd come in later and he did—came in and sat down and never bothered me again. His name was Kitch Bannatyne—one of the guys on our side, later a vice-president. But it was no big deal. Kitch knew he had it coming.

remarkable results. Some of the contractors really gained a lot—they hadn't realized how much the company had been cheating them. And don't think this didn't have a hell of an influence on the way union members and non-members alike looked at this new breed of union officers. That one change alone made good union men out of a bunch of guys who until then weren't particularly interested.

In this period we also had a slow-down at the fertilizer plant in Trail over how many bags to load. Until then, the way it worked was that after a certain number of bags at an agreed base rate, everything else was at an extra—bonus—rate. But the company kept raising the number of bags that had to be loaded before the bonus cut in. So one day the men said, "Fuck you. We'll load this many bags and after that it's bonus or we don't work." So they loaded exactly that number and stopped. It was harder for the union to maintain the necessary unity in this dispute than it was in the mine action because there were more bosses around.

CM&S was convinced the guys were just goofing off, that they could load more than they were letting on. So they took four young guys from the management staff and put them on loading.

Now you have to understand what this job involved. When I worked on it before the war, one of the guys I worked with was Jeff Nicklin, an athlete who'd been hired specifically to play on the lacrosse team. Jeff and I were good friends. During the war he was a Lieutenant Colonel of the First Canadian Paratroop Batallion. After the war when I was working in the milkhouse, a friend came back with a picture of Jeff hanging from a tree, stitched with bullets right across the chest. He'd landed in a tree on top of a German machine gun nest.

Anyway, Jeff was great at lifting bags. When things got slow on the crew, this guy would have us all doing calisthenics, hoisting hundred pound bags, one in each hand, just for practice. That was the kind of strength this job demanded. So when the four staff guys came to show the regular labourers how to work, they couldn't match them. In fact, it damn nearly killed them and the company settled with us shortly after.

After several months, when the raiders were confident they had enough cards, they applied to the Labour Relations Board (LRB) for certification as the bargaining agent for all the Trail plants. The Steelworkers' aim, of course, was for speedy action and a quick certification.

Normal procedure was to assign an officer to investigate; an LRB representative, Bob Forgie, soon appeared in Trail. Mr. Forgie quickly became known as the Little Certifier because he was five foot and a bit tall—a tough little bastard who liked his Scotch whiskey. I liked him because he didn't stand for any bullshit. I also got the impression he didn't like the Steelworkers very much. Whether he intended it or not, he helped us by taking a long time to check things out.

Meanwhile the Steelworkers were crowing loud and long that before many more weeks passed, they would become the bargaining agent for the smelter. They claimed to have signed up 2,400 members in the first two days of the sneak attack. There was little doubt they had signed up members by the hundreds, since the company allowed them complete freedom on the job to do so. Yet between the early signup campaign and their application for certification, many workers had reacted with anger when they discovered they had been lied to and misled.

Bob Forgie didn't actually count the cards—he did the background work, making sure of numbers and signatures. He got a list of employee names from the company to check the size of the bargaining unit (which took considerable time) and then he checked the collective agreement. His job included reporting back on the non-payment of dues to Steel and the lack of a proper oath—that sort of thing. Several weeks later he submitted his report to his immediate supervisor, a fellow Scot named William Fraser. Bill Fraser was head of the Board and a pretty good guy—very tough, very fair minded. Fraser was no friend of anything smelly. He used to scare the hell out of his staff. When the LRB eventually came to conduct the vote, there were about seven young guys working for him, and old Fraser was there cracking the whip.

But first, Forgie did his job and he left and time passed. Generally, when certifiers came around it was because of a conflict between a union and an employer, but in this case it was two unions. The application was one of the biggest handled by the Board, so I guess they didn't want to make any mistakes. Of course, the delay suited us in Mine Mill just fine. We used the time to do a lot of heavy hitting on plant conditions.

Finally, after several weeks, the LRB received Mr. Fraser's report and a formal hearing was arranged for April between Mine Mill and the Steelworkers at the Labour Relations Board in Victoria. There, the Board would hear witnesses from both sides as to whether or not the application by Steelworkers should be approved.

By this time, the momentum of the raid and our fight-back were showing signs of a change in Mine Mill's favour. In addition to all the work we'd done in the local, we'd also received supportive resolutions, telegrams and cheques from all over North America, including from the Vancouver Trades Council, the International Brotherhood of Electrical Workers, Carpenters, Machinists, Teamsters, Pulp and Sulphite Workers, Fishermen, Seamen, Marine Workers and Boilermakers, Civic Employees, Firefighters, Longshoremen, Painters, almost every single local of the United Mine Workers of America and of Mine Mill itself—even rank and file Steelworkers and their own Vancouver local had sent support. So it was with some optimism that we took a twelve passenger limo and drove to Victoria with Harry Drake as our driver.

The Steelworkers arrived with a lawyer from Washington DC named Tom Harris. Our lawyer was John Stanton from Vancouver. On the Steel side there were only two guys from the local—Billingsley and Bill Melvin. Melvin was one of the officers who'd defected. Bert Gargrave, the organizer paid by the CCL, was also there. None of them ever said a word.

The members of the Board were Chairman Pitcairn Hogg, Fraudenia Eaton, George Wilkinson, Hary Strange, Harry Murdoch and Fred Smelts. Smelts always took his little dog to hearings with him and it sat by his chair the whole time.

There were six witnesses for Mine Mill: Bob Penner, Ed Stott, Colin Donaldson, Major Treneman, George LeFort and Clarence Bouthelier. These guys all stood up and told how they were tricked into revoking their 480 membership and signing a Steel card because they were told Local 480 had ceased to exist. As the President of 480, I produced evidence that showed how, after the raid, four hundred and thirty-three workers realized they'd been lied to by Steel and had given me the slips to show they'd quit Steelworkers. This reduction in Steel's numbers would have left them with a minority, so they were no longer eligible for certification on this basis.

Stanton also argued that the Steelworkers had no jurisdiction in Trail because their constitution didn't include "smelterworkers" in the membership eligibility criteria, only "all working men and working women . . . employed in and around iron, steel and aluminum manufacturing, processing and fabricating mills and factories." Not a word about lead and zinc.

Stanton kicked the shit out of the Steel lawyer. He told him to get his ass back to where he belonged and that he had no right to practice law in Canada. But the real excitement came when, without any warning, one of our members, Major Treneman, suddenly gaffled the American lawyer around the neck and wouldn't let him go. He quoted a poem at him:

Here's to the American eagle
That great and noble bird
It flies all over the United States
And on Canada drops its turd.

By this time everybody in the room is hooting and hollering and the dog is barking. The members of the Board are screaming at Treneman to let go, but he still has a headlock on the lawyer. The Steel guys don't dare move, because we would have punched them out if they did. Treneman carries on:

Here's to Canada's future
She's beautiful, fertile and rich.
We don't need the turd from your noble bird
You American son-of-a-bitch!

Finally he let go and the hearing adjourned in some disarray. Pitcairn Hogg quit yelling. Fraudena Eaton stopped squeaking, Fred Smelts quit laughing, Smelts' dog stopped yapping and the Steel reps slunk out forlornly. Major Treneman promptly slugged down half of the bottle of scotch liquor Ed Stott had brought. The Mine Mill reps sailed out walking on air.

Back in Trail we celebrated by bringing in a first class orchestra from Spokane and holding a huge Smeltermen's Ball at the new arena. Buddy DeVito MC 'ed it. The Steelworkers celebrated by accusing BC's Labour Relations Board of supporting 'Communists.'

The LRB sat on that decision for a long time, and finally they ruled there would be a vote in June of 1952. It was almost a two-year delay, but that would work in Mine Mill's favour.

SAFETY AND HEALTH

Meanwhile, we went to work. The executive before us had done nothing for the union—I almost said "little" but it was really nothing whatsoever—in the field of safety and health and we had a pretty fertile field in which to work because of all the hazards at the smelter.

We started with forming a strong Safety Committee. We didn't call it Safety and Health yet (or later still, Occupational Health and Safety) but we set down certain rules including the requirement that every plant had to be gone over with a fine tooth comb for hazards once a month. We also started a policy that no one could be penalized for pointing out safety hazards (what we now call 'whistle blowers') because a lot of guys had been discriminated against when they brought up safety issues. We tried to make the point that

INSPECTION!

One time Ken Smith, the District Secretary of Mine Mill, came to town. I'd just been to a meeting at City Hall and was all dressed up when I went to his hotel room for a drink and to catch up with the news. Smith was notable for his leadership qualities. His ability to successfully arbitrate between different people and their points of view was universally respected. It was a sign of affection that we used to tease him unmercifully about his extra large ears. He and I sat up late over his bottle of Cutty Sark and when we finished that, I got another one from the bootlegger and we drank that too, so we never did get to bed that night.

The next day was Wednesday and along about six a.m. the phone rings. It's Tommy McIntyre. He'd phoned Lil who said, "He's at the Crownpoint Hotel with Ken Smith." So Tommy phones Ken's room and there I am, all duded up in my white shirt, suit and tie and Tommy says, "You son of a bitch, get up here."

I said, "Tommy, I'm not dressed to go on a safety inspection."

Meanwhile, Smith is rolling around on the bed, laughing like a bastard. He whispers at me, "You're the best dressed safety man I ever saw!"

Little Tommy McIntyre wouldn't let me get out of it. He made me go out on that Wednesday inspection with a blue serge suit and nice shiny shoes and a big hangover. But I was working for the members so I had to do as I was goddamned well told and away I went.

from now on the Safety Committee would have the backing of the whole union, which it had never had before. Then we took up certain issues that were of concern and corrected those—wherever we could, as fast as we could.

Fred Pearson was our first chairman of the Safety Committee. Fred had been at university prior to his war service overseas, but it didn't seem to have had any bad effects—he was still pretty left-wing. He did a lot of good work, organizing inspections and so on and was a real burr under the company's saddle, so much so that they beguiled him into going on company staff and shipped him over to Kimberley. But by that time, we had several other good young guys working on safety.

George LeFort was chairman after Pearson; he was more pragmatic and aggressive than Pearson. Then there was Tommy McIntyre. Tommy took that company apart—he was a goddamned ferret, the way he used to get his little body into every dirty hole in the various plants in his search for safety hazards. He'd come out black as hell. He was the best chairman we ever had and he was still chairman of the committee when I left Trail in 1960.

It was McIntyre who came to the union office and raised hell with me. He said, "Al, this safety and health business is so important that the god-damned president should be actively involved." And that's how I started going around once a week, every Wednesday, with the Committee to a different department or plant, so the guys would know that the union was on the job and was there to service them, unlike the last executive who sat in the office and conspired with the company by telephone.

One of the very first issues we took up around safety was the provision of protective clothing. Until then, except in places of major hazard like the zinc tank rooms where CM&S paid for rubber boots, gloves and aprons, the company made men pay for their own safety clothes. We showed them the then-Workmen's Compensation manual where it said that wherever there was a risk to a worker, "the company shall provide and the men shall wear" protective clothing. The company objected, of course, and we took it right to the Board where I argued that the meaning of "shall provide" was "to be supplied by the company" without any strings, so why were the workers paying for it? Jack Corner, the old mayor of Rossland and a personal friend of mine, represented the WCB. We beat the company on that one—they had to pay for protective clothing, especially shirts and pants, from then on. That was a big victory. It happened in our first year in office and gave the Safety Committee a hell of a boost. After that, the guys respected the committee and it started to get more support. Also, a lot more people showed a willingness to be on it.

It's funny. I don't have a whole lot of education—I quit school when we immigrated to help support the family—but I found presenting these labour tribunals and arguing in front of lawyers, fairly comfortable. I guess my work at the Legion was good training—I took to it like a duck to water. We had a good team, too. George Mukanik was the union's Grievance Committee secretary. George did the research and I presented it. He prepared the ammunition and I fired it. And of course, we planned—we were always well prepared.

I liked it. I liked debating with the company lawyers, arguing and winning for the members. I guess it helped that English and Latin had been my two favourite subjects at school in the UK. If I had my life to live again, I'd love to be a lawyer. We didn't win them all, George and I, but we won a good proportion, and every time we did, we won more members to the side of Mine Mill. I recently read in the newspaper about a guy in a smelter in Alberta getting burnt to death because he had no protective clothing on—in this day and age—and we won that damned thing forty years ago!

Then there was the $64,000 comma. For years it had been company practice to pay only three of the shifts that worked every holiday, but the complication was that our shifts didn't run midnight to midnight. They ran from seven a.m. to three p.m., three p.m. to eleven p.m. and eleven p.m. to seven a.m. So the fourth shift, the one from eleven p.m. to seven a.m. that they didn't traditionally pay, actually worked seven hours of the holiday.

We had a long debate over this in the union hall and most of the guys thought the intent was clear, but I wasn't convinced we could change it from the way it had always been done. However, the Grievance Committee insisted. They said if it had been in the company's favour all these years we would certainly hear about it, so finally I said, "Okay," and that was the first time we faced the company in an arbitration. They had their lawyers and we had us. I was spokesman for the union and in the end, it all came down to the misplacement of a comma. The chair of the Arbitration Board was a young lawyer named Leigh McBride from Nelson, The brother-in-law of the company lawyer and later a lawyer for Cominco himself. This time, McBride came down in thr union's favour—the company had to pay all four shifts in both Trail and Kimberley. We called it the $64,000 win.

After that, our guys had confidence that ordinary guys like us could take on the company's fancy lawyers and beat them.

When we formed the Safety Committee, the company formed one too and we carried out joint meetings. After a few union wins at the Compensation Board, the company started to take us seriously and put a lot more safety reps on their side. The shit flew when these two committees got together—they'd tour the plant together once a week then have a meeting, put everything down in the minutes and send it to the Workmen's Compensation Board.

Some of the worst conditions on the Hill were in the zinc tank rooms. One of the effects of working in the tank rooms was that the zinc mist rotted out your teeth. We put more pressure on the men to protect themselves, including their teeth. Up until now, there were no dentists worth going to in Trail so most of the guys went to Spokane to a company called Dr. Cowan and the Peerless Dentists. Peerless advertised a lot up in Trail—they even sponsored the Trail Senior baseball team. But we didn't think the guys should have to pay their own dental bills when the problems were directly related to their work. After the union got onto it, we brought two or three good dentists into Trail and made sure they were paid by the Workmen's Compensation Board when problems were a result of employment. Until then, I don't think the company took this issue seriously at all.

We did a lot of good work with that committee. We made things a lot safer in the plants and saved the workers a lot of money too, by not making them buy their own safety clothing any more. We kept after the hazards in the zinc tank rooms too, until they finally put in a system where most of the work of stripping the refined zinc was done not by people but by machines. Of course, that also saved the company money because the process as it was originally, was very, very labour intensive.

In the chemical and fertilizer plants we also dealt with the hazard of sulphur dioxide gas. Guys were gassed, not a lot, but sometimes an escape of gas would make them sick. There was always danger of explosion as well.

It was during this time that I first became aware of the ravages of silicosis in BC's hard rock miners. Early on, two miners, Jim Stuart of Salmo and Walter Secora of Kinnaird, both died of silicotic complications, but to the best of my knowledge, neither they nor their families ever received a penny of compensation. The Workmen's Compensation Board at this time was very obnoxious, very slow to accept the reality of miner's chest diseases. We were in a hell of a fight with them over silicosis. Their definition of the illness was so technical and so limited that it was almost impossible for anybody to qualify and it wasn't until the 1950s that the infamous Zucco case really brought this issue to the attention of the public.

Jack Zucco worked all his life as a miner, shift boss and foreman for various mines around BC including the Sullivan Mine in Kimberley. The miners used to say the ore in that mine was as hard as the back of God's head.

In 1949 an X-ray showed the presence of tuberculosis in his lungs and he went to Tranquille Sanitorium in Kamloops, from where he filed an application to the WCB for a silicosis pension. It was rejected. Over the next several years until he died of what we were convinced was advanced silicosis in April

SILICOSIS IRENE

Irene, last name unknown, was a familiar figure in those emporiums to which thirsty hard rock miners were attracted in the 1950s. A tall, well built brunette with fair skin, dark blue eyes and raven hair, Irene had a pleasing personality, a relatively current knowledge of politics, religion and the usual 'who's-doing-what-to-whom' as well as a better-than-average capacity for the Oh-be-Joyful juice.

Unfortunately, as mining waned in the late 1950s, so did Irene. When she became ill, the miners got together in an effort to help her. Says Joe L. to Whispering Bob M., "How would it be if we took a collection and bought her an annuity on which to retire?"

"Not a bad idea," says Bob, "but perhaps we should discuss it with the boys." So several were canvassed and all agreed it was a hell of a good idea until one asked, "Where are we going to raise the money? The whole industry has gone to rat shit and we are all on, or just running out of, pogie. What are we going to do?"

Finally they agreed, "This is a Workmen's Compensation claim. Irene deserves an Occupational Disease Pension." It took some debate before the terms could be properly set out.

Q. Who was Irene's employer?
A. The mining industry.
Q. What was her job?
A. Shaft sinking.
Q. How long was she thus employed?
A. Two decades.
Q. Nature of injury?
A. Silicosis.
Q. What were her wages, earnings, etc.?
A. Standard bonus and rates of pay.
Q. Term of disability, how long?
A. Indefinite.
Q. Family doctor's name?
A. Dr. Manson.

We figured Doc Manson, an old tramp miner and organizer, should be honoured to be associated with such a hard-working, deserving recipient. So after a great deal of hilarity the claim was signed, sealed and sent to the WCB. Months elapsed and when the anticipated letter arrived from the Claims Department, the claim was denied on the following grounds:

No X Ray evidence of silicosis.

No evidence of loss of income.

No description of ore body where shaft sinking duties performed.

No registration of Miner's or Blaster's certificate of fitness.

A meeting was held in the Blackstone Hotel and it was reluctantly decided not to appeal.

1958, Jack Zucco and his wife, Bea, fought to have the WCB recognize his silicosis and grant him a pension. Instead, the Board—in spite of the diagnoses of several well-regarded doctors and specialists—repeatedly insisted there was no proof of silicosis, and over the course of several appeals, rejected Zucco's claim.

Although Zucco, as a staff employee of CM&S, was no longer a union member, Les Walker who was by then the full-time Compensation Officer for Mine Mill, took Zucco's claim and worked hard to obtain compensation for his wife and children as part of the on-going struggle to have silicosis recognized by the Board as an occupational disease related to hard rock mining. At one point, Les Walker and I and several other Mine Mill officers joined Mrs. Zucco in pickets of the Board offices and on the steps of the BC legislature. She took her four kids and camped out on the steps for several days in an attempt to get some justice for her claim.

After Zucco died, they exhumed his body, ashed his lungs and showed that his lungs were full of a residue of dust and chert—the host rock of the Sullivan ore body. Finally, and still reluctantly, the Board accepted the case. So with the union's help, Mrs. Zucco and her family achieved some justice. Instead of being forced onto welfare as so many of her predecessors had been, the Zucco family finally received the economic assistance that was their right.

In 1951, public reaction to the despotic administration of the wcb as illustrated by the Zucco case forced the Social Credit government to appoint Justice Gordon McGregor Sloan Chief Commissioner to oversee a Royal Commission into the "policies and practices" of the BC Workmen's Compensation Board. Our union, led by Ken Smith, the District President, with Fred Pearson and Les Walker, was in almost constant attendance at this Commission, examining and cross-examining witnesses. Murphy appeared once to criticize the lack of appeal for bad medical decisions. Sloan introduced him with, "Now here's Murphy on medicine." I appeared as well. Mine Mill especially pressed for more emphasis on the prevention of accidents and for rehabilitation, both of which were almost unheard of at the time.

Several other BC unions also made strong recommendations for change. Bill White from the Marine and Boilermaker's Union and the Railway Engineers showed up and did a good job, as did the Fishermen's Union and the iwa. The BC Federation of Labour did little to help in that commission, though they did enlist Tom Berger, later Justice Tom Berger, to present a brief for them.

In 1964-66 there was a second Commission of Inquiry into the BC Workmen's Compensation Board, this one chaired by Mr. Justice Charles Tysoe. Again, Mine Mill was one of the most active unions present, to the extent that Tysoe mentioned in his final remarks that "the only person representing labour who was in anything like regular attendance before me was Mr. Walker, of the International Union of Mine, Mill and Smelter Workers."

At that time, the senior guy representing the BC Federation of Labour was Pat O'Neill. It was obvious as soon as he started to talk that O'Neill knew nothing about compensation. I don't think he knew the difference between a Form 6 and a writ of *habeus corpus*, but he tried to bullshit his way through. He kept saying, "I'll come back to that," and "I'll answer that later." I tried to help him by questioning him and trying to salvage a bit of his pride, but it was a waste of time.

Mine Mill introduced several important cases to that Royal Commission in an effort to show a pattern of over-legalistic wcb administration in cases of miner's chest diseases. When one of our witnesses, 'Toots' Chenoweth, pedaled a tricycle into the august presence of the Commission, some of the big shot company lawyers almost fell out of their chairs laughing, but when Toots told his story, they weren't laughing any longer. After twenty-five years as an underground miner, Toots was unable to work any longer due to occupational arthritis and silico-tuberculosis for which part of one lung had been removed. In 1953, due to the silicosis, he had been granted a WCB pension of $140 a month "for life," but when he recovered from the tuberculosis he was abruptly informed that his pension was reduced to seventy dollars and he had to go on welfare.

Toots had such severe disabilities that the only way he had of getting around was the tricycle. The motorized scooters of today would have been important to people like him. Justice Tysoe commented later that the Board "used neither its heart nor its head" in making the decision it did to cut Toots' pension in half.

Another claim that was partially dealt with by Commissioner Tysoe involved the Chairman of the WCB, Mr. Eades. Before becoming chairman, Mr. Eades had successfully pleaded the case of his brother who had underground exposure to silicosis in Britannia Mine and who had originally been barred from coverage under the Act due to the fact he had not submitted a claim within the five year limit after the exposure ceased. Mr. Eades' argument was accepted by the Board and the claim paid.

Les Walker injected the Eades case into the Royal Commission (for which he was castigated as "hitting below the belt") at the request of the Britannia Local. They claimed that many long-term miners with valid silicosis claims were being denied, while Eades, with something like five years or less of exposure, had had his claim accepted. Les was trying to show that the Board's exercise of "discretion" was somewhat selective and unfair.

Some changes were made in the WCB as a result of our presentations. We slowly got the qualifications for silicosis removed and we kept working on it. Before Sloan the definition stated that, " 'Silicosis' shall mean a fibrotic condition of the lungs caused by dust containing silica and evidenced by specific X-ray appearances accompanied by a substantially lessened capacity for work." (Section 8(5).) This improved after Sloan defined it as: " 'Silicosis' means a fibrotic condition of the lungs caused by the inhalation of silica dust and accompanied by a lessened capacity for work." (Section 8(5).) It improved again after Tysoe, who removed the reference to "a lessened capacity for work" and I maintain it should now rightly cover all dusts, so instead of "silicosis" it should discuss "pneumoconiosis."

But the union's biggest achievement was our success in having Section 54A (later Section 55) added to the Statutes. 54A allowed for a Medical Appeal Board; it was Mine Mill that persuaded the government to put that in.

The fact that many unions, including the BC Federation of Labour, didn't put a lot of energy into these inquiries was partly their attitude to health and safety at the time, and partly, I think, a result of their attitude to Mine Mill. They didn't want anything to do with anything Mine Mill touched.

Typical of this is what happened when, around 1952, Lyle Wicks, the Minister of Labour for the newly annointed Social Credit government, called a meeting of all BC unions to discuss industrial relations issues around the Industrial Conciliation and Arbitration Act. The cental labour bodies sent a message saying they wouldn't attend if Mine Mill was going to be there. That was the atmosphere of the day. They'd expelled Mine Mill from the CCL and the BC Fed in 1949 and everywhere we went, we were pariahs. We were holding off the Steel raiders with one hand and with the other, doing this work with occupational health and safety, doing our best to get the Act improved for the benefit of all BC workers. There's no doubt in my mind, we could have won a lot more gains for labour if we had been united to bring about the changes we all knew were necessary.

At the time none of us knew much about how to deal with the progress being made by science in exposing workplace occupational health hazards. Falling and breaking a leg or having an arm cut off, well, that was obviously work-related, though, according to the employer, it was always your own fault for being careless. But if your teeth rotted out, or you started getting weak from lead poisoning or coughing from asbestos, you were just told to stop whining. It was commonly understood—by some unions as well as all employers—that some people got sick at work, not because of dangerous fumes or working conditions but because they were weaker, more suscepti- ble, than others. In other words, if you were ill, it was your own fault.

Over the course of the next several years, we got smarter—or at least, the union did—but in Britain, where they're now doing genetic testing on employees, it's a version of the same thing, sixty years later. People were saying then and are saying again now in Britain that it's not because workers are working with chemicals and conditions that kill living things, that they get really sick—it's because they're "genetically susceptible" to disease. Hell. Raise the limits enough and we're all "susceptible."

Meanwhile, the fight for individual claims by Mine Mill continued un- abated. John Stanton was Mine Mill's chief attorney in most of these cases and together he, Les Walker, Ken Smith and Harvey Murphy made up the Mine Mill team.

Our leadership in Local 480 put far more energy and more activity into the issue of plant safety than there'd ever been before. In about 1954, four workers—all brothers—in the Silver Refinery succumbed to a particularly virulent form of chest cancer. They were all long-term employees and despite widespread fears that a particular carcinogenic element was being produced and that these four deaths were related, our efforts to secure medical and other support and, when they died, pensions for their wives and families, were blocked at every turn. The authorities insisted that cancer affects everybody—it was just their bad luck. And even if it could be proved that somehow the work place was at fault, no Workmen's Compensation Act anywhere provided coverage on occupational cancers at that time.

This caused me many a sleepless night and it wasn't until that fall that a possible solution presented itself from an unusual source.

At this time, the only medical practitioners in Trail were at the C.S. Williams Clinic. With one or two exceptions, the doctors there were avidly pro-company and anti-Local 480. Particularly poisonous was Dr. Mike Krause who once drove his car into a union parade and broke Roy Penson's leg. However, there was a new-comer at the clinic named Dr. Alvarez who had quickly distinguished himself as a superb surgeon who showed complete indifference to company-union differences.

By sheer coincidence, that fall when several other union officers and I were returning to Trail from a meeting at the Bluebell Mine, we met Dr. Alvarez on the ferry crossing Kootenay Lake. He was returning from a hunting trip in the East Kootenays with Bill Waddell, a friend of mine. We discussed the plight of the Silver Refinery widows and some of the fears of the remaining workers that that whole plant was perhaps toxic, and Dr. Alvarez suggested a course of action that had never occurred to us.

Instead of focussing on the rights of the widows, he suggested we should stress to the company the necessity of proving or disproving once and for all the fear of the existence of an air-borne cancer causing by-product of the silver refining process in that plant.

The company agreed and hired an epidemiologist named Sutherland and thus was born the Sutherland Study, following which, all four widows were granted pensions based on WCB rates but paid independently by CM&S itself. (In other words, in this case, the company acted as its own insurer.) As we had hoped, the study favoured the widows as well as eliminating the worries of the current employees as far as future exposure was concerned. It showed that the conditions at the time those men were working had, indeed, led to cancer as a result of exposure for most of their working lives, but that a recent renovation of the plant had eliminated the hazard.

This was particularly gratifying to the union because not only were the fears of men currently working in the plant abated, but Sutherland wisely ruled that the plant's effect on employee health be continuously monitored. To the best of my knowledge today, over forty years later, not a single additional case has been reported.

Mine Mill's appointment of Les Walker as a full-time safety and health officer after 1960 was one of the first, if not *the* first, for a union in Canada, perhaps in North America. There are many instances of Walker's defense of disabled miners that have never been told. Among them was a dispute between him and a doctor, who later became head of the Workmen's Compensation Board's medical department, regarding a silicotic miner who had had one lung removed that showed silicotic modules and a primary cancerous lesion. The Board had the nerve to argue that since the damaged lung was removed and the remaining lung showed no clinical evidence of silicosis, therefore the man had no silicosis and the Board could deny his claim for compensation!

Changes have continued. Until I left Trail in 1960, the company had always taken the measurements the worker's health relied on, including measuring the lead stipple counts, gas emanations, toxic dusts and so on, and we just had to take their word for it. But in the '70s the union began to take and record its own measurements of gas and pollutants under leaders like Keith Graham.

PENSIONS AND PROGRESS

Pensions was another thing we tackled damn quick in the fightback in Trail in the 1950s. We had a pension plan through CM&S, but it needed drastic surgery. We understood it wasn't vested, which was in complete violation of the law. Without vesting, a guy might work for years but if he left the company, like Gar Belanger did, he lost every penny of his pension. So you might work for ten, twenty years then quit or get fired for any reason and you walked away with nothing. The company got away with this non-payment of pensions for years until we got in and forced them to change it.

In 1951, at Murphy's instigation, we applied for and were granted a joint certification with our sister Local 651 in Kimberley. It was their daily shipments of lead-zinc concentrates that provided the bulk of the raw material to the Trail smelter. Murphy argued that joint certification with the pro-Mine Mill miners at Kimberley meant the Steelworkers would be required to sign up a majority of the Kimberley miners as part of their raid on Trail. The Steelworkers did try to do some dirty work in Kimberley, but they got run out of town pretty quick. At one point, old 'Seahorse' Johnson jumped on a guy on the main street in Kimberley just because he looked like Gargrave, the head organizer for Steel. Everybody laughed like hell but the old guy meant well. Eventually we got joint bargaining for the Trail, Bluebell, Kimberley and Alberta Nitrogen (in Calgary) plants, and in each one, Murphy initiated committees where every member was invited to get involved and at least have input in bargaining demands.

All this work was so that the members would come to feel Mine Mill was 'their' union, in a wider sister and brotherhood of unions. Traditionally, the usual turn-out to a union meeting was twenty or thirty members. Of course, when negotiations started to heat up or there was an election or a hot issue, meetings filled up. When I became president, we worked hard to try and get members out. As part of that, we made our executive members more accessible to the membership, partly by broadening the local executive to include board members from each residential area, partly by regularly publishing in the *BC District News,* the names of every current executive member and the address of their local so members could easily communicate—especially since these names often changed. We gave the Steelworkers a hard time because they wouldn't publicize their local executive names and addresses or give out their Constitution to the same guys they were trying to organize.

After the raid in 1950, attendance went up sharply because guys wanted to know what was going on. We encouraged this by forming Districts so we could have local meetings that were more accessible to members, but we always had a tough time getting workers involved. Still do. What we did, though, was that we got more people involved on committees, councils, and as shop stewards. For example, when it came time for proposals for bargaining, we didn't just rely on our official bargaining committee or on elected staff—we formed Policy Committees. These were separate from the elected Bargaining Committee that sat down and negotiated with the company. The

Policy Committee for each unit was wide open—it consisted of any union member who wanted to be on it. So when we were deciding on bargaining demands, we first had several meetings, setting policy with the Policy Committees and only then did the Bargaining Committee formulate demands and meet with the company. Several hundred people would come to these Policy Committee meetings and there was sometimes some pretty vigorous discussion.

That Policy Committee, backed by a very strong system of shop stewards, was the best thing we ever did. This was something else our new executive instituted right after we were elected. Each department had shop stewards to look after the day-to-day concerns of the union, and each of those had a chief steward. The shop steward body functioned separately from the general membership and the executive, holding their meetings on alternate weeks from the membership. Most of them also participated in the Policy Committees.

I learned a lot from Harvey Murphy about bargaining strategy. Mainly I learned never to get ahead of the troops—not ever, ever to get ahead of the troops. By that I mean, never to propose things that didn't come from the members themselves or that a maximum number of members hadn't had time to talk about and consider. Also, incidentally, this way we were always in close touch with the membership's current concerns.

A lot of unions don't take this approach today, but I think it's one of the things that made us strong. I don't know why more unions don't do it now—perhaps they don't trust their membership or else they use a bunch of gimmickery and smart aleckness instead. Too many unions now go ahead and bargain without a clear sense of what their members really want or need, and when they get a settlement the executive thinks is adequate, they can't figure out why the membership are still dissatisfied.

Another part of making and keeping this connection with the members was that we also set up committees for every trade. Until now, Mine Mill's main strength had been among the unskilled and semi-skilled workers. It was part of the old distinction between craft and industrial workers—the whole struggle of the CIO against the AFL and their different attitudes to organizing. But even though the proportion of craft workers in Trail was relatively small, we still wanted the tradespeople on our side. To do that, we had to be aware of any problems they had, to make sure the company weren't getting cheap labour or undercutting the trades, so we formed committees for each trade, and the tradespeople responded well. There was soon a Boilermaker's Committee, a Welder's, Carpenter's, Leadburner's, Machinist's and so on. We also formed contract committees, entertainment committees and publicity committees, and we had the very effective Ladies Auxiliaries. Among many other things, the Ladies Auxiliary distributed regular bulletins to workers at the plant gates and didn't charge us a penny.

We knew we were weak in the Italian sector of the union membership, but after 1952 when Les Walker succeeded Dave McGhie as district secretary in Vancouver, we acquired a real gem to take his place as secretary-treasurer of Local 480—Remo Morandini. Remo was just a young kid, a journeyman

MINE MILL'S ENIGMA

As the new executive of the union we worked damn hard, averaging twelve and sixteen hour days. We learned fast and got better as we went along. Soon we had a lot of great people involved in the union, working on different committees, in different roles, at different projects. There was lots of activity at every level of the union.

We also had a little unexpected help. Bert Gargrave, the leader of the Steelworkers' raid, stayed in Trail during the week, but every weekend he flew back to Vancouver. We had a guy named Martin 'Sarge' Walsh who spoke two or three languages and could pick up a language, or an accent, very fast, and Walsh soon had Gargrave's English accent down perfectly. If you put one of them in one room and one in the other and asked them to speak to you, you couldn't tell which was which.

When we saw Gargrave get on the plane on Friday night, Martin would telephone the Steelworkers' office the next day, pretend to be Gargrave and ask what 'we' were going to do next and who's this and what department needs what—a nice little chat—and we got to know every damned thing they were planning. You know that story of the Enigma project during WWII when the Allies had broken the German codes but couldn't let on they knew, so certain plans were allowed to go ahead in order to keep the secret? Well, we had to keep this a pretty damn dark secret, too. Only Murphy, Martin, Remo and I knew about it. The Steelworkers never caught on.

pattern maker by trade. I didn't know him and the first time I saw him at a union meeting wearing dark glasses, I challenged him, accusing him of never having been properly inducted into the union. He just looked at me, a long flat look, and said, "You talking to me?" I quickly retreated.

Remo was a well-liked member of the community. He played French Horn in the Maple Leaf Band, was brilliant at math and was a pattern maker in the plant, one of the most difficult of the trades, making patterns for all the forms and pieces poured in the foundry. He had no fear of the boss. His dad, a cabinet-maker, was pretty militant, too. As secretary-treasurer, Remo took complete charge of the administration and functions of the local and a firm hold of the bottom line. I always stressed to him the importance of paying no spurious bills. I was one of the first to feel his sharp scrutiny. Early on I brought in a note showing the times I'd made business calls from home, and asked for reimbursement.

Remo says, "Where's the bill?"

"I haven't got a bill, just the times."

"No bill, no money," he said, and that was that.

After the lax days of a company union, some guys were in the habit of taking personal time off and calling it union business, which was costing the union money. Remo and I soon let it be known we wouldn't put up with it. One day I saw a guy, a shop steward, working on his car when I knew he was booked out on union business. By the time I got back to the office, he'd already resigned.

Remo Morandini was a perfectionist in all ways, including in instant calculation. During bargaining when the company negotiator, Ed Benson, went to his slide rule or 'slip stick' as Red Paterson called it, for figures, Remo would have the answer first, just out of his head. Remo was later the union's representative on the Medical Services Association of BC, the organization that took over the administration of the hospital and medical system. In the late '60s when Remo left the union movement to work for the WCB, he nominated me as his replacement on the MSA Board, and I served there until I retired in 1980.

LIVING WITH THE RED BAITING

Part of the reality of that time was that we always assumed there were informants around, especially at every union meeting. We had one guy we knew was an RCMP informer who was on the executive of the union, Stan Walsh (no relation to Martin 'Sarge' Walsh who imitated Gargrave.)

Stan used to go into the company office every Friday afternoon and make a report to Geoff Johnson, the ex-RCMP officer in charge of company security. The way I found out was through a guy I knew when I was vice-president of the Legion. Art O'Reilley had been overseas and now worked on staff in the CM&S pay office. One day he said, "Al, did you know there's a guy comes to the office every Friday to see Geoff Johnson? He must work around here because he always comes in in his work clothes, wearing a large woolen touque."

I said, "What's he look like?" And he described Stan to a 'T.' Stan was also the only guy in the zinc plant who wore a touque.

I kept this under my hat for a long while because there was a lot of pressure on politically. The raid was happening and we were just trying to dig in and make progress on as many issues as possible. I only told three or four people who were members of the Labour Progressive Party but we were very careful around him. It was never generally known among the membership that he was a labour spy. This was the dark side of union activities in those days—and I'm sure it still goes on. An article in the Vancouver *Province* newspaper on November 15, 1993 reported on a thirty-two year old RCMP report uncovered by the Sudbury *Star*. At the time, Steel was raiding Sudbury too, and the report, about a riot outside Mine Mill's hall at a pivotal time in 1961, said that many of the rioters were former Nazi storm troopers who had been "imported" by INCO. This didn't surprise any of us.

One of the things that helped us throughout was that Harvey Murphy was very astute with the media. In 1950 when Mauris Travis, the International Secretary-Treasurer, was arrested by the RCMP in the Douglas Hotel in Trail and escorted across the border the same night, it was scheduled to be a major story in the Trail *Times* the next day. But Murphy countered by calling in the reporter, a guy named Costello, and alleging that the CCF was engaged in a conspiracy to undermine the union. The next day, the paper made that their major story so it at least neutralized the issue of Travis. Murphy was always careful to maintain good relations with reporters. It helped that he had an intuition for the dramatic and the catchy. But even Murphy couldn't counter Pierre Berton.

Maclean's Magazine, April 1, 1951 7

How a Red Union Bosses Atom Workers At Trail, B.C.

Openly controlled by Communists, the Mine-Mill Union doggedly holds its grip on one of Canada's most vital industries. Its domain includes a carefully guarded heavy-water plant in the B.C. mountains. An anti-Communist rival claims a majority of the workers, but the Reds are still on top in a fight that could involve our security

By PIERRE BERTON

IN THE SMOKY little smelter town of Trail, huddled deep in the gnarled recesses of B. C.'s Kootenay mountains, one of the most significant union struggles in modern labor history is being fought out against a backdrop of atomic secrecy, Communist infiltration and charges of political opportunism.

Here, the United Steelworkers of America, the continent's most powerful industrial union, is challenging the right of the 57-year-old International Union of Mine, Mill and Smelter Workers to bargain for the men who work for one of Canada's richest corporations, the Consolidated Mining & Smelting Co., a subsidiary of the Canadian Pacific Railway.

The contest at Trail is something more than just another union squabble. In the first place, the Mine-Mill union has, for more than a decade, been run by the Communist Party for its own purposes. In the second, Canada's first atomic plant is at Trail. CM&S has been producing heavy water for U. S. atomic research—perhaps for a hydrogen bomb—for almost eight years.

So far the Steelworkers have failed to uproot the Communist-led union. They were given the job in January, 1950, when the Mine-Mill union was expelled by the Canadian Congress of Labor. But, after a year of B. C. Labor Board hearings, court cases, appeals and counter-suits, the Mine-Mill union and its Communist-dominated executive is still legal bargaining agent for Trail's 4,000 workers—even though only 1,700 of them actually belong to it.

Although the Steelworkers, in a whirlwind campaign, were able to win 2,200 sheltermen to their cause, the government-appointed Labor Relations Board of B. C. has declined to certify them. And the Trail employees themselves have as yet been given no opportunity to vote on which union they want to represent them.

Some strange things have been going on in B. C. since the union struggle in Trail began. A Liberal M.P. has come out publicly in favor of the Red-run union. A leading American Communist with a black patch over one eye, barred from Canada, has managed to stay at large four days in Trail. And the Canadian Congress of Labor has hotly charged that CM&S has given aid and comfort to the Communist union for the sake of a "bargain-basement contract"—a charge vigorously denied by the company.

Communist Harvey Murphy runs the Mine-Mill Union which controls 4,000 workers at Trail, including some in secret Project 9 — an atomic plant.

In the background looms the grey square tower of the company's hush-hush "Project 9" which has been producing heavy water for the U. S. since 1943. Project 9 and the great hydrogen plant with which it is linked, is set apart from the sprawling fertilizer plant and smelter works by a high picket fence, a sign that says "No Admittance Without Authority," several uniformed guards, the RCMP, and an elaborate screening process and pass system—part of which is under FBI surveillance. But there is good reason to doubt that Project 9 has been wholly isolated from the Communists who run the Mine-Mill union.

The key men in the Trail local are Communist Party members or Party liners. One of them works as an oiler in the heavy water plant itself. He was identified to this writer as a member of the Labor Progressive Party in 1945 and was recently on the executive of his union.

Another works in the adjacent hydrogen plant as maintenance man. He is not known to be a Party member but has consistently followed the Party line and has distributed copies of the Stockholm Peace Petition within the plant itself.

The plant is vulnerable to sabotage because of the great squat storage tank close by which holds 200,000 cubic feet of highly inflammable hydrogen. Nearby is an ammonium nitrate plant, producing thousands of tons of fertilizer. It can easily be converted to munitions-making. (It was a shipload of ammonium nitrate that blew up in Texas City in 1947 destroying much of the town.)

The smelter itself would be essential to Canada in the event of war. It processes all the base metals from the great Sullivan mine at Kimberley, 200 miles away. This mine is the world's largest producer of lead and zinc and produces half of Canada's silver. The miners are also organized by the Communist-led Mine-Mill union which is organized in gold and base metal areas throughout Canada—including the International Nickel Co. at Sudbury, Ont.

The significance of the atomic developments at Trail has not escaped the Communist Party. On March 10, 1950, its west coast organ, The Pacific Tribune, said editorially: "The atomic products of Chalk River and Trail can be made to serve the interests of humanity, but only if the jackals of big business within the labor movement are decisively ousted. That is why

First page of Pierre Berton's article on Project 9.

As the Steel raids gained national publicity, the press caught on that one of the plants at CM&S, Project 9, had been producing heavy water for the US since 1943. Heavy water was what they used for the early nuclear fission experiments that led to the atomic bomb. Everyone in Trail knew about Project 9 and its adjacent hydrogen plant. It was separated from the rest of the smelter by a fence, armed guards, a sign that said, "No Admittance Without Authority," and an elaborate screening process and pass system—part of which was supposedly under FBI or CIA surveillance.

Like vultures attracted to a decaying corpse, the lords of the press soon smelled scandal and sent their flacks and the anti-Communist warriors of the pen into Trail. The *Reader's Digest* sent out a notorious anti-union writer who at least had the decency to meet with both sides. Harvey and I both met with him. Of course the article was anti-Mine Mill, but it wasn't as vicious as the one written by Pierre Berton for *McLean's Magazine*. Of all the red-baiting doggerel that was produced at this time, Berton's was probably the most offensive. His article, published April 1, 1951, was titled "How a Red Union Bosses Atom Workers at Trail, BC" The title gave you a hint of the objectivity of the rest of it, but it didn't leave you dangling for long. The subtitle read, "Openly controlled by Communists, the Mine Mill Union doggedly holds its grip on one of Canada's most vital industries. Its domain includes a carefully guarded heavy-water plant in the BC mountains. An anti-Communist rival claims a majority of the workers, but the Reds are still on top in a fight that could involve our security." One-quarter of the first page was taken up by a large picture of a oily, evily grinning Harvey Murphy.

If something like that came out now we'd all laugh at it for blatant bias, but in those days the red hysteria was so widely accepted that the media didn't have to be subtle at all. The article went on to imply that our "Communist controlled" union was a danger to national security because of the presence of the heavy water plant at Trail. As it said, "an avowed Communist runs the union that runs the plant." About Harvey, Berton said, "He is a graduate of Moscow's Lenin Institute where Communists from many countries took special training in espionage and Party doctrine." About the years after the war when we were fighting to make Billingsley and company get active on behalf of the members, Berton said, "The tight Red core kept the general membership apathetic by fostering long, bickering meetings."

You had to wonder how Berton knew anything about "long, bickering meetings." I figure he got that either from one of the Billingsley crowd, or directly from the pamphlet the company put out in 1948, written by the Assistant General Manager, W.S. Kirkpatrick, in which he had implied conspiracy on the part of unnamed "Communists" by saying, "If matters are not going to their taste, they will keep the meeting going until after the majority has become fed up and left. Then they will force through their motions." This was an insult. That pamphlet came out at a time when we were trying to counter Billingsley's apathy by making him take some kind of action on the union's behalf, to improve the union! How else could we do that except by badgering him in union meetings? I've already said there was no provision for motions at the end of the standard agenda for union meetings. But this is the way inuendo works. It's based on partial truths and implication and no one dares to challenge it, out of fear. If they did, they would in turn immediately be branded 'Communist.'

Berton went on to say that "The key men in the Trail local are Communist Party members or Party liners. One of them works as an oiler in the heavy water plant itself. He was identified to this writer as a member of the Labor Progressive Party in 1945 and was recently on the executive of his union." That oiler was Jerry Carter. Berton was right about one thing—Carter was a good old-fashioned Nova Scotia union man, but being a union man doesn't make you a seditious traitor. He used to come to all the Mine Mill meetings and he stayed with Mine Mill when Steel raided us, but other than that, he wasn't politically active. Jerry may have been an old drunk but from that day on he was the 'Red Oiler' and a hero to the rest of us.

I can't tell you how angry that article made us. It was just one more in a

CROSSING THE BORDER

Jack Scott, who was openly a Communist, was elected by the local members to be one of their representatives at a Mine Mill convention in San Francisco. When he arrived at the US border he was brought into Immigration and asked all kinds of questions including whether or not he was a Communist. Taft-Hartley allowed US Immigration to forbid Communists and other 'subversives' from crossing the border so Jack, knowing he'd never be allowed to cross if he admitted it, said, "No. I'm not a Communist."

The Immigration officer said, "You're lying. We know about you. We knew you were coming." Scott figured it was the RCMP who told them but they said, "No. We didn't get it from them. The president of your union told us." And while Jack waited, the guy went to the files and came back with a letter signed by Claire Billinglsey, president of Local 480, turning Jack Scott in for being a 'red.'

Here's a guy just back from overseas all shot up, who's been decorated with the Croix de Guerre, and here's Billinglsey, who sat safely on his githorne all through the war, turning his union 'brother' in to a foreign government as being a 'subversive' and a threat to Canada. Go figure.

Around the same time, Ken Smith of Mine Mill also went down to Seattle to catch a ferry to do some bargaining at the CM&S Tulsequah Mine near Juneau, Alaska. Ken was thrown in the bucket and sent home the next day. We eventually got around his problem by sending local officers from the B.C. to do the Mine Mill bargaining in Northern B.C..

long line of lies and misleading inuendos and half-truths flowing from Taft-Hartley. If there was one thing we were proud of in Mine Mill, it was the democracy of our union. Sure, Harvey Murphy was a Communist, but he sure as hell wasn't "keeping the membership apathetic." Harvey, along with the rest of us, was breaking his butt to get members more actively involved in their union, all to get them better conditions and more pay. How was that "threatening" the security of Canada? Bargaining, strikes, all major decisions including the selection of the union executive, were undertaken with a democratic union vote. We were very proud of that, and here was an outsider telling us how we were "controlled" by the Communist Party. I'd like to know how company people feel about the "control" exercised over them by management policy, a policy they don't get to vote on! In the end I think Berton's printed article was so one-sided and its perversions of the truth so obvious that it actually helped rather than hurt Local 480.

And there was another piece of the story that developed immediately after, that Pierre Berton might really have got his teeth into. There was a newcomer to Trail, a veteran with a young wife and family named Selmer Bean who, within a short time of being hired by CM&S in the early 1950s, became an avid and persuasive supporter of Local 480 in addition to being active in various left-wing causes such as the Stockholm Peace Initiative. It came as no surprise, therefore, when shortly before the end of his ninety day probation period, Selmer was laid off. The union grieved his dismissal on compassionate grounds that were morally unchallengeable—there were no on-the-job discredits, he was a veteran of WWII, he had a young family and

Meeting at Canada/US border when Asbury Howard (V-P, IUMSS) was denied entry, with Local 480. Front row (crouching, left to right): ? Arnold Laar, Bill (W.E.) Muir, Ed Calkin, Remo Morandini, Frank, Barnes, Dan Dosen. Second row (left to right): Johnny Irvin, Bernice Laarz, Evelyn Lewis, Mike Popoff, Ann Smith, Joyce Muir, Ken Smith, Asbury Howard, Percy Berry, Edna Sheard, Syd Sheard, Harry Drake (between Edna and Syd Sheard), Chuck Kenny (over Syd Sheard's left shoulder), Al Warrington (above Asbury Howard's right shoulder). Back row (left to right): John Starcevic, John Pertunia, George Mukanik, Garfield Belanger, Kinneken, Harold Bradbury.

so on—but the company stood its ground and everyone knew it was Selmer's off-the-job activities that cost him his job.

So what happened?

Joe Wilkinson, Head of the Unemployment Insurance Commission in Trail and an ex-Workman's Committee member under Selwyn Blaylock, took pity on the young family and found a job for Bean immediately—as a CPR switchman, switching railway cars in and out of Project 9 in Warfield. Yes, it was that most sensitive and secret part of the whole CM&S chemical complex and the very place that Pierre Berton had warned about in the article for *McLean's Magazine*. I bet the wires got pretty hot between CM&S, CPR, the RCMP, the CIA, the FBI and the Pentagon back in Washington, DC.

In Trail, however, the workers received the news with great hilarity. Here was Berton busy red-baiting poor old Gerry Carter as the 'Red Oiler,'a conservative from the Maritimes, when all the time Selmer Bean, red as a fox's arse, was moving with relative freedom in and out of the high security heavy water plant.

It was inevitable. Selmer soon got the final axe from CPR and he and his family left Trail for good. They were four more victims of the mass hysteria of the Taft-Hartly Act and the venom it spread into Canada.

THE LONG ARM OF THE LAW

After the war, any association with an organization accused of being 'red' could ruin whole careers. As Lillian Hellman so pungently remarked in the US, it was "scoundrel time" also in BC. The law was not exempt. After Art Evans breathed life into the union movement in Trail, Gordon Martin had been the first financial secretary of Local 480. When war broke out, Martin joined the RCAF and on his return to Canada, studied law at the University of British Columbia, graduating in 1948 with a Bachelor of Laws degree. Never relenting in his belief in Communism, Gordon was active politically throughout his university education. He articled with John Stanton who did a lot of legal work for Mine Mill, but when he applied to the Benchers of the Law Society of British Columbia for admission to the bar, his application was rejected. The Benchers wouldn't accept him because he refused to renounce his membership in the Communist party. A lot of people tried to talk him out of it, but he wouldn't hear of it, so he couldn't practise law in BC.

It wasn't long after this that another young graduate applied to practise law in BC Jack MacDonald had also served briefly as financial secretary of the Mine Mill local in Trail, but unlike Gordon, he was never a member of the Communist party. The son of a well-respected local lawyer, Jack had worked at the smelter during his university vacations, and in 1950 he worked at the Warfield plant, taking a year out from his studies. He had been attending union meetings regularly and when Billingsley and company absconded, Jack was elected financial secretary in the Shithouse Executive. He was secretary of the union bargaining committee during the first set of negotiations, and he and Les Walker were the two names listed as plaintiffs in the legal action the union had brought against Billingsley and the other officers. The reason for that was that we didn't want any known Communists listed in the legal proceedings.

In the fall of 1950, Jack MacDonald went back to UBC where he graduated with a Bachelor of Laws degree and articled with his father. In September 1951 when he routinely applied to the Law Society of BC to be called to the bar as a lawyer, he was informed he first had to undergo a special examination by the Credentials Committee of the Law Society in order to satisfy them that he was a "fit and proper person." This was standard. Everybody had to be a "fit and proper person" but they never bothered with most people—they just assumed that they were. However, Jack was now in the grip of the same nit-picking scissor-bills who had already wrecked Gordon Martin's career.

At a hearing held in the Vancouver courthouse, Jack was questioned closely by T.G. Norris, a prominent Vancouver lawyer, who asked Jack if he subscribed to the philosophy of Karl Marx and Frederick Engels. Norris quoted from the *Communist Manifesto*, taking one section out of context, and asked Jack if he agreed. He then asked Jack if he belonged to or supported the Labour Progressive Party of BC and asked him to identify, from a list of names of Local 480 members, which of them were Communists or members of the Labour Progressive Party. The list included Belanger, Ernie Weed and Pearson. My name wasn't mentioned. They'd name someone and ask, "Is he a Communist?" To each one, Jack replied he didn't know, and when they said, "Did you ever know anybody in Trail who was a Communist?" Jack answered, "Harvey Murphy," because Murphy had publicly proclaimed his affiliation.

But that wasn't the end of it. Over the next five months he attended two further hearings before the whole body of the Benchers of the Law Society before he was finally admitted to the bar in March, 1952. In the final hearing, they said, "We just want to get one thing straight, Mr. MacDonald. What will be your future relationship to the Mine Mill union?" They made it clear he wasn't to give any sort of political or moral support to Mine Mill. It was a complete exercise in intimidation.

Of course, by March all the best legal jobs had been filled, and in the small towns of the Kootenays, the whole thing labeled Jack MacDonald as a Party member, even though he wasn't. It followed him too. When Jack ended up going into social work, he was told at his first job that the RCMP had been around to ask the director if Jack was "stirring up the pot." And at another job, his boss eventually told him there was "some concern" about his political background. That was over ten years after Jack left Mine Mill.

T.G. Norris, the lawyer who questioned Jack, sat as a Bencher of the BC Law Society, the body that governs lawyers. He was also, at this time, the lawyer for the Steelworkers Union, working to defend Billngsley and the others against Mine Mill's civil suit in which Jack had been named as one of the two plaintiffs. My guess is that in putting together the case against Mine Mill, Norris got a lot of information from the Steelworkers about Jack's background as well as the Communist members of the union. When he asked, "Is so-and-so a Communist?" it was obvious Norris had been given the names by people determined to smear both Jack and Mine Mill.

BEATING THE RAIDERS

In spite of all this, it finally it began to percolate through the higher echelons of command in the USWA that their initial advantage was slipping away. They realised, for example, that the large Italian-Canadian group of CM&S workers were becoming more favourably inclined toward Mine Mill and that Remo

Morandini and Buddy DeVito were largely responsible. Shortly after, they parachuted into Trail an Italian-Canadian Steelworker named Terry Mancini. He had worked in Sault Ste. Marie in what was then the Algoma Steel Plant. Because Terry was from out of town and knew no one in Trail, the Steelworkers had a hard time finding him any help, but finally they persuaded big Roland 'Cash' Cachioni to help out. Rolly was a nice guy, well liked, and although he worked in the lead refinery where a good many company stooges hid out, Cash was pretty well neutral in his public position. It ended up as a match between Terry and Cash versus Remo and Kitch Bannatyne but it was really no match at all. It wasn't long before Terry went back to Sault Ste. Marie, and Cachioni left the Hill shortly after to get involved in the promotion of a chrome mine.

We felt we were in pretty good shape by the time May 1952 rolled around and the LRB decided it was time for the vote between Mine Mill and Steel. On that day, we had prepared a sack of buttons and some of our people, including Murphy and I, went around town and up and down the Gulch playing bocce ball with the Italian guys, meeting them in the beer parlours and passing these 'Vote Mine Mill' buttons around. The Steelworkers were either so sure of themselves or else so unprepared they didn't even bother to put out a pamphlet. In the secret ballot vote the next day, the guys on the job responded magnificently. Steel was caught flat-footed. We had the Labour Relations vote and we beat 'em. The vote was 1949 for Mine Mill and 1669 for Steel with forty-eight voting for "no union." It was close but not uncomfortable and a good jump on the one-third support that we'd begun with.

In February 1950 it hadn't been easy taking up the leadership of Local 480, and many of the men in the local didn't support us. When Billingsley and his lot took off, a lot of the guys said, "Well, that's just too bad," and figured we were goners. But we fought back and we beat 'em in spite of the fact that they had far greater resources than we had. On September 22, 1951, when they were only half-way into the raid, Charles Millard, Steel's national director, said in the Vancouver *Sun* that, up to that date, the Steelworkers had poured more than $500,000 into the fight to oust Mine Mill from the Canadian mining field. He said they had "succeeded in capturing the Northern Ontario gold mines" but "failed in base metal operations," which included Trail. In fact, he said, "one of the biggest fights" had taken place in Trail.

The tide had slowly started to turn when it became clear what a rotten way the raiding Steelworkers had used to try to get in. If they had played their cards right, all they needed to do was to call a mass meeting and get someone to move a motion that they discontinue their membership in Mine Mill. Then the existing executive under Billingsley could have led the whole union into Steel. If they'd done it democratically and up-front, they could have won it right there in 1950.

But they didn't have the courage to do that. Instead, they snuck around and came up with this full page ad in the *Times*. They got arrogant. They figured that because they had such a majority, they didn't have anything to worry about, that people would just sign up. But even men who weren't pro-Mine Mill or left-wing at all, guys who were uncommitted at first, condemned the way the Steelworkers conducted that raid and in the end, a lot of them voted for Mine Mill—not because they liked us. any better, but because of what the others did. I guess too, that some of them were coming to see that Mine Mill had something to offer, after all.

It was tough to beat the Steel raid in Trail, but it was a victory for democracy and for trade union decency. Leaders like Percy Berry, Doug Murdoch (later President of the Alberta Federation of Labour), Remo Morandini and other newcomers to the union as well as members of Local 480 from the pre-war days, successfully beat back that first raid and, later that year, negotiated a second agreement even stronger than the first.

There's no doubt the nucleus of the struggle for Local 480 of Mine Mill were the veterans of the second World War. We had already won one battle, now we simply had another and we won it in the streets and in debates and in the voting booth—we even had to win it a few times with our fists. We had some great fighters! We were good at it. We should have been—we'd spent several years perfecting our skills on a more deadly enemy than the likes of Claire Billingsley or even Judge Clyne.

Now we were called on to deepen the position of the union, to make it a part of the community and a viable force for the good of everybody. This would turn out to be the biggest challenge of all: to prove beyond the shadow of a doubt that we'd been right all along.

All this organizing activity in Trail cost money. We were very short of funds and wanted to raise the union dues, but we were cautious because sometime in the '40s, Billingsley had asked the members to vote on a fifty cent increase in their union dues and he was badly defeated.

In 1952, with union dues at three dollars per member per month, Les Walker and I wrote out a program of action and presented it to the local, who adopted it. Then we asked for an increase in dues of an additional two dollars per month to help pay for it. This was quite a jump and we had to work hard to convince members that it was a good idea, but it passed—barely. With the help of that dues money, we could now build a new labour hall and carry out our health and safety program, among other things. We immediately initiated a fund to finally build our own headquarters in Trail. We wanted it as a rallying point and social centre so we'd no longer have to fight landlords who refused to rent to 'reds.' Bud DeVito helped us find the location—the J.D. Anderson property in Trail. We'd been sitting up late, talking, when Bud remembered this property and of course, we had to see it at once. People would have thought we were *really* up to some funny business if they'd happened to wander by the Anderson property at three a.m. that morning, as we peered in the windows to see if it was suitable.

Of course, we had no money, but the realtor agreed to sell it to us on time, provided we could immediately pay so much down. We had no spare cash so to raise the money we asked the union leadership and others if they would buy a fifty dollar share.

The fact that Local 480 pulled off what looked like a pretty surprising feat of organizing had a broader effect than just on the Hill. Our organizing inspired other workers too. Following our example, hotel and civic workers in Trail and the surrounding district also began to organize in this period. A friend, Aubrey Burton, led and won the struggle for a civic worker's union that later shared an office in our new union hall.

Meanwhile, the Steel raids continued—and the atmosphere of hatred of anything or anyone suspected of having anything to do with Communisim. The Steelworkers were on the radio like we were, but most of what they had to say was confined to red-baiting. In those days, just to care about injustice, just to want a fairer deal at work or in your church or community, made you instantly suspect. The atmosphere was electric. Familes split up, brother against brother. You were keyed up all the time. 'Trust' and 'Peace' became dirty words. Sometimes it came down to fist fights, not so much in the union hall as in the streets. Trail was a grim, broken city. I guess by then we were sensitive to everything. Everything hurt.

Even our kids had trouble. At the Laura J. Morrish Elementary School in East Trail, the parents of most of the students were employees of Consolidated Mining and Smelting. Our eldest daughter, Geri, was seven or eight years old and one day her teacher, Miss Augustine, took it upon herself to lecture Geri in class as to the error of her father's ways and his role as president of a "Communist-dominated union." Geri came home in tears. Lil and I called for a meeting with the school principal, Mr. Perkins, to make sure this didn't happen again.

We later found out that Miss Augustine's brother was active in another local of Mine Mill. The principal's brother, Howard Perkins, was president of a local of Mine Mill in Nelson District, and Claire Billingsley's brother, Jack, was a solid Mine Miller and president of the Blubber Bay local on Texada Island. So when I say the town was divided, brother against brother, I mean it literally.

One of the kids at Geri's school was particularly bad at calling her names but Geri fought back, and I gather she set him in his place pretty fast. Maybe her dad was a Communist, but the other kid's dad was in jail, so Geri had a good come-back! If it bothered Wayne, our eldest, he didn't let on. Sometimes the Jewish kids got beat up in our area and it was Wayne who ended

RAISING CASH

During the time we were raising money to buy the Anderson property for a union hall, I was approached by Andy Dembicki, a ripe, cranky old devil of a miner who never showered. Andy was a loner. Whenever Mine Mill was trying to sign people up, he never committed. But on this day he said he was going on vacation and did we have enough money yet for the down payment on a union hall?

"No," I said, "not yet."

"How much are you looking for?" he asked.

"We're asking people for a fifty dollar share," I said.

"No. I mean how much more do you need?" Then he brought out his chequebook, signed his name and the date to a cheque and said, "You fill in the amount," and turned around to leave town on his vacation.

I argued with him, but Andy was adamant. We were going to get that property for a union hall even if he had to pay the whole damned thing himself. We filled in the cheque for fifty dollars— but it was through that kind of commitment we were soon able to raise the money we needed and Mine Mill in Trail never again paid monthly rent to anyone. We also adopted a policy of free rent to other unions and were happy to share our space with the Teamsters, hospital workers, civic workers and others.

up becoming a protector to one of them. I think there was probably more of that kind of thing going on in the school yard than we ever knew.

Our kids handled it well, I thought—they argued. Geri could argue with anybody, but Lil and I were careful that none of our kids were coached or educated to be anything other than what they are. We never tried to teach them Communism or any other dogma, because when I was growing up, I didn't want anybody indoctrinating me, either. I had enough of that in the Catholic Church. There was only one rule in our house: there wasn't to be any prejudice. It didn't matter if the other guy was white, black or green—everyone deserved respect no matter how different he or she might be from you.

WORKING WITH MURPHY

As president of Local 480 through the 1950s, I worked very closely with Harvey Murphy. Murphy was invaluable to the Western District of Mine Mill because he was more experienced than any of us, especially after 1950 when we found ourselves suddenly in charge of a union. Murphy educated a lot of people, including me and Ken Smith, the elected Mine Mill western president. Smith, originally an underground miner, was likewise pretty green when he started.

Murphy was very well read and had a broad knowledge of economics. He subscribed to several papers, including the *Globe and Mail* and the *Wall Street Journal*, and he was always on top of the local as well as the national and international situations. If you ever travelled in a car with him, he was constantly switching radio stations, jumping from news program to news program. And the next time he had a speech, he'd incorporate all that recent, local information. He had a great memory.

He was also brilliant, tactically. In February 1952, for our regular provincial convention in the Denman Auditorium in Vancouver, we invited Paul Robeson, the black singer, actor, peace and civil rights activist, to come across the line and address our convention. Local 480 was very active in the Stockholm Peace fight at this time, and Robeson was known not only as a supporter of world peace but as a man who spoke everywhere for the dignity of ordinary working people. Robeson was the son of an escaped slave, the second black man to be named college football All-American and the third black scholar ever to attend Columbia Law School. For years he had performed around the world, singing in many different languages with a single theme. "The idea of my concerts," he said, "is to suggest that all men are brothers because of their music." He was internationally recognized for his courageous stance on civil rights in the US and the world, the first major concert artist to refuse to perform before segregated audiences. He linked the plight of black Americans to the oppression of all working people and made those views an integral part of his concerts. By the 1940s he was among the top ten highest paid concert artists in the world. Then, in August 1950, the US government decided his travels were "contrary to the best interests of the United States" and revoked his passport. He could no longer carry out his extensive international commitments, including annual attendance at the Eisteddfod, the concert of Welsh miners' choirs.

When Harvey Murphy invited him to Vancouver, no one on either side of the border thought Paul Robeson would have any trouble getting into Canada. A passport was only for travel outside North America—until now. Robeson was stopped at Blaine and had his passport withdrawn because he was a "danger and a threat to the US government." This seems almost unbelievable now, but that was the extent of the paranoia in those days. And this was only one of the many times that the Canada/US border would be used against Mine Mill.

Murphy immediately got George Gee, the head of the Electrical Workers 213, to rig up telephone amplification so Paul could speak to the conference long distance, which he did. When he sang over the telephone that great miner's song, "I Dreamed I Saw Joe Hill Last Night" which is a hymn to the memory of Joe Hill who organized hard rock miners in the western US and in BC at the turn of the century, it brought the house down. But there was more.

Right there at the convention, with two hundred delegates as witness, Murphy made a promise to Robeson. "This summer," he said, "and for every summer after that until they let you pass freely, Mine Mill will meet you at the Blaine border. We'll have a truck and sound and you can sing and speak to the people on both sides of the border. Together, we'll beat this boycott."

And he did exactly that. All that spring the union worked hard to promote Paul Robeson's concert at Peace Arch Park at Blaine. Olive did all the groundwork. There were letters to unions and affiliates on both sides of the border promoting the concert as a way not only to hear a great voice, but also to register their anger at the US State Department's refusal to let a citizen leave their own country. It was a demonstration for peace, a way of protesting the actions of any government that would deny its citizens the right to move about and speak freely.

It was a tremendous amount of work but on May 18, 1952, we parked a flat-bed truck twelve inches inside the US side of the border in Peace Arch Park, with a Canadian and an American flag flying on the Arch above. We put an upright piano on the truck and hooked up speakers everywhere so a large audience could hear. Murphy and others, including Olive, sat on the truck with Robeson all that day. Olive got such a sun burn, she still can't stand the sun on her skin.

We didn't announce it but several of us, mostly veterans, came the night before and spent that night and all day in the hills around the park, ready with weapons. There'd been some serious violence from people trying to shut down Paul Robeson's concerts in the US and we didn't want any of that here.

Dozens of buses came, all we could charter, in addition to maybe 5,000 cars from all over BC—Nanaimo, the Okanagan, the Kootenays—lined up in a three mile long traffic jam. People came in the tens of thousands from Canada and thousands more from the US—Tacoma, Olympia, Spokane, Bellingham and Blaine! There were reporters from *Life Magazine* and the

Office Memorandum • UNITED STATES GOVERNMENT

56275/730 Inv. JFG

TO   : Memorandum for the File   DATE: January 17, 1952

FROM   : ▓▓▓▓▓▓▓, Investigator

SUBJECT: Paul Robeson

▓▓▓▓▓▓▓ received a telephone call from ▓▓▓▓▓ of the Canadian Embassy at which time Mr. ▓▓▓▓▓ informed him that he had received information that Paul Robeson was planning to go to Vancouver, B. C. in the near future. He wanted to know whether there had been any exchange of correspondence between the Canadian Government and the U. S. Immigration Service regarding this individual. Mr. ▓▓▓ asked me to check the file for this information and call Mr. ▓▓▓ back for him.

Robeson's file was obtained from the Confidential file room. No correspondence was found in the file from, or to, any official in the Canadian Government. It was noted, however, that there is an outstanding lookout directing that this subject's departure from the United States be prevented. As the lookout is dated August 4, 1950, and was posted at the request of the Passport Division, Department of State, I called Mr. ▓▓▓ of that office to ascertain whether they still desired Robeson's departure prevented. In Mr. ▓▓▓ absence, a ▓▓▓▓▓▓▓ in his office checked with Mrs. ▓▓▓ and notified me by telephone that their request to prevent Robeson's departure was still in effect. Robeson's passport has expired and they are not particularly interested in having same lifted as it will not be renewed under any circumstances.

I called Mr. ▓▓▓ and informed him that we have been asked to prevent Robeson's departure from the United States. To assist us in this I asked that he inform me as to when Robeson was expected to proceed to Vancouver and for what purpose. ▓▓▓ stated that the information he had was very vague. He believed it originated with a newspaper man here in Washington. However, it was stated that Robeson was to attend a concert in Vancouver, the last of January, 1952.

In view of the foregoing it would appear to be advisable to re-alert the Field Office as to our outstanding lookout regarding Robeson. The file will be handed Mr. ▓▓▓ for that purpose.

▓▓▓G:mc

Reader's Digest, from Canadian and US newspapers and there were cameras from KING-TV in Seattle. Forty thousand people waited in the park and scattered around on the hills with blankets and picnic baskets, kids running around everywhere and there was a vast gridlock of cars and buses—all come to listen to the 'red' singer.

Olive Anderson at work in Toronto as Murphy's secretary, assistant and occasional organizer.

At two thirty p.m. Murphy introduced Paul Robeson to the crowd, saying, "What is being done here will ring—is ringing now—around the world." And he was right.

After that, everywhere Paul Robeson went, he praised Mine Mill up and down, and he always sang Joe Hill. The Left got so much mileage out of that—thousands more people heard and knew about Paul Robeson than if the authorities had just let him come and sing to a few hundred miners and their wives in Vancouver! And Harvey Murphy did that. If he'd never done anything else in the labour movement, that was one glorious strategy that came out of his fertile imagination. And it worked because they forbad a man the simple freedom of crossing his own national border. Robeson later credited that concert with being the ticket that tipped the scales in his favour.

At the third annual concert in 1954, Robeson announced that US authorities had agreed to let him travel to Canada and that he would soon be allowed

Paul Robeson.

to travel anywhere. It's a matter of Canadian shame that when, in 1956, the Mine Mill local in Sudbury booked Robeson to sing and speak at their convention, it was the Canadian government, not the Americans, who dragged their heels and made various threats to the effect that he could perform but not speak. Later, a seventeen-concert tour sponsored by the Labour Progressive Party of Canada had to be cancelled because the Canadian government, as reported in the New York Times, refused to issue Robeson a visa. So there was government red-baiting on both sides of the border.

It was Murphy who created the space for all this to happen. Later, he had a recording made of those concerts and circulated it to even more thousands of people in Mine Mill locals and other organizations across the country. And now an American company, Folk Era, has reissued the first two concerts and some of the speeches made there, as a CD, "Paul Robeson: The Peace Arch Concerts."

Do you want to know something funny about Harvey Murphy? He was never known to go into a bank. When he got his pay cheque, he'd always ask someone else to cash it for him. When Les Walker was district secretary he used to do all his banking for him. It wasn't that Murphy didn't have time—he'd stand outside the bank, waiting for Les to finish, to give him his money. I don't know why. Maybe it had something to do with how much he hated capitalism. I guess he thought I was going to do the same thing for him when I later became secretary. What a surprise he got!

I always respected Murphy—but he was hard to like. He liked me I think, because I was his chief lieutenant in many ways. I think he felt comfortable around me, partly because I was sort of his bodyguard and he knew nobody was going to take any liberties with me around. But in some ways he was a strange man—people would do things for him and he'd have no gratitude, no respect. Sometime after 1950 we'd had a meeting in Trail and after, as usual, we'd gone to the Legion. Al Warrington and I were having a game of darts while Murphy and Gar and Tillie Belanger, Vic Quiding and his wife and a few others were having a beer. When the time came to leave, there were a couple of guys sitting by the door. One was Chuck Bradbury, an ex-lacrosse player from Trail who I knew before the war, and Ralph McNeil. As Murphy passes him, Bradbury says, "Get out, you Communist sonofabitch. I shot people like you in the Second World War."

I was right behind and said, "And maybe I shot githorns like you, Bradbury."

JACK DEMPSEY AND 'THE HARP'

In the 1950s, Mine Mill held an international convention in Denver, Colorado in which festivities on the final night brought together Doug Gold, secretary of the Kimberley, BC miner's union, myself and an excellent Mine Mill organizer from Ontario named Tom (no relation to Barney) McGuire, who had been affectionately dubbed 'The Harp' by hard rock miners on both sides of the border. Broad daylight the next morning saw Gold and I attempting to get The Harp on his home flight to Los Angeles but, to put it bluntly, Harp was in no condition to fly. In fact, he was in no condition to do anything. He was on a bench on the airport tarmac—out cold.

Airport terminals of the 1950s were nowhere near as sophisticated as they are today, and when Harp's plane arrived from the east, the passengers disembarked for a breakfast in the terminal restaurant. Most of them paid no attention to the tableau at the bench, but when I looked up and noticed the great boxer, Jack Dempsey, approach, I said, "Hello, Jack." Dempsey said "Hello," back and kept walking.

"Who was that?" demanded Gold.

"That was Jack Dempsey," I replied. "I think I'll go in and join him for breakfast." And I did.

Doug joined me and we were soon sitting beside Dempsey introducing ourselves. Dempsey visibly warmed up when he found that we were Canadians. He listened gravely to our problem of Harp being denied a seat on the flight because of his condition—unless he was accompanied by a sober companion.

Dempsey explained he'd had had a rough time of it economically for a few years after losing his title, and it was an invitation to referee a wrestling match in Montreal, Quebec that enabled him to re-establish himself in the athletic world from which he launched his business enterprises, notably a restaurant in New York. He said he was forever grateful for the opportunity that was offered him in Canada when his career was stagnating in the US.

I asked him if he would help us in getting The Harp to LA. Dempsey never hesitated—he said he was glad to.

Minutes later, with Dempsey standing by, we were again attempting to revive The Harp. The dialogue went something like this:

Me: "Harp, wake up. Jack Dempsey is taking you to LA."
Harp: "Fuck Jack Dempsey."
Gold: "Harp, please don't say that to the Manassa Mauler."
Harp: "Fuck the Manassa Mauler."
Me & Gold together: "Harp, you don't know what you're saying. Jack Dempsey is trying to help us to help you."
Harp: "Then fuck you too."

At this point Dempsey suggested we get Harp on his feet, and it was not long before The Harp realized he was in good hands and became co-operative. And that was how Tom McGuire returned home from one miners' convention. Nothing earth-shaking, just the simple act of a good man who had himself been through the mill.

Bradbury got quite aggressive and said, "Yeah? I'll fix you if you want to come outside." So out come him and MacNeil, and Murphy and the others stood across the street watching while I put Bradbury in the hospital. MacNeil didn't move. I asked him if he wanted to join the dance, but he declined.

After Bradbury got out of the hospital, he went to the Steelworkers Union who took his story to court and had me prosecuted for assault and battery.

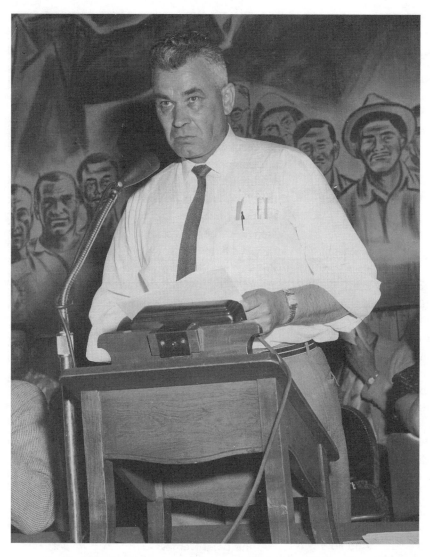

Githorns beware! At a union convention in 1954.

Jack MacDonald's dad defended me, but the verdict went against me—they said I waylaid Bradbury on the way home. I was sentenced to one day in jail that I never served because that was the day in court. Afterward, the magistrate phoned me up and apologized for the way it appeared in the paper.

A while later, Murphy and I were in Ontario and I was driving the Mine Mill executive to a meeting in Port Colborne when Murphy told them in the car that I kicked the guy when he was down. The lying bastard. I was driving so I couldn't turn around and belt him, could I?

I was taught how to fight by a Welsh boxer before I came to Canada and I was good at it, though the rules don't seem to apply so much here in Canada. The way they operate here is you get the guy down and just put the boots to him, but I learned to fight fair, on my feet. You fight standing up, not when people are lying on the ground. Murphy knew I wouldn't fight like that—he was belittling my defense of him, contemptuous of what I did for him. That's the kind of man he could be.

TO EUROPE

In 1954 the BC District Union of Mine Mill received an invitation from the French Metallurgical Workers Union to send two Canadian Mine Mill representatives on a fraternal visit to France with the aim of promoting understanding and friendship between Canadian and French workers in our industry. The union accepted and two delegates were chosen by secret ballot—Mike Solski from Sudbury would represent eastern Canada, and I was chosen to represent the west. Brother Solski was held up by some difficult bargaining in Sudbury and never did make it to Europe, but I had an interesting trip.

As the guest of various trade unionists, I travelled to Paris, Munich and Vienna and although I'd always heard of these as cities of lightness and culture, the devastation of war was still very visible. People were always very polite, but they seemed apathetic and subdued, and I assumed this was due to the fact they were still very obviously recovering, both physically (there were many amputees, both men and women) and emotionally, from the war.

In Vienna I attended an international convention of the World Federation of Trade Unions (WFTU) with hundreds of delegates from seventy-three countries, including China, Japan, Italy, the Soviet Union and Great Britain. As a guest of the French Metallurgical Union, I was the only representative from North America. Many of our concerns were reflected elsewhere in Europe—I compared notes about lead poisoning with the delegate from Sweden, discussed efforts to raise the cultural as well as the material well-being of workers with the brothers from England, and took the floor to tell the delegates about key issues for the Canadian Mine, Mill and Smelter Workers, particularly the problems of unemployment and of American domination of Canadian resources.

When the convention ended, I joined a Canadian delegation of trade unionists who were to travel through eastern Europe and the Soviet Union. The group included members of the Marine and Boiler Makers Union, the United Auto Workers, the Union of Fur and Leather Workers, United Electrical Radio and Machine Workers, and the Carpenters. Everywhere we went, we were treated with unstinting hospitality, and I was impressed with the vast extent of the efforts to rapidly rebuild countries after the war, although I wasn't always impressed with the working environment in some of the factories. When we visited the tombs of Lenin and Stalin in Red Square, I was delighted to find that one of the founders of our union and its first financial secretary, William 'Big Bill' Haywood, is buried at that spot. I had my picture taken beside the plaque in the Kremlin wall that bears his name.

Everywhere, women worked alongside men. I was especially impressed by the participation of women—often up to thirty per cent of the work-force—in the shipyards and in heavy industry. I was told this was because of the huge mortality rates Soviet men suffered in the war. When I expressed greetings from Canadian workers at one smelter we visited, a woman stepped forward and told us to bring greetings to all Canadian women from Madame Zencova of the Kirov Aluminum Plant. I promised to put her in touch with Sister Kay Dosen of our local Ladies Auxiliary.

We also saw the results of Soviet efforts to rebuild after the systematic damage done to industry by the retreating Germans. We visited construction sites, smelters, a steel pipe mill, the Dneiper Dam near Kiev, a steel mill, shipyards, a children's summer camp, a daycare centre, the port of Odessa, a machine factory, clinics and sanitariums and a collective farm. Connected with several of the plants were full educational, cultural and entertainment facilities. In the countryside, on billboards that in North America would be advertising hamburger joints or liquor, there were calls for international

June 1954 at 'Big Bill' Haywood's tomb in the Kremlin wall, Moscow, USSR.

peace. I was convinced they weren't there just for our benefit, but for their own people. Such an internal concern with world peace was entirely at variance with what we were being told at home. We finished our visit to the collective farm with a magnificent dinner and large quantities of the liquid depth charge called vodka.

In Stalingrad we went to the Heights which had been left churned by the fierce battles that took place here and that were the turning point of the war. The ground was still strewn with rifle and machine gun bullets, exploded hand grenades and mortar fragments, and was a burial ground as well as a battle ground. It was very moving for those of us who were veterans. One of my strongest impressions from this trip was the absence of the constant editorializing and indoctrination I had become used to in Canada, about the Soviet Union and the People's Republic of China being enemies of the United States. The absence or rejection of this idea was not just in veterans or workers, but everywhere. The outlook and the atmosphere of the people of North America and those in eastern and western Europe, were very, very different. It was obvious that the Europeans and Soviets knew war—the signs of it, human and otherwise, were still prominent seven years after it ended—and they clearly wanted no more of it and were very threatened by the numerous signs of America re-arming in Europe and generating hostility with the Communist bloc. The Canadian and American people don't recognize how fortunate we were between 1939 and 1945.

The final irony of my trip was that, after touching down in nine countries, the only place I had trouble at a border was at my own. When I flew back from Scotland via Montreal, my luggage was searched three times, I was stripped and skin searched and my daily journal and address book were confiscated. If there was such a thing as the Iron Curtain, after that trip I was convinced it primarily circled the North American continent.

BORDER CROSSINGS

The following year, 1955, was the year for our district, District 7, to host the International Mine Mill convention. The two largest and strongest locals in the district were Coeur d'Alene in Idaho and Trail, BC and since Spokane was about the same distance from both, we decided to hold the convention there.

Local 480 was very proud to co-host it. In fact, we laid on not one but two pipe bands from Trail. We named one band to go because we had members on it and then someone at the Legion said, "We've got a pipe band that has Mine Mill members on it, too!" so we sent the whole works. Most of the delegates at the convention had never seen bagpipes, let alone a pipe band before, and my sister Olive reported that when the two bands walked into that hall playing, everyone stood up. They went ape shit over it!

But I wasn't there. Seventeen of us from Trail including me, the president, and Remo, Secretary-Treasurer of the local, had been stopped at the border. After the experience with Robeson and later Jack Scott, it was becoming pretty routine that our people were getting stopped at the border but it was erratic—the customs guards stopped some people but not others, for no clear reason. Ed Lewis was stopped, but his wife was admitted. And Al Warrington who had just run in the provincial election for the Labour Progressive Party and was therefore the most publicly recognized, card-carrying Communist in the bunch, was let through. They didn't stop anyone from Vancouver, including my sister Olive, who was a Communist, or from Nelson or Kimberley—only Local 480 who was co-sponsoring the convention. One of the border guards showed us a list he'd been supplied with that was an exact copy of a list published in the union paper. We always assumed Billingsley sent it. In fact, we rigged up another phone hook-up, like we'd done for Paul Robeson, and Murphy, Thibault (the Canadian national president), me and others, spoke to the convention by telephone.

Right after this I got a letter from the United States government stating that, under the Walter McCarran Act, I was henceforth forbidden to enter the US because I constituted a threat to the internal security of the United States. And if I violated this order, I was subject to five years in jail and a $5,000 fine—a lot of money in those days, and I didn't have it. That Act wasn't lifted until 1993, but I haven't been even tempted to go across the border since.

In fact, in 1950 when I became president of Local 480, I had quit the Labour Progressive Party. The party decided it would be better if I wasn't a member because the pressure was pretty grim. Eventually it became known around town that I wasn't a Party member and technically this was true, even though my sympathies were still there and have never changed.

'JUICY' WHITE

In the 1950s at a northern Yukon mine, a mining engineer named Clarence Edward White—Clare to his friends—was standing in the chow lines at breakfast when he noticed one very large, very hung-over hard rock miner, pick up and down in quick succession six glasses of juice. White ordered the man's name taken down and sure enough, on his next paycheque there was a deduction for the price of the extra juice.

Well, the collective agreement at that mine had never been tested on this kind of issue, but the miners agreed that most of them never got to breakfast at all on their 'mornings after,' so why penalize a man who did? And the issue went to arbitration. The Board in its wisdom favoured the company, but only after agreeing that two or three glasses of juice would have been reasonable.

The company won the battle but lost the war. Total catering costs at that camp promptly doubled because everybody, but everybody, had three or four glasses of juice, three or four times a day, from that day onward. And from that day, Clare White was known as 'Juicy' to Canadian hard rock miners.

The 1955 Convention where we established Canadian autonomy for Mine Mill.

INDEPENDENCE

The International Mine, Mill and Smelter Workers Union was proud to be one of the most democratic unions in North America, and our relations with our International office in the US reflected this. Delegates elected from every local went to international conventions where officers were nominated and later voted on by secret ballot, and policy was democratically voted on by all the delegates. Everyone was then supposed to abide by those policies regardless of which side of the border they were on. Of course, some locals followed them more closely than others, but regardless, everyone knew the policy of the union—it wasn't imposed.

The union's position on the Taft-Hartley Act was to oppose it but people like Billingsley and others went against that when they either openly or implicitly supported the Act.

The Canadian side of the International Union of Mine, Mill and Smelter Workers always had considerable independence from the International, but in 1955 we made an arrangement whereby we would conduct our Canadian business entirely apart from the US. Partly this was because we were being raided on both sides of the border and there weren't enough resources, but in the US particularly (and later, we realized too late, in Sudbury in Canada) we were in a fight for our lives. In the early '50s and until 1955, Mike Solski, as president of the Sudbury local, and me from Local 480, started going to the States to attend Executive Board meetings because Murphy would be

PARTIAL LIST OF CERTIFICATIONS OF THE WESTERN DISTRICT OF IUMMSW
Mid-1950s

Local No.	Local Name	Certifications
289	Vancouver Metal & Chemical Workers' Union	1. Mainland Foundry 2. Lettson & Burpee 3. Port Haney Brick & Tile 4. Nichols Chemical 5. Atkins & Burbrow
480	Trail & District Smelter Workers Union	1. CM&S Co. Ltd.
564	Dawson Miners Union	1. Yukon Consolidated Gold Mines
578	Gypsum Workers Union	1. Gypsum, Lime & Alabastine 2. Perlite Industries Limited
649	Copper Mountain Miners' Union	1. Granby Consolidated Mining Smelting & Power Co. 2. Canam Copper 3. Granduc Mines Ltd. 4. CM&S (Fairview Mines)
651	Kimberley Mine & Mill Workers Union	1. CM&S (Sullivan) (Fertilizer) (Steel plant) (Bluebell) 2. Mineral King (Sheep Creek Mines) 3. Western Gypsum (Invermere)
663	Britannia Mine & Mill Workers Union	1. Howe Sound Company
685	Wells Miners Union	1. Cariboo Gold Quartz
694	Portland Canal Mine Mill Workers Union	1. Silbak-Premier Mines (Hi-grading)
800	Calgary Metal Workers Union	1. Westeel Products Ltd. 2. Calgary Iron & Engineering

Local No.	Local Name	Certifications
802	Yellowknife District Miners' Union	1. Giant Yellowknife Gold Mines 2. Con Mines (CM&S)
816	Texada Island Quarry and Mine Workers Union	1. Ideal Cement Co. Ltd. 2. Lafarge Cement of North America
851	Zeballos District Mine and Mill Workers Union	1. Zeballos Iron Mines Ltd. 2. (Privateer Mine-International Iron Mines)
882	Blubber Bay Quarry Workers Union	1. Gypsum Lime & Alabastine
900	Beaverdell Mine and Mill Workers Union	1. Highland Bell Mine 2. Camp McKinney Gold Mine Ltd. 3. Sheritt-Lee Mines Ltd.
901	Nelson & District Mine and Mill Workers Union	1. Canadian Exploration Ltd. 2. H.B. Mine (CM&S) 3. Reeves MacDonald Mines Ltd. 4. Violamac Mines Ltd.
913	Beaverlodge District Miners' Union	1. Eldorado Mining & Refining 2. Rix Athabasca 3. Cayzor Athabasca
924	Mayo District Mine and Mill Workers' Union	1. United Keno Hill Mines (Elsa) 2. United Keno (Transport Division: Whitehorse)
927	Cassiar Mine Mill and Allied Workers	1. Cassiar Asbestos
931	Trail & District General Workers	1. Crystal Laundry

turned back at the border. It was during those trips that we started to find out how bad it was down there.

The major incident that precipitated Canadian political independence in the union was a dispute that developed over the sale of zinc. Mine Mill in the US, supported by Senator Barry Goldwater of Arizona and powerful zinc mining interests such as Phelps Dodge and Kennecott, had supported an embargo against the importing of Canadian zinc. This was happening at the same time as Canadian Mine Mill were sending delegations to then-

*Al King and Remo Morandini
presenting formal strike notice
to CM&S in the 1958
'non-strike.'*

Prime Minister Louis St. Laurent opposing the embargo and proposing that if the US went ahead with it, we would put embargos on our water and asbestos shipments to them. The position of the two unions was directly counter to each other. That's when we decided to make our own decisions in Canada, separate from the US, even though we would maintain our brotherhood and stay in the same union.

In 1955 we were the first Canadian union to win voluntary and full independence from our US International parent body. This wasn't a break-away, as it has been with many other Canadian unions that sought independence from their International. Mine Mill in Canada still saw itself as a part of the same union as Mine Mill in the US. We still voted on International officers and so on, but we would be self-governing. We immediately set up a separate Canadian structure. Until then, the two most senior men in Canada had been the District Directors of District 7 (Murphy, in the West),

THE STRIKE THAT NEVER WAS

In 1958 there was a two-day strike in Trail. A guy from Calgary named D. 'Pat' Morris was head of negotiations for the company and he was very unaccustomed to bargaining. The union didn't want to strike and the company knew it. I can't even remember the issue, but Morris forced us to take a strike vote and almost immediately we settled the thing. That was on Friday, and Saturday was the day the strike was supposed to start but there wasn't time before then to get to all our people to take a ratification vote. And it was too late to stop the strike.

It was a pretty strange strike. No one ever saw a picket line because for most members, Saturday and Sunday were their days off, and besides, we'd already settled. The one problem we had was the banking of the furnaces so, since we were shut down over the weekend, we let the company keep enough staff working to make sure the plant didn't freeze up.

I still have the picture of Remo Morandini, the Secretary-Treasurer of the union and I, taking the strike notice up to the company office on Friday afternoon. We got the settlement even before we took the strike notice up, but we had to go through the motions. Afterward, Morris broke down in tears. He said, "I didn't think my boys would ever do this to me, would ever go on strike." It was the first strike at CM&S since 1917, even though it wasn't a strike. Murphy at that time was still chairman of the Bargaining Committee and spokesman for the union.

Murphy was very much opposed to taking strike votes, a tactic I learned from him. Some unions took strike votes prematurely, before or during bargaining, but Murphy didn't believe in that. In the thirty years I conducted negotiations I was in strikes started by someone else, but I never did have a real strike stemming from a bargaining dispute in any of the negotiations I conducted.

and District 1 (Nels Thibault, in the East). Now Murphy, with all his savvy, introduced the idea of a national Executive Council of ten members. When it became obvious that we couldn't afford to keep such a large council active, the Canadian national executive was reduced to five people that became the Executive Council: Nels Thibault, President; Harvey Murphy, Vice-President; Bill Longridge, Secretary; Bill Kennedy, eastern Board member; and Ken Smith, western Board member. When Thibault stepped down to run for president of his old Sudbury local and Ken moved to become national president after 1960, I followed as western district secretary and later, western board member.

With this new arrangement, Murphy moved to Toronto and my sister Olive went with him, as a secretary/assistant. She had one kid and I don't know what her husband Ed was doing at the time, but he agreed to go. Olive moved from Vancouver to Toronto at Murphy's request, but when she asked for reimbursement for her moving costs, Murphy said no. I have no idea why. That was just Murphy. It was another example of what I call Murphy's lack of respect for people.

Olive was a marvel at shorthand and transcribing. She'd sit all day taking notes on a whole convention, transcribe them that night and have a copy on the desk for each delegate the next morning with everybody's name right, working all night to do it. She was that good. I used to help her on the Gestetner. The miners all got to know Olive and thought she was wonderful. She used to give them money if they were broke, a real softie.

MOVING ALONG

While I was president of Local 480 during the 1950s, I began to help Bill Rudychuk and others organize various mines including the one at the head of the Arrow Lakes, and the Violamac Mine in Silverton.

Violamac is an abbreviation for Viola MacMillan, who owned it—no relation that I know of, to H.R. MacMillan of MacMillan Bloedel fame. Viola liked the miners, but she was crooked as hell. When she became president of the Canadian Prospector's Association, she registered her mine not as a company but as an association so the Mines Act wouldn't apply to her and, she hoped, so she wouldn't have to deal with the union, either. We told her we didn't care what the hell she was called, she had to sit down and bargain with us! The union was under a different Act and besides, the guys in that mine were very militant. They wouldn't have put up with baloney like that. She later went to jail for insider trading, but she was a great old gal and reasonable enough when we bargained with her.

I liked working with the miners. I had no fear of going underground, and I quickly got to know miners and their business. Sometimes I wonder how I became a smelter worker—I still think I should have been a miner.

All through the '50s I got phone calls from Murphy or Ken Smith giving me assignments, like organizing outside Trail. Thinking back, I guess they had their eyes on me for higher office even then. And Murphy kept appointing me as his representative to go to the International Executive Board meetings in Denver, Colorado to represent him. Until 1955, that is, when they wouldn't let me cross the border any more, either.

In those days, all of our locals had elections for a new executive every November. During the ten years I was president, there were some contests, but I was elected each time I ran. To tell you the truth, I don't think there were too many who wanted the job—but by 1960 I decided it was time to move on. There were several reasons.

Ten years is a good stretch, and by 1960 there were several capable young guys who were active in the union who'd learned a lot. The situation in 1960 was far different from the one we'd inherited in 1950. In 1950 we'd walked into an empty shell of a union whose officers had just deserted *en masse*, leaving no money in the bank, virtually no job stewards and our members being raided by a large and wealthy union.

By 1960 we had a large, strong local with an efficient executive, wide involvement of the membership in various committees at every level of the union, a strong system of job stewards, an impressive building owned by the members and an extremely effective secretary-treasurer, Remo Morandini, who kept a close tab on the doh-re-mi. We also had three million dollars in the bank. Everyone was paying dues but in addition to two or three women

THE JOE CAMPE CASE

Joe Campe was a good man who worked for many years as a heavy duty truck driver for the American firm that mined high grade lime on Texada Island near Powell River, BC. But Joe was beginning to have a series of driving accidents, the last of which caused the company to fire him on the grounds that he'd become a hazard.

Although somewhat sympathetic to the company's arguments, the union's membership instructed its officers to file a grievance for unjust dismissal. The grievance eventually went to an Arbitration Board whose decision, when it came down, was a clear victory for Campe. The arbitrator ruled that Joe Campe had reached a stage of failing eyesight and co-ordination that in his present job led to risk of injury to employees and company property. But Campe was to be retained with no loss in pay as the company gardener until his regular retirement.

How did such an enlightened decision favoring a worker come about? It happened that on the ferry trip from Vancouver to Texada Island, the adjudicator, a retired Canadian Army officer, and myself met and discussed certain mutually interesting topics. Although Mine Mill was not a member of the BC Federation of Labour at the time, we were always interested in the provincial labour scene. Not long before this, the President of the BC Federation of Labour, Pat O'Neal, had publicly complained that the record showed this particular adjudicator's judgments were a full ninety percent in favour of the companies and only ten percent for the unions.

Said I, "Wasn't that stupid of O'Neal to print that percentage crap in the Vancouver papers?"

Sighed he, "Indeed it was."

The remainder of the journey passed in a friendly manner and when the adjudicator's judgment came down, I was probably the only unsurprised individual in BC.

---

in the office, we only had two full-time officers—the president and secretary-treasurer—whose wages were set at a journeyman's rate of pay. Mine Mill could never be accused of being a union of fat cats.

And there was pressure on me to take on more province-wide work. By 1960 I'd sat on several conciliation boards and helped organize several mines. So when Ken Smith, who had been secretary of the BC District Council, moved back east to become president of Mine Mill nationally, I ran as secretary of BC District. When I got elected, Lil and I moved the family to Vancouver. Harvey Murphy was by now living in Toronto as director of the western district and Les Walker was in the job of full-time compensation officer in Vancouver, looking after Mine Mill compensation claims.

It was shortly after I left Trail that I legally changed my name from Albert King to Albert Lorenzo King. I'd never had a second name and I wanted to honour the Italian-Canadians who'd been such good friends to me in Trail, so I picked a good Italian name. I'm very proud of being "Lorenzo." I use it a lot.

WESTERN DISTRICT SECRETARY

In 1960, as secretary of the western district, I'd looked after BC, the Yukon and the Northwest Territories, but in 1961 or '62 when the national executive was reduced from a ten to a five-person body, I became western Board member responsible for all hard rock mining and smelter operations from Manitoba west and from the US border north, including the two territories. For this, I had the help of four organizers and three office staff in Vancouver.

The work wasn't much different from what I'd been doing before, but I had a lot more responsibilities. One of the more unpleasant was that there were several staff members I had to replace because they weren't helping the organization. These included Jack Moffatt, who lost us the Granduc mine, Dick Archibald and Boo Nedderfield. The other was Barney McGuire.

Both McGuire and Moffatt, who used to be president of the BC District Union, had done a lot to organize Mine Mill in the early days. They, along with a few others like old Doc Manson, are legends for how they came to organize the remote mining camps. But mining conditions in the '60s were very different. When I came on staff in Vancouver, Barney had been driving a bread truck in Edmonton and later trying to organize real estate workers. When Murphy came back out west, he put Barney on staff for a while under my direction and sent him to Oliver where we were trying to organize a talc mine owned by a Seattle company. We were having a hell of a tough time getting them organized. I'd signed up about six guys that I knew, so with this foot in the door I sent him in there to try and get it all signed up. It was a crucial time because we were trying to get the job done before the manager in Seattle caught on to what was happening and put the fear of Christ into the workers.

But Barney got married at about this time and took his wife on their honeymoon. He never went near Oliver. When I went down to see how the campaign was going, it wasn't going anywhere—he was in Penticton with his new wife at union expense, so I had to let him go. He didn't argue because he knew he had it coming. Steel hired him later. He worked for them until the merger happened, then they let him go, too.

Barney and I never had any acrimony, but the women in the office were pissed off with him. One time after he was working for Steel, he came in to the Mine Mill office. The two staff, Olive Anderson and Gladys Bjarnason, had rolled up thirty pennies in silver paper and when Barney came to the office, they gave it to him: thirty pieces of silver for his treachery in going to Steel. Feelings ran very high in those days.

In place of the four I let go, I hired organizers like Archie MacDonald, Vince Ready and Neil MacLeod, plus other guys on an on-and-off, part-time basis. Metro Nazarchuk worked for us for a while. Bill Rudychuk wouldn't come on staff so long as Murphy and Smith were around, but when I started, Murphy was still back east so Rudychuk came on board.

Other field support included Stan MacRae, Paddy 'Take Five' Toner, Mike Shields, Henry Amyotte, Lou Regenwetter, Tony Belcher and others. In the Kootenays were Doug Gold, Bill Booth, Jim Patterson, Clem Thompson, Jack Musgrove and Bill Muir. Bill Berezowski, a miner from Keno Hill in the Yukon, was taken on staff to assist the locals in Saskatche-wan, Alberta and the Territories. Neil MacLeod was a big addition because he'd worked in open pit operations. After a while I made him the Director of Open Pit Mining Operations and he did an excellent job of it. These were all young miners, fairly new to the labour movement, but they were excellent organizers.

This new energy was important because from the early 1950s on, an intense battle was in progress right across Canada for the right to mining certifications. In the west, we were in a continuous struggle not just with the Steelworkers, but with other unions, particularly the Labourers, Teamsters and Local 115 of the Operating Engineers. These three formed a devilish coalition they called the Three-Way Pact that took advantage of the struggle between Mine Mill and Steel to take mining certifications away from both of us. The way they set it up was deceptively simple. They'd approach the management of a mine and say they wanted to take the place of the union—Mine Mill—that was 'clearly' Communist dominated. Maybe they also promised better co-operation. Anyway, they made a deal for management to start hiring only those guys who were members of their three unions. Then when the raiding period began, those members would simply vote out Mine Mill and vote in the Three-Way Pact. Management loved it—more division among the unions, the chance to get rid of a 'red' union and to bring in a union they figured might not push them so hard.

Another policy devised at this time to control the unions was called "pre-contract bargaining" or "pre-contract agreements." It was perfected by Mr. W.A.C. Bennett, then premier of BC. At the time, the BC Industrial Conciliation and Arbitration Act (ICA) gave all organized workers a guarantee that no work or wage conditions could be imposed on them without their agreement. So what happened? Premier Bennett, together with a consortium of companies and a very co-operative Building Trades Council just went ahead and, in New York City, signed a ten year contract for the development of BC dam jobs in the Peace River area.

It was a form of slavery, and at that time, in complete violation of the Industrial Conciliation and Arbitration Act. On the Peace project, people were paid on the basis of a contract negotiated in New York City before they even started. This was what confronted Mine Mill in BC from 1960 on.

THE PEACE RIVER DAM

On the huge hydro electric dam project at Hudson Hope that was a part of the Peace River Dam, there were already men working when the pre-con-

King's Wrecking Crew, 1967. Left to right: Stan MacRae, Norm Harsford, Al King, Paddy Toner, Vince Ready, Archie MacDonald.

tract deal was struck. They were diamond drillers, members of Mine Mill's Local 1005, who were testing the bedrock for footings. When the collective agreement was imposed, not just Mine Mill but also the company, Connors Diamond Drill (owned by CM&S), were so angry that they came with us to the Labour Relations Board. They felt a responsibility as employer because under Bennett's deal, their long-time employees would lose their pensions by having to switch from Mine Mill to another union. Backed by the government, the LRB stood firm. When we accused them of violating their own act, Chairman Bill Sands never batted an eye. "Sue us," he said. He knew full well that the embattled Mine Mill was in no shape to sue anyone.

Nor were the building trades about to interfere on behalf of Mine Mill. There were several reasons for this: one was that, in a period of high unemployment, those unions needed every job they could get. They were certainly no friends of the raiding Steelworkers because they had been recently cheated by Steel out of their certification at the Kitimat smelter project, but they were, by long tradition as AFL craft unions, opposed to industrial unions like Mine Mill.

Also, three of their member unions—the Labourers, Operating Engineers and Teamsters—had combined as the Three-Way or Tri-Pact, to invade Mine Mill's jurisdiction while we were preoccupied defending ourselves against our main opponent, the United Steelworkers of America. The Tri-Pact unions would lure our guys away by promising them construction jobs when the mining work was over. So, to make a long story short, we lost any involvement in the Peace River Dam project.

THE ZEBALLOS MINE

In the 1930s, Mine Mill had held union certification for the Zeballos gold mine on the west coast of Vancouver Island. Under the terms of the old ICA Act, once a union had a certification it never died, so in the 1950s when the new owner, Falconbridge, sent a crew to reopen the mine, we assumed it was ours. However, the company got the crew to apply for certification under the Three-Way Pact and in the meantime we refused to recognize them. When the mine started production, our guys (who were working underground by then), went on strike over the issue of health and safety because one of our miners, Don Fraser, had been blinded on the job. I was there running the strike for our members and we really had the company and the Tri-Pact by the balls. We weren't certified so they couldn't take any legal action against us, yet our guys were the ones doing the underground work. It was crazy. Mine Mill picketed while the Mounties paraded up and down in the ditch below our picket line to prevent "labour violence."

That strike goes down in the history books because when we finally had the vote to certify, the guy who came to count the ballots burned them, and that was the end of that. Possession is nine points of the law, so we just kept on going as if we'd never been disturbed. I'm sure the vote was ninety per cent in favour of Mine Mill over the Three-Way Pact, anyway.

That was another place where we encouraged families to get involved in the strike. I had high school kids as stewards on the picket line—kids love a good fight—and then their mothers got interested. So the whole family ended up involved in the struggle against the boss, and that's how it ought to be.

But the Three-Way Pact unions as well as Steel continued to challenge us on every new property, and fought to take away from us the properties we'd already organized. The ones we lost were to the mining companies conspiring with the Three-Way Pact—Phoenix, Peachland and Boss Mountain—though we later took back Peachland and Boss Mountain. Steel were in the process of raiding Cassiar, Craigmont and Endako but we merged before those came to a head. So, in the '60 s we never actually lost a mine to a Steel raid in the west.

It was the new young organizers who helped us hold our own in the western district—that, and the fact that we did a lot of accident prevention work and health and safety work. Mostly they weren't on staff and we couldn't pay them much more than expenses, but this union was formed by guys like that, just going from job to job, organizing wherever they went. We got along well together. I guess I could be about as haywire as they were so they cottoned on to me. The new organizers did such a good job that people started calling them "King's Wrecking Crew."

Archie MacDonald and Vince Ready secured Mine Mill certifications at Mt. Nanson and another mine on the Saskatchewan/Manitoba border. This was particularly satisfying because until then, that part of the country was dominated by the Steelworkers. And a strike and a lockout at Britannia Mines in the mid-sixties went a long way toward improving conditions there and strengthening the loyalty of miners toward Mine Mill.

We organized all the diamond drillers in the three western provinces and the territories into a new Local 1005. With Lance MacPhee as their business agent, supported by Norm Badger, Danny White, Slim Donovan and others, there were now fifteen diamond drilling companies under certification to Mine Mill—every diamond drilling company there was—and in 1965 they had a very successful strike.

Then we organized the Development Miners Local 1037. The development, or tramp miner, is a special breed. He's the one who goes in wherever a new mine is opening up and prepares the mine. He sinks the shafts, drives the drifts, and raises and generally gains access to and from new ore bodies. It's highly hazardous but highly paid work, which is why a lot of miners liked to do it. It was as tramp miners that Vince Ready, Archie MacDonald, Stan MacRae, Jack Durac and most of our other young wildcats worked.

Raids on Mine Mill certifications in Yellowknife, Whitehorse and Uranium City were often led by two ex-Mine Millers named Joe Rankin and Jimmy Russell. Russell had been secretary of Local 240 of Mine Mill in Kirkland Lake when they were originally trying to get certified. He left there to work in the steel plant in Hamilton and helped organize there—that's how he became a member of the Steelworkers Union. Mine Miller's drank a lot of Rankin's and Russell's liquour but in the end, most of them refused to sign their Steelworker union cards.

There was also a full-scale raid by the Operating Engineers at CM&S 's newest (and largest) mine at Pine Point in the Northwest Territories, but Mine Mill maintained its position there and a new collective agreement was signed in 1964.

By 1966 we had all the diamond drill crews and shaft development companies (seven of them in the province). We organized or held onto Phoenix, Princeton, Boss Mine, Kennedy Lake, Pine Point, the Wedge Mine in New Brunswick, and most of the mines in the Northwest Territories, including Keno Hill, Giant, the Con Mine and Cassiar, where we were able to get the threshold limit values of asbestos down from seven and eight and nine, to two.

WORKING WITH MURPHY

Murphy had quite an ego. Some time after I'd left Trail to become District Secretary of Mine Mill, Harvey and I had been to make a presentation to the Cabinet, as we often did, and afterward we went to the Press Room. Arch Snow was the CBC guy who covered the labour beat at the Parliament Buildings in Victoria, and the routine in the past had always been that Murphy would make statements and answer any questions. But this time, Snow says to Murphy, "How about we have a new face. Why don't we hear from Al King this time? He's the Secretary of your committee. You don't mind, do you?" So I did the interview.

Murphy didn't talk to me for three months. I laughed like hell over it. His ego was bruised! And I was his chief supporter.

THE ALMOST MINER

In 1965, the town of Stewart was a typical northern Canadian village in which life revolved mostly around the waxing and waning of the mining industry. Early in the winter of 1965, an enterprising ex-miner opened up a trailer-type bunkhouse and bar in anticipation of the influx of miners to the newly reopening Granduc property. One of his first customers was a well known BC miner named Dave Wilkinson who arrived on his way through to employment at Granduc. Spotting the newly-opened bar, Big Dave wasted no time. He was soon passing the time of day with another thirsty individual, an older traveller who had got there ahead of him.

After a few rounds of the Oh-Be-Joyful, the subject got around to mining, and it transpired that the other guy was from Eastern Canada and very set in his ways. Big Dave, an experienced development miner and a Mine Mill union man, just didn't see eye-to-eye with the guy and hot argument ensued.

Finally, the older guy says to Big Dave, "Who the hell are you anyway and what are you doing here?"

Big Dave says, "My name is Dave Wilkinson. I'm from Bralorne, BC and tomorrow I head into Granduc to go to work. Now who the hell are you?"

The other guy says, "My name is Bob Baker from Ontario. I'm the new manager at Granduc Mines and you're fired, you son-of-a-bitch."

Whereupon Dave stands up to his full six-foot-five, 220 pounds and retorts, "Don't call me a son-of-a-bitch, you son-of-a-bitch. I wouldn't work for you under any circumstances."

And he didn't. In the end, the union got into the act and threatened severe reprisals unless Wilkinson's expenses and time loss were fully compensated by the company. The company was only too glad to comply.

BENSON LAKE

Before the Three-Way Pact got too active, we managed a nice little piece of justice at the CM&S mine at Benson Lake. We had previously been certified in this mine, but in 1961 the company wanted to reopen it, which meant rebuilding and expanding the infrastructure—cabins and lunchrooms and so on, for the crew. We all knew the ore would be handled in Trail where Mine Mill was already certified, and CM&S didn't sign a pre-contract agreement because they preferred to do business with a single union. My impression was that once Mine Mill became the certified bargaining agent in Trail, we had a pretty good relationship with the company. They trusted Murphy and me to keep our word and were confident that if everybody stuck to their part of the collective agreement, production wouldn't be slowed or halted.

So we went to the company and said, "Look, your Kimberley employees are going to develop this mine as Mine Mill members so we want you to use craftsmen who are also members of Mine Mill, but under the craft union construction contract." We asked for the craft union rate because at the time it was higher than the Mine Mill trades rates. In order to keep the site under a single union and avoid labour unrest on a new property, the company reluctantly agreed.

At this time the Taft-Hartley poison was lingering, and some of the

International craft unions were blacklisting their members for any so-called 'radical' activity. Good tradespeople who had been blacklisted included George Gee, Cliff Worthington (Tom Berger's father-in-law), Jack Green and Bill David of the Carpenter's, Jim Kinnaird (who was later president of the BC Federation of Labour) and Dusty Rhodes of the International Brotherhood of Electrical Workers (IBEW) and others, all good tradespeople prevented from working because their own union International blacklisted them. I think they got blacklisted if they simply ran against an incumbent officer or did anything at all progressive that made their American officers itchy.

It gave me great pleasure to hire a bunch of these blacklisted building trades people and put them to work on the Benson Lake job. That felt like some kind of justice.

I was their representative and when Jack Green got fired, I filed a grievance. When Jack heard about it he came to me and said, "Don't bother. In the building trades we're used to guys getting laid off. The union doesn't take up a grievance for a guy getting fired, for Christ's sake!"

"Well," I said, "this union does," and I got the sonofabitch reinstated.

In return, we imposed our safety rules and everybody did what they were supposed to do in a safe way—or else. And the tradespeople came to our meetings as Mine Mill members, signed up in our union. That was one of our happier interactions with the building trades unions.

BOSS MOUNTAIN

In the mid-60s after we'd lost the Sudbury and Thompson locals in northern Ontario and things were getting tense, the national executive, in desperation to get some dues money coming in, tried to initiate one of those same pre-contract agreements with Noranda. Smith, Longridge and Murphy had a meeting with Noranda back east, when Noranda was planning one of their first workings in BC, a molybdenum mine at Boss Mountain, east of Hundred Mile House. It turned out they were amenable to someone coming in to organize and out of this came the possibility of a contract like the Three-Way Pact were doing—a pre-contract agreement with Mine Mill—for which all they needed were some warm bodies and three names. Rudychuk had tried going in to this mine earlier, but they'd set the dogs on him, two big Dobermans, and if the snow hadn't been three feet deep, they'd have killed him.

So now, under this new agreement, I was assigned to go in and sign the guys up. It was January and snowing, so I had to stop at Hundred Mile or at Williams Lake, I forget which, to rent a truck. I almost got killed on that drive in. When I got to the mine I went to the office where a guy, all brass buttons, stopped me and asked, "Who are you? What are you doing here?"

I said, "My name is Al King and I'm an organizer for the Mine, Mill and Smelter Worker's Union." Suddenly he was all friendly.

"Oh," he says. "The miners are in that bunkhouse over there so you can go right over and sign 'em up." I went over and talked to the boys. They told me about the working conditions, how they were getting the usual shit from the company. The more I talked to the men, the more I felt sick at my stomach at what I was about to do and I couldn't do it. I refused to sign a single one of them up because I don't believe in that kind of unionism.

I drove back to Vancouver and when I phoned Toronto, Longridge damned nearly went through the roof. Called me incompetent. I said, "Go do your own goddamned dirty work, asshole. I'm not going to do it for you." I'd been so critical of the Three-Way Pact over exactly this kind of unionism.

Instead, we waited for the Three-Way Pact to get into that mine and then we raided them—Vince and Archie and I—and we took it away from them in about 1964. The same at Peachland, another molybdenum mine. We waited for the Three-Way Pact to get in and sign the guys up and then we went in and raided them—took it away from them like they'd been doing to us. As far as I know, that's the only time Murphy and Longridge tried that pre-contract business. They did it out of desperation.

John Stanton in particular has been very critical of Murphy at that time, accusing him, among other things, of signing agreements with poor wage rates. But even the Steelworkers never criticized his ability to negotiate—they said Harvey Murphy was the smartest guy Mine Mill had. Besides, Murphy never signed any agreements in my area. During my time as western Board member, I signed them all.

GRANDUC

One of the largest mines being raided in the '60s was the Granduc in northwestern BC. It was a new base metal mine owned by Newmont and still in the development stage.

The miners worked several miles underneath the Leduc glacier, but in February 1965, with no warning, a huge avalanche tore down the mountain and swept away part of the west-end portal camp. Twenty-six men on the surface were instantly buried beneath tons of snow.

Though Granduc was being raided at the time, it was still a local of Mine Mill, and it was my duty as head of Mine Mill in BC and administrator of the union's Death Benefit Plan to go to the scene of the disaster. I was also worried because we didn't yet know the names of the missing and two of our organizers, Vince Ready and Archie MacDonald, were working there at the time.

It was a challenge just to get to Granduc. Prior to the building of the present highway, the only way to get to Stewart, BC, the nearest centre, was by water or float plane, so the RCMP arranged a quick flight for me from Vancouver to Stewart. A large number of press people arrived at about the same time I did, including a big, friendly guy named Peter Gzowski to whom I took a liking. But at that point, the RCMP weren't letting any press into the mine site.

When I got to Stewart in the afternoon, the weather made it impossible to fly in to Granduc immediately, so early the next morning, those of us

TAKING CARE OF BUSINESS

Shortly after the Granduc disaster, the widow of one of the deceased miners, a man named John Scott (no relation to Jack), arrived in my office in Vancouver with a handwritten, water-stained, unposted letter that had been found in her dead husband's pocket. It was addressed (she thought) to Mine Mill. But it wasn't addressed to Mine Mill. It was addressed to the Teamster's Union. Snow had made the ink run and the woman saw the word "union" on the envelope and assumed it was directed to her husband's current union, Mine Mill.

In the letter, John explained to his wife that he was now working secretly for the Teamsters union, trying to to organize a raid to get Mine Mill out of Granduc. Maybe this was because his brother Kenny was an organizer for the Teamsters. Ken was a good pal of Vince and Archie and I. We used to meet when he was raiding us—he didn't raid very hard—and we'd sit and drink together.

I thanked Mrs. Scott and took the letter to Ed Lawson in the Teamster's office. Harvey Murphy and Ed Lawson were friends; they used to talk to each other in Ukranian. But on this trip, I reviled Lawson and his union for their lack of 'brotherhood.' When I left Lawson's office, I asked if he thought Mine Mill should pay death benefits to Mrs. Scott.

"Don't pay it, Al," he said.

We paid it. We weren't about to penalize a deceased worker's family because of her husband's falsity.

allowed to go to the mine assembled at the heliport. We had strict warnings to just take in adequate winter gear and no excess baggage. This didn't sit well with Bob Baker, the mine manager, who had been away when the accident took place. Baker had a big load of personal effects to take back, including a large cardboard case full of Scotch whisky. The rule was was "no excess baggage," so neither Baker nor his Scotch was on board when the helicopter took off for Granduc. I never saw mine manager Baker again, though by the time I returned to Stewart, I would have liked more than a nodding acquaintance with one of his bottles of Scotch.

When we arrived over the camp site, the glacier was completely socked in. Visibility was near zero and they had to set out a series of salamanders—those burning barrels you see at a strike—to get us down. They'd poured oil on them to make the smoke look darker than the fog, and the pilot set the machine down into this ring of smelly, oily smoke atop a hurriedly-prepared landing pad. Days later, when they were taking that spot apart, they discovered a tough old Finnish carpenter trapped underneath. I guess when they prepared the emergency landing space, they just picked the flattest site they could find in the middle of all the wreckage. Miraculously, the man survived with only minor injuries—I think he lost a couple of toes.

The main body of survivors from the mine had already been taken off the site by the coast guard and I was relieved to hear that Archie and Vince were among them. When the avalanche struck, it was daytime and Archie was safely at work, underground. The only surface building that wasn't entirely destroyed was the bunkhouse in which Vince, on the cross shift, was fast asleep. He was in the far end, and he and a few others with him there survived, but most of the building was swept away. Everyone else was killed. It was a terrible event.

One of my duties while I was there was to help the RCMP identify bodies. Even as an overseas veteran of the war, this was not an easy job.

When the Granduc mine resumed operations after the tragedy, the company hired Three-Way Pact members so when the vote came, it was stacked. Mine Mill was defeated—we got creamed—and was replaced by the Three-Way Pact. That's why I later fired Jack Moffatt, because he was in there sleeping—lying in his bunk reading a pocketbook while other unions were signing them up.

But the miners soon saw the colours of their new union. Under their next agreement, the company was allowed to violate the eight hour, portal-to-portal agreement that Mine Mill (as the Western Federation of Miners) had pioneered and forced into law. Under that agreement, miners were paid their eight hours wages starting from the time they arrived at the mine mouth, or portal. In other words, travelling time—which in Granduc later consisted of a six-mile-long underground tunnel—was paid as work time. But under their new union, workers now travelled on their own time and were obliged to work underground for nine and ten hours—eight hours plus travel time.

Later, the Three-Way Pact paid their debt to the company in the form of political assistance when, in the early 1970s, the NDP government passed Bill 31 which took away some of the vast benefits the mining industry had enjoyed until then. The company sent the new union's local president and an entire delegation of union delegates to Victoria, all wages and expenses paid, to lobby the government to repeal Bill 31.

SUDBURY

Despite the Three-Way Pact and boss collusion (of which Granduc was a prime example), the fortunes of Mine Mill in the base metal mining industry in western Canada were slowly improving while those in Ontario were deteriorating. In fact, the situation in Sudbury was in crisis, although for a long time we didn't really appreciate this. Of all the places in the union that were vulnerable, that would have been the last we suspected. Sudbury Local 598 was the biggest Mine Mill local in North America. It had money. It had resources. It had halls, a camp, cultural programs, a strong Ladies Auxiliary. When Trail was being raided in 1950, they'd supported us, but otherwise we didn't have much to do with them except in conventions. INCO and CM&S were both subsidiaries of Canadian Pacific, so we were close in policy making, but we didn't think they were in any grave danger—until the strike.

After the passage of Taft-Hartley in 1947, Steelworker tactics of 'boring from within'—undermining Mine Mill by electing leaders sympathetic to Steel—were the focus of activity in northern Ontario. The same red-baiting and divisions caused by the Steelworkers' raiding in Trail occurred in Sudbury Local 598 and Port Colborne Local 637. In 1948, two years before the tactic was tried in Trail, the entire Port Colborne union executive board

Joint bargaining meeting to discuss wages and strike action, summer 1958.
Seated left to right: Al King, Mike Solski, Percy Berry (Trail), Clem Thompson (Kimberley), Tom McIntyre (Trail), Ken Smith (Western board member), Jack McKinley (Bluebell Mine, B.C.), Nels Thibault (National Pres.), Hilly York, John Clarke (Montana, Pres of Int. M.M.), Bobby Mitchell (Kimberley), Arnie Bennett (Britannia), Harvey Murphy (National VP), Jim Forgaard (Salmo). Standing left to right: J. McGregor (Bluebell), Remo Morandini (Trail), Ed Clemmer (Kimberley), Jim 'Red' Patterson, (Kimberley), Leo Fuerst (Salmo), J. Twells (Salmo).

openly aligned with the raiding Steelworkers and defected. As in Trail, this didn't result in the loss of the local to Steel, but in the emergence of a new union leadership loyal to Mine Mill. Three times, Steel failed in their raids on Falconbridge, the last in 1966.

However, the refusal of Local 598 to allow the Falconbridge miners an independant local was trouble some. The Falconbridge mining operation near Sudbury consisted of some 2,500 workers who felt their voices were lost amid the approximately 15,000 miners from INCO plant in Sudbury. The fact that the Falconebridge miners didn't have their own local caused a simmering discontent.

From the early 1950s to 1959, the president of Sudbury Local 598 was a strong Mine Miller named Mike Solski. Where the previous president, Nels Thibault, had been easy-going and convivial, Solski was harsh to his subor-

THE SUDBURY STRIKE

Mike Solski proved to be less than effective as a strike leader. He seemed to operate in a different key from other leaders. For example, he sneered at the donations of food and clothing that Mine Mill traditionally collected for striking miners and their families and neither he nor his executive were able to mobilize the women. He himself always wore a shirt and tie.

In his history about Mine Mill, he doesn't mention a personal odyssey he later told me about, that he undertook to Washington DC. Without conferring with the Canadian officers of Mine Mill or with John Clarke, the International President, Solski went to Washington to ask a one million dollar loan from James Hoffa, Sr., President of the Teamsters Union. Perhaps it wasn't out of line in Mike's eyes to make such a request because he assumed he could promise speedy repayment once the strike was over. After all, he was president of a 17,000 member local. Hoffa told Solski he didn't deal with local union presidents.

"Send your International President," he ordered.

I don't know if John Clarke ever followed this up. I think a Teamster donation was made, but it wasn't one million dollars and it wasn't a loan, either.

dinates and sledge-hammer crude in his approach to problems. He was a forceful administrator, obviously dedicated to his union, but he carried out his responsibilities with a domineering attitude that demanded total obedience from his local executive and committees. Local 598 convention delegate's behaviour had to be in strict accordance with Solski's wishes. This inflexible style of leadership was one of the factors that provided fertile ground in which the enemies of Mine Mill sowed their seed.

In 1958, Local 598 in Sudbury and 637 in Port Colborne voted to go on strike against INCO. The rest of the union leadership, particularly in the west, thought it a most inopportune time for such a move. The Canadian economy was in a slump, national unemployment rates were scandalous and employers were determined to hold onto any profits for themselves. There was a glut on the international metal market and prices were down. It didn't seem the right time, economically, to take on the company.

In the west, Murphy got around this situation by negotiating a nine-month agreement for Trail, Kimberley, the Blue Bell Mine and Alberta Nitrogen in Calgary. A nine-month contract was almost unheard of at the time but it was another of Murphy's strategies, designed solely to buy us time so we could move into a better bargaining position later. He got us five cents an hour that was put into a retirement plan you could take out on retirement or cash in at the end of the contract. I'm still getting my money from that five cents.

We also negotiated wage increases and other contract improvements at Bralorne and at Gypsum Lime & Alabastine in New Westminster, BC and at the Con Mine in Yellowknife but in general in 1958, the labour relations atmosphere was tense. Certainly, Steelworkers in Hamilton, Autoworkers in Windsor and Oshawa, Railway workers and others were turning down employers' offers and asking for more, but Canadian companies were responding with a 'hold the line' fight again labour.

In this atmosphere, the guys in Sudbury asked for ten cents an hour and improvements in the pension plan. The company responded with major layoffs and a reduction of the work week from forty to thirty-two hours with a resulting loss in wages. Solski, who was chairman of the joint bargaining committee, broke off negotiations with INCO and, as the Constitution required, asked for strike authority from the national Executive Board.

In his book, *Mine Mill: The History of the International Union of Mine, Mill and Smelter Workers in Canada Since 1895,* Solski suggests he had no choice in calling a strike vote at this time, that the company simply refused to bargain and his local was being undermined by wildcat walkouts and the ongoing agitation of the Steel raids. Whatever the reason, when he asked the national Executive Board for strike authority, a heated battle broke out with Murphy, Smith, Longridge and the Western District members adamantly opposed. Apart from the issue of the Steelworkers, this is the only time I can recall a dispute of this magnitude dividing the union.

It probably didn't help at this crucial time that Harvey Murphy and Mike Solski heartily disliked each other. I never understood why. Solski was aggressively opposed to Murphy on just about everything. Harvey was extroverted, manipulative, experienced and crafty, while Solski was introverted, harsh and green as grass as a trade union officer under his elegant exterior. They were like oil to water; bitter differences erupted from time to time between them. No matter what the reason, it's sad that Mike Solski's obstinacy and Harvey Murphy's aggressiveness couldn't be joined in a single defence of Mine Mill.

A18c The Province   Monday, November 15, 1

Inco imported Nazis in '50s

Details in old RCMP report

Canadian Press

SUDBURY, Ont.— Inco Ltd. imported former Nazis who disrupted union activities at its Sudbury mining operations during the 1950s, an RCMP intelligence document obtained by the Sudbury Star says.

Some of these anti-communists helped wreak havoc during one of the most violent episodes in Canadian labor history — raids by the United Steelworkers of America on the International Union of Mine, Mill and Smelter Workers.

A 32-year-old RCMP report, about a riot that occurred outside the Mine-Mill union's hall in August 1961, says many of the rioters were former Nazi storm troopers and Hungarian freedom fighters who had been "imported" by Inco.

The riot occurred during a pivotal period in the international unions' battle to represent Sudbury-area miners, a battle that was eventually won by the Steelworkers.

The report, prepared by the RCMP's former security and intelligence branch, was obtained under the Freedom of Information Act.

Inco spokesman Jerry Rogers said he could not find any supporting evidence in the company archives.

"We couldn't see anything," said Rogers, adding: "There isn't anybody around any more from those days."

During the anti-communist hysteria of the 1950s, the RCMP's security and intelligence branch had orders to monitor the Communist party of Canada and trade unions.

Inco's alleged actions are a "plausible scenario," said historian Alti Rodal, who reported on immigration policy for a 1986 commission on war criminals. During the Cold War, officials gave preference to immigrants with anti-communist credentials, including former Nazis, he said.

Published in the Vancouver Province, November 15, 1993.

In the end, when they couldn't get Canadian approval for strike action, the Sudbury officers went over the national executive's heads and brought in the vice-president of the International, Orville Larson, to lend some moral weight. They were going to strike anyway, but they needed a degree of legitimacy, so they got the Big Swede to come up and speak in favour of their decision to strike.

Solski later wrote as if the Mine Mill national Executive Board approved of the strike from the start, which was a damn lie. The problem was that, once the vote was taken—and it was a strong one of eighty-three percent in favour—the national Executive Board had no alternative. At the last possible minute we passed a motion to support the strike with the entire Canadian union in full support. All of us on the national payroll were placed on fifty dollars a week strike pay, the same pay as the strikers. That's when Lil went to work as a cashier at the Hudson's Bay; she continued there until she retired. In the west, Clem Thompson and I were placed in charge of strike support in the Kootenays; we raised over $70,000 in a time of major layoffs in BC due to the poor mining conditions.

I remember Solski, as president of Local 598, and Nels Thibault, the

JIMMY RABBIT

In one of John Stanton's memoirs, he accused Harvey Murphy of signing a poor agreement with the Craigmont Mine in 1962 and of being a boss collaborator, demanding the firing of Mine Mill members who wouldn't support their union against raiders. 'Boss collaborator' is the last thing Harvey Murphy could ever be accused of. Stanton says he got this from Big Dick Vladetich who was orginally a Mine Mill supporter but later became a boss. Vladetich apparently reported to Stanton that when he was sharing a hotel room with Murphy in Merritt, he overheard Murphy talking on the phone to some guy in the Mining Association, telling him to fire Jimmy Rabbit. Jimmy Rabbit was a first class asshole who had defected from Mine Mill to become an organizer for Steel.

The whole thing is a fantasy: Dick Vladetich worked at the Craigmont Mine and he and his wife Muriel lived in Merrit, so why would he share a hotel room with Murphy? Even if Murphy was there, even if they were sharing a room, if you were in a room with a guy and he was talking on the phone, could you figure out the gist of the conversation, let alone who he was talking to? Besides, Dick Vladetich had

mined underground all his life and was deaf as a stoat. And the guy who handled the whole campaign in Merrit and at the Craigmont Mine was me.

I'm pretty sure it was me on the other end of the phone, not an employer. I remember a long conversation with Murphy about what to do about Jimmy Rabbit. Under the terms of our Collective Agreement it was a condition of employment that you had to maintain your membership throughout the term of the contract. But Rabbit, who later became a Minister in Bill Bennett's Social Credit government, was the only member of his executive who violated the union oath of office by leaving Mine Mill for Steel. I argued with Murphy to leave Rabbit alone and not make a martyr of him and in the end that's what we did.

That's the only incident I know of where Murphy was accused of being a boss collaborator. Harvey Murphy, despite his warts—and who hasn't got them—fought the bosses every day of his life. Not too many other people can say the same.

national president of Mine Mill, both coming to Trail to try to persuade us into joint strike action against both INCO and CM&S, but every man who worked in Trail could see for himself the long metal sheds bulging at the seams with unsold metal. As I recall it, poor Thibault was just about torn in two. He didn't think Sudbury and Port Colbourne should strike, but they'd already voted and he couldn't speak against it.

The ensuing battle in Sudbury—the strike and its aftermath in which the faction sympathetic to Steel finally captured control of the local—was one of the dirtiest, most venal struggles of the Canadian labour movement.

Clearly, the record of that time shows the provocative attitude of INCO toward the union and its members and the full story of the massive conspiracy against Mine Mill in Sudbury has barely begun to be told. One of the most active organizers in what he declared "a fight between Christianity and Communism," was Alexander J. Boudreau, alumnus of a Jesuit school and director of extension courses at the University of Sudbury. The University of Sudbury is the Roman Catholic college of Laurentian University. Supporting Boudreau was the Very Reverend Emile Bouvier, president of the University of Sudbury, who had already published a book hostile to labour. Boudreau initiated a series of courses that would be only the beginning of his intimate involvement in the destabilizing of the Mine Mill local. More, in 1993 the Vancouver *Province* picked up a Sudbury *Star* report on a thirty-two-year-old RCMP intelligence document that detailed how INCO had imported "former Nazi stormtroopers and Hungarian freedom fighters" to disrupt union activities in Sudbury in the '58 strike, and I am convinced there is more, much more, to be told.

The pressure was on the local to resist unfair and unprincipled attitudes by the company, and there's no doubt the Ontario Labour Relations Board was strongly biased against Mine Mill. But it was a shock to everyone that such a strong, militant local as 598 could be humbled, as it was, in just three months of strike. Ordinarily, a three month miner's strike is not uncommon. It only serves as a preliminary to deeper and lengthier industrial warfare when the strike is over and the miners are back at work, united. For example, in the mid-1960s, Britannia mines in BC endured a twelve month lockout, a few months back at work and then a solid twelve month strike against their employer, American-owned Anaconda Copper. The union emerged from that strike stronger at the end than when it began.

The strike in Sudbury and Port Colborne in 1958 was suicide. After it was settled, the presidents of both local unions, Mike Solski of 598 and Mike Kopinak of 637, were defeated in the next local elections. Solski and his entire executive were defeated by a slate headed by a man named Gillis (who once ran for the Conservative Party). We had a hell of a time with him. Among other things, Gillis and his supporters weren't too fussy about sending their per capita dues into Mine Mill, mostly because they openly supported the Steelworkers. Because Sudbury was such a large local, this put even more strain on Mine Mill's already reeling national finances. Without the Sudbury dues, Mine Mill's income instantly fell by two thirds.

Eventually the Sudbury members had two votes on whether to stay with Mine Mill or go with Steel: we lost the first, in 1962, by fifteen votes. By coincidence, this was the same as the number of guys on the local's executive. In spite of a hostile Labour Relations Board and even though we lost just about every legal battle we were in in Ontario at that time (the lawyer for the Steelworkers was the well-known CCF'er and avowed anti-Communist,

STICKING TOGETHER

The night we finally lost Sudbury, a dozen of us including me and Ray Stevenson (who did communications work for Mine Mill in Ontario) went back to my room for drinks. We soon got the word that a few Steelworkers were coming around to gloat. I had a little fur cap at the time—I still have it—and when the Steel guys came in, I remember setting that cap on my head before putting my back to Ray and having it out with them. They just wanted to throw their weight around a little but Ray and I wiped the floor with them and felt a lot better for it afterward. As Ray tells it now, that little cap never left my head. The others got into it too, even Elsie Murphy, Harvey's daughter-in-law. She was a big lass and at one point she held a broken bottle to a Steelworker's throat. That settled him right down.

David Lewis), we proved that some of the cards on that first Sudbury vote were forged. The guy quarterbacking the campaign on the Steelworkers' side was Lynn Williams, who later became President of the Steelworkers, and the guy doing the actual dirty work was an ex-hockey player named Jim Robinson, a notorious drunk. He came out west years after the raids, boasting about how he forged enough cards to swing the vote in favour of the Steelworkers in Sudbury.

I know there were more dirty tricks because when dozens of Ontario men came out to Trail during that period looking for work, one of them, Bob Gray, was here working in the Craigmont mine, but when we checked, he was also on the list as having voted in Sudbury. That was just one vote, in an election that was only lost by fifteen.

In 1965 we forced a second vote, but we lost again, more definitively. I think by then the guys just didn't want the battles to go on, and they knew that if Mine Mill won, it would continue.

With the loss of Sudbury, the national union found it increasingly difficult to keep up the fight against Steel and the other raiders. More than any other single factor, Sudbury's insistence on the 1958 strike and its consequences deeply hurt both the Canadian and US sections of the union.

STAVING OFF THE RAIDS

In the early 1950s, the main lawyer for the western district of Mine Mill was John Stanton. We had used him many times before the war, in Trail and Vancouver, and he was eventually placed on an annual retainer. Another lawyer we used at the time for many of our compensation cases was Tom Berger, who later became Justice Tom Berger.

But after 1960, Murphy got the idea that, in order to win our fights with large corporations, we should get corporate law firms to be our representatives, that they would have the 'in's' that labour law firms might not have. It was purely a strategic thing. I had just started as secretary of the BC District and was scarcely knowledgeable about law firms, but Harvey had spent most of his life dealing with them. I'd been impressed with his strategic skills elsewhere, so it was okay with me when Harvey decided to use a big Vancouver corporate firm called Bull, Houser, Tupper for many of our cases. Sometimes we also used John Laxton. I don't know if Murphy was right, but it meant we didn't need John Stanton any more, and I ended his retainer contract.

ON THE FRONT LINES

Throughout the raiding period of the '50s and '60s, there were many nasty incidents. One of them was an encounter at the Craigmont mine when several of us were distributing pamphlets. A Steelworker named Bud 'Tiger' Arnold —a man with a reputation as a goon and a serious kickbox fighter—showed up with a station wagon full of liquour. Arnold immediately squared up against me and even though I was almost twice his age, he was the one who ended up on his back with his pamphlets strewn all over the gravel.

John Stanton has accused Murphy of staving off raids by persuading companies to sign new agreements before the open period of a contract. Raiding was only allowed in the open period and he accuses Murphy of "using a loophole in the law" by confirming contracts before then so that raiding was impossible. Again, it wasn't Murphy who was doing the bargaining out west at this time, it was me.

One of the managers I first negotiated this early confirmation of contracts with, was Frank Holland at Giant Mascot Mine in Hope, BC. When we reached an agreement thirty days before the expiration of the old agreement, I got Frank to put the new wage scale into effect on top of the old agreement so the miners immediately got the new and better package. Another time I bargained with Jim Clifford at Craigmont. He was hired by the mining companies to negotiate collective agreements and he wasn't a bad guy. We put that agreement into effect a full three months prior to the expiry of the old agreement. There was one more settlement like that, over a fifty cent wage increase at Britannia. Nonetheless, settling the contract had no effect on the open period, although no raids were being conducted at the three mines at the time.

From 1960 on, the Mine Mill officer who oversaw all the western district negotiations and all union business, was Al King. I'm not boasting. That was my job. Murphy might have negotiated collective agreements with one company that had two mines, for instance, the same copper company that had Britannia also had Princeton. And Cominco. But the small mines he always left to Ken Smith and when Smith left, to me. When I didn't do it, I had somebody like Bill Rudychuk help me.

MERGER

In 1966, after almost twenty years of unremitting pressure from every section of American society, the weary American Mine Millers from President Al Skinner on down to the last rank and filer, had had enough. The two parties called it quits and when the merger details were completed, the International Union of Mine, Mill and Smelter Workers in the United States joined and became part of the United Steelworkers of America. In doing so, Steel did not decapitate Mine Mill. They defied the provisions of Taft-Hartley that required all suspected Communists to be removed from union leadership, and allowed Mine Mill leaders to stay in office. In Canada, we were left to ourselves to ponder these events.

Meanwhile, the Canadian national director of Steel, William Mahoney, and Larry Sefton, Director of District 6 (Ontario), had for some time been proposing a similar merger between Steel and Mine Mill north of the border. This idea would have seemed incredible ten years earlier, especially considering that it was the same Bill Mahoney who'd led the western Canadian raids against Mine Mill. (William 'Bill' Mahoney was the Canadian national director of the Steelworkers Union and Joe Molony was the US vice-president).

The main argument the Steelworkers had for merger was that the labour movement should stop fighting internally—which, God knows, all of us would agree with—and unite all mining operations under a single union. It's now my belief that another reason behind this new attitude was that the almost unlimited funds that were used to finance the raids on Mine Mill had dried up.

For a long time our answer to Steel's inquiries about merging had been, "Stop your raiding and we'll discuss it." The International President of Steel, David 'Wavy' McDonald, had always made this impossible by wanting blood—he not only vowed to keep up the raids, he insisted that one of the conditions of merger be adherence to Taft-Hartley. That would have decapitated our leadership, and neither Mine Mill officers nor members would agree to that. It wasn't a question of who was and who wasn't a Communist—it didn't matter. Lots of good people who weren't Communist had gone to jail and lost their careers. Someone just had to accuse you; Clinton Jencks was a good example.

The secretary of the CCL at the time, Donald MacDonald, was a rabid red-baiter. A lot of those higher up, Mosher (President of the CCL), Phil Murray (President of the CIO in the US) and the Canadian labour attaché in Washington, Pat Conroy, were worse. Nonetheless, Mine Mill had earlier written to the CLC stating we were prepared to accept their rules and regulations, but they weren't willing to take us back unless we went inside the belly of the Steelworkers.

But by 1965, times were changing. For one thing, new leadership of the Steelworkers in the US under I.W. Abel took a very different attitude to Taft-Hartley. Though I was on the fringe, being out west, the key thrust to merger, as I understand it, came from Abel and US Vice-President Joe Molony. It's my recollection that Molony was the guy who finally said, "This Taft-Hartley business is bullshit."

The 1960s was also a more progressive era than the '50s especially among young people. A lot of rank and file members were tired of the endless raiding and wanted both unions to start fighting for their members instead of fighting each other. And by the late '60s, everyone was taking a bite out of us, even the Food and Restaurant workers. The decision of the mining companies to co-operate with the Three-Way Pact and their success in raiding us, was another part of it. After 1965 and the loss of Sudbury and Port Colbourne, we were getting no dues from virtually the entire province of Ontario. Mine Mill was broke. If we were going to fight companies that were getting steadily bigger and more entrenched, well then, maybe the only thing that could take them on was a bigger, stronger union. Our fear was that if we kept on the way we were going, we'd end up without *any* union. And finally, very slowly, the hatred bred by Taft-Hartley was ebbing and accusations of being Communist didn't have the same explosive power they once had.

As unionists, we had connections with individual progressive Steelworkers right across the country. Many of them, people like Nick Smith and Corey Campbell in the west coast steel mills, wanted us to merge because it would strengthen them, too. So some people saw it as a win-win situation. But the change that made a key difference was that the new Steel leadership—Abel and Molony—were finally willing to ignore Taft-Hartley and accept the existing Mine Mill leadership.

In January 1966, one month after bargaining rights for the INCO workers changed in Sudbury from Mine Mill to Steel, Mine Mill held a convention in Trail to discuss what would happen to the union with the loss of Sudbury. The alternatives that came up and that the national officers were instructed to investigate were: to remain as we were; to set up a labour central as an alternative to the Canadian Labour Congress; to move Mine Mill's national office to BC and operate as a strictly western union; or to merge with another union already in the metal mining field. An Officer's Report presented to a special conference in June 1967 explained the officers thinking on all these points. We had quickly abandoned the idea of a "retreat behind the mountains of BC" because we believed that workers need to be united on more than a regional basis. We also felt that the question of forming another labour central was wrong in principle because the main effect would be to further foster division. Also, no other union was prepared to seriously consider or join such a move.

So the national executive pursued the third alternative and began to pursue active discussions with representatives from three different unions: the Confederation of National Trade Unions, the International Building Labourers (one of whose locals is the Rock and Tunnel Workers) and the United Steelworkers of America.

Despite several friendly meetings in Quebec with the CNTU, no proposal for merger or affiliation was forthcoming. As for the Labourers, it was immediately obvious that affiliating would simply mean that the 13,000 members of Mine Mill would unite with, at most, a few hundred rock and tunnel workers so we would still face the problem of being divided from the majority of workers in our industry. (This would also have been true if we'd pursued affiliation with the CNTU.) That left the Steelworkers.

We approached them with some trepidation and, let's face it, outright hostility as the result of eighteen years of hard, and at times, vicious conflict. But we persevered, first, because they'd signed a no-raiding clause, and that was always our condition for talks, and second, because unity would mean that more than ninety per cent of all the metal mining industry workers in Canada would be under a single union. In a sense, what followed was history repeating itself. At the turn of the century, the One Big Union and the Industrial Workers of the World had evolved out of the Western Federation of Miners which in turn evolved into Mine Mill. Now Canadian Mine Mill was considering merging with Steel.

There was never an issue more throughly debated than the merger of the International Union of Mine, Mill and Smelter Workers with the United Steelworkers Union. Every local president put out bulletins, called meetings and invited discussion. In Trail following the signing of the terms of merger, Bob Keiver, President of the local, held three separate meetings—one with the Executive Board, shop stewards and active members, a second with the general membership, and finally a special membership meeting where national officers who'd been negotiating with Steel were invited to come and answer questions.

We had two national conventions where the idea was specifically discussed. The first, in Edmonton in the fall of '66, ratified continuation of merger talks with the Steelworkers. On April 29, 1967 the National Executive of Mine Mill unanimously approved a merger document with the United Steelworkers of America, effective July 1, 1967. It was placed before the membership at a second special convention called for Winnipeg on June 23-24, 1967.

THE 1967 WINNIPEG CONVENTION ON MERGER

The Officers' Report that opened the Convention said, ". . . the workers who work this industry can no longer afford the luxury of several different unions or division among themselves, when they face the entrenched and immense power of this industry in Canada and the United States . . . and indeed on a world wide scale." The officers pointed out that seventy-four years earlier, when the Western Federation of Miners was born, metal mining in North America was in its infancy and owners were in fierce competition with each other in a relatively small metals market. Even so, independent local unions weren't strong enough to match the strength of the owners and that was why the Western Federation of Miners had come together. Now, we were in a much more dangerous position of international metal monopolies, huge metal markets and a tremendous growth in technology and production per hour. And from the growing influence of these blocks of capital was coming ever-increasing pressure on governments to curb the trade union movement. All this called for the broadest possible labour unity and the officers were unanimously recommending merger.

All the leaders of the union spoke—the presidents of each area, staff and veterans—and agreed it was the way to go, that we were being forced into a position of weakness that the mining owners were taking full advantage of.

Most of the opposition came from Falconbridge Local 598. It was clear from the beginning when Joe Astgen, Vice-President of Local 598 refused Ken Smith's request that he be a sergeant-at-arms for the convention. Not only Joe, but every member of Falconbridge refused to act as sergeant-at-arms. The Falconbridge members stood up regularly throughout the conference, opposing what was going on at every step. In some ways, I can't blame them. They'd just come away from the third unsuccessful raid by Steel, and if you'd asked the Trail local in 1952 to merge with Steel after we'd just won some hard raiding batttles, we would have said "No way," just as clearly.

In the debate, the Falconbridge miners plus others who spoke against merger, referred to all the dirty things Steel had done—that they had forged cards, and so on. Basically they argued that we shouldn't join people with that kind of trade union ethic.

The debate was pretty emotional. The Officers' Report ended with, "It is with profound pride in you, the membership, and it is with equally profound confidence in the future, that we recommend the acceptance of these terms of merger. History will show that we are builders of unions, that we are architects of unity for the working people. In our view, there is no reason for any apology, there is no reason to mourn. The classic words of Joe Hill as he faced the copper bosses' firing squad, may well be recalled: "Don't mourn for me—organize! . . . . We will never forget what we are or where we came from and we will now go on to building a new kind of union for all our people. The matter is in your hands."

Under the proposed terms of merger, all present local union officers of Mine Mill could continue until 1970 to be elected annually according to Mine Mill practices. There would be no disruption of locals and all local assets would continue to be held by the local union. All national officers and local organizers would continue to serve the membership—there would be no break in continuity, no strangers—and the Steelworkers Policy Conference guaranteed Canadian autonomy in electing Canadian officers by Canadians.

In the end, the key issue that made people take it seriously, especially among members in the secondary leadership, was that we didn't have to sacrifice our leaders. This was the real defeat of Taft-Hartly. It had called for the removal of any possible Communist leadership from the unions, and here were the Steelworkers ignoring it, saying our existing leadership could stay. As far as I know, it was the first time an international union ignored Taft-Hartley after having complied with it for a time. This was extremely important—and a relief to the members who, under Steel, wanted the same leadership as under Mine Mill. The final vote at the convention was ninety-five in favour, thirty-one against and seven absent or not voting. My old local in Trail strongly supported it. I swallowed my pride and voted for the goddamned thing too, because in my mind, there was no alternative.

Finally, in August there was a Canada-wide mail-in referendum in which, consistent with our commitment to democracy, every member of

Mine Mill was entitled to vote by secret ballot on whether or not to merge with the Steelworkers. The vote came down in favour of merger by almost three to one. In the end, many Mine Millers voted for the merger in the belief they would keep their Mine Mill leadership. In fact, it would turn out they didn't, for a variety of reasons. One was fear in the reactions of certain staffers and, in the end, the spitefulness of some Steel staffers toward ex-Mine Millers.

We officially merged on July 1, 1967 but the story of Mine Mill doesn't end there. Although we had taken a democratic vote of every member of the union nation-wide and discussed it at length at conventions, there were three defections to the merger: the Falconbridge section of Local 598 in Sudbury and two small locals at Domtar in New Westminster, BC and the BC Diamond Driller's local. I always opposed their action. If they weren't ready to accept the results of the vote, they shouldn't have taken part in the debate and the whole decision-making process, as the Constitution demanded it. There were a lot of members who voted against the merger, but once the vote passed, the majority had spoken and I believed then and I believe to this day that—unpalatable as it was—we were all then duty-bound to carry out that democratic decision. The welfare of our members and their families came first.

When a conference was held in Sudbury in 1993 to celebrate the one hundredth anniversary of the Western Federation of Miners and Mine Mill, I was invited but refused to go. Mine Mill prided itself on its democracy. Many times we lost votes but in sisterhood and brotherhood, you accept a defeat as well as a victory and abide by the majority decision. Falconbridge and the two other locals refused to do so, so I wouldn't go to the conference.

Not until 1995 did the Falconbridge local finally vote to join—not the Steelworkers but the Canadian Auto Workers union.

THE MOVE

The merger of the International Union of Mine, Mill and Smelter Workers and the United Steelworkers Union officially went into effect on January 1, 1968 when the Vancouver office of Mine Mill at 2414 Main Street moved lock, stock and barrel over to the Steelworkers' offices at 33 East Broadway, some three blocks away.

It was a drastic change for all of us, including the Steelworker reps. "Does this mean we can't raid any more?" was the incredulous response of one of them, Ron Douglas in BC. It's a sad commentary on the union movement at the time that that was all poor Ron knew—raiding.

The decision about what would happen to existing Mine Mill leadership was made in San Francisco. I gather it wasn't an easy meeting because at one point, Ken Smith walked out. In the end, the top three officers of Mine Mill—Smith, Murphy and Longridge—were given what were called 'key staff' positions, something higher paid than ordinary staff rep.

A long time after the merger, I heard a rumour that the executive of Mine

Mill only went to Steel so they could get a good package for themselves, but that's a crock. At the time, we didn't know what the salaries and rates of pay were for Steelworkers; I didn't ask. I don't know what the three top Mine Mill executive got though I know they got more than Kennedy and I did, as was proper.

The important thing, and everybody knows it, is that the decision, when it was made, was a democratic one made by the entire membership. We had plenty of discussion even before the final convention and then the vote, and at that time, I didn't hear anyone accuse us of doing it for our own profit. That accusation came later, and it's true the salaries were almost double in Steel compared to what we were used to in Mine Mill. In the 1960s my salary as a national board member was between $6,000 and $7,000 a year and my salary as a Steel staff rep was $10,000 plus a leased automobile. In Mine Mill we got mileage, but we had to buy our own cars. So the money was all right, but that sure as hell wasn't the reason we did it.

As I remember, the staff of the western district of Mine Mill at the time of the merger were Berezowski, MacLeod, MacPhee, Walker, McLaren, Regenwetter, Belcher, MacDonald, Rudychuk, Ready, Nazachuk and myself. Archie MacDonald and Vince Ready soon moved on: Archie became

Final transfer of Mine Mill to Steel at Local 480, Trail. Front row, left to right: Don Dunphy (skulking), Frank Jurick, Steve Chambers, 'Pen' Baskin, Bob Keiver (Pres. of 480), Harvey Murphy, Hilly York. Back row, left to right, Joe Luke, Jack Kelly, Norm Gabana, Remo Morandini, Jerry Flanagan, Jack Cox.

one of the top flight staff people in another union, and Ready is known across Canada as one of the premier arbitrators and mediators of labour agreements. Harvey Murphy moved into the USWA offices on Broadway Street and retired around 1970. He died quite suddenly in the mid-70s. Kenny Smith did some bargaining but started drinking heavily and after a long life of service to workers, died of a condition complicated by his silicosis. It gave me some satisfaction to get his widow a pension from the WCB. Longridge wasn't heard of much after 1967. So while it's true the merger didn't officially 'decapitate' Mine Mill, the effect was very similar.

Until now, thirty years later, I haven't been able to write about the personal abuse and mistreatment we got when we joined the Steelworkers. They tried to make it so obnoxious for us that we'd quit, and Olive did just that. Full time Mine Mill office staff at the time of the merger were Olive Anderson and Gladys Bjarnason but Gladys chose to retire, leaving only Olive. She'd been a top-notch secretary, Murphy's personal assistant and occasionally an organizer for him—and the Steelworkers put her on reception, answering telephones. She tolerated that for about three years and then she quit. She lost her daughter, her only child, at about that time. and the two things together were too much, so she and her husband left Vancouver entirely to move to Vancouver Island.

The Steel reps, even the janitor, didn't make it easy. When our files were brought over from the other office there was no effort to make room for them upstairs. They were put in the basement, and if we needed anything we had to go down there to get it. The janitor was an old drunk named Cooper who used to come down to the basement and watch us as if we were doing something shady. And they all laughed. Thought it was a big joke.

The entire time I worked there as a staff rep based in Vancouver, they never really backed off. Until I retired in 1980, the National Director, Lynn Williams, made my life as uncomfortable as he could. Williams had been the master-mind of the raid, and whenever he came to Vancouver and called staff meetings, the ex-Mine Mill guys—Vince and Neil and Rudychuk and I—were not invited. We were always the outsiders.

Once when we had a regular staff conference just north of Toronto, I knocked on Williams' door and said, "Can I see you for a few minutes? Why do you have staff meetings in Vancouver and not allow ex-Mine Millers to attend?"

He sat ramrod still, staring straight ahead and saying nothing. I repeated the question. "Why do you have staff meetings at the coast and exclude ex-Mine Millers?" He said nothing. Not a single word. He stared straight ahead as if I wasn't there, as if he was hearing a ghost, until I turned around and left. It was like that.

On the BC staff of Steelworkers, with one exception, there was no sense of letting by-gones be by-gones. They simply hated us. I decided I wasn't going to let it get me down and I would just keep working. I thought of getting out, but what could I do? I had a wife and kids still in high school and they had to eat. We were living in a little vet's house in Vancouver and I couldn't go back to Trail.

THE SAD SAGA OF "CHAMPAGNE CHARLIE"

Things were getting tough with Local 168 of the Hod Carriers and Labourer's Union in the winter of 1969 and spring of '70. Hordes of unemployed construction workers were besieging their Vancouver union office. Jobs were scarce and the future gloomy.

Not so in the interior of the province, however, because Charlie, demon organizer of Local 168, was on the job. There wasn't much of an unemployment problem here, either, because the people Charlie was trying to 'organize' already had jobs and were already organized by the Steelworkers Union.

Did this deter Charlie? Not a bit. "Come join us," he said "and very soon I'll have you all on a highly-paid construction job at the Mica Dam." He forgot to mention that for the 1,500 jobs expected sometime in the future at Mica, there were multitudes of hungry candidates already paying Local 168 dues and waiting patiently in the Lower Mainland.

Miners get around a bit, though, and when some of the thoughtful ones mentioned this matter, Charlie was hard pressed for an acceptable explanation. However, the nagging doubts once raised had to be dealt with, so Charlie, ever resourceful, devised a brilliant method of removing them. He decided to sponsor a sumptuous banquet with all the trimmings so that the doubting Thomases would forget their qualms. To hell with the cost, decided Charlie, these boys have got to be organized.

So it came about that a resplendent Charlie hosted a feast in the best hotel dining room in Merritt. And of course it had to be done again so that afternoon shift was not left out. Equality, that was the thing for Charlie.

How did it go? Perfectly but costly. Charlie got carried away and decided that beer or rye were just too ordinary so, "Champagne!" he cried. "Champagne to go with the New York cut sirloins. Local 168 is going first class." And champagne it was—Mumms 37.

You know miners—it took a hell of a lot of giggle juice to give the boys that good old feeling, and by the time this procedure was repeated for the other shift, Charlie's organizing exploits were the talk of the town. Shades of Ginger Goodwin and Arthur Evans, this dazzler Charlie was the all-time meteor of trade union organizing history.

But wait! Charlie had miscalculated! The last fond belch and rumble had hardly faded when the Labour Relations Board conducted the vote between our Charlie's Local 168 and Local 1037 of the Steelworker's Shaft and Development Miners, and sometime between feasts, a plain representative of the Steelworkers Union had come in without fanfare—certainly without champagne—and interfered with Charlie's plans. Out of that dozen or more damned ungrateful guests that poor Charlie entertained so lavishly, he got only three votes and the Steelworkers were victorious.

Years from now, grizzled old miners will relate with a glint in their wise old eyes how Charlie, the rocket organizer of Local 168, became known the length and breadth of hard rock mining as "Champagne Charlie".

For weeks and months I wrestled with what to do. Meantime, I received a letter from Cominco (who'd changed their name from CM&S in 1966), cutting off my relationship with the company because I was no longer an elected Mine Mill officer.

That was the most agonizing period of my life. I thought of going into a different field of work but what? I was a smelter worker, fifty-two years old, with no training for sales or anything else except union work. I hadn't even finished my high school education. I guess I could have got a job with another union but . . . .

Penrod 'Pen' Baskin headed the office in Vancouver. He'd worked with my brother Jack back in Trail before the war when we were all pretty young. When Baskin met me he asked if I was Jack King's brother and I said I was. Baskin was a decent guy, the only one who was friendly toward me, so when I finally couldn't take it any more, I phoned him and said, "I can't stand these bastards. I've decided to pull the pin."

Baskin said, "Before you do, I'd like you to come down and have breakfast with me." So I went. And he said, "For Christ's sake, Al, I need somebody like you to be my lieutenant in the mines. None of the staff I've got have any experience in the mines." He said, "Please stay on. Besides, time will pass."

And he was right. A lot of people laughed at Pen Baskin, but he was a good trade unionist and he left monuments behind him: the pension plan and the Steelworkers Co-op building in Vancouver. He was also right in that it did get easier over time, partly because they learned they needed me at Steel; soon after the merger, I organized and signed important collective agreements in two northern mines, Keno Hill and Anvil, and at the gold mine near Whistler, Northair Mine.

1969-70 NEGOTIATIONS

During the Steel raids on our union, both east and west, Steel had repeatedly stressed to our members how skilled their contract negotiators were, and many of the Mine Mill rank and file were attracted by the idea of the major clout a large and powerful union like Steel, with its bargaining expertise, might offer them.

I wasn't impressed. In 1969-70, negotiations for all the westcoast metal plants, including some of the foundries, were headed up by Don Dunphy and Monte Alton for the union. On the other side, the employers were united in an organization called the Metal Industries Association (MIA). The MIA spokesman was working to get Steel to modify their demands on the grounds that their competition in Washingon and Oregon had wages and fringe benefits substantially below those offered in BC. They took Dunphy and Alton on a US junket to prove this was so, and the result was a two year agreement with a six per cent annual wage increase, voted on and accepted by the workers in the plants affected.

In the meantime, Pen Baskin asked me if I would negotiate agreements for two ex-Mine Mill foundries named Mainland and Letson-Burpee, and though I had no experience in the metal shop and foundry industry, I reluctantly agreed.

The bargaining commitees of both plants were most co-operative. We first opened negotiations with Letson-Burpee, who promptly offered us the established six-and-six offer accepted by the foundries. We adjourned to think about it, but we didn't put it to a vote. Instead, we proceeded to negotiate separately with Mainland Foundry—a much larger and less aggressive employer—and eventually accepted a two year agreement based on a seven and one half percent per year wage increase. Jimmie Cameron, the owner of Mainland, was a decent employer. When he later sold the foundry, he gave one million dollars from the sale back to his employees, to be split among them.

With the Mainland settlement in our pocket, we went back to Letson-Burpee and conducted a vote on the six and six offer. It was unanimously defeated and it didn't take long for Letson-Burpee to settle on the same basis as Mainland so that everybody was happy.

Well, not everybody. The shit hit the fan in the Steelworkers office. Poor Pen Baskin was subject to considerable pressure from Toronto for embarassing Alton and Dunphy. He realized that punishing King for negotiating too much money was absurd, and he couldn't have the first (six per cent) collective bargaining agreements revoked, so Baskin quietly did nothing.

Despite this, Alton was still appointed negotiator for the huge Cominco mining and smelting operation in BC that I would have liked, and was certainly more familiar with.

Later, in the 1970s, the Steelworkers raided the United Mine Workers, the coal miners in Alberta, in the Crowsnest Pass. I was one of several guys who weren't too happy with that situation. Apart from the fact that I knew too much about being raided to be comfortable with anyone else being on the receiving end, I also felt uneasy because I'd always admired the coal miner's union. Back in the early 1900s, John L. Lewis of the UMW and Big Bill Haywood of Mine Mill had made an agreement that the UMW would take all coal jurisdictions and Mine Mill would look after hard rock, and we'd stuck to that. We always had a very brotherly relationship whereby we gave each other transfers so if we got each other's members in our locals, we wouldn't charge initiation fees, and if there was a disaster, we helped each other. I just didn't think the Steelworkers should raid the coal miners and I told them so at the time.

I liked organizing. I had organized a mine in New Brunswick and the Pine Point Mine in the Northwest Territories, and now I looked after Con, Giant and all the Yellowknife locals. They were some of the more difficult ones. The mine in Uranium City in northern Saskatchewan wasn't too easy, either. It was composed mostly of men the company had flown in directly from Shannon Airport in Dublin, and they hated anybody who wasn't Irish. I was not only Irish, but one night when I was invited to a late night lunch,

WHATEVER IT TAKES

Not long after we merged, in 1971 or '72, I was sent to sign up the men at the Princeton mine. This had been an underground mine that closed when they ran out of ore and now was being opened as an open pit. I wasn't too sure about how to approach open pit miners and someone advised me, "Just take up a case of beer. The boys will do the rest." When I got there, someone pointed me at the bunkhouse, but when I went in, they weren't drinking beer at all—they were smoking marijuana. They invited me to sit down. I offered them my beer, they offered me a puff and I signed them all up.

But someone must have changed his mind and turned me in, because a few days later I got a phone call from someone in the union's head office, who accused me of smoking dope on the job.

"I'm an organizer," I told him. "I'd smoke dried pig shit if I had to, to sign people up!" and I heard no more about it.

PERSONAL POLITICS

As for personal involvement in party politics, I was always left-inclined, but I had been very surprised when as the young and green president of Local 480 Mine Mill in Trail, I'd received invitations from two parties to become their candidate in provincial elections.

First came a well-dressed pair of advance agents for the brand new Social Credit Party, newly spawned by W.A.C. Bennett—Pierre Painter and a prominent fruit farmer from the Fraser Valley. They failed to ignite any desire in me to join their party despite their assurances that I would be a prime candidate, settling instead on Robert Sommers, a music teacher from Castlegar who did, indeed, become the successful candidate for their party and who helped them ease out the CCF, nineteen seats to eighteen.

Next to visit the embattled offices of Local 480 were a very active Liberal MP named Art Lainge and his youthful colleague, a UBC luminary by the name of Ray Perreault who later became a prominent Senator. They were a polite and plausible pair but these august gentlemen failed to make a Liberal politician out of me, either.

It was not until the late '60s or early '70s that I was politically enticed again. I'd had a tough day, trying to talk some sense into a thick-headed Mine Manager at Keno Hill in Mayo in the Yukon. It was very cold—minus seventy degrees with a strong wind blowing—and we were all afraid to go to bed, afraid the overheated pipes in the hotel would explode, so we were sitting up, drinking beer and bullshitting when a long distance call came from the CCF Club in Trail. They wanted to know if I would be their candidate in the upcoming provincial election. At that stage of my life, I wasn't too interested in politics, though I was still a left-winger. When I told them this, they put my brother Ray and then Bud DeVito on the line. They told me that if I didn't run, they didn't have any possible winner. Finally I said, yes, I would accept the nomination under two conditions: first, my wife had to agree, and second, the USWA had to grant me a temporary leave of absence so I could campaign, and a semi-permanent leave of absence if I was elected.

Well, Lil reluctantly agreed, but director Larry Sefton of the USWA refused to grant any leave, whatsoever, and that was the end of my political career. It didn't bother me a damn bit, despite the strangeness of Sefton's decision.

it lasted for two days—not because of booze but because someone brought out a guitar that no one knew how to play. Well, I challenged them that I knew more Irish songs than they did and they took me on. And you can guess what happened between "The Londonderry Air" and "Bold Robert Emmett". We got along great.

I contined to organize miners. I also continued to do Workmen's (later Worker's) Compensation claims for the union and after a while they started boasting that they had a guy who could win them. Then I started helping other unions do the same. Mine Mill had been barred from the BC Federation of Labour almost the entire time I was active in the union, so one good thing that came out of our merger with Steel was that, as a member of a union now affiliated with the Federation, I got to attend the 1968 BC Fed convention where I was put on the Health and Safety Committee. We did some good work there.

THE SANDY ANDERSON CASE

One day in the mid-seventies, I received a phone call at the union office from Sam Brown. Sam was a Teamster union officer who represented his union on Workmen's Compensation Board matters. As part of the Three-Way Pact of Teamsters, Labourers and Operating Engineers, his union had been raiding ours for several years and our relationship was cool. But Sam was contacting me to help one of his members. The man's father was an ex-Mine Miller from the Pioneer Mines at Bralorne, and when he died, the Workmen's Compensation Board refused his widow any pension, despite the fact that her husband had been on a WCB silicosis pension for many years.

Now, how could any respectable union officer refuse assistance when a former member's widow was being denied her legitimate rights? Besides, despite the on-again off-again union battles, many of us in Mine Mill had a friendly relationship with several of the Teamster's field staff. Ken Scott, Big Zimmerman, Walt Doshkosh and others were all good guys to sit down and have a drink with. One thing you could say about the Teamsters—if you had to hit the bricks, they wouldn't let you down.

In any event, the processing of the Anderson case took a strange course. This was before disclosure rules were in place and after we were granted a hearing in front of the Board of Review. We assembled as much medical support as we could in order to prove that Sandy Anderson had indeed died of silicosis. Fortunately, the man had been a patient at the Hanna Medical Clinic in Burnaby, and through my personal relationship with Dr. Hanna, I discovered that the young doctor involved had made no mention of silicosis on the death certificate. I simply approached him and persuaded him to amend the certificate to correctly identify silicosis as the contributing factor in the death.

When the Board of Review sat down to review the case, their file didn't include the amended version of Mr. Anderson's death certificate. Fortunately again, the chairman of that board, a young lawyer, was green as grass. He immediately accepted the fact that the doctor had initially erred and the three-person panel reached a unanimous decision to reverse the denial of the widow's claim. Very seldom did we get one as easy as that!

The first chairman I was with on the committee was a fellow named John Hashe from the Woodworkers (IWA- Canada). After him we put in another IWA guy named George Kobell. He had been to the CLC Labour College in Ottawa. I thought he was a pretty good guy, and I worked under him until my brother Bill, who was by then the NDP Minister of Labour, appointed him as labour's representative on the Workers' Compensation Board, but he failed to distinguish himself in that position. After that was Hector Poirier, a good guy, also IWA, but he wasn't in the best of health and retired early. Then I became the chairman.

In 1976 I withdrew to make room for a bright and energetic young audiologist and the first woman who ever chaired the committee, Marianne Gilbert. Under Marianne, that committee had a dramatic impact on the attitude of workers and employers to health and safety issues in this province. Until then, the approach to safety had been one of compensation: if you lose a limb, who'll pay for it and how much? But Marianne was one of the first to get us thinking 'prevention.' She got the idea across first with hearing loss. If a worker loses their hearing you can buy them a hearing aid, sure—but wouldn't it be better to cut down noise levels in the workplace or at the very least, provide him or her with earplugs to prevent the loss in the first place?

In 1977 the committee presented a report called *Perspectives for Health and Safety in British Columbia* that proposed this new approach to the BC Fed Convention, and followed it up with an education campaign. Several of us travelled around the province with international experts like Jeanne Stellman who wrote, *Work is Dangerous to Your Health,* to emphasize to workers that they should concentrate on preventing injuries, not just getting compensated for the damage when it was too late. The only good thing Lynn Williams, then President of the Steelworkers Union, ever did for me was to okay giving a copy of Jeanne's book to every member of the union. I recommended it and damned if he didn't do it!

It was a very exciting time for those of us involved: Marianne, Cliff Andstein, Carolyn Askew (Gibbons), Astrid Davidson, Bruce Elphinstone, Keith Graham, George Heyman, Verna Ledger, Dave Lomas, Fred Roycroft and Norton Youngs. Unfortunately, not only for Marianne's family but for the labour movement as a whole, we too-soon lost her to cancer.

The Mine Mill union very early commited itself to the health and safety of workers and I intend to document it in a separate history. But from the time of our merger with the Steelworkers Union I continued to work among miners particularly in the areas of occupational health and safety.

So on account of Pen Baskin, I stayed in the Steelworkers Union. But in general it was a rotten period and with the one exception of Baskin, I don't have good memories of any of those men: Monte Alton, Don Dunphy or Ron Douglas. For all of us, it was a pretty bad period and it was a terrible thing for me, personally. Before I ever heard of Harvey Murphy, I was fighting for Mine Mill. I'd joined it and helped organize it when I was still a kid, the youngest member in the local. It still agonizes me, the fact that I had to come to support the merger with Steel and lose Mine Mill. But it had to be done. I'm no Jesus Christ, but it had to be done. And looking back, I guess it was quite a defeat for them, in their eyes, that after all those years, they couldn't keep raiding and they could never defeat Mine Mill. In the end, we merged by our own free will and our own vote.

PART III

Looking forward

I started writing this memoir because I think there have been too many erroneous accounts of Mine Mill's history and the people involved in it, and I wanted to set the record straight from my point of view. I also think it's important for trade unionists to know the history of Mine Mill because of the terrible effect of the raids and the disunity they created in the entire Canadian labour movement. I hope that younger people will draw the lesson that raiding is only destructive and that they should stick with their union—the one that does the job. The Canadian labour movement is weaker today because of the divisions of the 1950s and '60s. It's also weaker because it lost a fine, militant union, one of the most democratic that ever existed. Even the enemies who helped to bust it, admit that. The loss of Mine Mill and other progressive unions such as the Canadian Seamen's Union was a loss to the entire union movement.

A lot of the struggles in my life were due to the fact that I was a Communist, and I think a lot of the reason for people's opposition to us as Communists was because we posed a real threat to traditional ways and the self-perpetuation of the powerful. Think about it—there's never been any other party but Liberals or Tories in power in Canada federally, and not much different provincially, and all these entrenched powers fight to maintain their security and well-being. It doesn't matter what you are—if you challenge that security, even for the good of a greater number, you'll be seen as a threat. And they have ways to convince people that the good of the Tories and the Liberals is everybody's good!

It seemed simple to me. I joined the Communist Party because I believed we needed a union and because I thought the Communist system was better for my kids and for the future of this country. For me it represented security, the ability to resist Blaylock and people like him who would profit personally without sharing with the bulk of people who did the actual work. I didn't think then and I don't think now that the capitalist system we have is fair in distributing its vast wealth among all its people. It's just a matter of conscience.

In fact, I never was a very good Communist, or a Catholic either, because my rebellious nature would intervene. I used to balk at certain things. Still do. I can't stand the habit of putting a single ideological label on a person and then treating them according to that. You can't classify people that easily—it's an unwarranted interference with their basic rights and freedoms.

I hate regimentation, and for most of my life as a left-winger and a socialist, I've detested most, if not all, of the strictures imposed by authoritarian figures. I eventually joined the NDP but I'm no better as a left-leaning NDPer—some of the things the present so-called Socialist party does, appall me. All through my life, I've had trouble jumping when certain people said jump.

For example, when we nominated Bud DeVito, a veteran, to run for the New Democratic Party in Trail, I supported him because he was and is, a friend of mine and a very good guy who always supported the union. But Nigel Morgan, who was the General Secretary of the BC Communist Party, decided it had to be a Labour Progressive Party person who ran. I just didn't accept Nigel's decree and got into a lot of trouble for criticizing his decision. Morgan got Al Warrington, another veteran, to run against DeVito. Al was equally a good friend and active in the union. But he was a better Communist than me, willing to accept decisions made elsewhere that affected us in Trail.

I wouldn't do that for any party, including the Communists, because it was just plain stupid. It was stupid to have two equally progressive guys run against a Liberal so we could split the vote of the workers and let the Liberal get in. And if that was effective Communism in a community like Trail that was heavily working class, I wouldn't go along with it. The Communism I wanted in my community represented security, the ability of ordinary people to resist people like Selwyn Blaylock and the company and the autocracy of people like those we had then in Ottawa and still have today.

In the early days, people thought Communism meant inviting the Communists of Russia to walk in to Canada and take over. For example, they made a big deal about the Soviet crèches, arguing that children were taken away from their parents and forced to stay in these places where they could be brainwashed. Well, today we call them 'childcare centres' and lots of people in North America use them without considering them a Communist threat. In fact, the Liberal Party of Canada, for God's sake, ran for national office in 1993 on the promise of a national daycare program. Sometimes it all depends on who's doing the talking.

I think the Communists have done a lot of stupid things but the capitalists more so—maybe because they've been at it longer. But overall, to me, the word Communist simply implies communal. It's a code of behaviour that allows people to live in community, in peace and harmony with each other. And you can't live in peace and harmony when a third of your population is hungry or doesn't have a decent roof over its head. So I didn't mind then and I don't mind now being called a Commie—Commie by conscience and Commie by living in my community. As the great Art Evans said, "I'd rather be called a 'red' by the 'rats' than a 'rat' by the 'reds.' "

I will never apologize to anyone for my perspective; it's mine and mine alone. I'm a member of the working class and proud of it. The people who don't work for a living—who've never turned a screw or dug a potato or made a song, the ones who were born into plenty—what a bastardly bunch they are. If it wasn't for the workers, the ordinary people, they'd starve. I figure the higher you go, the lower you get. That's my way of looking at things.

But I must say I had a strong and unpleasant case of *deja vu* in 1996. In that year, the US government passed a bill called the Helms-Burton law that forbad other independent governments, including Canada, from trading with Cuba. It was blatant interference in the sovereignty of other countries. It shocked me because it mirrored so closely the precedent of the McCarran Act of 1950 that limited people's right to freely move across the Canada-US border. But where was the uproar? Where were the unions and the press? They hardly said a word—just like when they let us be tormented in the labour movement after the Americans passed the Walter McCarran Act.

I'll be forever in the debt of the labour movement and the Canadian Legion because it was they who really educated me—not officially, of course, but as vice president of the Legion and chairman of the Legion Housing Committee after the war and then in Mine Mill. These organizations paid for my education by giving me the time and opportunity to read and write and research and do public speaking. They taught me responsibility. This memoir is partly my thanks and my repayment to them. Thanks largely to them, writing articles and briefs and appearing as an advocate in front of boards came pretty naturally to me and I enjoyed it. And I sure liked doing it, arguing for the workers, for ordinary people and their families.

When I visited the metal union in France with its six million members, there were only three people on the national executive—the executive were only figureheads. I liked that. The real union was in the plants where the shop stewards led the political life of the unions. I think the bureaucracy of trade unions today is what is partly responsible for the mess we're in. Business unionism—workers capitulating to instructions coming from on high, taking no active part in their own union is not unionism. I think Mine Mill understood that.

Mine Mill had a history of being one of the most honourable and effective labour unions in North America. Some of those who joined the high-paid posse who sought its destruction were, to put it kindly, suffering from 'a pigment' of their imagination. Their fear of Communists and of 'red domination' destroyed an excellent union and created enormous personal hardship and loss to all those working in the mining industry in Canada. Energies that should have gone into fighting the boss instead went into fighting each other. In spite of all the accusations of Communism, Mine Mill as an organization had absolutely no ties, agreements or official connection with any political party between 1938 when I joined Local 480, and 1968, when it ceased to exist as a national union body in Canada. This is not to say there were no Communists among its officers and members. There were probably Fascists and Nazis as well, but the union itself was and stayed politically independent.

The real reason, I believe, for the virulent attacks on Mine Mill from the mining industry of North America was their fear of Mine Mill as a powerful and unrelenting adversary in the struggle for workers' rights versus profits. Anti-Communism not only legitimized business's goals, it also undermined labour's united opposition to the business agenda of absolute power and control.

The forces organized against Mine Mill and her sister, left-wing unions in the United States and Canada— governments, business, immigration, the pulpit and the press—were probably the greatest ever pitted in peace-time against a relatively small union organization. To their everlasting shame, some unions also became willing accomplices in this dirty business. It was a great injustice and the outcome was predictable. In retrospect, it is remarkable that Mine Mill both in the United States and in Canada maintained its independence and identity as long as it did. The struggle lasted for almost twenty long years and should never, ever be repeated.

My association with my former colleagues in Mine Mill was memorable and productive and our membership, in my opinion, was well served. We had our internal differences, of course, but we tried not to let them interfere with our work. It was not selfish motives that inspired the officers of Mine Mill, in the end, to endorse the merger with the Steelworkers; our membership were always our first concern.

Today, I'm concerned about some of the developments I see in modern unions. At heart, a union is a weapon of capitalism. Sitting down and bargaining with the boss is a form of setting out the terms of your own slavery. But of course, I still fought for a union and I continue to fight today, because in comparison with the situation we've come from, we now have at least some control over our own conditions of work. Before unions, there was none at all.

For years I fought against becoming a member of the USWA, but today, through the leadership of solid trade unionists like Lawrence McBrearty nationally and Ken Neumann in western Canada, as well as many others, I see the Steelworkers Union, like high grade steel, emerging from the dross of decades of indifferent leadership. I have had nothing but fair dealing from current Steel officers and staff.

I want to stress the importance of international unionism. Today, even more—far more—than when I was most actively involved, the same people are bosses on both sides of all international borders. Only a strong unity and like-mindedness from labour can counter that. Of course, it depends on the practice of unionism. Some unions have made a mockery of true international solidarity, but if it's democratic, which it was in our union, then international sisterhood and brotherhood is a vital basis of strength. The merger of the three great metal-working unions: the United Steelworkers of America (USWA), the United Auto Workers (UAW), and the International Association of Machinists (IAM) effective January 1 of the year 2000, is an unprecedented step forward in the history of the North American labour movement. It is through such difficult but vital mergers, that our unions will be strong. As their Unity Declaration says, "Without the countervailing power that only organized workers can achieve, the economic freedom and political democracy that are the foundation of the good life we have come to enjoy are in serious peril . . . . In sum, our enduring vision of a world of dignity, security and prosperity for the many—not just the few—requires nothing less than that we create a new union for a new era." I have seen this done before. It is time to do it again.

In my own lifetime, I've been lucky in that I happened to be the right person in the right place at the right time to do a little for the good of ordinary working men and women. Among unions, it was an honour to work for the International Union of Mine, Mill and Smelter Workers. In fact, in later years if anyone asked, I never said I worked for Steel; I worked for the members—the miners and their families. I guess I always will.

WHERE ARE THEY NOW?

Olive Anderson. When her husband Ed died, moved back to the Kootenays where she still lives, near her family.

Kitch Bannatyne was killed in Vancouver by a car.

Garfield 'Gar' Belanger. After being fired by CM&S, worked in local mines then retired to Kaslo and Nelson, BC. He died in Nelson in the mid-1990s, still fighting for progressive community causes.

George DeGroff. After being a solid union supporter and very strong Communist, became a religious fundamentalist and moved to Klamath Falls, Oregon.

Dan Dosen. After retirement from the smelter, worked as a janitor in the Mine Mill hall in Trail.

Harry Drake. After being blacklisted by CM&S, worked as a logger and miner in the Kootenay area until he died in about 1990.

John Gordon. After the 1950 raid, retired to Victoria, BC.

Bill Longridge. Retired to Toronto where he died.

Jack MacDonald worked as a social worker in the BC criminal justice system and then as a Social Work professor at the University of British Columbia until his retirement in Burnaby, BC.

Archie MacDonald became Vice-President of BC Rail.

Remo Morandini. In the late 1960s left the union movement to join the Workmen's Compensation Board as head of the Cranbrook office in the Kootenays. He was killed in 1988 while riding his bicycle.

Harvey Murphy worked for the Steelworkers Union until he retired in 1970 and died in his sleep in Toronto in the mid-70s.

Leo Nimsick. One of the charter members of Local 480, he served for many years as a CCF and then NDP MLA for Rossland-Trail and was Minister of Mines under Dave Barrett's NDP government. He is retired and living in Cranbrook, BC.

Fred Pearson. After being fired by CM&S, he moved to Vancouver Island where he married and later retired to Comox, BC.

Vince Ready has a national reputation as an extremely effective labour arbitrator and mediator working out of Vancouver, BC.

Lou Regenwetter became one of the top flight staff people in another union.

Bill Rudychuk worked for Mine Mill and then the Steelworkers in the Yukon Territory until about 1995 and died a year later, leaving his legacy for workers' education.

Ken Smith. After the merger he did some bargaining for Steel. After developing silicosis from working in the Britannia mine near Vancouver, he retired on a silicosis pension.

Nels Thibault left the national presidency of Mine Mill to fight the right-wing for the leadership of the Sudbury local. After losing that battle in 1965, he rejoined the national staff of Mine Mill as an organizer. He was later elected president of the Manitoba Federation of Labour and received an honorary university degree in recognition of his work for labour.

Bud DeVito. After the Steelworker raids in Trail, he ran successfully for civic office becoming the Mayor of Trail and dedicating himself to the service of his community. Is now retired and living in Trail.

Al Warrington retired from Cominco and continues to be active in community service in Vancouver, BC.

JOE HILL

Music by Earl Robinson
Words by Alfred Hayes

I dreamed I saw Joe Hill last night
Alive as your and me.
Says I, "But Joe, you're ten years dead."
"I never died," said he.
"I never died," said he.

"In Salt Lake, Joe," says I to him,
Him standing by my bed.
"They framed you on a murder charge,"
Says Joe, "But I ain't dead."
Says Joe, "But I ain't dead."

"The copper bosses killed you, Joe,
They shot you, Joe," says I.
"Takes more than guns to kill a man."
Says Joe, "I didn't die."
Says Joe, "I didn't die."

And standing there as big as life
And smiling with his eyes,
Says Joe, "What they forgot to kill
Went on to organize,
Went on to organize."

"Joe Hill ain't dead," he says to me,
"Joe Hill ain't never died.
Where working folk are out on strike,
Joe Hill is at their side.
Joe Hill is at their side."

"From San Diego up to Maine
In every mine and mill,
Where workers strike and organize,
That's where you'll find Joe Hill.
That's where you'll find Joe Hill."

I dreamed I saw Joe Hill last night
Alive as you and me.
Says I, "But Joe, you're ten years dead."
"I never died," said he.
"I never died," said he.

Joe Hill was an American songwriter and organizer for the Industrial Workers of the World, one of the offshoots of the Western Federation of Miners. On January 13, 1914 he was arrested and charged with the murder of two grocers in a holdup. Following a trial that was filled with irregularities and based on entirely circumstantial evidence, Joe Hill was convicted and executed by the State of Utah on November 19, 1915. In his final message to union headquarters, Joe Hill wrote, "Don't waste any time in mourning—organize!" On the night before his execution, an unknown speaker at a rally in Salt Lake City said, "Joe Hill will never die, do you hear it everybody? Joe Hill will never die." These words inspired Robinson and Hayes to write this song.

APPENDIX

THE STRUGGLE:
A Brief History of Local Labour Movements and the Rossland Miners' Union Hall

By Rosa Jordan

(Author's note: In 1985 Local 480, Trail, printed The Struggle: A Brief History of Local Labour Movements and the Rossland Miners' Union Hall, *a history of the birth of unionism in the Kootenays. The author, Rosa Jordan, has given kind permission for us to reprint here the part of that history up to the 1930's as well as of the restoration of the hall.)*

In 1890, gold was discovered in the Kootenay Mountains of British Columbia, just a few miles from where the Columbia River flows out of Canada into the state of Washington. News of the find exerted its usual magnetic force, and within five years, thousands of men had converged on the area, arriving by foot or horseback along trails not yet widened into wagon tracks, or by boat on the Columbia River to the Trail Landing; from there, climbing ten miles and some 2000 feet in elevation to the mining camp of Rossland. By 1895, over 4000 claims had been staked. Ore initially was taken by pack mule down to the Trail Landing, but by '93, a road had been constructed, and it was hauled out by 40-horse-team wagons. On the banks of the Columbia, Kootenai Indians loaded the heavy ore onto wood-burning boats which would take it to the smelter in distant Butte, Montana.

Conditions of life in the tent-camp of Rossland were harsh, but most of the men who came had lived in other mining camps and knew what to expect: no medical facilities or other amenities, high prices for food and lodging, scarcities of just about everything except liquor. They worked doggedly, sometimes alone but usually cooperatively with other prospectors, spurred on by the possibility of "striking it rich" and the necessity of finding gold before their money and provisions ran out. They were independent men, and they had their dreams.

Very soon all that would change. The many prospectors who did not make a strike would be broke, worse off than when they arrived. The few who did "strike it rich" invariably sold out within a year or so for a few thousand dollars. The buyers—newly created companies dominated almost completely by US capital, and later sold to British and Canadian interests—would be the ones to develop the mines and extract millions in precious metal. These companies would become the employers of now poverty-stricken men whose dream had not come true, and who needed, more than anything, a job.

Living conditions for the men who worked these mines were rough and primitive, the labour heavy and the work dangerous. As the town of Rossland developed, living conditions improved. (By 1898, Rossland had a water system, and by the following year, two nuns had collected enough donations from the miners to build a hospital). Working conditions, however, did not improve. The question arose, in the minds of many, of whether it was necessary to struggle quite so much for so very little.

Because most of the workers had come from other mining areas, they were familiar with something which get-rich-quick investors regarded as even more dangerous than the life-threatening conditions under which their employees worked. This was the concept of unionism.

In the summer of 1895, Ed Boyce, president of the Western Federation of Miners, visited Rossland, and in July, Rossland miners formed the first Canadian local of the WFM. The WFM was a militant and progressive union whose membership was made up of both Canadians and Americans, and open to people of all ethnic groups. At a time when virtually no group—not the (usually absentee) owners of the mines, not churches, not businesses, not federal or provincial governments—was willing to take a stand on behalf of workers for better wages and safer working conditions, the only organizational ally which a worker had was his union.

A BUILDING SECOND TO NONE

Rossland's Western Federation of Miners Local No. 38 was formed in an era when legal protection and recognition for unions was non-existent and persecution of union members was rampant. In the face of such opposition, it wanted supporters and detractors alike to know that unions in this area were to have a history that would not be transient. So in 1898, the members of Local 38 voted to build themselves a great hall on the main street of Rossland. (And almost immediately, the BC government decided to build a massive, multi-spired court house at the other end of the street to reflect its intention of maintaining control over the supposed "lawlessness" of union men.)

Rossland miners—men working 10-hour days and earning less than 25 cents an hour, assessed themselves a day's wages to cover the costs of building their Union Hall. When completed, the Hall was an edifice that even the local paper (which generally ignored the union except to take swipes at its leadership) conceded was "the most substantial building of its kind in the Kootenays...in point of strength and solidity, second to none in this district...seemingly good for half a century of usefulness."

On January 25, 1899, Local 38's executive reported: "Lots purchased, $658. Architect E.J. Weston hired; Foundation cost, $938. Superstructure bid accepted, $3,560; Borrowed $3,000 from Mr. O'Brien Redding, cost of loan including three months interest in advance, $146.75; Borrowed $700 from five individuals, now repaid; Three hundred chairs for upper hall, $293.75; Including architect's fee, total cost of building, $6,537.75."

It had taken a strong union to build such a Hall, and the physical presence of such a structure strengthened the labour movement it served. Members of the Typographical Union, Tailors, Carpenters and Joiners, Knights of Labour, Blacksmiths and Helpers, and Cigarmakers all took part in its Grand Opening on July 16, 1898, but it was the Western Federation (called by some "the most militant union ever known") which owned the hall and took the lead in much of British Columbia's and Canada's historic labour legislation.

"IF MINERS ARE HUMAN BEINGS"

For half a century North American miners had been fighting for an 8-hour day. In 1986, the Western Federation of Miners (which because of its highly democratic bias was committed to political activism) had succeeded in getting the 8-hour day legislated for mine and smelter workers in Utah, but there was as yet no such law in Canada.

In 1898, abut a month before the Miners' Union Hall opened, leaders of the Rossland union met at a local blacksmith shop and planned a political strategy for bringing about the 8-hour day in Canada. On the promise of Rossland hardware dealer Jim Martin that he would introduce the necessary legislation, union members turned out at the polls to elect him to the provincial legislative assembly. Jim Martin approached another M.L.A., Joseph Martin, and persuaded him to author 8-hour-day legislation. Meanwhile, another member of the Rossland local, James Wilks, was elected vice president of the Trades and Labour Congress of Canada. Wilks contacted BC's Minister of Mines (Fred Hume from Nelson) and secured from him a promise to enact an 8-hour law for underground workers. Hume tacked Smith's bill on as an amendment to a Metalliferous Mines Inspection Act. Historic though it was (being the first 8-hour day legislated for underground workers in Canada), it passed quietly through the assembly on February 27, 1899, with virtually no debate.

The sensational wealth being produced by the Kootenay mines was well known. Both local and international press regularly carried stories fueled by owners' boasts and celebrated reports of profitable dividends paid out to shareholders. According to the *Rossland Miner*, gold valued at almost three and a quarter million dollars was taken from Rossland mines in the year of 1899. Yet mine owners were outraged that workers who risked (and frequently lost) their lives in extracting the bullion from the bowels of the earth should seek better pay and safer working conditions.

The mine owners' association immediately launched a campaign to have the Eight Hour Day Act repealed. The enforcement of such a law would cause at least a 20% loss in productivity, they said. The mines would close.

The Western Federation locals of the Kootenays (in addition to the one in Rossland, there was now one in Sandon) responded with the following, read in the B.C. Legislature:

"If miners are to be considered in the same category as so much machinery or some kind of animal that lives on black bread and hog fat, needs no books, can live in a rude hut, or sleep in a mining company bunk house without being dissatisfied, then there is no cause for quarrel over how many hours he shall or shall not work. Conceding him to be a human being, a modern man able to read, think and appreciate the good things of life as others do, then we contend that eight hours are sufficient for men to work underground."

The B.C. government considered the situation for a time, then dispatched a Royal Commission to investigate. Up in the Slocan Valley, mine owners had reacted to the Eight Hour Day Act by reducing wages from $3.50 for a 10-hour day to $2.50 for an 8-hour day. Outraged, mine workers had struck. Management countered the strike by (illegally) bringing in trainloads of strike breakers. When striking miners in the Slocan realized that they could not get the government to enforce the Alien Labour Act that would prevent the importation of strike breakers, they accepted a wage cut, settling, finally, for $3.25 a day.

In Rossland, however, miners met in their Union Hall and planned a different strategy. Starting at the Columbia-Kootenay Mine and then spreading to others in the Rossland area, workers began a quiet campaign to do more work in the eight hours than they had been doing in ten. They documented production, and when hearings were held in the Rossland court house on February 26, 1899, the union presented conclusive evidence that the 8-hour day had actually REDUCED costs for the mine owners, while increasing productivity.

The 8-hour day was one of two major union victories born in the Rossland Miners' Hall. The second occurred in 1900 when Rossland miners elected Smith Curtis as M.L.A. and he, two years later, succeeded in getting the province's first Worker's Compensation legislation passed. The Act was limited, in that it provided only a $1,500 benefit to the families of miners killed in mine accidents, but it paved the way for the British Columbia Workmen's Compensation Act of 1917.

These legislative successes enhanced the Rossland Miners' Union Hall as a focal point for labour-oriented political activity in western North America. Joe Hill, a labour organizer and songwriter later framed for murder by Utah's copper bosses, met with union organizers here. (Hill's last message to union friends before being executed by a firing squad was, "Don't mourn me—organize.") America's most famous lawyer, Clarence Darrow, came to Rossland in search of evidence for the defense of an Idaho miner. Labour organizers from throughout western North America, being pursued by the notorious, company-employed Pinkerton detectives, were given refuge in the Hall.

In December 1899, the Western Federation of Miners (which now had 13 locals in Western Canada) held its convention at the Rossland Miners' Union Hall. The convention called for enforcement of the Eight Hour Day Act. It also endorsed the *Rossland Industrial World* as its official newspaper, and voted to develop a program of organizing libraries and lectures to educate its membership and to collect statistics on unemployment, employment and wages.

THE STRIKE OF 1901

Working conditions, even by the standards of the day, were wretched. Hand drilling left its mark in battered hands and broken arms, but machine drilling wrecked havoc on the human body in more ways—everything from strained backs to the miners' scourge, lung disease. One drill was named the "widow-maker" because it threw up so much dust that its operators rarely survived lung disease for more than a few years. In addition to health hazards posed by new and unperfected technology, machine drilling caused many workers to be demoted to the lower paid jobs of "muckers" or shovellers.

The Le Roi, richest of the Kootenay gold mines, was now owned by the British American Corporation of London, part of an early multinational company controlled by Whittaker Wright. Wright's manipulations of worthless securities managed to plunge the company into bankruptcy by October 1901. Wright later was convicted of fraud, but not before he had removed millions of dollars of profits from the Rossland mines to cover his failing empire. This had a brutal effect on Rossland miners as wages were cut, equipment was left unrepaired, and dangerous short-cuts were used to make up drained-off capital.

By 1901, Rossland minders considered their condition intolerable. Ore valued at well over four and a half million dollars would be taken from the Rossland mines that year, yet most workers were not making $3 a day. Wages had dropped with the re-introduction of the contract system. Some mines had instituted a policy of firing and blacklisting union men and replacing them with non-union workers.

In April of 1901, union members met at the Rossland Miners' Hall and took a strike vote. It was narrowly defeated (partly because if there was a strike, men working under the contract system would have lost wages owed them). In July, the issue came to a vote again, and the decision was to strike. The demands were (a) a raise in muckers' wages from $2.50 to $3 a day, and (b) an end to company discrimination against unionists. In addition, the strike in Rossland was intended to support a strike going on at a sister local at the smelter in Northport, Washington.

The mining companies immediately imported trainloads of strikebreakers from the U.S.—a blatant violation of the Alien Labour Act. The Western Federation headquarters in Colorado sent $20,000 to assist Rossland's striking miners, but pointed out that a million dollars would be not be [sic] enough to tide them through the strike as long as management could get strike-breakers.

At Union request, then-Deputy Minister of Labour William Lyon Mackenzie King came to Rossland to investigate violation of the Alien Labour Act. According to Union Secretary Frank Woodside, "We supplied hundreds of affidavits of violations of the law. After several days of investigation he met with our executive and told us there was no doubt of flagrant violations."

Yet King did not order the companies to comply with the law. According to Woodside's account, King "told us to call off the strike, and all the members of the executive would get good jobs. We told him that if this was his decision after all the evidence we had produced of violation of the Canadian law, that he had better go back home before striking miners who were waiting for some action found out his attitude. He left that night."

During the conflict, a Bank of Montreal official had suggested to King that it would be better all round if the Alien Labour Act were not enforced. However, King's diary indicates that what really influenced him to ignore violations of the Alien Labour Act was his understanding, after discussing the matter with various cabinet ministers, that "the government does not wish to enforce any such law."

Strikebreakers continued to pour in, many of them non-English-speaking immigrants from the coal fields of Michigan who were not aware that there was a strike in progress, and who did not have the money to leave once they were here. Although some refused to work when they learned of the strike, most were forced by economic necessity to take the jobs available, regardless of pay and conditions. The union's strike fund was soon depleted, and by January 1902, the Rossland Local was out of money and its members voted to return to work. "You could not blame the men if they accepted less," wrote the union secretary. "We have had to cut them down almost to starvation."

Three years later, a union member writing of the 1901 strike conveyed the hardships of that year in a single sentence: "No man living outside Rossland can imagine the troubles our brothers in this town have been through."

Even so, the mining companies were not satisfied. After the strike of 1901 went down to defeat, Centre Star and War Eagle mines sued the union and members of its executive for damages.

Shortly after the case went to trial, Rossland's union-supported M.L.A. Smith Curtis introduced the "Trade Unions Protection Act" aimed at protecting unions against injunctions and their funds from liability. The act was to be made retroactive to "any action now pending." It did not pass, but on the day it was defeated, Joseph Martin brought in a similar bill, which was passed into law on June 20, 1902.

BAD TIMES AND WORSE

Legislation had passed which would keep future unions and individual union members from being held liable for any losses suffered by companies as result of a strike, but this came too late to help Rossland's Local 38. In the Rossland courthouse, mining companies had won their suits against the union and the members of its executive. Damages were set at $12,500, and the Miner's Union Hall was seized along with union funds. Local 38 went into receivership. (Union dues were reduced to ten cents a month as a way of keeping the organization alive without its accumulating additional assets to be seized, but without resources it obviously could do very little for its members). Two years later, the executive of Local 38 was still appealing to sister unions for assistance to miners, "married men with families who lost their homes during the strike."

Although the Miners' Union Hall had been awarded to the companies, registration of ownership was not changed, and in the negotiations which followed, a compromise was reached which allowed the Union to continue using the building. The Hall remained a focal point for union activists throughout the west, for although Local 38 was crippled by bankruptcy, the Western Federation of Miners throughout the U.S. and Canada continued to lobby for child labour reform, abolition of contract labour, equal pay for equal work, enforcement of the Eight Hour Day Act, and better working conditions. Disillusioned with a government which had failed to bring "incorporated greed" under control and to recognize the legitimate rights of working people, the WFM became increasingly socialist in outlook.

The Western Federation of Miners strongly supported the American Labor Union, and at one point American Labor Union leader Eugene Debs spoke to workers in the Rossland Miners' Union Hall. The American Labor Union was opposed to elitist and craft unionism, and launched a campaign to organize semi-skilled and unskilled workers. It began its Canadian campaign in the mining camps of the Kootenays where there were a great many unskilled workers. By the end of 1902, the American Labor Union had made good progress in the Kootenays, organizing such groups as cooks. bartenders, teamsters, lumbermen, and general labourers. However, the ALU derived most of its support from the WFM, and collapsed when the WFM itself began to fail.

The decline of the Western Federation of Miners occurred in 1903 and 1904, as a result of a long and losing battle in Colorado. Large assessments for the Colorado strike caused a drastic decline in union membership, even in the Kootenays.

In 1907, the prices of lead, silver and copper collapsed on the international market, and 1,200 miners in the Kootenays lost their jobs. A number of Rossland mines closed, not to reopen for many years. Miners moved away, taking their ideals of worker unity with them.

THE TRAIL SMELTER

Those Rossland mines which remained open continued to produce. In the years of 1902 to 1916,

Rossland mines produced between 200,000 and 300,000 tons of ore a year, representing 50% of British Columbia's total gold output. Value of this production fluctuated between two and a half and four million dollars per year.

The production of ore from the Rossland mines was so great that a smelter had been built in Trail, a town on the Columbia River just ten miles down the mountain from Rossland. The smelter was a multi-million dollar concern which by now owned most of the mining properties in Rossland, plus several dams and its own power plant—all of which were part of the economic empire of the Canadian Pacific Railroad.

While the industrial might of Consolidated Mining and Smelting Company was regularly touted by local newspapers as an unmitigated blessing to the communities of Rossland and Trail, there was another side to the story. In 1911, the wage for a smelterman was $2.75 a day, regardless of how many hours he worked. The Eight Hour Day Act, which had been on the books more than a decade, was generally ignored. Smeltermen worked 365 days a year. Stanley Scott, professor at Notre Dame University in Nelson, has described the conditions under which smeltermen worked at Consolidated Mining and Smelting during that period:

"Many men were hired after slipping a foreman $20. To hire one, of course, meant another man was fired. No one was ever sure of continued employment. Few jobs were far removed from the blistering heat of 160 degrees of the lead furnaces. Huge 12-ton pots had to be tapped by hand. Numerous workers literally caught fire while performing these tasks. If someone got hurt his friends took care of him because the company didn't have anything to do with that. Lead poisoning began to affect workmen as early as 1900. No first aid existed on the Hill. If someone broke an arm or a leg, both common injuries, then a big, strong friend would load him on his back and take him to the hospital. Naturally the healthy friend lost wages, if not his job, for the trip to the hospital was on company time."

As far as living conditions in the area, it was noted that "Down-wind from the smoke stacks the ethnic communities at the foot of the hill suffered dreadfully, while management, safety guarded by town and mill security, retired each evening to Tadanac, a village constructed by immigrant labour but by 1916 forbidden to them."

What could be done? The crushing Rossland strike of 1901 and the blacklisting of workers who struck was well remembered by men in the Trail smelter. Further, many smeltermen were immigrants who feared that if they dared to unionize they not only might be fired, but deported.

Things begin to change in 1915, with the arrival of WFM organizer Ginger Goodwin. In a remarkably short time, Goodwin managed to overcome the long-standing animosity between craft and industrial unionists. In 1916, soon after the Western Federation of Miners changed its name to the International Union of Mine, Mill and Smelter Workers and opened its membership to smelter and millmen, Trail workers organized into Local 105 of Mine Mill. They immediately demanded a wage increase of 50 cents a day, which they received, but conditionally. (It was indexed to the price of metal and fell if prices fell.)

THE STRIKE OF 1917

In September of 1917, the Mine Mill held its convention in Nelson. Resolutions made at that meeting urged enforcement of the Eight Hour Day Act. Members also protested an amendment to the Workers' Compensation Act, being put forth in the provincial legislature, calling for a reduction in compensation to the dependents of Orientals. The convention's major political focus was opposition to World War I conscription.

Two months later, when the Trail smelter management refused union demands to enforce the Eight Hour Day Act, workers there went on strike. The company fired all 1,200 of those who struck. Within six weeks the strike crumbled. Some 500 workers were never recalled. All the strike leaders were blacklisted.

During the strike, Goodwin, who being slightly crippled had been declared unfit for military duty, was suddenly declared fit and conscripted. He fled the area. A few months later he was tracked down in the hills of Vancouver Island by a special constable and shot to death.

The following year, a flu epidemic swept Trail. The smelter crew was cut by 50% in a matter of weeks, leaving so many stricken that there were hardly enough able-bodied men to bury the dead. Local 105 of the Mine Mill was decimated by this succession of disasters, and soon was broken. It was quickly replaced by a "company union" (a concept evolved by William Lyon MacKinzie [sic] King in 1914 when as a "labour expert" he was employed by John D. Rockefeller to break a strike in Colorado.)

It was subsequently noted by the *Rossland Miner* that "despite the manifold difficulties presented by the strike, the flu epidemic and poor metal prices . . . the total value of the Company's production for 1918 exceeded $10,500,000."

DEPRESSION MINING

The need for metals during World War I gave the Consolidated Mining and Smelting Company incentive to continue operating Rossland mines despite their depleted condition. After the war, high unemployment plus labour disorganization made it possible for the company to make up for declining production by cutting labour costs, and thus continue to operate profitably.

In 1924, the company reopened some mines which had been closed for years. "Conditions in these mines are the worst," complained a One Big Union bulletin. "It is not safe for a man to walk around in the stopes, owing to the fact that the timbers are falling apart from dry rot."

However, production from the mines was continuing to decline, so the company had no real incentive to invest more than was absolutely necessary in their upkeep. In 1929, the company closed its last Rossland mine.

By the summer of 1931, B.C. had 27.5% unemployment—the highest in Canada. There were 36,000 registered unemployed in the province. Yet during the Depression, gold, of all things, experienced a small boom. When commodities were at

their lowest level, manipulations in the world's financial centres actually caused gold to increase in value. Rossland was full of abandoned mines and laid-off miners, which made it convenient for Consolidated Mining and Smelting to adopt a scheme which companies had used in the U.S. to extract ore without the expense of reactivating old mines. It leased mines to former employees on a royalty basis. This provided the company with a limited-risk way of working its aging claims. The leaser, not the owner, paid the overhead, so the owner's share of the find, however small, was just that much more than he would have made with the mine closed.

"The company was doing you a big favor to let you have a lease," explains Roger Terhune, a Rossland miner whose family managed to secure a lease on the Le Roi mine. "Everybody was having a tough time. There was nothing. And in those days, if you didn't have work, you just went hungry. You were very fortunate if you got a lease."

1934 found several hundred Rosslanders working at their own risk in mines which, having been closed for years, frequently were in states of serious disrepair. Even so, it was not the worst of all possible conditions. The leasers had some control in their hours of work, and chose their own working companions; in a sense, they were self-employed. That year the Rossland mines yielded one million dollars worth of gold. The following year, most of the leases were withdrawn, though a dozen or so were allowed to operate until 1937.

THE MINERS' UNION HALL REVISITED

The Rossland of tent-dwelling prospectors had given way to a permanent settlement of miners and their families who clustered in neighborhoods according to nationality. On the high side of town lived the English, the Italians, the Scandinavians, the Scots, the Americans, and the Canadians. Further down the mountainside was the Red Light District (presumably multi- national) and below it a Chinese community which provided most of the town's fresh fruits and vegetables. The business district of Rossland was twice gutted by fire, and each time was substantially rebuilt. As the years passed, Rossland grew into a cohesive and integrated community, surprisingly modern for one in so remote an alpine setting.

During the heyday of Rossland's mining operations, the Union Hall had played a central role in the life of the community. Erna Coombes, the first Caucasian girl child born in Rossland (in 1902), recalls seeing a "magic lantern" show there. She remembers that a boxing match with heavyweight champion Jim Fitzsimmons was held there, one which her young brother was so passionate to see that he persuaded a large black man to smuggle him in under his greatcoat. She remembers as one of her regular childhood errands, going to the side door of the Hall, to the office of Local 38, to pay her father's union dues.

However, by the time the Great Depression hit, mining had wound down in Rossland and the Hall was no longer used for union business. It was rented to the Knights of Pythias, and became known to a new generation as the K.P. Hall. This generation would remember it for dances held there (some of the best big bands in the West, in route between Vancouver and Banff, found it convenient to include the Rossland Union Hall on their itinerary.) Rosslanders who recall the Hall in the decades between World Wars also speak with nostalgia of weddings, musical performances, and flower shows held in the Hall during those difficult Depression years.

Even in the depths of the Depression the Rossland Miners' Union Hall never quite lost its sense of purpose—that purpose being to provide a meeting place for people seeking a democratic means of improving their lives. Elections were regularly held there, as were meetings of the Unemployed Relief Workers.

In 1932, the Miners' Union Hall hosted the area's first meeting of the Co-operative Commonwealth Federation (CCF). The Rossland constituency was to become B.C.'s first chartered member of what was then the province's only major party to declare itself pro-labour and anti-racist. (Most other provincial parties at this time were vehemently opposed to franchising {so called} Orien-

tals.) Harry Lefevre, who participated in the organization of the CCF in this area and attended many CCF meetings in the Miners' Union Hall, recalls that their first choice for candidate was a high school principal who was instructed by the local school board not to become involved with the CCF if he wanted to keep his job, so another candidate had to be chosen.

MINE MILL MAKES A COMEBACK

By the Twenties, the Trail smelter had magnanimously granted its employees the 8-hour day; however, men were required to work 7 days a week. Harry Lefevre, who began work at the smelter in 1926, recalls that he worked a year and a half before he was allowed one day off. Average salary for the 56-hour week was $25. Only a portion of that was paid during the Depression, when, rather than lay off, the company cut employees to half or three-quarters time, depending on whether or not they were married.

A "company union," firmly under the control of management, was the only forum through which smelterworkers could speak. "It wasn't really a union at all, just sort of a committee," said Harry Lefevre. "I got on it because I wanted something done about pensions. But of course, what I said fell on deaf ears." It was this committee, not the company, which organized what little medical care there was for workers injured on the job. "We deducted 25 cents a month from every worker's pay and put it in a fund to pay doctor bills. There was no ambulance either. The workers bought themselves an ambulance by passing the hat around for donations."

The Mine Mill Union, which had been broken in Trail by the 1917 strike, struggled to reestablish itself . . . .

THE MINERS' UNION HALL REBORN

It took more than half a century to firmly establish an organization in this area dedicated to the unity and well-being of working people. By the time this was finally accomplished, the Miners' Union Hall, meant to symbolize just such unity, was in a state of decay.

Encouraged by a young architectural student who recognized the historical value of the Hall, Local 480 helped establish a "heritage society" to oversee its restoration. Between 1978 and 1983, $630,000 was raised from such diverse sources as the B.C. Heritage and Lotteries Fund, TIDSA (a government agency for the promotion of tourism), Canada Works, Cominco, private donors, and union locals across Canada. The idea was that this great Hall would someday serve as both a museum of, and a monument to, those early union struggles.

The Miners' Union Hall has now been restored (with as much authenticity as possible, given necessary concessions to modern public health and safety standards). It reopened to the public in the fall of 1983. Since that time it has hosted musical and theatrical troupes, dances, exercise classes, craft displays, art exhibits, fashion shows, and events of Rossland's annual Winter Carnival, Golden City Days, and Mountain Music Festival.

In 1984, the Hall's Lodge Room, where historic and sometimes clandestine (no names were recorded in the minutes for fear of being blacklisted) union meetings were held, was restored to a functional state. It is now used by the Rossland Heritage Society to host a monthly "Joe Hill Coffee House." Variety entertainment is provided by Canadian and American folk musicians whose performances frequently include labour ballads. Eighty-five years ago one of the performers might have been young Joe Hill. Now it's songs by him or about him, such as, "I dreamed I saw Joe Hill last night," that one hears, carried by voices young and old to the great beams of the Miners' Union Hall . . . .

For more information about the Rossland Miners' Union Hall, you may contact:

Rossland Heritage Society
P.O. Box 1453
Rossland, B.C. VOG 1YO
Canada

COLLABORATIVE LEARNING IN MIDDLE AND SECONDARY SCHOOLS

APPLICATIONS AND ASSESSMENTS

Dawn M. Snodgrass
Mary M. Bevevino

EYE ON EDUCATION
6 DEPOT WAY WEST, SUITE 106
LARCHMONT, NY 10538
(914) 833–0551
(914) 833–0761 fax

Library of Congress Cataloging-in-Publication Data

Snodgrass, Dawn M., 1955–
    Collaborative learning in middle and secondary schools : applications and assessments / Dawn M. Snodgrass, Mary M. Bevevino
        p. cm.
    Includes biographical references and index.
    ISBN 1-83001-84-6
    1. Group work in education—United states. 1. Middle school education—United States. 3. Education, Secondary—United States. 4. Educational tests and measurements—United States. I. Bevevino, Mary M. II. Title.
    LB 1032.S62 2000
    371.39′5—dc21   99-045593

10 9 8 7 6 5 4 3 2 1

Editorial and production services provided by
Richard H. Adin Freelance Editorial Services
52 Oakwood Blvd., Poughkeepsie, NY 12603-4112
(914-471-3566)

Also Available from EYE ON EDUCATION

Personalized Instruction
by James Keefe and John Jenkins

Teaching in the Block
by Robert Lynn Canady and Michael D. Rettig

Writing in the Content Areas
by Amy Benjamin

The Interdisciplinary Curriculum
by Arthur K. Ellis and Carol J. Stuen

Research on Educational Innovations, 2nd ed.
by Arthur K. Ellis and Jeffrey T. Fouts

Best Practices From America's Middle Schools
by Charles R. Watson

The Paideia Classroom: Teaching for Understanding
by Terry Roberts with Laura Billings

Supervision and Block Scheduling in the Block
by Sally J. Zepeda and R. Stewart Mayers

Encouraging Student Engagement in the Block Period
by David Marshak.

Teaching Mathematics in the Block
by Susan Gilkey and Carla Hunt

Teaching Foreign Languages in the Block
by Deborah Blaz

Supporting Students with Learning Needs in the Block
by Conti-D'Antonio, Bertrando, and Eisenberg

Socratic Seminars in the Block
by Wanda H. Ball and Pam Brewer

**The Educator's Brief Guide to the
Internet and the World Wide Web**
by Eugene F. Provenzo, Jr.

DEDICATION

This book is dedicated to Mrs. Evelyn Himes, Mr. Harry Kitzer, and Mrs. Agnes Kitzer. Though they have left our physical presence, their love continues to fill our hearts, and their lives serve as inspiration to our own.

ACKNOWLEDGMENTS

We offer our sincere gratitude to our publisher, Mr. Bob Sickles, for giving us this opportunity to share our experiences with colleagues. We are grateful for the technical assistance of Erin McGowan, and the support of students at Edinboro University of Pennsylvania and educators in the Edinboro area who allowed us to include their application ideas. It is our good fortune to work with these innovative minds and kind hearts.

MEET THE AUTHORS

Dr. Mary M. Bevevino and Dr. Dawn M. Snodgrass, former teachers at elementary, middle, and high schools, are currently Professors of Education at Edinboro University of Pennsylvania where they teach undergraduate and graduate courses in teacher preparation. They also serve as codirectors of the Center for Excellence in Teaching at Edinboro University and are coauthors of *An Educator's Guide to Block Scheduling: Decision Making, Curriculum Design and Lesson Planning* published in 1999 by Allyn and Bacon.

TABLE OF CONTENTS

PREFACE

Collaborative Learning in Middle and Secondary Schools: Applications and Assessments provides a detailed examination of collaborative learning as an effective instructional tool and guides middle and secondary teachers in collaborative planning and assessment. The authors have been careful to separate cooperative learning from collaborative learning because each of these can contribute in unique ways to student learning. Specific connections for teachers who are teaching in block schedule formats are made throughout the text. Discussion of social skills important to productive collaboration is followed by a brief review of cooperative learning as a tool for teaching older students. A significant amount of information is provided in the areas of both teacher decision making and student assessment so that the assessment process can be carefully woven into instruction. The authors have examined teacher planning and student assessment in depth with emphasis on professional decision making and the responsibilities of collaborative and cooperative teachers. The inclusion of assessment tools provides teachers with the materials needed throughout the stages of teaching and learning. The information here will assist middle and secondary teachers in their decision making and their use of student-active strategies in their profession: teaching peers, students, parents, and, most importantly, the teachers themselves.

Collaborative Learning in Middle and Secondary Schools: Applications and Assessments is the result of over 45 combined years in public education. The experiences of these years in many classrooms have taken the authors across multiple grade levels and into many curriculum areas. As teachers themselves, they have long recognized the need for clearly written information, straightforward advice, and specific guidance in the understanding and implementation of alternative teaching approaches. The authors understand the diversity of classrooms today as well as the demands placed on teachers at all levels to involve students in the learning process while moving them to higher levels of understanding. Preparing students for the world they will enter requires a tremendous amount of knowledge, understanding, and flexibility on the part of every teacher involved in their education. This book is designed to provide information that makes sense to teachers today and can be taken into the classroom tomorrow.

1

COLLABORATIVE LEARNING

Last week five of us sat in the library after school for our monthly meeting, a loosely organized cluster of teachers using *student-active methods* (SAM). Our government instructor, Brent Ortiz, coined the term and insists that the "M" is really for Mavericks. But our informal purpose hasn't been to press other teachers to break out of their favorite teaching strategies; we're just sharing what works and talking through our collaborative and cooperative learning strategies. Jane Richards, our biology teacher, started the ball rolling.

"I've done peer editing with my classes, and last semester I actually made up some learning stations for bacteria and viruses. I think they've worked well. I tried role-playing for my unit on the environment, but my students just didn't get into it."

As we tossed around the strategies that each of us had used, it became clear that we all use collaborative learning strategies to some extent, some successfully and some not so well.

"I like using pairs work in algebra," Wayne Ethridge noted. "I just finished linear equations and a lot of class exercises were done in pairs. My students are used to it. They know what to do and what I expect. Maybe that helps to make it successful. Role-playing, huh? Did you every try making a list of what they have to include in their roles? I think that helps them conquer their fear of looking silly in front of their peers."

Reg added, "I do that, and it does work; but my real problem has been explaining what I'm doing and why. Have any of you had to explain to parents what you're doing? Last year I had parents questioning me about the collaboration their students described to them. They were worried that I wasn't standing at the board explaining all the time. One actually said that's what they pay me to do. Talking to all of you since September has helped me clear up my own thinking, though. This year parents seem to accept my explanations. I must be communicating better! I know it's because I'm listening to what all of you say."

The SAM group has met on a regular basis to discuss their experiences with collaborative and cooperative learning. Two years ago, the main questions of the faculty centered on the terminology of the two approaches. Most teachers saw them as the same approach with two names. No one was much good at verbalizing the differences, so they were hard to explain to faculty who were already resistant to trying an activity that meant students had to talk to each other or that rows had to be moved.

Cooperative learning activities and collaborative strategies do have much in common. In *Learning Together and Alone* (1999), Johnson and Johnson describe the characteristics common to both approaches:

- They involve a task or activity suited to group investigation.

- They utilize small groups.

- They involve cooperative behavior.

- An element of productive interdependence exists.

- Individual students are held accountable and responsible.

(Davidson, 1994, in *Creativity and Collaborative Learning*.)

Collaborative strategies, however, are different from cooperative learning. They are designed with the assumption that students participating in the activities are competent in the social skills required to work in peer groups. It is important, then, to address social skills as we implement cooperative learning strategies designed to develop this social competence. Berry (1991) suggests that both the Civil Rights Movement and the Women's Rights Movement were actually the products of collaborative initiatives. These movements were able to succeed because their members contributed their perspectives and understanding of the common issues. Through controversy and discussion, they were able to move forward and accomplish what had not been done before.

Collaborative learning operates on the principle that the students will each contribute meaningful chunks of information to the group with which they are working. Complex models of collaboration can move students beyond the simpler structures and expectations on which cooperative learning is founded. Collaborative learning strategies are effective as instructional tools that encourage all students to participate actively in making meaning of information that is to be learned. Collaborative learning not only promotes the quantity of knowledge gained but also provides for the development of a greater depth of understanding of that knowledge.

In collaborative learning, students work jointly to share information and perspectives. Teachers encourage their students to share their interpretations of content information and personal perspectives about that information. In collaborative learning, students use other students as resources but are also encouraged to question their peers' views. Collaborative learning often encourages dissent among group members so that meaningful discussion about content knowledge can occur. Determining multiple responses to questions or multiple solutions to problems further promotes collaborative learning. The diversity of knowledge brought out in collaborative learning groups enriches students' original knowledge base. Collaborative learning makes positive, productive use of student differences. Bruffee (1995) concluded that collaborative learning requires students to use "levels of ingenuity and inventiveness that many students never knew they had" (p. 48).

Lunsford (1991) suggests that collaborative learning leads students to higher achievement overall. Lunsford supports the following conclusions about the role of collaborative learning approaches in student learning:

- ♦ Collaboration promotes problem finding as well as problem solving.

- ♦ Collaboration aids in learning abstractions.

- ♦ Collaboration facilitates transfer and assimilation.

- ♦ Collaboration fosters interdisciplinary thinking.

- ♦ Collaboration leads to sharper critical thinking.

After participating in collaborative learning groups, students may retain their initial personal views, but the diversity of information that they investigated will enrich these views. Students may also alter their views as a result of participating in collaborative learning groups because of the impact of their peers. As students share information and gain knowledge, views within the group may still vary. Collaborative learning values and, indeed, promotes divergence supported by information and knowledge.

Collaboration occurs as small groups of students address course concepts. Clark and Starr (1991) describe the various types of small groups that teachers often use. Students form small groups to complete some type of committee work; to participate in review games; to facilitate a discussion; and to pursue special interests. Clark and Starr suggest that small groups could be introduced by first creating very simple assignments such as the construction of a bulletin board or the distribution of this week's lab equipment. Clustering students into small groups provides teachers with many additional benefits. Figure 1.1. lists several of these benefits.

**FIGURE 1.1. SUMMARY OF SMALL GROUP BENEFITS
AS DESCRIBED BY CLARK AND STARR (1991)**

Small groups are useful for...

♦ One-on-one instruction time

♦ Giving students opportunities to work with a diversity of peers

♦ Developing problem-solving skills, independent learning, and self-directed planning

♦ Covering a large amount of information

♦ Providing in-depth experiences

♦ Nurturing study skills and research experiences

TEACHER DECISION MAKING

"When should I use collaborative strategies, which ones should I use, and what makes collaborative strategies better in a certain lesson than other approaches?" The answers to these questions depend on the teacher's analysis of the curriculum, the variety of teaching strategies that could address a curricular concern, his or her own strengths, the students in each classroom, time elements, and a host of other variables.

Henson (1993) suggests that teachers consider the following questions as they make decisions about their teaching strategies:

♦ Who makes the decision in your district about the nature of this course, the content to be covered and the overall goals to be achieved?

♦ Who determines the length of time you can spend on any one part of the course's content?

♦ What degree of control do you have over the nature, content, goals, and time related to this course?

♦ What are your goals for the course?

♦ What content do you want students to learn in this course?

♦ What experiences do you consider crucial for your students in this course?

♦ Are field trips or speakers beneficial in achieving the goals of the course?

♦ To what degree are you required—or do you wish—to follow the textbook chapters?

♦ What units should be part of this course and in what sequence should they be used throughout the term or year?

♦ How much time do you consider necessary to study any one part of the course's content in depth?

♦ What is the best strategy to use for each of the goals you have for student learning in this course?

♦ In what ways will collaborative strategies increase the learning and the developmental goals of your classroom?

Teachers sometimes do not realize the extent to which they really are the experts in the classroom for this particular content, these particular students, and this setting. Henson reflects on the need to use decision making in long-term planning:

> As you might suspect, the teacher plays a significant role in making all these important decisions. According to Joyce (1979, p. 75), most of the important decisions by teachers are long term in their influence, as opposed to the influence of lesson-by-lesson planning. This means that the quality of education each of your future students (and these may number in the thousands) will receive will depend on how much you are involved in long-term planning. (Joyce, 1993, p. 16)

Milner and Milner (1999) agree with the advantages of long-term decision making and planning. "Research shows that what separates able teachers from excellent teachers is the latter's ability to develop long-range plans"(p. 402). When planning units for a course, simple and complex collaborative strategies should be considered.

SIMPLE COLLABORATIVE LEARNING MODELS

Several collaborative learning strategies are simple to plan yet interesting for students, a good change of pace in the classroom, and effective learning tools. Having students brainstorm and using buzz groups, peer editing, and role-playing are among the easiest strategies to plan and implement.

BRAINSTORMING

Putting students into small groups to generate ideas and examples is an effective strategy for encouraging students to analyze, synthesize, and evaluate course concepts. For every idea that a student contributes, other group members generate three more. Each time this occurs, students experience the realization that responses to any question can be varied and that their own view is not the only possible way to look at an issue.

When students come together to brainstorm, they address an initial prompt given by the teacher and use their own personal experiences and prior knowledge to suggest topics or directions to solve the presented problem. When Marci Elkin wanted her seventh-grade English students to start their writing workshop assignments, she had the challenge of moving her students from the "I can't do this. I don't know what to write!" stage to the prewriting stage. She decided to form small groups giving them the direction to think about and discuss childhood memories. Marci watched and listened as students generated lists of memories; students moved from the writer's block stage to realizing that deciding what to write about doesn't have to be hard. This nonthreatening way "in" to a writing assignment has another benefit: Students listen to each other's experiences and realize that not everyone has grown up the same way. Because group members must accept all students' memories for the list, students begin to experience understanding, and they have the eye-opening opportunity to listen to a diversity of experiences and views of others. For some, it may be the first time they have thought about the fact that not everyone believes the same things are important and not everyone comes from the same type of background.

This simple collaborative strategy provides the students with a more positive first experience in the writing process. It gives them breadth of types of childhood memories instead of only their own. The benefits of brainstorming extend beyond the list for writing; the students practice listening to others and have the opportunity to compare and contrast what they think is memorable with the childhood experiences of their classmates.

BUZZ GROUPS

Using buzz groups can prepare students for the next classroom activity: a large-group discussion. In his American history class, Reg Moski plans to discuss the Japanese internment camps in the 1940s. He capitalizes on the students' hostility toward the new school proposal to make all students wear uniforms, using the issue to prepare them for his lesson. Before launching into whole-group discussion, he writes the following question on the board, "To make sure that no freshmen are influenced by upperclassmen to boycott the new uniform rule, upperclass students will remain in the cafeteria each morning until all freshmen are in their homerooms. Upperclassmen will not be permitted in the halls after school when freshmen are at their lockers. They will be required to wait in their eighth-period class until all freshmen have left the building, causing them to exit 10 minutes after the regular dismissal bell. What is your opinion of the new rules?" He directs them to gather in their small groups to share their opinions on the proposed school "regulations" for five minutes.

Because this is an unannounced assignment, the students will be sharing quick impressions and opinions. Before coming to the whole-class discussion on segregating groups of citizens thought to be capable of undermining the nation's war efforts, the students will have already voiced their opinions and listened to views of their small-group partners on a similar issue rooted in their own environment and experience. They already have a depth of understanding not usually achieved in the classroom when such personal links are not first explored. They can make connections between their own situation and historical events on a much larger scale. Reg observes, "I find that buzz groups really oil them up. Discussion isn't like pulling teeth after the buzz groups have responded." Buzz groups can be used to address a variety of assignments such as suggesting ways to solve a problem in the community or creating a list of questions to ask a guest speaker.

NOTE

Although buzz groups are easy to plan and to implement, teachers need to be very concerned about the makeup of the group members. Putting four strongly opinionated students in one group can cause arguments to flare up quickly. If the students are not sufficiently skilled in handling controversy, the purpose of the activity may be lost in the emotional turmoil. Also, adhering to time limits is important. Teachers can become so impressed that everyone is talking that they assume learning continues to take place. It is true that tangential conversations can be very valuable, and teachers should recognize that benefit. In reality, teachers need to assess the context of the conversations taking place, looking for fruitful digressions and allowing them. At the same time, teachers need to keep track of time and pull back students who may be going off in totally unrelated directions.

PEER EDITING

For any writing assignment, whether it is a writing log for geometry class or a position paper for government class, peer editing provides an excellent small-group activity that promotes analysis and asks students to exercise critical judgment. In addition, the sometimes-delicate process of providing helpful comments without dwelling on negatives gives students invaluable experience in productive social interactions.

Constructive peer editing is very hard for students to do. It requires teachers to first train students to read each other's work with the object of helping that person create a better product. To encourage such positive analysis, teachers can provide guidelines for students to follow and display them in the classroom. Peer-editing rubrics are presented in Chapter 5; Figure 1.2 also lists suggestions.

FIGURE 1.2. SUGGESTIONS FOR PREPARING PEER EDITORS FOR THEIR WORK

- ◆ Read the entire piece before considering any comments.

- ◆ Negative comments will not be tolerated.

- ◆ Use information-gathering questions such as, "I'm not sure. What do you mean?"

- ◆ List two things you like or feel are good about the piece.

- ◆ Give one suggestion for the author to consider adding.

- ◆ Go over the rubric for this assignment and check all criteria covered in the piece.

- ◆ Circle anything left out for the writer's benefit.

- ◆ Review your editing with your partner.

More comprehensive rubrics, such as the Pennsylvania Holistic Writing Guide, can also be used. Providing peer editors with guidelines and insisting that they adhere to the rules encourage students to experience more in-depth learning and productive social interaction. American schools are sometimes criticized for offering students learning that is very broad in scope but very shallow in depth. These critics say that teachers do not encourage students to apply critical thinking skills. However, when students engage in peer critiques, they have to employ higher-order thinking skills. Not only do they see the way other students tackle the same assignment, but they also experience modes of expressions and examples that they may not have thought of themselves. Reading the work of others can promote a wider understanding of the assignment and an appreciation for the value of other students' views. Asking the partner for clarification and starting a dialogue limited only to positive comments on the margin of the paper help students understand the process of working together for mutual success. A checklist of proofreading points might form the basis for the analysis during the second peer-editing session that is held after the students have revised their work based on the first peer-editing conference. Many checklists, suggested peer-editing strategies, and points to consider exist, and teachers use a variety of them depending on the age group of their students (Ashworth, 1992; Golub, 1988; Milner & Milner 1999; Posamentier & Stepelman, 1995; Shrum and Glisan, 1994).

ROLE-PLAYING

Some teachers have had positive experiences with role-playing while others have not. Jane Richards' biology students were not receptive to her attempts at using role-playing to illustrate the opinions of the different interest groups on the issue of protecting the wetlands. Wayne's suggestions that she try giving students more direction and having them list information or address certain issues are good points to consider. Spontaneous role-playing is often very uncomfortable for adolescents. They are already in a constant state of anxiety over the way their peers perceive them. Letting loose and adopting a "role" is often just too much of a leap, especially for high-school students. However, specific directions about certain points to cover or issues to discuss help to distance their personal anxieties from the implementation of the assignment. Once students become used to role-playing and realize that everyone is playing the part of someone else, they tend to relax and enjoy the opportunity to be someone else for a few minutes.

Foreign-language teachers use the role-playing collaborative strategy often because simulating conversational language opportunities is crucial. Students can be assigned to groups of four, but it is also common to have pairs of students in role-playing situations. In Rick's Spanish I class, the students study a unit on foods and the restaurant. He plans a restaurant scenario with a table, chairs, place settings, and menus. Waiter and tourist roles are assigned. On cards, Rick has given each student a list of items. That list guides the students so that they can use the vocabulary of the restaurant and foods to simulate the experience of eating out in Madrid. Figure 1.3 presents sample cards.

Role-playing is useful when the students pair up to conduct interviews of each other. Jane might have better success if she splits her biology class into pairs, giving each pair cards. On one card is the agenda of the land developer. On the other card is the agenda of the farmer. This simple list becomes a guide for students to follow as they adopt the roles of representatives of the two factions in a wetlands controversy.

FIGURE 1.3. SAMPLE ROLE-PLAYING CARDS

Bienvenidos a Madrid Greetings Info. on the restaurant Taking the order Two questions about the tourist's reason for visiting Madrid Switch cards; reverse roles	Bienvenidos a Madrid Greetings Questions on specials Giving the order Answering the two questions Switch cards; reverse roles

This role-playing activity can turn easily into a group interview with the whole-class audience questioning the representatives. In this application, each representative will have his or her card indicating the agenda to be explained and defended. Students in the audience are responsible for asking at least one question in this informal group interview. Through this process, the class listens to two sides of the issue and probes the wetlands controversy in greater depth by asking questions. The teacher can function as the resident expert when necessary, so that questions that are too involved for the representatives to address completely can be clarified by the expert.

Students seem to listen to each other and to consider the views of their peers more closely than they attend to the opinions of most adults. The group interview capitalizes on this, expanding student understanding of the issue and at the same time exposing them to opposing views, both of which may have merit. Thus, an element of judgment enters as students consider the representatives' positions, draw on new information or insights given by the resident expert, and ask questions. Such a collaborative activity can provide a greater depth of understanding than the textbook chapter presents.

FISHBOWL SMALL GROUP COLLABORATION

This strategy combines the efforts of small groups with individual presentation as students to consider an issue, decide on the group's viewpoint on that issue, and send a representative to the center of the room to present the opinion of the group. The representative presents the prepared view and also has the opportunity to engage in spontaneous dialogue with the other fishbowl presenters.

> **NOTE**
>
> Teachers can also use this strategy in preparation for a later, more formal debate.

Jane Richards can involve all of her students in the issues of wetlands protection versus farming use or developmental land use by using the fishbowl strategy. She first divides the class into small groups with some prearranged criterion in mind. Students in each group decide the view they will present and their argument's points. They will then choose a spokesperson to give their point of view in the fishbowl. The whole class listens to the representatives of the groups as they give their group's viewpoint and supporting reasons for their decision. After listening carefully to each participant in the fishbowl and taking notes on the various views and supporting reasons for those views, students return to their small groups—or begin an individual assignment—to create a position paper on the issue. Figure 1.4 shows the structure of the three-part fishbowl just described.

Students have trouble when trying to interact immediately in speaking activities that require them to use content knowledge and apply that to spontaneous interaction. Teachers wishing to discuss controversial issues and put students into roles that explore the several sides of an issue can employ role-playing first, then engage students in three-part interviews and finally plan a fishbowl activity to introduce the class to informal debate.

Using the fishbowl allows the teacher to encourage several critical-thinking skills while also promoting clarity in argumentation. All three activities can prepare students to engage in more formal debate settings later in the unit or later on during the year.

PAIRS COLLABORATION IN PROBLEM SOLVING

Mathematics classes provide an excellent opportunity for pairs collaboration in problem solving. Waychoff (1996) uses pairs collaboration in his unit on linear equations, displayed in Figure 1.5.

FIGURE 1.4. THREE-PART FISHBOWL ACTIVITY

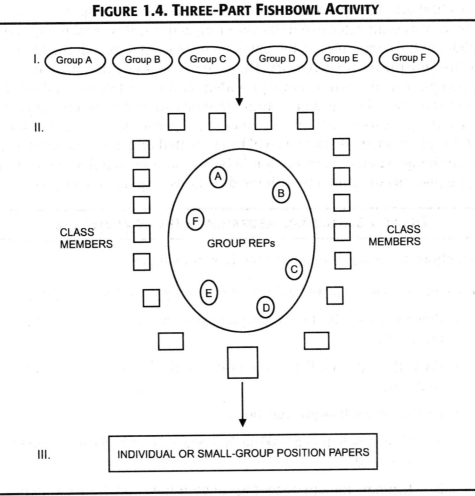

FIGURE 1.5. PAIRS COLLABORATION FOR PROBLEM SOLVING IN ALGEBRA

Calculator Worksheet

1. Students will work with their partner for pair activities.

2. Each partner will use the TI 81 graphing calculator to graph the equations listed on the board, record the viewing rectangle used, and estimate the x and y intercepts.

3. Partners will discuss possible strategies to achieve the objectives in #2.

4. Students will be evaluated with the TALK (Donato, 1992) Checklist and by the degree to which they contribute to the class discussion following the activity.

5. Time limit for the actual activity (10 minutes).

Waychoff also uses pairs to collaborate on a computer project for the same unit. Since this is an extensive data-collecting activity, it will take two days to complete. In the computer lab, the pairs are instructed to search the Internet to locate housing prices in a given city. They are to pick a city that they feel would be a good place to live. Students are provided with a list of World Wide Web addresses to facilitate their searches. Students must collect data including prices of homes and square footage from a number of properties in the city that they selected. Emphasizing that students will be evaluated on their computations, answers to the questions, computer lab behavior, and productive interaction in pairs, he presents the students with the directions displayed in Figure 1.6.

FIGURE 1.6. PAIRS COLLABORATION IN THE COMPUTER LAB

Directions for completing your search of housing prices:

♦ Using the data collected in your WWW search, do the following:

- Plot the data collected on graph paper and draw the best-fit line for the data.

- Write the equation that corresponds to the best-fit in slope-intercept form.

- Answer the following questions:

  1. How much does a 5000 sq. ft. home sell for in the area you researched?

  2. Estimate the square footage of your house and estimate what it would be worth in that housing market.

  3. What are the x and y intercepts of this graph?

  4. Estimate the price of a 7500-sq. ft. home.

  5. Estimate the square footage of a $200,000 house.

Students can use pairs collaboration in the computer lab to engage in problem solving and to practice other critical-thinking skills. Also, Schipke (1991) encourages student pairs to use the computer to create journal entries based on critical-thinking goals and then to share them with partners. These activities lead students to become aware of the value of the development of in-depth thinking, join in meaningful conversation, state their own opinions and think independently, analyze their own views related to those expressed by others, and make decisions. This approach to critical thinking relies on sequential procedures beginning with writing, then collaborating to share responses either in group discussion or between partners, and finally evaluating what they've done. The steps shown in Figure 1.7 might be explained as a cyclical process.

FIGURE 1.7. COLLABORATIVE COMPUTER LAB JOURNALS

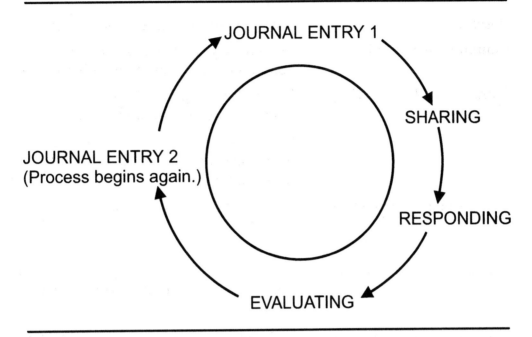

Schipke suggests giving students a list of questions to use in a specific assignment to help them develop critical-thinking skills as they engage in self and partner analysis, discussion, and observation of divergent views. Questions might require students to examine the details of their entry or to state the educated guess that they are making in their responses. Students can analyze any concept that they have accepted as true in order to arrive at their conclusions and give examples that support the view they have taken on an issue. If, in analyzing their assumptions, students see that they cannot support the views they originally had, they have the opportunity to reshape their responses. Teachers can ask students to collect and provide data to include in their response to the writing prompt and to then compare their observations with those of their partner or others in the class. During the partner discussion or the larger group discussion, students who have already analyzed their own views use the same tools to study the opinions expressed by their classmates. The 12 critical-thinking skills and sample questions designed to develop each skill appear in Figure 1.8.

FIGURE 1.8. QUESTIONS TO ADDRESS CRITICAL-THINKING SKILLS IN COMPUTER LAB JOURNAL WRITING

Critical Thinking Skill	*Sample Question*
1. Observation	What specific details are you listing?
2. Examining Assumptions	What have you assumed to be true? Is your assumption based on verifiable fact?
3. Gathering and Classifying Data	Where did you gather information? Is your classification outline logical?
4. Making Comparisons	When asked to compare two characters, have you stated their similarities and differences?
5. Considering Classifications	Is there another way to organize your information? Would it be just as good, better, or not as logical?
6. Making Educated Guesses	What do you think has happened or will happen? Have you stated your hypothesis clearly?
7. Making Critical Judgments	Did you explain your reasons for picking one view over another?
8. Interpreting Information	When you examined your data and the statements you have made as a result, do the data verify your judgment?
9. Creating Imaginary Scenarios	Is your creation believable? What details have you included to make it so?
10. Using Marking Codes	Have you identified and labeled your assumptions, judgments, values statements?
11. Solving Problems	Have you collected enough data to come to a logical conclusion? Did you have to address any subproblems in order to solve the problem? Do your data support your conclusions?
12. Summarizing Information	Have you included all data needed to support your view? Have you stated the summary clearly? Are there any data included originally that are not needed for the summary?

Teachers can evaluate pairs collaboration as students are working at their computer stations. For example, Donato's TALK checklist illustrated in Chapter 6 might be used. Students can complete self-evaluations or submit checklists based on the steps of the critical-thinking journal cycle. Teachers can also collect journal samples, grading them on the criteria established for the continuing journal activities or for a specific journal assignment.

Schipke (1991) suggests these activities:

♦ Have students identify the assumptions that a character made about a situation or character in a story, book, play, or poem (p. 89).

♦ Have students compare their views of how a character is portrayed in a book and a movie (the character's physical appearance, behavior, etc.). Are the print and visual presentations alike or different? On what points (if any) do they agree or disagree? (p. 89)

♦ Have students imagine what it would be like if they were to meet a particular character from a story, book, play, or poem they are reading, and then have them write a detailed account of the character and the encounter (p. 91).

Monroe (1993) suggests that biology students might use the computer lab either individually or in pairs and larger groups in order to review content or to expand on content covered in class. He summarizes the use of a networked lab in which a letter from a fictitious relative is posted. In his example, "Aunt Gladys" writes to tell a student that she has heard that he is terrific in biology. Therefore, she assumes he can explain all that she and "Uncle Elmer" want to know. She cautions him that both she and her husband have little education so the response to her question will have to be very clear. The biology teacher then poses the Aunt Gladys question for students to answer. Criteria include the citing of at least two references, a clear and to-the-point explanation, and possible information gleaned from the class's "resident expert," the biology teacher. Students can also include other resident experts, but none of the expert testimony can be counted as one of the two cited references. Some of Monroe's questions include the following:

♦ I was watching one of those Marlin Perkins shows about sharks, and he said that sharks will attack a metal boat, but they usually won't attack a wooden one, unless they're provoked. Why? (p. 106)

♦ Cousin Elmer John just bought a purebred Doberman, and it turned out to have some kind of hip disease. My neighbor Veronica Shmeltz's purebred St. Bernard had the same problem, and so did Barney Harbottle's purebred German Shepherd. Is this a coincidence? If not, what is the disease, and why do purebred dogs get it? (p. 107)

♦ Cousin Elmer John just had to go to the doctor because he stepped on a nail, and the doctor gave him a tetanus shot. And I wondered, how do shots work? Why does getting a shot give you immunity against disease? Does the shot for a viral disease differ from a shot for a bacterial disease? Why haven't doctors been able to make a shot for colds? (p. 108)

Students respond to Aunt Gladys and then deposit their responses in the networked lab's drop folder for the teacher's evaluation.

Posing Aunt Gladys letters could also take the form suggested by Shipke (1991), asking students to gather information, create a journal response, compare it with their partner's response, and participate in a discussion about the issue.

PAIRS COLLABORATION IN THE INFORMATION GAP ACTIVITY

Another pairs collaboration strategy involves the predicting of information when one partner has a complete set of data such as a map, a diagram of the water cycle, or a drawing of a house plan, for example. The student with the incomplete copy needs to question the partner holding the completed data sheet so that the questioning student can fill in the information missing on his or her copy. Shrum and Glisan (1994) label this an *information gap activity* and suggest that foreign-language students can improve their vocabulary; sharpen their speaking, listening, and writing skills; and develop their questioning and analytical thinking skills by participating in it. The student writes the answers to questions such as "How many rooms are in this house?" or "On the second floor, my copy shows just one big room. Is that right or are there more? How many are there? What are the dimensions of each room?" Looking at the incomplete copy, the questioner might ask, "I have only a sofa labeled as the furniture in the living room. Is there a chair?" In this manner, the questioning student completes the data sheet. The partners can then evaluate their work as the partners by comparing both information sheets to determine the accuracy of the inserted data used to fill in the "gaps."

THE WRITING RELAY

A simple collaboration strategy for writing can be used in any content area. Students can develop creative thinking by participating in this activity and building a story from a *story starter*. The first person begins with the teacher prompt, in this case a story starter, and adds one sentence to move the story along. Each person in the row adds a sentence. The paper comes back to the first person in the row. If the story is not finished, the row repeats the process until it is. When all rows have completed their relay-writing stories, they share their creation with the class.

If the teacher wants students to use their prior information or life-experience knowledge to create a list related to the topic to be studied next, the writing relay works well. Logsdon (1996) uses the writing relay as a warm-up exercise for her seventh-grade life science class as they study ecosystems. She passes out a sheet of paper to the first person in each row with the direction that the student needs to write down one fact about water (other than "it's wet") before passing the paper back to the student behind him or her. The paper continues down the row until the last person writes a fact about water not previously listed. After each row's paper is complete, the students pass it up to the first person in the row. The teacher lists the facts on the board as the students contribute information from their lists.

COMPLEX MODELS OF COLLABORATIVE LEARNING

SIMULATIONS

Simple role-playing combines with more complex problem solving in the simulation activity. When the simulation is constructed to approximate a real situation and when it is carefully planned so that students can carry out their assigned roles with full understanding of the agenda of their character, this collaborative activity can be a very powerful strategy for learning.

As with every classroom strategy, teachers decide the rationale for using a simulation game. Simulations can be used to introduce concepts as well as to review factual information. Planning a good simulation takes thought and time. The reason for including it should be that it provides the best experience for students in the learning of a particular concept or the reinforcement of specific information.

After the teacher determines the goals to be achieved through the simulation, the next step is to decide on an event or a setting for the activity. Clark and Starr (1991) explain that the choice of a current event has the advantage that the students have a better understanding of the event, and they may recognize and even be aware of the agendas of the various people involved. It may also be easier to construct since the teacher has recently seen the people involved through television interviews, has followed news commentary, and has read about the controversial elements of the issue. Its disadvantage may be that the students may be too close to the event. And emotional reactions, biases, and shifting perceptions of the event may be occurring as new information comes out about it.

Instead of choosing a current event or historical situation, the teacher may decide to construct a hypothetical situation. Since the students play roles based on agendas created by the teacher, they may not experience the conflicting emotions that a current event might encourage.

The teacher constructs the situation, the problem to be solved through the simulation activity, the roles of all the major players and their agendas, and also the roles of the support players and their agendas related to the major player. The teacher also creates directions for the game and gives them to the group before the game. Covering the points listed in Figure 1.9. will help to ensure a successful game.

FIGURE 1.9. STEPS IN PLANNING A SIMULATION GAME

1. Decide the rationale for using this activity.
2. Pick a current or historical event or construct a hypothetical situation as the setting for the game.
3. List the concepts or the review information to be introduced or reinforced by the game.
4. Create a problem to be solved through the activity.
5. List all major roles to be played and the power positions, and write a description of each player's agenda.
6. Assign support roles to students based on allegiances to major players; write a description of the agenda for each major player's support group.
7. Make up the directions for the game procedure.

Simulations can be run in small groups or in whole-class settings. In either case, teachers need to allow the game to progress once the rules have been explained, the students have their roles and agendas, the time limit is established for the game, and everyone understands that the problem must be solved by the end of the game. The teacher allows the students to run the game and interjects only if the game breaks down or if a behavior incident occurs. With students taking on the personae of their characters and spontaneously interjecting commentary into the game, statements that they make may bring up related issues for the group to address as they seek to solve the teacher-posed problem.

Used as an introductory activity, the simulation game can prepare students to think in depth about a complex concept, which the teacher will explore following the game. In the following simulation, students experience the problems faced when players with different agendas need to make decisions that may not favor their individual agendas.

The teacher of a world history class wants the students to understand the problems that caused nations to polarize in the years before World War I (Bevevino, Dengel, & Adams, 1999). Creating a simulation that involves siblings who need to make decisions involving space, money, jobs, and power prepares the students for later analysis of the issues of territorialism, economic pressures, employment issues, and powerful personalities contributing to the war. After the simulation, the teacher ties in the family problems and power struggles as a microcosm of the worldwide situation. The students use their prior knowledge and experiences to solve the problems posed in the game. In groups of four, they follow two major rules: each sibling must work to come to a productive compromise and any solution they accept must provide some benefit to each of the members.

The hypothetical scenario for the game indicates that the four students are siblings, 17, 13, 9, and 5 years of age. They live with their working parents in a two-bedroom apartment. After they assign themselves to the roles, they open an envelope that contains the agenda of that role. Figure 1.10 lists the four assigned roles.

**FIGURE 1.10 ASSIGNED ROLES FOR SIBLINGS
FOR THE SOCIAL STUDIES SIMULATION**

Role 1: The 17-year old: You have football (or soccer) practice on M, T, and Th at 6:00 pm. You work at McDonald's on Saturday from 3:00 to 11:00 pm. You drive. You also have a significant other so you wish to go out on (and pay for) a date once a week.

Role 2: The 13-year old: You go to Girl Scouts (Boy Scouts) each Th at 3:30 pm; you also play intramural basketball on M at 3:00 pm; you need new basketball shoes and you've been told by your parents to save at least half of the money yourself. They'll pay the rest.

Role 3: The 9-year old: You have a Brownie Troop meeting (Cub Scouts) each T at 4:00 pm; you like to play at a friend's house each Saturday from 8:00 am until 1:00 pm; you know you can attain a higher grade in science if you construct a model of the eruption of Mt. St. Helens, and you need money for supplies.

Role 4: The 5-year old: You want to go with your friend to gymnastics lessons on Saturday at 10:00 am; you have also lost your favorite stuffed animal so you've cried for days, and think buying a new version of Fluffy will make everything better; but since you were the one who lost Fluffy, your parents want you to save some money toward the purchase.

After reviewing their individual roles, the players begin their problem-solving simulation with the directions shown in Figure 1.11.

FIGURE 1.11. SIMULATION GAME—SOCIAL STUDIES

In this simulation, your mission is to decide the following:

1. Space allocation in your bedroom including assigning bunk beds (2 sets), desks (2), drawer spaces (5 large, 7 small), closet space (2).

2. Work assignments including transporting (and staying with if needed) all children to their activities; other work assignments include setting the table nightly, washing dishes each night, cleaning the bathroom twice a week, removing garbage daily, cleaning the kitchen floor twice a week, keeping the bedroom clean, washing clothes once a week, folding and putting clothes away once a week, monitoring phone conversations to 5 minutes per call, packing school lunches S-Th. nights, checking that everyone's homework is done four times a week, mediating arguments among siblings.

3. Allocation of funds includes $10 per week for all allowances together; the parents have also decided that extra jobs around the apartment will receive an additional payment of $1 per job. The four of you must decide what types of extra jobs exist and which sibling will earn the extra money per his/her qualifications to do the job.

Remember: At the conclusion of the game, you must be able to defend your solutions to the space, work, and funds allocations according to the two criteria of productive compromise and mutual benefit.

Other simulations are often based on town-meeting scenarios. The purpose for this particular scenario is to review the types of taxes just studied in class. The group may gather for a village meeting in order to explore funding for a new school; they will look at various types of taxes such as income tax, sales tax, user fees, excise tax, estate tax, and real estate tax. The teacher assigns major players and provides their agendas. Support players are created to emphasize the agenda of each of the main players. A mayor, whose role is to limit the time for each person to speak, brings up any taxation method not suggested by the other players and moves the citizens toward a solution for their problem before the meeting ends. The rules of the game include the need for each person to speak; the inclusion in the discussion of each type of tax studied; and requirement that alternative solutions be examined and one choice made by a majority vote before the end of the "meeting." The student leading the meeting needs a very detailed description of his or her role. In Figure 1.12, the setting is Northwest Pennsylvania in 1870, and the directions list the leader's background, duties, and subject matter to be included.

FIGURE 1.12. SIMULATION GAME: RAISING MONEY FOR EDUCATION

Simulation

Mayor's duties for the village meeting on raising money to employ a teacher for the town's children. (You have 4.)

Background: The date is October 6, 1870. The children of the village haven't had a teacher in three years since Mr. Jones' Great Aunt Izzie died during the record-breaking blizzard of 1867.

You are the village's medical person but not a doctor. No one pays you money. Instead they give you dried cow dung for fuel and extra vegetables when possible. However, your wife has just died, leaving you with her small nest egg saved from the sale of pigeon eggs from the birds roosting in the eaves of your house. This money barely covers the monthly financial obligations of raising four children.

Your duties: You are to conduct a 45-minute village meeting at the end of which some solution must be reached to pay the new teacher, who is asking $8 per month plus 1/6 of each family's cow dung supply to heat the shack behind the saloon. That is the only space available for the classroom. He will also live there. He has agreed to bring his own supplies: one book, three pencils, a small packet of paper, and a dunce cap free of charge.

The decision as to what way the money is to be raised must be made today before the stage leaves for Waterford, or he will take the job which they are offering him at $5 per month and all the free liquor he wants. He also will be permitted to sell for his own profit any leftover cow dung not used to heat the school.

The new school teacher candidate wants to stay here because he is in love with Mrs. Callahan, the town's librarian, whose husband is in the state penitentiary for horse stealing and will be hanged next week. (He will be leaving a small inheritance for Mrs. Callahan.)

You will open the discussion and allow each speaker to have the floor for no more than a minute at a time. Speakers may request to speak more than once, but everyone needs to speak at least once.

The following are taxes that you should suggest for raising the money if the citizens do not bring them up: Property tax—*Who pays? How much must each landowner pay per year?* Income tax—*Who pays? How much must each person pay per year? Will anyone be exempt?* Sales tax—*On all goods? On all except food? On medicine? At what rate?* Excise tax—*On fuels? On liquor? On tobacco? On something else? How much?* User fees—*On what? How much?* Estate tax—*On inheritances? Should it be retroactive? How much?* Wage tax—*On which citizens? How much? Other ideas?*

Other major players need agendas, some of which support other players, and some of which clash with the goals of other players. The creation of players and agendas is limited only by the teacher's imagination. Figure 1.13 shows major player roles for the sample village meeting simulation.

FIGURE 1.13. MAJOR PLAYER ROLES FOR THE VILLAGE MEETING SIMULATION

Mrs. Callahan: You are about to be widowed since your husband is in the state penitentiary and will be hanged next week. You will receive a small inheritance of $2 per month. You own your own home and are the mother of two children of school age. In addition, you are the town librarian, and your salary is $1 per month. The new teacher candidate is in love with you. In addition, Mr. Wickerly is also interested in you.

Mr. Wickerly: You make your living by raising cattle to sell to the markets in the surrounding villages. Your farm is on the other side of the bridge that leads into town. Three times a week, you drive cattle over the bridge on your way to the villages west of your farm. You are a landowner, and you also rent out three cottages, one of which is rented at 50¢ per month to Mrs. Williams. Your monthly income is $50. However, you are a philanthropist. You give generously each month as much cattle dung as people want as long as they cross the bridge from the village and clean your barn. You hate teachers since Mr. Jones' Great Aunt Izzie told every one that you were just like your no-good uncle Lem. You see no reason for children to be educated since you've done fine with little learning. Also, you have romantic notions about Mrs. Callahan. She is young and strong. Possibly, she could have even more children to help on the farm. You know that the new teacher applicant is a rival for her attention.

Mr. Jones: You are the village's banker. You make approximately $45 per month. You own the building housing the bank, the house in which Mrs. Domingo lives, and your own house. You support this new teacher candidate and the idea that the town needs a school. However, you are interested in village politics and feel that Mr. Confusco has too much power. You would like to be the school superintendent. You don't intend to leave this meeting without getting a promise from the citizens to appoint you to the superintendency. You also love your money and want to spend as little of it as possible.

Mr. Penman: You are the village storeowner. You have four children, all of whom are now grown. You earn $15 per month, but you also support your sister, Mrs. Suffersilently. She has three children, would like to have more, and is married to Herbert Suffersilently who would like to start a newspaper in town but can neither read nor write. Since his dream of being an editor has not come true, he spends his days drinking in the saloon and his evenings talking with his wife about the joys of large families. You have heard them talking and are sure that they will move to Waterford if the new teacher is not hired today.

Mrs. Suffersilently: You are Mr. Penman's sister. He supports you, your husband, and your three children. You would like to have four more children, but Mr. Penman disapproves. Your husband drinks all day because his dream of becoming a newspaper editor has not come true. He can neither read nor write. You want a school so that he can learn these skills and so your children can go to school. You resent your brother's prosperity and are sure that you could take care of your family if your husband could start his newspaper business. You disagree with everything your brother says.

Mrs. Byrd: You run the saloon and make approximately $20 per month after paying Mr. Knotingly $5 per month to throw obnoxious people out of the establishment. You have two children, one of whom does know how to read and could be ready to become the local teacher after another year of practicing. The other child is 9 years old and has never been to school. Your daughter has refused to help her sister learn to read. You own the shack behind the saloon and are willing to allow the village school to be held there.

After creating major players whose agendas will coincide or conflict with the types of taxes to be reviewed in the game, the teacher clusters the other class members into support groups for the major players. The support group players also need to know their agendas. Figure 1.14 illustrates some supporting roles for the village meeting simulation.

The teacher creates major players and support players according to the number of students in the class so that everyone has a role to play. As with role-playing, cards should be given to the players so that they can refer to their own agendas before and during the game.

Debriefing after this simulation includes a review of group processes, clarification of the use of any of the tax types, and observation on the effect of individual agendas on community decision making.

FIGURE 1.14. POSSIBLE SUPPORT ROLES FOR
THE VILLAGE MEETING SIMULATION

Mrs. Landbottom: You are a good friend of Mrs. Callahan. You support whatever she says. You do not think people appreciate her enough so you are very enthusiastic with your praise of her ideas. In addition, you have already decided that the new teacher applicant is a much better choice to replace her husband than Mr. Wickerly would be.

Mrs. Williams: You are a married woman who has not seen her husband since he disappeared on a hunting trip three years ago. You live across the bridge in a cottage rented for 50¢ per month from Mr. Wickerly. To support yourself and your three school-age children, you catch small game and rodents to sell to the townspeople each day. You want your children to go to school. To do so, they will also have to cross the bridge twice a day.

Miss Domingo: You are a good friend of Mr. Jones. In addition, he holds the mortgage on your house, and you have no money left over at the end of this month to pay him. Therefore, you support enthusiastically any suggestions he makes, no matter what it is.

COLLABORATION THROUGH BRITISH-STYLE DEBATE

Formal debate is by its very nature a mix of collaborative and individual assignments. Ubbelohde (1991) suggests that teachers wanting to incorporate debate as an instructional method might try the less formal British-style debate format, made famous because of its use in the British Parliament, before or instead of formal debate. This less formal structure requires students to address a controversial topic posed by the teacher. The teacher divides the class into two groups: one in favor of a certain course of action and one opposed. Each side prepares its argument and chooses a spokesperson to present its view and supporting documentation.

Each spokesperson has an equal amount of time to present the team's view. In the case of a proposition, however, the teacher might emphasize the need for proponents to prove the value of their proposition by assigning 5 minutes to the spokesperson from that team and 3 minutes to the spokesperson advocating no change from current practice. After the two spokespersons present the views of their sides, the floor is then opened for questions or comments from the remaining members of both groups. The sides must take turns in asking questions or making comments on the speakers' stands. Figure 1.15 presents a suggested format for the British-style debate.

> **NOTE**
>
> When the topic falls into the category of a proposition to be made, the bigger burden of proof rests with the team advocating the proposition. For example, the team representing the need to protect the nation's wetlands may advocate federal sanctions against farmers who drain wetlands on their farms. The opposing team would then argue against such federal sanctions against citizens.

FIGURE 1.15. SUGGESTIONS FOR PLANNING A BRITISH-STYLE DEBATE ON THE ISSUE OF WETLANDS USE

Teacher-Chosen Issue: The Placing of Federal Sanctions on Farmers Who Drain and Use Wetlands

- In preparation for the debate:
  - Split the class into two groups according to the pros and cons of imposing federal sanctions.
  - Instruct the teams to gather information, expert testimony, and personal experience to support the side assigned to the team.
  - Pick the spokesperson for each team.
- During the debate:
  - Allow the speaker proposing the federal sanctions 5 minutes to present his or her team's view and supporting evidence.
  - Allow the speaker against the imposing of federal sanctions 3 minutes to present his or her team's view and supporting evidence.
  - Instruct students from both teams to ask questions and to make comments in an alternating format on the views presented.

COLLABORATION THROUGH FORMAL DEBATE

The simplest type of argumentation can occur through role-playing. The argumentation becomes more complex as teachers use the three-step interview and the British-style debate. The most complex debate strategy is the formal debate. Trowbridge and Bybee (1990) suggest that science teachers consider using the formal debate strategy at times when they want students to gather information and analyze varying opinions on an issue. They advise that teachers pick science-related controversial issues, such as Jane Richards' wetlands discussion. Trowbridge and Bybee (1990) ask teachers to pick small groups of no more than four students assigned to any one view of the issue. Before the debate occurs, students in the groups have to gather data, discuss their facts, and identify their assumptions, their values judgments, and their "if…then" statements. The teacher needs to tell the students which team will be their opposition on the day of the debates. On the day of the debate, the teacher gives clear and specific rules to govern the activity. Figure 1.16 lists several stipulations for teachers to include.

FIGURE 1.16. RULES TO FOLLOW DURING FORMAL DEBATE

Opening will be limited to one speaker from Team A and one from Team B.

- Time: 3 minutes for each speaker.

Rebuttals will be limited to one speaker from Team A and one from Team B.

- Time: 2 minutes for each rebuttal speaker.

Closing statements will be limited to one speaker from Team A and one from Team B.

- Time: 1 minute for each closing speaker.

Total Time: 12 minutes per debate.

No one is allowed to interrupt a speaker.

> Note: When the opposing opening statement speaker is giving his or her address, the rebuttal speaker from the opposing team and the fourth member of that team work together quietly to add responses to the rebuttal speaker's prepared rebuttal so that any opposing arguments not anticipated ahead of time may be inserted before the rebuttal is given.

Formal debates can be conducted in various content area classrooms. The English teacher may structure a debate on the value of reading the classics. The government teacher may choose to structure a formal debate activity to address discrimination in the 1990s. The Spanish teacher can use formal debate to emphasize the need for understanding among cultures. The health teacher can incorporate debate to explore federal funding to specific AIDS research versus the same funding applied to general cancer research. The computer science teacher can address the concerns of the public about increasing technology by structuring a formal debate in which students advocate increased technology or decreased use of technology relative to its effects on society.

The series of debates may be conducted with peer evaluations during each debate or by the class voting for the most convincing team at the conclusion of all debates. In a formal debate, the follow-up may also be the small-group position paper or individual writing assignments that allow the students to reflect on the various sides presented and make judgments on the controversial issue.

COLLABORATION THROUGH LEARNING STATIONS

Setting up a learning center or a series of learning stations is a good way to accomplish several goals. Callahan, Clark, and Kellough (1992) describe three types of learning centers: those dealing with skill building; those providing a variety of activities to explore a concept; and those giving student the opportunity to pursue open-ended goals such as enrichment and creativity. Learning centers are a way to individualize instruction and to provide activities that address individual learning styles. When students utilize a learning center or participate in a series of learning stations, they experience a measure of self-direction, addressing each activity through prepared directions and displays and often using self-correcting answer keys.

Learning stations require careful planning and construction. Teachers need to consider the reason for having students participate in a series of activities instead of involving them in whole-class discussion, mini-lecture, or other learning strategies. If the goals are to provide for individual learning styles, for reinforcing skills, or for exercising critical thinking and creativity, the learning station format can help to achieve those goals. Milner and Milner (1999) point out that four features are needed for the planning of successful learning stations:

- ◆ Choice

- ◆ Variety

- ◆ Movement

- ◆ Interaction

Using content and critical-thinking goals and the size of the class, the teacher determines the number of learning stations to be used. Groups of four are the ideal size because the participants may collaborate on activities, work in two pairs for some assignments, or work individually on assigned tasks. Thus, a total of six learning stations could be used for a class in which 24 students are enrolled. Teachers can create an extra learning station so that students have the option of doing six of the seven. In some cases, that type of choice is acceptable for achieving the goals of the stations. In other cases, the choice is the small group's decision of which station will be their first destination. An element of choice can also be included by giving each group a chance to pick one of the cards on which the teacher has written the number of each station. The group picking Station 4 begins there while the student groups picking Stations 1, 2, 3, 5, or 6 begin at their respective locations.

Time is an important factor in the planning of learning stations. Activities that have approximately equal completion time facilitate order and movement. For example, a station could use a total of 20 minutes to brainstorm a list of possible factors related to handling natural disasters and begin a prewriting a journal entry. Within that 20-minute time limit, 5 minutes might be allotted for brainstorming as a group of four, and 15 minutes could be devoted to individual journal entries on the issue. The rest of the writing-workshop project might be extended over the next two weeks in the regular class setting, culminating in an informative essay on the types of preventative and reactive measures the community should take in order to respond to a flood, earthquake, or hurricane. Planning the stations with these extended possibilities allows the students to move on to the next station in 20 minutes, the time allotted for each of the other station activities. If the class is a group of seventh-grade students, each station activity may last only 10 or 15 minutes each. Chemistry students participating in five performance stations in which they are testing the effects of solvents may complete two stations in a block of 85 minutes the first day, with two more stations to be completed the following day and one station during the first half of class on the third day. On the other hand, high-school juniors studying the concept of the American Dream in literature may complete only one station a day for six days.

After deciding on the goals, the types of activities to be used in the learning stations, and the time element, the teacher concentrates on construction. Because students move to stations, each location needs to be clearly labeled. Stations are student-active, self-directed activities so the instructions must be clearly displayed, and materials must be available. Self-correction keys make multiple activities easier to evaluate and should be used whenever possible. The key should be located at the station as well. Station work is usually very motivating because it is so active and appeals to a variety of learning styles. Students like the feeling of being somewhat in control as they proceed through the stations. Making the stations visually attractive adds to their interest. Stations can be created, stored, and reused if they are well constructed. For example, a large poster board laminated and folded into a tent at each location can provide color, focus, and space for directions and materials. On the laminated surface, glued pieces of Velcro provide fasteners for laminated direction sheets, station numbers, and other visuals. Careful construction in this manner can allow the teacher to remove the station directions and other information, placing new directions and information on the tents for their next use as learning stations that may address a different content, creative exploration, or skills focus of the curriculum. On the back of the tent, two large envelopes contain any self-correction keys or provide a place for students to put their assignments if a teacher-evaluation is planned. Figure 1.17 illustrates a sample learning-station tent.

FIGURE 1.17. LEARNING STATION CONSTRUCTION

(on the front)

| (Directions) | **STATION 4** | (Picture or Article or Diagram) |

(on the back of the tent)

Answer Key   *Place Work Here*

Teachers can plan for easy management of learning stations if they provide students with a checklist to address as they move from one station to the next. The students submit the checklist to the teacher after they have been completed all the stations. The same instrument provides the teacher with a continuing record of each group's progress. Putting the check beside each listed activity and placing the student's signature on the bottom of the checklist creates a format for individual and group accountability. Chapter 6 illustrates two checklists for stations.

Learning stations can be useful in all content areas. Science teachers are already familiar with the learning station concept since they have always set up stations for students. In many cases, the collaboration between pairs of students is a factor of the number of microscopes or the amount of equipment in the classroom. Students using collaboration in learning stations, however, not only explore concepts in more depth and exercise critical-thinking skills, but also realize that learning takes place through many approaches. Ackman (1997) illustrates this in her learning stations to explore bacteria and viruses as shown in Figure 1.18.

FIGURE 1.18. LEARNING STATIONS IN BIOLOGY:
BACTERIA AND VIRUSES

Station 1:   Review of factual information on viruses in pairs by using flashcards available at the station location.

Station 2:   Individual reading of information on bacteria; decide on main points in pairs; summarize main points in an individual writing log paragraph.

Station 3:   Identification of eight types of bacteria with eight microscopes and slides already set up; identification and example of an organism are done individually. Example: Slide 1: Gram-positive cocci-staphylococcus aureus; students use the self-correction key; if they have time to do so, they review any slides that they misidentified or for which they gave an incorrect example.

Station 4:   Sorting activity will be completed by using the two sets of labeled strips provided at the station to put the strips into the categories of disease and causative agent for bacteria and then for viruses. Students work in two groups of four, checking their categories with the other group's work and then using the answer key provided at the station to validate their group's categories.

Nauman's (1997) series of learning stations to explore short stories read by her seventh-grade students includes both individual assignments and small-group collaboration. She assigns students to groups of five and requires them to do all four stations. Nauman's stations explore the following aspects of the short story: vocabulary and point of view; plot, setting, and character. Her students have read only part of the short story before participating in the stations. She has also included a sponge activity to be addressed when students finish any station before the time has run out. They are to complete a journal entry on women's roles in society, answering the question, "What do you think has happened to women's roles in our society since *The Upheaval* was published in 1917? Has the public's attitude changed toward the two kinds of women represented in the story?" Nauman's learning station organization is shown in Figure 1.19.

FIGURE 1.19. SHORT STORY STATIONS FOR SEVENTH-GRADE ENGLISH

Station 1:   Each student picks a word from the provided word list; students look up their words; each student writes the definition and creates a sentence for that word, shares his or her definition and sentence, comparing both with the answer key, while the other group members write both into their notes. In a round-robin, the students rewrite a scene from the story from the point of view of the character that the group selects from an envelope of character cards. These will be shared after all groups have completed all station work.

Station 2:   Each student will write a prediction for the story's ending; the group will compare answers and come to a consensus as to which prediction seems best according to what they know up to this point about the story. Along with the prediction, the group must list facts and observations about the story that support their decision. At least three examples from the story are to be included. The group's prediction is to be placed in the folder on the station table.

Station 3:   Students use one copy of questions provided at the station to explore setting. They individually create a picture to illustrate the setting based on the physical environment and the mood created by the writer of the story. Markers and paper are provided. Students leave their setting question sheet at the station in a folder. They take their picture with them for later discussion and sharing.

Station 4:   Students turn assigned parts of the story into a short play by creating a script for that scene of the story, complete with dialogue and stage directions. Each student has a role assigned that represents one of the characters in the story. That student decides what his or her character will say and do. The characters are to be portrayed as closely as possible to the way they are described in the story. One copy of the completed script is to be left in the basket at the station after all group members have signed it, indicating their own assigned character and attesting that they contributed as directed to the creation of the playlet.

Teachers may think of learning stations as having only concept-centered or exploratory and creative applications. However, learning stations can provide several passes through a grammatical concept such as the use of the preterite tense in Spanish. Although the activities at each station vary in approach according to the group or individual assignments, each station targets the preterite tense in some manner so that students experience repeated skill building in tense construction. Small groups of four practice reading, writing, speaking, and listening skills as they apply the preterite tense in the learning station activities illustrated in Figure 1.20.

FIGURE 1.20. PRACTICING A GRAMMATICAL CONCEPT THROUGH LEARNING STATIONS

Station 1: Each student takes a worksheet provided at the station and picks a card from the station envelope. He or she completes the conjugations of -ar, -er, and -ir verbs in the preterite for the three verbs on the chosen card. Students pass their worksheets to a partner and compare endings for the three verb types. They then consult the self-correction key provided to check the accuracy of their conjugations.

Station 2: The four students watch a video of Juan and Marta's visit to the mall. After viewing the video, they turn to individual journals and retell, using their own Spanish, what the two shoppers did and saw.

Station 3: In pairs, the students read an article from a Spanish newspaper. After creating two questions to ask the other pair at the station, they pose their questions in Spanish. The other pair does the same. They then work again as pairs to use markers at the station, highlighting all verbs in the article that are used in the preterite. They self-correct their preterite identification with the self-correction key provided.

Station 4: All four students listen to an audiotape of sentences in the preterite read by the teacher. They repeat each sentence in the pause time on the tape. They then listen to the teacher read the sentence once more for reinforcement before asking them to listen to the second sentence and repeat after her. A series of 10 sentences and pronunciation practice are completed.

INQUIRY LEARNING: THE LEARNING CYCLE

Inquiry learning using the learning cycle model comprises a series of activities, collaborative work by small groups and pairs, and individual assignments. It differs from the *group investigation model* pioneered by Thelen (1967, 1981), and applied by Sharan and Sharan (1992), which addresses a complicated issue and instructs students to study its various subtopics in research groups. After carrying out their research using the group investigation model, the groups prepare and present their information to the entire class. However, the learning cycle encourages students to construct meaning from their prior knowledge and experiences and to incorporate new information given by the teacher in order to solve problems. The four basic characteristics of inquiry learning include the following:

♦ It is a complicated style of learning.

♦ It is concerned with solving problems.

♦ It does not require one solution to a problem.

♦ It uses a flexible set of activities.

Involving several critical-thinking processes, this approach to learning is both personalized and contextualized. Instead of learning new concepts in isolation, the students address assignments that make them apply their prior knowledge and experiences along with those of their group members to the new concepts, expanding their overall knowledge base and understanding. Students learn because they are involved and active. Trowbridge and Bybee (1990) describe the goal of the learning cycle as allowing "students to apply previous knowledge, develop interests, and initiate and maintain a curiosity toward the material at hand" (p. 306). In considering a problem or a situation posed by the teacher, students employ a variety of critical-thinking skills. They must formulate questions in order to seek out information and then construct hypotheses to address the posed problem. In the learning cycle format, the students suggest and try out solutions. The teacher has several duties in the planning and implementation of the learning cycle. These duties are listed in Figure 1.21.

FIGURE 1.21. TEACHER PLANNING AND IMPLEMENTATION DUTIES FOR THE LEARNING CYCLE

The teacher

♦ Creates the situation or selects the problem;

♦ Chooses the group members;

♦ Serves as a catalyst for students as they progress through the series of activities;

♦ Encourages the positing of student hypotheses;

♦ Emphasizes that one problem might be addressed by a variety of solutions and that all solutions might have merit;

♦ Acts as a guide and new information source as students test their hypotheses;

♦ Creates activities in which students can apply what they've learned or use the new learning creatively to enhance classroom learning.

Learning cycle lessons are three-phase plans that may be completed in one period or may use more time to finish. Teachers may plan a variety of approaches such as cooperative learning activities, simulation games, mini-lectures, guided discussions, independent projects and lab experiments as they address the three components shown in Figure 1.22.

FIGURE 1.22. PHASES OF THE LEARNING CYCLE

PHASE I: Exploration:

In the first phase, the teacher poses a situation or a problem for students to solve. Students rely on prior knowledge and experience to generate hypotheses concerning the problem.

PHASE II: Invention:

In the second phase, students share their hypotheses in a whole-class discussion format; the teacher presents new concepts that will add to students' understanding. The mini-lecture format is often used to accomplish this.

PHASE III: Application or Extension:

Students add the new information to their prior knowledge in order to solve a new problem or create a project based on the material that they have explored and discussed, and to which they have added teacher-generated new concepts.

> **NOTE**
>
> Formal, unit-grade-determining evaluations should not occur until students have completed all three phases and have had sufficient time to internalize the concepts presented.

Teachers and students can evaluate the learning activities in a variety of ways. Students can evaluate their group's work in Phase I; they can complete initial journal entries to hypothesize individually before joining their groups; individual students can complete a self-evaluation at the end of the three phases. A quiz to check for understanding of new information might follow Phase II; problems done in Phase III might be evaluated, or a test may be given in which students demonstrate understanding. Teachers can pose informal questions during Phases II and III to provide evaluation opportunities. Lab performance can be evaluated by lab reports; checklists for participation and social skills development might be used when the activities call for small group collaboration or pairs work.

In a 12th-grade English class, philosophy combines with the study of literature to create a challenging learning cycle lesson. In Figure 1.23, students explore logical fallacies in the three phases.

**FIGURE 1.23. LEARNING CYCLE:
LITERATURE AND LOGICAL FALLACIES**

Phase I: Exploration

- ◆ The teacher gives several sentences containing faulty reasoning.

- ◆ Students may be asked to work alone, in pairs or in small groups to answer the following question:

    After reading each sentence carefully, ask yourself if the statement is logical and explain why or why not for each decision you make.

Phase II: Invention

- ◆ The teacher guides the discussion about the sentences analyzed in Phase I as students offer opinions on each sentence and its logical or illogical implications. They defend their opinions with explanations and offer alternative wording.

+ Using the mini-lecture format, the teacher explains types of faulty reasoning including the visual fallacy, the slippery slope fallacy, the fallacy of two wrongs, and the circular reasoning fallacy.

Phase III: Application

+ The students analyze "The one-Legged Crane" from Boccaccio's *Decameron* for faulty reasoning. They complete a journal entry in which they identify the faulty reasoning used in the tale.

(or)

Phase III: Extension

+ Students work in pairs to create examples of the four types of faulty reasoning; pairs exchange their examples with another pair; they then analyze those examples and try to determine the type of faulty reasoning used.

+ Each student picks two of the group's combined eight examples of faulty reasoning. Working alone, each student writes the examples sentences again so that the sentence will be expressed logically.

Students studying German can experience the learning cycle as part of their unit on travel. Through the three phases, students have the opportunity to use their speaking, listening, reading, and writing skills. The three phases are personalized and contextualized because students are using the closest large city as their destination and also locations throughout the school as shown in Figure 1.24.

FIGURE 1.24. GERMAN TRAVEL UNIT:
THE LEARNING CYCLE

Phase I: Exploration

+ Students are asked to write in German a description of the easiest way to go to Erie, PA, from the front parking lot of the school.

+ Question Posed: A person has stopped you outside the school building. He asks you the best way to get to Erie from your location. Using your own German vocabulary base, write a description of the directions you would give.

Phase II: Invention

- ◆ Students share their written directions with the whole class. The teacher puts selected phrases from their contributions on the board.

- ◆ The teacher leads the students in a TPR exercise in which they turn in directions given by the teacher and point to directions of locations according to the compass.

- ◆ The teacher asks what vocabulary the students feel they need to make their directions better and then introduces directional vocabulary including north, south, east, west, northeast, southeast, northwest, southwest, right , left, highway, street light, street sign, stop sign, and verb commands.

Phase III: Application

- ◆ Students are to pick a card from several provided by the teacher. On each card is a different destination within the school. Each student writes a set of directions without revealing the final destination. The students exchange directions and attempt to follow them. The students return and tell where they ended up. They exchange cards to see if they have matched the destination listed.

- Note: *As a debriefing, the teacher and students discuss the destination directions and problems that students had in following the written directions. Any confusing points are clarified.*

Middle schoolers studying parts of speech may internalize the concepts in more depth if a learning cycle lesson is planned. For example, pronouns might be the topic of a learning cycle. The following learning cycle involves small group collaboration, pairs collaboration, discussion with the creation of a pronoun classification chart, mini-lecture, and hands-on sorting and classifying activities. In Figure 1.25, the variety of activities not tied to the textbook exercises appeals to the students, and the movement and hands-on activities reinforce the classification process.

FIGURE 1.25. ENGLISH GRAMMAR THROUGH THE LEARNING CYCLE

Phase I: Exploration

- ◆ The teacher assigns students partners.

- ◆ The teacher passes out an envelope to each pair; the envelope contains several cards, all of which contain only one word.

- The students open the envelope and spread out the cards on their desks.

- Question posed: In what way could you arrange these words in categories?

Phase II: Invention

- The teacher writes the categories on the board as the pairs explain what they did.

- The teacher is creating a pronoun category chart for personal, possessive, interrogative, demonstrative, reflexive, and indefinite pronouns without labeling the categories as such.

- In a mini-lecture, the teacher explains that there are several categories of pronouns; using the chart already on the board, the teacher labels each category as the students take notes.

Phase III: Application

- The teacher erases the board chart and asks students to mix up their cards, and then sort them again according to categories.

- The students then receive a second envelope with six pronoun categories. They match their categories with the labels from the envelopes as the teacher circulates to evaluate their work.

CONCLUSION

Collaborative learning strategies offer many benefits to students. The nature of collaborative learning allows the student to go beyond the scope of a cooperative learning activity. Collaborative activities promote problem solving and the identification of new problems. Such activities facilitate the transfer of information and aid students in the internalizing of abstract concepts. Through the personalization and contextualizing of activities, students link their previous knowledge and experiences to the new learning so that information is not learned in an isolated manner. Many critical-thinking skills are developed through the use of collaborative activities as students share views, defend choices and judgments, and make creative applications of course content. Simple and complex models of collaborative learning foster opportunities for learning to occur in depth with applications that extend beyond the classroom.

2

COLLABORATIVE
PLANNING AND
COTEACHING

"I'm so glad you agreed to come to our meeting," Robyn greeted Dr. Gordon. "We want to pick your brain about some projects we're thinking about. Everyone, this is Erin Gordon, the student teaching supervisor that I told you about from the college."

Erin smiled and addressed the group. "You wanted to talk about doing some collaboration, according to Robyn. Let me tell you about my most recent collaborative effort. I walked into the elementary school office to sign the visitor sheet last week and received the obligatory name tags which stated in bold red and white letters, VISITOR. Though I'd been coming to this same school every Thursday for eight weeks, I was still a visitor. I headed to the first-grade classroom, which was my destination, and was met by two students coming around the corner. Huge smiles lit up their faces as they recognized me. 'Hi, you're going to our room, aren't you…my puzzle is almost done…I worked on it during indoor recess yesterday… you can take it to your big kids pretty soon, right?' We arrived at the classroom door, I raised my hand to knock, and the little boy with whom I had been walking said, 'You don't have to knock on our door, just come in with us.' All of a sudden I was a visitor no longer. I was accepted by these students as part of their classroom, as part of their school day. I couldn't wait to begin the next lesson with me, their 'real' teacher, and them. I also couldn't wait to get back to the university to share the newest responses from 'my' first-grade students to my university education majors."

"I've heard some great projects that you've started with teachers," Wayne commented. "We're not nearly ready for that! But we wanted your ideas about some coplanning and collaboration on a basic, simple level. I'd just like to make some collaborative progress with the other math teacher in the 11th-grade program."

"And inclusion has helped me to see that I need to work more closely with the special ed teacher," Jane Richards admitted. "We just can't seem to balance out what both of us need to do. I'm so used to planning collaboration for my students that I thought collaborating with a colleague would be easy. It isn't. Maybe I'm too used to being in my own room, doing my own thing, and relying only on my own ideas. And I think that most of us are like that—isolated."

INTRODUCTION

Today's classroom consists of one teacher and many (often *too* many) students. This picture reflects the common experiences of many middle and secondary teachers who also work in near isolation, closing the classroom door and proceeding with the job of teaching. When another adult does enter, it is most often for the purpose of evaluating the teacher's performance or for providing assistance to individual students with identified special needs. The thought of another teacher working alongside seems like dangerous daydreaming—a pipe dream of most educators who feel they can't possibly meet all of the needs of their students. Fortunately, in more and more schools across the nation, teachers are breaking out of this traditional isolation and seeking ways to work together. They are planning cooperative and collaborative learning experiences for their students and enlisting the participation of other teachers in the effort.

Collaborative instructional approaches and cooperative learning strategies foster the social and academic skills that students need to be successful in their daily lives. And just as students benefit from the development of these skills, teachers can reap the benefits of both the process and the product of working collaboratively with peers. By participating in a collaborative experience, teachers feel a sense of collegiality or community. Collaborative learning activities promote learning through sharing of information and individual perspectives, and collaborative teaching fosters creativity and effective instruction.

> **NOTE**
>
> When teachers capitalize on the benefits of collaboration, everyone benefits.

Each teacher brings personal background experiences and behaviors to bear on the act of teaching. These aspects of individuality help to shape teaching style, impacting methodology and content. But what if teachers were able to expand on their own experiences and knowledge by listening to the knowledge and experiences of other professionals? Imagine the wealth of experiences and talents within any one faculty from which each individual teacher could draw. Collaboration can be the way we each contribute to and take from this treasure.

Knowledge of any content area is enriched when the teacher broadens his or her view to include the diversity of information brought out in a group of teachers. Collaboration can help to create positive conversation among peers, which will stimulate personal and professional growth. Talking with peers about teaching and listening to their classroom approaches provide all teachers with a chance to learn and foster the desire to grow and change.

NOTE

"If we turn to each other…we may discover that, through professional collaboration, we can effect the changes we need to make for ourselves and for our students to succeed" (Heidorn and Rabine, 1998, p. 46).

COPLANNING

To foster collaborative learning in students, teachers need to see and participate in successfully planned lessons. To this end they can successfully employ coplanning with their peers. If teachers have some experience with coplanning, they may realize some of the many benefits of working with fellow professionals. When coplanning, teachers become more aware about what is taking place in other classrooms. Teachers receive detailed information about their own students' behaviors and abilities in other subject areas. Teachers can recognize that all students have both strengths and weaknesses, therefore developing tolerance of individual differences and approaches to effectively address these differences. In coplanning, teachers can share strategies that are helpful to students, each adding successful strategies to their own classroom collection. Teachers who participate in coplanning build a network of support for each other as they work together to address the many problems that today's students bring to the classroom. Ultimately, both teachers can realize the personal and professional satisfaction that results from working together instead of in isolation.

COPLANNING ACROSS THE GENERATION GAP

One of the most infrequently tapped resources within any single school faculty is what the combination of veteran teachers and new teachers can offer. Although each faculty member has a treasure of his or her own to offer, veteran teachers as a group have a significant wealth of knowledge born from years of experience. And as each faculty member provides a unique perspective, new teachers as a group add perspectives born from youth and recent student experiences. Combining these characteristics in educational collaboration results in a powerful resource for improved teacher effectiveness.

Bridging the teaching generation gap requires a willingness on both sides to communicate their needs and their interests. Both groups must open themselves to the possibility that the other has something of value to offer. Veteran teachers need to realize that a new idea might be worth trying in their classroom, just as new teachers must recognize that there are tried and true ideas worth using with today's students. Figure 2.1 is an example of shared strengths.

FIGURE 2.1. COMBINING FACULTY STRENGTHS

Bob	*April*
30-year teaching veteran (Other Strengths)	Second-year teacher (Other Strengths)
1. Motivating lecturer in American Literature	1. Used cooperative & collaborative ideas in student teaching and 1st year
2. Rapport builder with students	2. Uses effective guided questioning to foster discussions
3. Travels to sites famous in American Literature	3. Member of NCTE—reads most recent application ideas in *English Journal*
4. 15 years as SAT coach	4. Very computer literate
5. Teacher evaluator for writing sections SAT	5. Spent summer studying literature in England
6. Actor in local community theater	6. Has attended and presented at writing workshop conferences

In collaboration they can teach a unit on Mark Twain using the following:

- Lecture delivery of factual material concerning Mark Twain's life,
- Video presentation of actual sites used in Twain's stories,
- Jigsaw cooperative learning strategy to compare Twain's significant works,
- Internet research about political and economic influences on Twain's stories, and
- Writing workshop for students to create character insertions in Twain's stories.

Building professional relationships among veteran and new teachers requires organization on the part of interested teachers and support from school administrations. But the resulting programs need not be expensive, time consuming, or difficult to arrange. To facilitate the communication, veteran and new teachers simply need time to be together. Figure 2.2 provides ideas to initiate faculty collaboration.

FIGURE 2.2. FACILITATING FACULTY COLLABORATION

1. A faculty room area that welcomes both new and veteran teachers can provide an area for formal and informal conversations. Teachers can gather around a "Talking Table" to discuss the weather or an upcoming school event, bring forth questions about students or curriculum, to review texts or educational materials catalogues, or share a cup of coffee.

2. A bulletin board can be set aside for the use of new and veteran teachers who are seeking specific information or materials. Teachers can post requests and responses at any time.

3. In-service days can include time set aside for new and veteran teachers to reflect on information gained in the day's program and brainstorm ways to use the new information.

4. Faculty e-mail addresses can be assigned through schools so new and veteran teachers can discuss issues when they don't share common free time during the school day.

Once teachers on both ends of the generation gap begin to communicate, coplanning becomes a next step. Sharing new and well used instructional techniques can result in student learning that encompasses many levels of understanding and addresses many student needs. Sharing these techniques also benefits teachers who expand their repertoire of effective instructional strategies.

In a faculty of 40 high-school teachers, a random pick found the expertise and experiences represented in Figure 2.3.

A social studies teacher may use a lecture format to effectively convey factual information concerning significant commanders of the American Civil War and locations of important battles. Complementing this lecture information, an English teacher may use role-playing to have students write possible prebattle dialogue among commanders and soldiers and role-play the scene of the night prior to battle. A foreign language teacher may present information about language used in a restaurant by having students listen to an audiotape and complete a worksheet, while a mathematics teacher may employ a think-pair-share activity to create meals within a given monetary limit from menu items prepared on the worksheets. There are many advantages to coplanning (see Figure 2.4).

FIGURE 2.3. FACULTY TREASURE CHEST

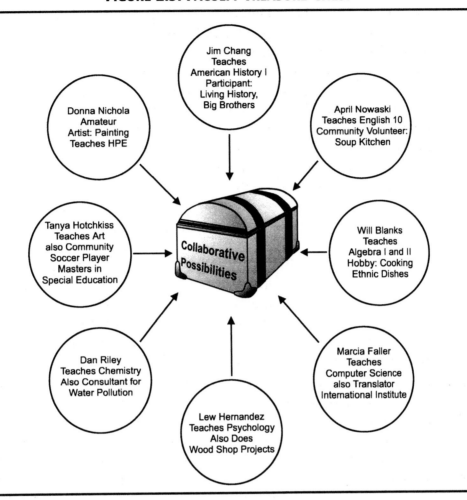

FIGURE 2.4. ADVANTAGES OF COPLANNING

For Teachers	*For Students*
Increased awareness of other classes	Connections among classes
Greater knowledge of students	Academic strengths known by all teachers
Teaching strategies added to repertoire	Instruction presented in a variety of ways
Peer support in planning instruction	Academic needs known to all teachers
Fun	Increased variety of activities in classes

The experiences of academic collaboration can bring challenges that may initially frustrate some teachers. However, viewing this temporary frustration as an important step to improvement will keep teachers moving forward together. Coplanning does not mean examining contributions in a way that all of them become totally acceptable to each of the members of the coplanning group. But rather it implies that all members of the group understand the ideas provided by their peers and are willing to investigate an acceptable means for incorporating these ideas into effective instruction. Because of the diverse opinions and ideas that surface in coplanning sessions, teachers have opportunities to honestly examine possibilities. Indeed, it is the diversity which teachers bring to coplanning that is its strength.

That coplanning capitalizes on the strengths of collaborative learning approaches helps teachers to be more interactive in their work with their peers. As students must share within the groups to which they are assigned, teachers must be willing to share within their peer groups. The new perspective that a peer can bring forward can provide a fresh insight to past practices and a real reason to alter approaches. But these perspectives must be received with interest, by teachers who want to understand that which is being shared. Exhilarating, professional discussion provides the means by which all ideas are considered for their potential use in the classroom.

Teachers need to see and participate in successfully planned collaborative lessons. For collaboration to be successful, teachers need to be as prepared as possible to plan for maximum use of knowledge and strategies available to them. In this collaborative planning, educators can maximize benefits for all children in all classrooms. The benefits for children can occur through the use of interdisciplinary thematic units by teachers in several curricular areas, collaborative products from regular education and special education teachers, and multiage activities from teachers in varying grade levels.

COPLANNING WITH TEACHERS AND STUDENTS WITHIN A SCHOOL ON INTERDISCIPLINARY THEMATIC UNITS

The interdisciplinary thematic unit as it applies to the middle-school curriculum is explained by Kellough, Kellough, and Hough (1993, p. 90) as

> the tool used to link the learning experiences of middle-school children in ways that engage them fully in the learning process. *Interdisciplinary* means that the core subjects as well as the cocurricular activities and exploratories are involved. *Thematic* means that the same topic is used to develop the teaching plan (content and instruction) for each of the different subjects in which the students are enrolled.

Unit refers to an extended teaching plan (several days to several weeks), in which a variety of goals and objectives are established that are centered around a common concept, topic, or theme.

Whether the unit is planned for middle schoolers or high-school students, the teachers involved collaborate on the issues, concepts, events, persons, or locale to be integrated into a unit of study. All teachers wishing to do so can integrate their content area into the joint effort.

Interdisciplinary thematic units are often based on a current issue such as the environment. They can be organized around a concept such as prejudice or courage or responsibility. Many times they are organized around a national event such as the American Civil War or a worldwide event such as the Olympics. For example, students can study cultural heritage and practice mathematics skills, English writing skills, and research skills; learn about art and music related to that heritage; and share with their classmates food particular to that cultural heritage. Teachers can plan interdisciplinary thematic units around a famous person such as Martin Luther King, Jr., and include the reading of his *Letters from a Birmingham Jail*, the exploration of the historical events of the 1950s and 1960s, the comparison and contrast of employment statistics from the early 1960s with the 1990s, and the evaluation of the impact of federal acts and judicial decisions related to the Civil Rights Movement. Teachers can plan interdisciplinary units based on the sequence shown in Figure 2.5.

Collaboration occurs as teachers work together to plan an interdisciplinary thematic unit. When students observe teachers working collaboratively, they learn a valuable lesson about adults: just as students produce meaningful work in their cooperative learning and collaborative class activities, so do teachers produce meaningful products by collaborating with each other. Students see an example of the way professionals can work in real-world situations to utilize each other's strengths and to create products that benefit others. Students see the teachers who emphasize team building and the advantages of collaboration actually doing what they teach.

This is a particularly good approach, for example, to a study of the American Civil War. Traditionally, the war is studied chronologically, and students concentrate on the sequence of events. The interdisciplinary thematic approach, however, allows students to look at the complexity and the variety of issues and repercussions that made the American Civil War important to the development of the nation. With more teachers addressing these complexities and bringing their collective expertise to the topic, windows of in-depth understanding can open for students.

**FIGURE 2.5. POINTS TO CONSIDER WHEN
PLANNING AN INTERDISCIPLINARY THEMATIC UNIT**

BEFORE IMPLEMENTATION

1. Agree on the *nature* or *source* of the interdisciplinary thematic unit.

2. Discuss *subject-specific frameworks*, goals and objectives, curriculum guidelines, textbooks and supplemental units, and units already in place for the school year.

3. Choose a *topic* and *develop* a timeline.

4. Set *two timelines*. The first timeline is for the team planning only. The second timeline is for the implementation of the unit and addresses both students and teachers.

5. Develop the *scope* and *sequence* for content and instruction.

6. *Share goals and objectives.* Each team member should have a copy of the goals and objectives of every other member.

7. Name the unit.

8. Share subject-specific units.

DURING AND AFTER IMPLEMENTATION

Discuss successes and failures...and determine what needs to be changed, and how and when, to make the unit successful. Adjustments can be made along the way (formative evaluation), and revisions for future use can be made after the unit (summative evaluation).

(Kellough, Kellough, & Hough, 1993, pp. 96–97)

Rich opportunities for students and teachers to participate in both cooperative learning and collaborative activities occur when teachers plan for an interdisciplinary unit. For example, an integrated unit can include a cooperative learning jigsaw activity in history while students collaborate in pairs to search the Internet in mathematics, participate in the first two phases of a learning cycle in science class, and do small-group research in English. One of the biggest advantages of the integrated interdisciplinary unit is the opportunity for in-depth learning through both cooperative learning and collaboration.

In addition to the opportunities for cooperative learning activities and collaboration which the interdisciplinary thematic unit offers, the implementation of this type of unit on the high-school level can include student input on the focus of the study.

In Chapter 1, Reg Moski decided to use buzz groups in his American history class. Moski formed the buzz groups to initiate a meaningful link between the controversy over uniforms and regulations isolating upper-class students and the subsequent discussion of internment during World War II. Teachers who wish to give students some power in the selection and direction of the interdisciplinary unit can also forge those meaningful connections.

The buzz groups can be involved in the choice of the interdisciplinary unit focus while the teachers still control the boundaries that will be acceptable choices. First, the teachers create a list of issues, concepts, people, or events that they have decided are acceptable choices for inclusion in a unit that would conform to their school's curriculum. They then allow the students to discuss the possible choices in buzz groups, reporting back to the teachers the results of their discussions. The teachers can then structure the unit around the choices that the students indicate to be the most interesting.

With student input, the teachers then use the unit focus to construct the plan which they will all implement in order to create opportunities for in-depth learning. Figure 2.6, on the next page, illustrates the student-student, teacher-teacher, and student-teacher collaboration made possible with an interdisciplinary thematic unit.

Humphrey, Crain, and Bergfield (1991) created an interdisciplinary thematic unit at North School in O'Fallon, Missouri. The unit involves the middle-school English, social studies, and mathematics teachers in a unit focusing on the American Civil War. They have planned a unit that lasts 24 days. Sample content and assignments designed by the three teachers for three of those days are summarized in Figure 2.7 (Kellough, Kellough, & Hough, 1993).

FIGURE 2.7. INTERDISCIPLINARY THEMATIC UNIT ON THE CIVIL WAR: CONTENT EXAMPLES—SUMMARY

	Social Studies	*English*	*Mathematics*
Day 9	Research—reports on Civil War topics	Discussion of *Across Five Aprils*, Chapter 3, and questions	Introduction to graphing of information related to the Civil War
Day 16	Missouri in the Civil War	Chapter 8 of novel	Computer lab: MECC graphing primer
Day 18	Research project due for both classes; Appomattox; Civil War Trivia; baseball review	Research projects; Chapter 10 of novel	Training for color graphs; printing of black and white graphs

**FIGURE 2.6. STUDENT-STUDENT, TEACHER-TEACHER,
STUDENT-TEACHER COLLABORATION:
INTERDISCIPLINARY THEMATIC UNIT STRUCTURE**

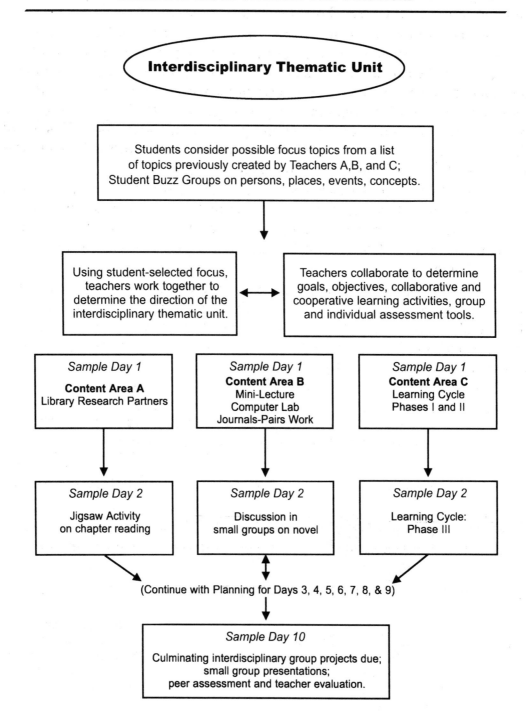

The subject-area content summarized for the three days on page 52 and for the other days of this unit can be planned to include a wide variety of cooperative learning activities and collaborative strategies. Since Missouri and the border states are part of the unit, role-playing, small-group interviews, or the fishbowl strategies can address Lincoln's traditional reputation as the Great Emancipator and the conflicts over slavery in those states. Small group research can contribute to the research projects which will receive credit in both the social studies and English classes. Partner assignments in the computer lab can enhance the opportunities for students to share information and explain processes in graphing. The computer lab can also be the site for the English class students to compose their journal responses to questions on the novel and on the war posed by the teacher. The pairs can then read and respond to each other's work before a whole-class discussion takes place on any chapter of the novel. Final research reports and displays of graphs can serve as unifying factors if used as a culminating activity in which students share their products.

Hendren, Keely, Mason, Sullivan, and Weissenberg (1993) designed their middle-school interdisciplinary thematic unit to provide in-depth learning about earthquakes for their students and to produce an earthquake guide for their student body. The subject areas include mathematics, language arts, science, social studies, and reading with science and social studies as the predominant classes for instruction and the other classes used for support activities. The five teachers planned a seven-day unit that was based on the learning that students would experience in the integrated activities. Content included the history of earthquakes, the New Madrid Fault, how to prepare for an earthquake, what to do at home and away from home during a quake, what safety supplies might be needed, and what to do after an earthquake. The first three days focused on the study of earthquakes, the Earth's tectonic plates, probability and severity of earthquakes in New Madrid Fault area, and preventative measures as well as actions to take during and after a quake. The following three days were devoted to the production of the safety guide with editing and rewriting being done in the language arts class while graphs emphasizing the Richter scale and estimations of earthquake predictions were done in math class. The computer lab was used to produce the final copy of the guide.

This unit provides many opportunities for cooperative learning activities and collaborative strategies. The research on earthquake information might be done in small groups with each group investigating one aspect of the subject. The creation of the guide lends itself to the writing process with peer editing as a component. Working as computer lab partners, students can search the Internet for information on the most recent earthquakes. They can then work in their small groups to produce maps to illustrate earthquake activity (Kellough, Kellough, & Hough, 1993).

Interdisciplinary units on the high-school level can provide critical-thinking practice and in-depth learning of important concepts. Focusing on the theme of the search for justice and dignity, the California English Curriculum (Taylor, 1985) demonstrates the integration of several literary pieces, such as *Death of a Salesman, I know Why the Caged Bird Sings, Farewell to Manzanar,* and *Ozymandias* to explore the concept of dignity and the struggle of the fictional characters for justice. The theme and literary selections described in the "The Search for Justice and Dignity" can be used to create an interdisciplinary thematic unit in which the English, American history, and sociology teachers address the same concepts. The subject-area content for the three classes can be arranged as illustrated in Figure 2.8.

FIGURE 2.8. INTERDISCIPLINARY THEMATIC UNIT: JUSTICE AND DIGNITY

Class	*Content*
English	Exploration of the American Dream:
	Death of a Salesman
	I Know Why the Caged Bird Sings
	Farewell to Manzanar
	Ozymandias
	I Have a Dream
American History	Segregation and Discrimination in 20th-Century United States:
	Japanese Internment During World War II
	Civil Rights Movement of the 1960s
	Women's Movement
	Equal Opportunity
	Affirmative Action
Sociology	The Structure of the American Family in the 20th Century:
	The Effects of Isolation on Individuals and Groups
	Cultural Similarities and Differences in Family Relationships among Ethnic Groups in America
	Changing Demographics in the Latter Half of the 20th Century

A unit on the search for justice and dignity can provide many cooperative learning experiences and collaborative learning assignments. Figure 2.9 provides a list of suggestions.

**FIGURE 2.9. SUGGESTED COOPERATIVE LEARNING ACTIVITIES
AND COLLABORATIVE EXPERIENCES FOR THE INTERDISCIPLINARY
THEMATIC UNIT ON DIGNITY AND THE SEARCH FOR JUSTICE**

Class	*Suggestions*
English	In journal-response pairs, explore students' own experiences of discrimination related to the main characters in *I Know Why the Caged Bird Sings*.
	Compare Willy's view of the American Dream in *Death of a Salesman* with that of an older relative in your family.
	Conduct an interview to gather data. In small-group discussion, compare your relative's responses with those collected by the other group members.
American History	Research information with your partner on your assigned event in 20th-century America. Prepare to give a short report to the class in which both of you contribute information from your research.
	In buzz groups, prepare a list of questions to ask the guest speaker.
	Conduct a class interview of four famous 20th-century figures who were involved in controversial events. The famous "interviewees" will be students assigned to research those historic figures.
	In small groups, prepare for a British-style debate on the U.S. government internment practice during World War II.
Sociology	In the jigsaw, choose a decade to research, concentrating on demographic trends of urban and rural populations. Report back to your base group.
	Compare and contrast demographics information.

An interdisciplinary thematic unit organized around a famous historical or literary figure allows content applications in many subject-area classrooms. A unit on Shakespeare may involve, for example, the English, social studies, psychology, drama, music, art, industrial technology, and home economics teachers working in decision-making groups to design a unit that will conclude with a Shakespearean Festival to be put on for the entire student body. Examples of content to be explored in this unit are described in Figure 2.10.

The Shakespearean Festival unit provides multiple activities that promote collaboration within small groups in individual classrooms, as well as cross-discipline collaboration in the planning and implementation of the festival for the whole student body.

Decision-making among teachers can be an excellent way to model what we teach. If students see us functioning as a team, and if that teaming produces in-depth understanding and enjoyment of learning, they may be more responsive to the advantages of working together. By planning and implementing interdisciplinary thematic units, we can demonstrate to students that none of us is as knowledgeable and talented as all of us can be if we work together.

TEACHER COLLABORATION ACROSS GRADE LEVELS

An all too familiar lament of upper-grade teachers is that "these students were never taught to…." As common are the complaints of lower-grade teachers that "secondary teachers have no idea what we have to teach down here." Neither complaint may be true, but the comments persist because of perpetuated misconceptions from a lack of first-hand knowledge of the reality of classrooms beyond our own.

Teachers from all grade levels can benefit from sharing the experiences of their classrooms and collaborating in their teaching (see Figure 2.11 on p. 58). Just as teachers from different curriculum areas within a school can learn from each other, so can teachers who are willing to reach across grade levels learn from their other grade peers. Certainly teacher collaboration epitomizes the belief that adults can learn from each other.

When teachers from different grade levels collaborate for student learning, there is necessarily a difference in instructional focus. A lower-level teacher, who is primarily responsible for approximately 25 students during a school year, may concentrate significant efforts on addressing affective development while promoting academic gains, while an upper-level teacher, responsible for perhaps 125 students during that same year, focuses on content instruction and cognitive development, giving less attention to affective components. Thus, an important part of cross-grade collaboration is for teachers to merge their affective and academic goals in a way that creates a supportive classroom experience

FIGURE 2.10. INTERDISCIPLINARY THEMATIC UNIT: SHAKESPEARE—SUBJECT AREA CONCEPTS

English	*Social Studies*	*Psychology*
Julius Caesar; Biography of Shakespeare	History of Elizabethan England; Social conditions	Personality types; Contemporary explanation of the four humors
Projects for display during the festival	Creation of handbills proposing social improvements to be handed out at the festival	Setting up of four booths in which student psychologists give advice from a modern perspective on diagnosis of the four humors
"Autobiographies" of selected characters in *Julius Caesar*		Creation of pamphlets on personality types referring to characters in *Julius Caesar* as examples
Selected sonnets	Characteristics of Elizabethan entertainment	Influence of powerful figures on those around them

Drama	*Music*	*Art*
Production of scenes from *Julius Caesar* during the festival	Performance of music from the period for the festival	Design of the stage and festival grounds; creation of banners, signs, art to be displayed during the festival

Industrial Technology	*Home Economics*	*Health*
Construction of a model stage and booths for the festival	Creation of a menu of foods to be prepared by the class for festival	Research on the life span, eating habits, diseases, childhood mortality as compared with the same factors in today's world; Setting up a medical booth to give fairgoers advice to promote their health

---

FIGURE 2.11. COLLABORATIVE GOALS AND ACTIVITIES ACROSS GRADE LEVELS

Academic Intentions		*Activities*
Creative Writing	Upper Level	Creating rhyming poems
	Lower Level	Identifying rhyming words
Geometry	Upper Level	Combining geometric figures
	Lower Level	Identifying simple shapes
Art History	Upper Level	Studying artists' geographic influences
	Lower Level	Seeing master artists' works
Grammar	Upper Level	Using descriptive language
	Lower Level	Listening to stories
Reading	Upper Level	Dramatic reading with expression
	Lower Level	Listening skills

---

where all students and the participating teachers have opportunities to hone productive behaviors and positive attitudes.

Some cross-grade academic programs seem somewhat obvious and have been used in many school districts. Reading and writing collaborations have paired upper-level students from creative writing classes with lower-level students engaged in learning how to read. Cross-grade reading programs have connected slower readers in upper-level grades with prereading students who are just beginning to recognize print. The upper-grade readers have the opportunity for meaningful practice of fundamental reading skills, and prereaders experience the fun of read-alouds. Pen-pal collaborations are also somewhat commonly used to facilitate both reading and writing skills of students in upper- and lower-level grades.

Content areas beyond the language arts also provide excellent opportunities for cross-grade collaborations. An upper-level fine arts teacher may collaborate with a lower-level social studies teacher to investigate locations represented in master works. Upper-level students learn about art and artists, culture, and geography with a real purpose, that of teaching young children. Young children receive exceptional exposure to the same subjects by means of an influential role model. A course in geometry for upper-level students can be easily reinforced by having those students teach simple shapes to younger children. Working collaboratively, students can develop two-dimensional designs or three-dimensional robots combining shapes they've investigated together. In the area of personal health, older students who have experiences with peer pressure and knowledge of difficult social choices can be tremendous resources for younger children just beginning to feel that social pull. With teacher guidance and monitoring, both groups can realize the impact of decisions made on the basis of peer pressures.

Once teachers have determined their combined goals, it is important to communicate these goals clearly to students. Older students may be somewhat used to teachers identifying their learning objectives, but even young students can understand the purposes of an activity when it is conveyed in specific terms. Teachers and students alike must all approach the collaboration with these goals clear in their minds so the techniques used will be selected because they specifically address the goals established.

In these cross-grade collaborations, it is inevitable that relationships among the student participants will develop. Fostering positive relationships, the connections that will benefit all members, therefore becomes of critical concern. Students and teachers must understand some things about each other. They must be tolerant of differences and aware of similarities. The culture of the classroom, the experiences of the students, and the expectations of the teachers must be clearly identified within the context of the classrooms through which the collaborative activities will occur. Promoting relationships that will secure this understanding requires an investment of time and attention. Teachers must take time to discuss their students, their classrooms, and their expectations with each other. When teachers feel comfortable in their understanding of each other and the classrooms involved, the relationship must be extended to students.

Students must be given time to engage in minimally structured conversation with their cross-grade peers to begin to build the relationships on which the success of the collaboration will depend. Prior to structured academic programs, activities can be used that will encourage discussion. Teachers may provide short and general interest inventories which older students can administer to their younger partners. These inventories serve as sparks for opening conversations, thus beginning the construction of positive, productive relationships. An example of an inventory is provided in Figure 2.12.

FIGURE 2.12. INTEREST INVENTORY

What is your name?   Do you have a nickname? What is it?

My name is ___.   What do you think my nickname is?

I like the colors ___ and ___.   What are your favorite colors?

After school I like to ____.   What are some things you do after school?

I used to read books about ___.   What are the names of some books you like?

Do you like to play ____?   What sports do you like?

Once students have begun their collaborations, they will learn a great deal about each other. This personal knowledge can serve as a valuable tool in promoting academic growth if the collaborating teachers employ periodic activities combining academic skills and students' interest. These activities should be predetermined by the teachers so they can be integrated with the primary academic goals of the collaboration and not treated as add-on activities. Some ways to provide for relationship building among students and teachers and for promoting academic development in several content areas are provided in Figure 2.13.

FIGURE 2.13. RELATIONSHIP-BUILDING FORUMS

---

1. Provide days where cross-grade classes can shadow each other during the school year, providing exposure to content in many areas.

2. Build minimally supervised discussion time into each cross-grade visit to promote constructive dialog, listening skills, tolerance, and understanding.

3. Encourage pen-pal writing between classroom visits to practice writing and reading skills.

4. Hold a parent program where cross-grade peers can meet each others' family members to develop public speaking and interpersonal social skills.

5. Invite cross-grade peers to attend extracurricular activities such as choral programs, theater productions, and sporting events to provide experiences in diverse subject areas.

Collaborating with cross-grade peers must ultimately be for the purpose of promoting academic gains in both the lower- and the upper-grade students. Indeed, the match between teachers occurs because of the specific learning both want their students to experience. As upper-level students practice academic skills, lower-level students receive initial exposure to the fundamental components of those skills. Because upper-level students need to understand concepts in great depth, teaching the simpler constructs behind the concepts encourages their understanding.

TEACHER COLLABORATION
ACROSS SCHOOL DISTRICTS

As students and teachers within a school realize the benefits of their combined efforts, it is worth investigating an extension of these collaborations by considering what the school districts nearby might have to offer. The range of opportunities for academic enhancement is increased as teachers from different school cultures join for similar goals. Students who are striving to experience the world can be guided in their experimentation by coteaching activities that join schools and their students.

Robyn, a high-school English teacher, recalls her high-school experience with collaboration:

> When on the high-school debate team, we worked in our writing class on the development of pro and con arguments addressing current topics presented to us by a neighboring school. Once a month the teams from the two schools met to deliver their debates orally, and following each meeting our teachers would sponsor a cookie and punch gathering. Beyond developing my writing skills and learning a tremendous amount about current events, we were able to meet students from other geographic regions and cultural backgrounds. We spoke with students whose first language was not English for the first times in our lives. We witnessed fashion and behaviors which were previously foreign to us. Our first encounter with a physically disabled student occurred in these programs, as did our first attempt at drinking punch from crystal glasses and using cloth napkins. Our academic gains were well complemented by our increasing social development which was fostered in this program.

Twenty years ago, Robyn experienced a cross-district collaboration using pencils, papers, and a school bus. Today computers and their applications to education provide countless opportunities to join school districts that are geographically near and far. Beyond simply incorporating computers into a curriculum, the technology provided by computers opens lines of communication that were previously unavailable to all but the most serious of computer techies.

The establishment of a network into which all students can tap is an important component of cross-school collaborations. The computer network enables all students to participate in dialogue that promotes academic and social skills.

Ubbelohde (1991) developed a plan that combined two schools in the development of students' writing skills. Activities included electronic mail debates and sharing of students' writing through the development of continuous stories. Two high-school teachers and their ninth-grade students participated in the collaborative program which had three activities. The participants realized many academic benefits, including the development of logic and reasoning, use of persuasive language, reading comprehension skills, and hands-on computer use. Beyond these academic gains, students can benefit from the diversity that peers from other school programs can share through their writing.

The written debates require students to temper their adolescent emotions with logical arguments and reasonable charges, demonstrating respect for others' views, skills not often practiced with peers seen on a daily basis. Figure 2.14 presents a summation, originally developed by Ubbelohde (1991), of the student guidelines for participating in cross-school collaborations.

FIGURE 2.14. DEBATE GUIDELINES

1. Each team assumes the role of either the group responsible for proving the identified resolution or the group negating that same resolution.

2. Any individual can respond if the reaction presents only one point of view and all responses remain focused on the issues.

3. Each school must be given the same number of opportunities to respond.

The continuous stories require students to follow logical story development by initiating plot ideas of their own and developing ideas of their peers in other schools. Characters are created and then developed as a result of multiple perspectives, encouraging students to consider others' viewpoints. Figure 2.15 summarizes Ubbelohde's eight steps for successful continuous story collaborations.

Not only can school districts nearby benefit from collaboratively planned activities, but global collaborations can also be created that serve all students and teachers involved in the advancement of student understanding of the world in which they live. These collaborations can take many forms and are facilitated by the connections possible with the computer technology available in many schools, but need not rely on computers to succeed.

FIGURE 2.15. CONTINUOUS STORY GUIDELINES

---

1. Any student from the other school may continue the story.
2. All continuations should be of equitable length.
3. Any student can add a character by developing the character. Only a character's creator can remove that character from the story.
4. Each story will have a limited number of entries. The student who makes the last entry must provide the story's ending.

Not only can school districts nearby benefit from collaboratively planned activities, but global collaborations can also be created that serve all students and teachers involved in the advancement of student understanding of the world in which they live. These collaborations can take many forms and are facilitated by the connections possible with the computer technology available in many schools, but need not rely on computers to succeed.

Joining students from another country who are learning English and English-speaking students who are learning a foreign language can provide opportunities for all to practice. The students could begin their collaborations by using simple conversations to introduce themselves to each other. As this conversational communication continues, it can be expanded to include discussions about geographic regions, customs, traditions, politics, and other culturally specific issues. Students from both countries practice their writing of the foreign language as they transmit information and their speaking skills as they report on their communications to teachers and peers. These types of activities can be communicated via written materials, audio tapes, or electronic mail. Even telephone conferences can be used to implement this sharing of language.

Wright (1991) describes a computer conference project that joins students from different countries with the goal of improving writing proficiency. Students in both elementary and high schools practiced their writing for a real audience of readers as well as their teachers. Going beyond a simple pen-pal program, several classrooms can work together to pick and choose writings that are of interest to them and appropriate to their academic needs. Students in this program have many opportunities to improve their writing skills while learning more about people from other cultures and the world beyond their own.

COTEACHING WITH REGULAR EDUCATION AND SPECIAL NEEDS TEACHERS

Inclusion has met with a variety of responses from both special educators and regular education teachers. Some are trying to work together enthusiastically while others fear that their students will be shortchanged by inclusion. Still others work on a major player/minor player arrangement in which the regular education teachers teach and the special educators come in, helping their students and others in more of an in-class tutorial position. In other situations, the regular education teachers send their students to the resource room for help during the regular class instruction.

Some suggest that teachers will figure out how to work with inclusion because they are professionals, and they are employed in schools with other professionals. The reality is that inclusion will only be successful when teachers are motivated to want to work together and are able to successfully initiate coteaching with their fellow teachers. Teachers will be able to work in inclusion settings with a higher possibility of success if they are provided with guidance in how to work effectively with other teachers or with paraprofessionals in coteaching lessons.

When coteaching, both the regular education and the special needs teacher can realize many benefits. For example,

- Both teachers become better informed about what is happening in the classroom and in the special educator's program.

- The regular educator receives more in-depth information about the special needs students, and the special educator learns how his/her strategies can be helpful to all students.

- Each teacher adds more successful strategies to his/her own repertoire.

- Teaching in a partnership mode allows both to observe and expand on the strengths of the other.

- Teachers have more student-individual contact opportunities, which can increase motivation and develop student self-control.

- Finally, a sense of belonging can occur since the special needs teacher is working side by side with the regular education teacher.

As teachers increase their teaching effectiveness through coteaching, students also benefit. Figure 2.16 identifies some of the student benefits from teachers who coteach.

FIGURE 2.16. BENEFITS OF COTEACHING FOR STUDENTS

- ◆ Participating teachers are aware of special needs and abilities.

- ◆ Assignments from participating teachers are coordinated.

- ◆ Multiple teachers can help students with assignments.

- ◆ Feedback on individual tasks is received from different teachers.

- ◆ Content material is examined from multiple perspectives.

Unfortunately, with all of the potential positive outcomes of coteaching, some teachers who have attempted coteaching report multiple problems with the implementation of lessons. Even though these teachers have the motivation to collaborate and have worked with a number of planning strategies, they sometimes feel dissatisfied with the resulting lessons for a variety of reasons. Some of the common reasons for this dissatisfaction include the following:

- ◆ The work in planning is not assigned equally.

- ◆ The materials to be used are created by one more than the other.

- ◆ The teaching becomes regular-educator-dominated in spite of the plan.

- ◆ The special educator does not use the classroom procedures that are followed every day by the regular educator's students.

- ◆ Students become confused by mixed signals from the two teachers.

- ◆ Resentment can occur when one teacher creates many of the materials used by the second teacher without acknowledgment.

The lesson planning guide in Figure 2.17 addresses the problems associated with coteaching. This guide requires that both teachers engage in the decision-making process to determine the objectives and the modifications to objectives for each lesson. It sets up a possible sequence of activities to be planned to address the objectives.

The guide provides for the specific assignment of planning of activities, indicating which teacher will create the activity and who will present content during that activity: the regular educator, the special educator, or both. Because work assignments have proven to be uneven, there is a section for materials that delineates which teacher will gather or construct each listed item for the lesson.

The methods for evaluating student progress must be listed and specifically designated as to which teacher will be responsible for constructing and imple-

---
FIGURE 2.17. COTEACHING PLANNING GUIDE

Coteaching Lesson or Unit

Note: This is a plan which is prepared and taught by both teachers.

Regular Classroom Teacher:

Special Education Teacher:

What Subject Will Be Taught?

Student Objectives:

Modifications to Outcomes for
Special Needs Students:

Answer the Following:
How Often Will the Inclusion Teacher Be in the Room?

What Activities Will Be Used to Teach the Unit/Lesson? List Them.

Who Will Plan Each Activity?

Activity	*Planner*	*Presenter*	*(One or Both)*
Anticipatory Set			
Activity 1.			
Activity 2.			
Activity 3.			
Activity 4.			
Closure			

Materials Needed? (List Them)	*Who Will Gather /Construct Each?*
Materials (1)	Who Will Gather/Construct
Materials (2)	Who Will Gather/Construct
Materials (3)	Who Will Gather/Construct
Modified Materials (4)	Who Will Gather/Construct

Evaluation Instruments: What Is Needed? Who Will Construct? Who Will Implement?

Evaluation Instrument (1)	Who Will Construct?	Who Will Implement?
Evaluation Instrument (2)	Who Will Construct?	Who Will Implement?

Student Responsibilities: (List)

Classroom Procedures/Rules/Expectations: (List)

Evaluation of Objectives by Both Teachers:

Self-Evaluation by Both Teachers:

menting the evaluative tool, whether it be a checklist of completed work, a test, a rubric for students to use, or a set of criteria for multiple ways in which a student can show what he/she has learned.

Another area that causes trouble appears to be the manner in which each teacher deals with occasions of student irresponsibility. Because of this, the plan includes a section in which both teachers must list the responsibilities they expect of their students during the coteaching lesson. A connected problem has been the manner in which each teacher deals with procedures of the classroom. When are students to sharpen pencils? When is silent work needed? Will students raise their hands to contribute? Can both teachers agree to insist on total attention before either begins to teach or to direct the students? Even issues such as the procedure for students to move desks for cooperative learning activities should be discussed so that both teachers agree on the order of procedures and so that teachers will not be uncomfortable with the directions of the other.

Detailed planning and the specific assigning of tasks to both teachers help everyone in the classroom to experience a successful coteaching experience. Experience with successful inclusionary practices such as coteaching will promote positive attitudes in regular educators and special educators and effective instruction for all students.

COTEACHING WITH ENGLISH AS A SECOND LANGUAGE STUDENTS

In *Rethinking the Education of Teachers of Language Minority Children: Developing Reflective Teachers for Changing Schools*, authors Milk, Mercado, and Sapiens (1992) note that,

> Language minority children are best served by instruction that is characterized by high levels of interaction framed within collaborative instructional modes. Such instruction appears to be attained by teachers who consciously and deliberately push students beyond their current individual capabilities toward goals that focus on social-cognitive processes rather than on lockstep skills mastery. (pp. 5–6)

ESL teachers know that language acquisition and development are enhanced by interactions in all areas of student learning. The opportunities for listening to informal student talk occurring within the context of collaborative activities give the ESL student practice in developing comprehension skills. Since the nature of small groups is informal, the ESL student feels less pressure to understand everything and to be on call for correct answers. The interaction in small groups also provides the ESL student with a variety of nonverbal expressions, gestures, and cues that contribute to understanding.

Milk, Mercado, and Sapiens (1992) include Hamayan's 1990 list of six areas in which the regular education teachers impact the language-minority student. The regular education teacher becomes all of the following:

- Mediator and facilitator of content learning

- Facilitator of the acquisition of English as a second language (through multiple avenues, including integration of ESL instruction with content area subjects)

- Language model

- Mediator of mainstream culture

- Advocate for student empowerment

- Collaborator with administrators and other teachers to provide valuable information about language minority students in their classes and about the content of their classes (p. 4)

The ESL teacher and the regular education teachers can plan collaboratively to help the language-minority student succeed in the middle and secondary classroom. The ESL teacher can provide valuable insights as to the level of language proficiency that the regular education teachers can expect from each ESL student. Teachers working together in teams facilitate successful integration of language-minority students in the regular educator's classroom. "Team-based approaches to resolving instructional challenges" (Milk, Mercado, & Sapiens, 1992, p. 10) help to address the problems which ESL students have when they are placed in the regular education classroom.

Regular education teachers can predict more about the ESL student's level of performance in the classroom when they understand the amount of time the student has been in the United States, the level of literacy that he or she possesses in the first language, and the family structures and customs of the student. The ESL teacher can address all of these issues. In addition, the ESL teacher can help with the student's preparation for involvement in small groups. If all teachers involved in a collaborative effort give the ESL teachers the activities and assignments as well as the assessment procedures ahead of time, the ESL teacher can help the student to understand the procedures to be followed and also help with the content to be addressed. The ESL teacher can help the instructional team to comprehend the needed conditions that must exist in their classroom so that the language-minority student can succeed.

Collaboration for the benefit of the language-minority student can also include the ESL student's family or community members. Teachers can brainstorm a list of suggestions to translate for non-English-speaking parents so that they can support their children's efforts at home (Quintero & Rummel, 1998).

Parents or interested citizens can participate by providing translation services, tutoring, or serving as volunteers in the classroom. Members of the student's own ethnic group can add immeasurably to the understanding of the entire student body by presenting information on culture, heritage, traditions and history of the student's first-language homeland. School and community collaboration can become an important factor in the ESL student's academic and social success. Such collaborative teams also demonstrate to the other students that language barriers and other differences need not keep people from working together productively.

TEACHER COLLABORATION FOR PROFESSIONAL GROWTH

Interdisciplinary thematic unit planning, cross-grade planning, cross-school planning, and coteaching promote professional growth because teachers have the opportunity to discuss teaching strategies, explore the teaching philosophies of their peers, and learn more about other subject areas. This collaboration permits students to see their teachers as professionals consulting with each other to produce meaningful units of instruction.

Professional growth is also fostered when comfortable professional friendships develop with other teachers within the same departments and with teachers in other content areas, in other schools, and even in other nations. Collaborative planning can encourage such professional interactions. The experiences that these teachers have shared in their collaboration sessions and the discussions shared about students, content, testing, and teaching approaches in general can promote further professional growth if teachers decide to also assess their own teaching. Once teachers have successfully collaborated on learning strategies for their students, it is a small step to suggest that two of these colleagues work together to assess each other's cooperative learning plans, collaborative strategies, and coteaching lesson implementation. Most teachers are always pressed for time, yet when asked for help by a colleague, they always seem to squeeze in time to do so. Teachers can take advantage of their natural "caregiver" personalities to share with and benefit from mutual collaboration in peer assessment.

Mentor programs for beginning teachers already exist across the nation. The intent of such programs is to pair an experienced teacher with a new teacher so that help will be available if the beginner needs assistance. Collaboration on interdisciplinary thematic units, coteaching, and peer assessment can be facilitated when mentor programs are already in place and functioning effectively.

Teachers can help each other on a more informal basis by simply sitting in on a class during the instructions for a cooperative learning activity or collaborative strategy, listening and observing colleagues and students for insights and suggestions. For two mutually agreeable teachers, a collaborative assessment can be an illuminating and very satisfying experience in professional growth.

First, the two teachers should discuss their approaches to collaborative approaches, cooperative learning activities, and coteaching. Then they need to share their favorite approaches and explain the goals they are addressing through their use. The next step is to discuss concerns that they have about their own implementation of the strategies in their classrooms. Once they have decided what they want the other to observe, they need to discuss a mutually acceptable time for each to observe the other in action.

Using a checklist such as the one in Chapter 5, "Collaborative Teacher Assessment Sheet," the two colleagues agree to observe according to the stipulations of the checklist, thus avoiding negative criticism. The checklist also asks the observer to list two alternative approaches that might be used to teach the lesson. Finally, the colleague observing offers two ideas that he or she has found useful in the classroom. The two teachers then meet to discuss the observation and to plan a time for them to change roles for another peer assessment. Teachers who feel comfortable enough to engage in peer observations can enjoy many opportunities for professional growth.

CONCLUSION

Collaborative teaching is an important extension for teachers who already use collaborative strategies and cooperative learning activities in their classrooms. Developing students' academic and social skills through these strategies enables teachers to better address the diverse needs of today's student population. Teachers working together to further that goal serves everyone well. As a colleague once asked, "After all, why should the kids have all the fun?"

3

SOCIAL SKILLS

"Sharing! Since I was three years old, my mother has said to share. My seven-year-old twins share a bedroom. We have fish that share food. Sharing is a small thing to ask of teenagers...isn't it?" complained Reg Moski as he slumped into a chair in the faculty room.

"That sounds like a loaded question, Reg," commented Brent. "Have a rough group last period?"

"Actually, they're usually good students, but I have a terrible time getting them to work together some days. Can't they just cooperate?" said Reg.

"Well, you might think so," responded Marci, "but it sure seems like I spend a fair amount of time teaching it. Actually, I'm teaching sharing, listening, praising...a host of other social skills that students don't seem to have mastered yet just so they can work together in our collaboration tasks and our cooperative group activities."

MORE THAN JUST ACADEMICS

Group tasks of any type involve students in situations requiring complex interactions. As students work to master a variety of academic content with their peers, they also employ social skills necessary to learning. Social research has long concluded that people who work together for one goal experience positive feelings for the members of their group. Piaget (1980) examined the role of social interactions as beneficial to cognitive development noting that when various opinions and perspectives are presented in collaborative activities, students are forced to reconsider their own ideas, thus expanding their understanding. Vygotsky (1978) proposed that learning is, by its own design, a social behavior. Adger, Kalyanpur, Peterson, and Bridger (1995) suggested that cooperative groups "provide the social structure so that students have someone to talk ideas over with as they learn together" (p. 91). Beyond academic investigations, Cohen, Johnson and Johnson, Slavin, and others concluded that cooperative approaches have also promoted gains in social skills necessary to learning.

ADDRESSING STUDENT BEHAVIORS AND ATTITUDES

Social skills address the behaviors and attitudes that students need to develop as they mature. These skills help them interact positively with peers, family, and people in positions of authority. The social skills not only assist students in completing the learning process set before them, but they also allow students to practice the behaviors they will need as adults. With the guidance of teachers and peers, students can observe and perform positive behaviors, can receive redirection when needed, and can see the immediate results of their own behaviors. In these ways students move ahead every day in the mastery of these important lifelong skills. Vygotsky (1978) concluded that once students can perform a task with peer support, they are better able to perform that task independently. The opportunity to grow in a supportive peer group is essential to moving students toward independence in learning and in life.

A wealth of research conducted in the areas of education, psychology, and sociology has demonstrated that groups of people working together are more effective at solving problems presented to them than are people working alone. Collaborative and cooperative tasks allow students to develop both their social skills and their problem-solving skills while working toward a productive end. John Dewey (1963) felt schools should employ approaches that would engage students in the processes of a democratic society so those students would be ready to assume their adult roles as contributing citizens. As students examine these societal issues in school, they are preparing to successfully enter society beyond the school. Preparing students to be contributors to a democratic society is a fundamental purpose of our educational system. Schools, by the nature of their composition, engage students in a variety of democratic processes. Unfortunately, students are not always prepared for this participation or cognizant of their roles in the processes.

Newcomb, Brady, and Hartup (1997) noted that the influence of peer groups can be a powerful resource for students and teachers. When teachers design collaborative and cooperative activities for students, they are providing the means by which students can explore the social concerns that directly affect them. With teacher direction and support, students can work together to develop the social skills necessary to be successful in a democratic society.

SOCIAL DIVERSITY IN CLASSROOMS

Classrooms today are of a far more heterogeneous nature than ever before. Significant changes in the population have resulted in classrooms with more students with limited English language skills; more students from dysfunctional families; more students with greater physical, mental, and emotional needs; and more students from different cultural and racial backgrounds. Traditional instructional techniques do not always provide the learning opportunities that ensure that students will benefit from these differences, even though the differences themselves are exceptional resources for learning. Collaborative and cooperative learning strategies capitalize on the diversity within today's classrooms. The sociogram described in Chapter 6 can help the teacher examine these differences and use them for the benefit of all students.

Bruffee (1987) suggested that collaborative learning assists students in learning how to be flexible and encourages them to adapt to changes—skills that will serve students well in a world that "requires greater flexibility and adaptability to change than ever before" (p. 13). Berry (1991) also suggested that a collaborative learning experience provides students with participation in situations that encourage them to make "productive use" of their differences. He reports that the multicultural interaction within groups encourages learning that is "unique and creative" (p. 73).

Using collaborative strategies and cooperative approaches within multicultural classrooms will promote greater understanding of the world in which students live. The experiences provided with these approaches will enhance awareness and develop understanding of culturally specific areas such as customs, religion, music, literature, and community values. When students gain knowledge about the diverse characteristics of their classmates, they begin to appreciate the differences that individuals bring to any situation. This can be directly applied to the world beyond the walls of the classroom as students encounter people with diverse backgrounds.

Cohen (1997) has made significant contributions to our understanding of classroom procedures that can facilitate the establishment of equitable classroom environments. Cohen concludes that the interaction that occurs among students within a class is instrumental to learning. When students are able to talk and work together, they are able to meet with greater success in their academic endeavors. The establishment of a comfortable environment, one in which students all feel they share "equal status" (p. 4), supports students who are "active and influential participants" (p. 4).

Parrenas and Parrenas (1993) examined the demographic changes in society that highlight the cultural diversity within individual classrooms. Their research concluded that cooperative approaches provide students from multicultural backgrounds, students with limited English proficiency, and students requiring second-language education with greater confidence, self-esteem, and social skills. Students bring to the learning environment many different values and a range of background experiences, and all can benefit from these differences.

COMPONENTS OF SOCIAL SKILLS

Cooperating while working toward a group goal requires social skills that are not necessary when working independently. When Reg Moski says he wants his students to "just cooperate," he may not realize that the skill of cooperation is really built on multiple smaller skills. Identifying the components of cooperation results in a list of behaviors expected of children such as taking turns, sharing materials, not interrupting, praising each other, and listening. Asking his students to "just cooperate" is really asking for a great deal. But when breaking the expectation of cooperating into smaller steps, students can readily move ahead with cooperative behaviors. Figure 3.1 lists social skills in the two categories of simple and complex because teachers may not always easily identify the skills.

FIGURE 3.1. SOCIAL SKILLS REQUIRED FOR COLLABORATIVE AND COOPERATIVE LEARNING TASKS

Simple Social Skills		*Complex Social Skills*	
listening	observing	respect	facilitating
sharing		compassion	compromise
taking turns		tolerance	leading
praising		supporting	appreciating
waiting		patience	

It is important to note that some social skills are very complex and actually comprise several simpler steps. Mastering complex social skills may actually be the result of the successful application of several simple skills. The social skills listed in both categories here are not inclusive. Teachers will discover social skills needed by students as the group processes unfold. When groups recognize they are not working efficiently, they may require social skills that have not been presented here. Teachers and students then determine the social skills necessary at that time to move the students forward.

Johnson and Johnson (1994) have differentiated between two basic types of social skills: task and maintenance skills. Task skills are those behaviors that enable student groups to complete the activity given them. Task skills could include such behaviors as sharing ideas, following directions, and checking for understanding. Maintenance skills are those behaviors that underscore the contributions of each of the members of the groups during the completion of the activity given them. Maintenance skills might include encouraging, checking for agreement, and respectfully disagreeing. Reg Moski's plea for his students to "just cooperate" is recognition of his students' need to both complete the cooperative task and assist each other in the process.

TEACHING SOCIAL SKILLS

Marci seems to recognize the need to teach social skills to her students.

Just as academic skills need to be taught, social skills also need to be directly addressed by the classroom teacher. It is not enough to tell students that they need to share materials. Students must know a great deal of information:

- ◆ What materials are to be shared?
- ◆ Who begins with the materials?
- ◆ To whom are the materials passed?
- ◆ How are they to be passed?
- ◆ In which direction are they to pass?
- ◆ How long will each student possess the materials?
- ◆ Who gathers and returns the materials?
- ◆ To what location are materials to be returned?

What may seem like an obvious behavior—"share materials"—may require detailed directions and close supervision. Specifying expected behaviors, modeling those behaviors, and guiding students in their practice of the behaviors are necessary to teaching those skills.

The clear delineation of expected behaviors and the specific steps by which students will move toward the social skills goals are very important. Besides explaining the behaviors, teachers might clearly post the social skills demonstrated by those behaviors in the classroom to serve as daily reminders and reference points for students. Figure 3.2 provides samples of possible behavioral guideline charts to facilitate middle-school students in their use of the social skills necessary to work successfully in groups. By allowing students to see up front what their goals are and how they must prove mastery of those goals, students are aware of what is expected of them. These guidelines help students maintain focus.

FIGURE 3.2. TWO GROUP BEHAVIOR GUIDELINE CHARTS FOR MIDDLE-LEVEL LEARNERS

Our **Musty** *Rules*	*On the* **SHELF**
Everyone **must** take turns speaking.	Speak in quiet voices.
Everyone **must** listen to each other.	Help others when asked.
Everyone **must** take turns using the materials.	Engage actively in group tasks.
Everyone **must** offer help when asked.	Listen to other group members.
Everyone **must** be responsible for participating.	Form your group quickly and quietly.

Jane Richards knocked lightly on the door to Reg Moski's classroom.

"Hi, Mrs. Richards, how can I help you?" Reg asked as he opened the door.

"I am sorry to interrupt your class, Mr. Moski," responded Jane.

"Oh, no problem, we're always glad to see you."

"Well, that's nice of you to say," smiled Jane, " I was in the office and looked out the front windows to see that your car lights are on. I tried to turn them off for you, but your car doors are locked. Would you like to give me your keys, so I can take care of the lights for you?"

"Thank you so much. I would appreciate that. It's awfully cold to be walking home after school today if I have a dead car battery," Reg said as he handed Jane the keys. Jane left and Reg turned back to his class.

"Mr. Moski," asked Shandra, "Are teachers always that nice to each other?"

"Actually, yes, most of the time we try to help each other out," laughed Reg. "You know—COOPERATE—just as I'd like all of you to learn to do."

Teacher modeling of expected social skills allows students to see the shape and form of these skills. Showing students within your classroom what these skills look like clarifies exactly what you expect to see from them and what they can expect to see within their groups. Modeling need not be staged nor contrived, though the use of role-playing can allow demonstration of specific skills needed. Integrating collaborative and cooperative behaviors into daily instruction immerses students in these skills before they are asked to use them independently. Figure 3.3 lists classroom opportunities to demonstrate the social skills necessary for productive group activities.

FIGURE 3.3. CLASSROOM DEMONSTRATIONS OF SOCIAL SKILLS

---

1. Use please and thank you when addressing students. Expect students to do the same with teachers and peers.

2. Have materials available to share with students. Cans containing used pencils, erasers, paper clips, and other daily supplies can be accessible for students to borrow from or add to.

3. Make it a practice to listen carefully to students when they speak. Use eye contact and positive body language to show students you are listening.

4. Praise students when it is deserved. Brief and private comments can be delivered as students are engaged in class activities.

Once students are aware of the academic and social goals toward which they are working, they need to know the steps that they will need to take toward those goals and the specific roles they will fulfill in moving through those steps. At this time all group members must clearly understand the responsibilities they have to themselves, to the teacher, and to their fellow group members. Teachers can guide this application of social skills by facilitating both the formation of groups and the initial contacts that students make within those groups.

When determining the composition of groups for a collaborative task or a cooperative activity, teachers might consider several questions relative to the activity. Responses to these questions can provide information that will allow teachers to form groups containing characteristics that should develop students' abilities to work productively.

- What is the academic goal of this activity?

- What social skills will be needed within each group?

- What academic skills will be needed within each group?

- Which areas of student diversity will facilitate the progress of groups?

- How many groups will be needed?

- How many members should each group contain?

- What roles will members of groups assume? (See Figure 3.4.)

Responses to questions such as these will direct teachers in forming groups that can work together to meet the goals set before them. Once these issues have been examined, teachers can select students for each group based on the needs of the activity to be completed. Student selection in this manner sets the stage to begin the development of a team attitude within groups.

One important way to build cooperation into group learning strategies is to assign predetermined roles to students within each small group as referenced in Question 7. Assignment of specific roles provides a tangible means by which individual students can participate as leaders by identifying specifically how they are to serve as the leader. This assignment also guides student group members in roles that move them out of positions of leadership, encouraging them to look to others to guide the learning process. The sharing of responsibilities within groups is not a skill that teachers can assume students are prepared to handle. However, the assignment of these tasks is an effective way to facilitate both the assumption of leadership and the development of competence in sharing responsibilities. Figure 3.4 provides a list of possible roles that could be used in learning groups.

FIGURE 3.4. ROLES FOR GROUP MEMBERS

monitor	timer	writer	praiser
speaker	recorder	checker	summarizer
reader	observer	paraphraser	material manager
taskmaster	go-for	questioner	

Researchers such as Johnson and Johnson, Slavin, Cohen, and others provide a great deal of information detailing methods that teachers can employ in the effective formation of small groups within a classroom. Information from Chapter 6 of this text also provides information to assist teachers in these formations.

TEAM BUILDING

Physically creating groups is not all that is required to promote the productive, social behaviors that students need to be successful within those groups. Students may not have prior experiences with students of different backgrounds and may not be comfortable in heterogeneous groups right away. Another factor to consider is that students may be comfortable completing school work independently and, therefore, are unsure of what is expected of them with groups. Many researchers in the areas of collaborative and cooperative learning strategies address the need for team building early in group approaches so students will understand how to work together efficiently. Foyle and Lyman (1989) refer to group-building activities that allow students to practice group participation skills when they first convene. Team building is a means by which students can make positive initial connections with each other. As students learn about other group members, they begin to recognize the resources available to them within their group. Adger et al. (1995) noted that the time teachers dedicate to teaching students how to work cooperatively is "well worth the effort" (p. 143) in facilitating successful group experiences. Developing rapport within groups leads to the creation of a safe environment in which students can progress academically and socially.

There are, perhaps, as many activities for providing team-building opportunities as there are teachers using them. However, each activity serves the general purpose of having students socialize with peers in a productive way. Simple tasks requiring students to learn the names of their teammates and more complex tasks employing multiple social skills serve to nurture a feeling of collegiality within student groups.

- ◆ Slavin (1995) suggests a simple activity of "Name Learning" to involve students in becoming familiar with all members of their group.

- ◆ Graves and Graves (1985) designed "Broken Circles" to engage students in an activity that promotes the behaviors of paying attention to peers and contributing to group goals.

- ◆ "Two-Minute Interviews," an adaptation of the "Three-Step Interview" strategy can be used to promote initial familiarity with partners. As student pairs ask questions of each other, then share information with the larger group, they are practicing listening, questioning, and summarizing.

♦ Dishon and O'Leary (1994) created a pairs activity called "What's In A Name?" which involves students in discussion promoting talking, listening, and summarizing information provided by group members.

♦ Snodgrass created "Stop, Look. and Listen" to engage older students in behaviors such as making eye contact and listening carefully as others speak to assist students in greater understanding of peers' communications. In this activity students must not only listen to peers, but also give positive feedback during group sharing. Figure 3.5. provides a brief procedural description of the stop, look, and listen strategy.

FIGURE 3.5. STOP, LOOK, AND LISTEN

---

1. Students are placed in pairs, each with a partner of diverse characteristics.
2. Each partner receives an index card with the categories of HEARD and SAW written on it.
3. Students take turns telling information about themselves as directed by the teacher. Ideas might include name, nickname, favorite free-time activity and career goals.
4. As one partner is speaking, the other makes notes on the index card about what is being said and what positive physical behaviors he or she observes (i.e., nodding, smiling, leaning forward).
5. Partners are then joined with other pairs to form groups of six. Within this larger group, the index cards are placed face down in the center of a table. Members randomly select one card, read the information aloud, and attempt to identify the group member to which the information refers.

CONCLUSION

Both collaborative strategies and cooperative learning activities have been recognized as effective instructional tools that promote active participation and academic success for students. Years of research in social psychology and in a wide range of academic arenas have also concluded that these same methods are effective means by which teachers can promote the social skills necessary for students to benefit academically. Teachers who employ collaborative strategies and cooperative activities and who remain aware of the dual benefits—academic and social—of these strategies can provide maximum learning opportunities for all students in their classrooms.

4

REVISITING
COOPERATIVE
LEARNING

Seeing Jane Richards and Jim Chang in the teacher's lunchroom, Brent Ortiz walked over and took a seat nearby.

"Well, Brent, how are your career day guests doing?" asked Jane.

"Well," replied Brent, "I can tell you that I continue to be surprised by what I learn from my former students."

"Wait, I've had a good day so far, so only share if you had a good surprise," said Jim.

"I'm not sure if it's good, but I think it helps confirm what we are doing in our SAM group," observed Brent. "Do you remember Taylor Swanson? He graduated and went to State University."

"Yes, I remember Taylor," said Jane.

"He's home on his spring break," continued Brent, "so I invited him to talk to my class about college. Students asked him about the studying he did in high school, and he told about an experience he had as a student here that really struck me."

"Uh-oh, I'm not feeling a good surprise in this," responded Jim.

Brent repeated the story that Taylor had told:

When I was in 11th grade student, we read a series of poems in American literature. The teacher then placed us in groups and directed us to write a poem for parents' night. We had two class periods to write the poem and prepare it for grading and to be displayed. Two members of my group, Erin and Michelle, were good-looking and very popular, and the other member, Joshua, was smart and pretty quiet. For two days, I flirted with Erin and Michelle, while Joshua wrote the poem. On parents' night our poem was displayed in the room with a big letter A and the comment, "This is exceptionally well done."

To this day, I cannot remember the content of that poem. I do remember my awkward attempts to discuss the poem with my parents while they beamed with pride for work I did not do, for an A I did not earn.

Brent paused, "Taylor went on to talk about the importance of students doing their best and all that, but I was already taken back by his story."

Jane sat back in her chair and said, "Wow, if there was ever reason to hone our cooperative learning activities, *this* is it. I think I'll pull out my old materials on cooperative learning and give myself a quick review."

INTRODUCTION

Taylor's experience with group work is an example of what researchers have been saying for decades. Educational researchers such as David and Roger Johnson (1994), Robert Slavin (1994), and Spencer Kagan (1992), among others, have long impressed upon teachers, students, and parents that cooperative learning is not just group work. Johnson and Johnson (1994) have provided detailed information concerning the significant differences between what is viewed as traditional group work and more contemporary cooperative learning group work. Figure 4.1 highlights some of the differences noted by teachers who have used group assignments in their classrooms and by researchers in the field of cooperative learning.

FIGURE 4.1. CONTRASTING GROUP WORK AND COOPERATIVE LEARNING

Group Work	*Cooperative Learning*
Students work on their own.	Students are dependent on each other.
Some students do all of the work.	Each student is accountable for the work and the learning.
Group composition is not related to task.	Groups are formed based on task to be completed.
Social skills are not taught.	The teacher provides instruction in social skills.
Teacher does not participate in the group work.	The teacher closely supervises groups.

In group work, students are able to work on their own. They may occasionally discuss their work with other members of their groups, but ultimately the work they produce is a result of individual effort and not the result of cooperating with peers. Students do not feel they are dependent on other members of their group or that they need each other to complete the task given to them by the teacher. Indeed, students often discover they can be successful only if they ignore the other members of the group or do the work of the other group members. Students may even move their seats or position their bodies so they can remain physically apart from the group. A frequent means of communication in these situations is, "Shhh, you're bothering me."

REVIEWING BASIC PRINCIPLES
OF COOPERATIVE LEARNING

Cooperative learning is a term that is used to describe a collection of instructional strategies involving groups of students working together to investigate content information with teacher supervision. DeJong and Hawley (1995) described cooperative learning structures as those that have small groups of students working together to meet a shared goal. Cooper and Mueck (1990) provide a definition of cooperative learning as a "structured, systematic instructional strategy" (p. 68) in which students work together for a common goal. Definitions of cooperative learning may differ slightly, but they all provide the common characteristic that every cooperative learning strategy centers around students working together to help each other learn.

To facilitate that process of working together, cooperative learning employs necessary, fundamental principles of operation. As Jim Chang refers to his characteristics checklist, he is reviewing the principles frequently promoted as important elements in creating successful activities.

Among cooperative learning proponents, there are some differences in characteristics perceived as necessary to the creation and implementation of successful cooperative learning strategies. But, when teachers and students enjoy cooperative learning experiences and when teachers can use cooperative learning as a successful instructional technique, the characteristics necessary to those strategies have been addressed. David Johnson and Roger Johnson often identify five principles that need to be present in successful cooperative learning activities:

- Positive interdependence

- Face-to-face interaction

- Individual accountability

- Small group and interpersonal skills

- Group processing

Detailed explanations of these factors can be found in *Circles of Learning* by Johnson, Johnson, Holubec, and Roy (1984). Sharan (1990) agrees with these four fundamental factors and adds the principle of group self-evaluation. *Cooperative Learning: Theory and Research* by Sharan (1990) provides a description of his interpretation of those principles of cooperative learning which he promotes as necessary to successful use. In *Cooperative Learning,* Robert Slavin (1995) identifies the five characteristics of group goals important to cooperative learning tasks:

- ◆ Individual accountability
- ◆ Equal opportunities for success
- ◆ Team competition
- ◆ Task specialization
- ◆ Individual needs adaptations

Figure 4.2 provides general information about the characteristics that teachers such as Jim Chang find useful in helping to avoid group work and in facilitating effective cooperative learning activities. Detailed information for each of the characteristics presented in Figure 4.2 can be located in the resources cited . As Jim told Brent at the SAM meeting later that week, "I figure that if I remember to provide for each of the fundamental principles in my cooperative learning activities now, one of my students may come to your career days in the future recalling tales of successful group writing in my class."

FIGURE 4.2. PRINCIPLES OF COOPERATIVE LEARNING

Appropriate Grouping refers to the combination of students within the small groups of a cooperative learning strategy. Teachers identify the content material, and the content focus dictates the group formation. Group formation is determined by the content to be examined. Cooper and Mueck (1990) stated that heterogeneous grouping of students promotes the most productive results of a cooperative learning activity.

Distributed Leadership requires that each cooperative learning structure is designed to ensure an equitable sharing of tasks to be completed. Because of distributed leadership, each group member must take a turn serving as the leader, director, or coordinator of the process at some time. Each group member has a time when the task of moving the group forward falls to him or her.

Team Building invites cooperation by developing in students a sense of belonging to their group. Group members practice working together and become familiar with each other. This creates a feeling of trust among students. Building a sense of collegiality assists students in productive decision making during the learning process. (Sharan and Sharan, 1992).

Positive Interdependence provides that the success of the group can only be achieved when each individual in the group is successful. All members of each group become responsible for the learning of every other member of their group. Because of positive interdependence, students must support each other in the steps involved in the group process. The product cannot be produced without each group member completing one part of the product (Johnson, Johnson, & Smith, 1991).

Skills Acquisition addresses the learning gains expected. Johnson, Johnson, and Holubec (1993) conclude that cooperative group activities that do not have structure and do not account for specific learning objectives will not engage students in a productive learning experience. Each structure used must be selected because of its appropriateness to the learning that students are expected to acquire. The skills must first be identified, then the structure that facilitates learning those skills can be selected.

Group Autonomy provides opportunities for students to make decisions within their groups. The composition of each group will color the process used to complete tasks so groups must be allowed to make choices about the process they will employ to get their jobs done.

Individual Accountability holds each student responsible for proving that he or she has learned the material under study. Slavin (1995) stresses that individuals must prove their learning without assistance from other group members. Individual accountability ensures each student will demonstrate academic and social growth.

Teacher as Facilitator alters the traditional teacher's job of giving information to the new job of directing the learning. The teacher leaves the front of the room for varying positions around the room. Instead of talking to the whole group for the majority of the class time, the teacher spends significantly more time listening to student groups and speaking with individuals. Telling students what they should do and what they should know is replaced with listening for what students need and responding to those needs.

Group Processing involves students in monitoring group progress and assessing group performance. The teacher builds into activities time for groups to examine how well they are working toward success. They identify obstacles and decide how they will address those problems.

USING COOPERATIVE LEARNING

Cooperative learning has a long history of use. In 1898, Norman Triplett published information concerning cooperation and competition. Further work by Deutsch (1949) investigated the psychology of cooperation. More than 1000 studies have been conducted to investigate the use of cooperative learning on student learning.

The theory that people working cooperatively often achieve more than people working independently is a generally accepted principle of social psychology (Deutsch & Krauss, 1965). Early investigation of the role of cooperation on performance was already under way at the end of the 19th century. Triplett (1898) explored the effects of cooperative and competitive behavior on the pace of bicycle riders and concluded that cooperation increased motivation to perform. Further laboratory research on the effects of cooperative performance was conducted throughout the 1920s (Mailer, 1929) and the 1930s (Anderson, 1939).

The theory and research developed through studies in cooperation have allowed for significant progress in our understanding of the roles of cooperation and competition in human performance. Deutsch (Deutsch, 1949; Deutsch & Krauss, 1965) is often credited with pioneering research on cooperation in learning. Deutsch defined cooperation as any situation in which a participant seeks outcomes that are beneficial to others with whom he is cooperatively connected. Deutsch's extensive work in the areas of cooperation and competition allowed him to conclude that cooperative behavior could improve attitudes and achievement of learners. Deutsch suggested cooperative learning experiences as opportunities to promote learning to a greater degree than competitive or individualistic experiences.

Research on specific applications of cooperation to school-age children and learning situations has yielded numerous positive results. As early as 1951, Stendler, Damrin, and Haines compared competitive and cooperative learning situations with children, observing that children in competitive tasks had negative behaviors, but a similar task done cooperatively produced positive behaviors in the same children. Johnson and Johnson began using learning groups in classrooms in the 1960s with both elementary children and adolescents. Their research into cooperative group structures and the positive results associated with cooperative learning encouraged the Johnsons to refine the use of cooperative learning in education. Many others in the field of education have also tested and modified conclusions relevant to the effects of cooperation on student learning (Cooper, 1990; Sharan, Ackerman, & Hertz-Lazarowitz, 1980; Slavin & Tanner, 1979).

Researchers in the United States, as well as in other countries, have spent years studying the practical applications of cooperative learning. Hundreds of studies conducted in school classrooms and published in a wide range of educational journals have shown the positive effects of using cooperative learning structures with students.

> Jane Richards is walking toward her classroom, reading as she goes, when she bumps into Wayne Etheridge.

"Must be interesting stuff, Jane," laughed Wayne, "I know I'm not invisible."

"Oh, excuse me, Wayne, I wasn't watching where I was going," explained Jane.

"Yes, I see that, but what reading material has your attention at the end of a school day?"

"Actually, I'm rereading some of the cooperative learning information we got at our in-service programs a couple of years ago. Can you believe I kept this whole folder?" said Jane.

Wayne responded, "I can believe you kept it. I just can't believe you want to read it again. What are you looking for in there?"

"Well, I guess I wanted to be sure I was on the right track with the cooperative learning activities I'm using in my classes. After listening to Brent's story about his former student and being so involved in our new collaboration projects, I started to feel a little uneasy about simple cooperative learning strategies that I thought I knew well," explained Jane. "I'm glad I did review this stuff. I found some great approaches that I haven't used since last year. I'm going to reuse a few of them."

Wayne thought for a moment, "Jane, would you mind if I borrowed that folder when you're done? A review of those strategies wouldn't hurt me, either."

Examination of cooperative learning theories and their potential for application to classroom instruction has resulted in the development of many practical programs of cooperation for use in school classrooms.

Using prescribed cooperative learning strategies provides opportunities for teachers to master the implementation of those fundamental principles of group cooperation that maximize learning for students. But students differ from class to class, from year to year, even from day to day; so must the cooperative learning tasks used. Teachers competent in cooperative learning instruction may want to alter those canned approaches in ways that better address the specific needs and interests of their own students, subjects, and personalities. In doing so, teachers use the guidelines that will assist in continuing the benefits that cooperative learning provides. Considering changes in a reflective manner will help the teacher make decisions that will improve instruction, not just change it. Beyond the general principles presented in Figure 4.2 (p. 89), teachers might consider several important issues:

♦ Why do I want to change the prescribed activity? Specifically, what about the activity is of concern to me? Am I unhappy with students' performance during the task as it is currently being used? Are academic objectives not being met with the task as it is? Are social objectives not being met with this task? Does the activity currently take more time than I would like?

♦ Do I have the resources to make the changes I'd like to make? What specific texts, supplemental print, video materials, computer programs, and equipment would I need for the changes I want? Where can I get these resources? Who is the contact person to arrange the use of these materials for my class? How much "lead time" do I need to gather these resources?

♦ How will students benefit from the changes I plan to make? What specific academic benefits will they receive? What identifiable social benefits will they receive? Will these benefits be enhanced because of the changes, or would they have occurred without any change?

♦ Do I have, can I locate, or can I create appropriate assessment tools for the revised activity? Can I have these means of assessment ready before students begin the activity? Are these assessments appropriate to the redesigned task?

♦ Does the revised activity still address the fundamental principles of effective cooperative learning instruction? Have I accounted for each of these principles in each step of the new task so that this task is truly cooperative learning and not a fallback to group work?

THE BENEFITS OF WORKING TOGETHER

The ability to cooperate has been touted by parents, teachers, child development experts, child psychologists and educational researchers as a building block for success in life. T. Berry Brazelton (1992) discusses the importance of children learning the "give and take of equality" (p. 437) in building relationships with friends. Brazelton identifies the development of the "rhythms of reciprocity" (p. 437) as children knowing the appropriate times to dominate and the times to submit in their interactions with peers. He claims that the ability to do so "is basic to important relationships in the future" (p. 438). Most people involved in the education of children would agree. Therefore, the long-standing focus has been on facilitating the development of cooperation of students in schools, and, as a result, on the widespread use of cooperative learning activities in instruction.

Cooperating with peers can sometimes involve giving up some old beliefs in order to be a contributing member of the group and to be helpful in moving the group forward. Indeed, sometimes teachers need members of cooperative learning groups to come to consensus in a given task. Sometimes the subject under study is characterized by convergency; there is a right and a wrong answer, and students need to agree on a single acceptable response. When Jane Richards uses a Heads Together activity in biology to review the parts of a typical animal cell, she does so as a means to reinforce factual information gathered in a class lecture. Jane does not want students to debate the value of each cell part, nor does she want a creative writing response concerning the fictional account of a nucleus accused of abusing the power as "boss" of the cell. Jane wants students to be able to recall the name of the eight cell parts found in a typical animal cell, identify the parts in a diagram of a typical animal cell, and explain the significant characteristics of each of those eight parts. There are specific right and wrong responses to those objectives, and the heads together cooperative learning approach serves as an efficient instructional tool for moving Jane's students toward those objectives.

CONTENT AREA APPLICATIONS OF COOPERATIVE LEARNING ACTIVITIES

All of the cooperative learning applications presented here are simple in structure and implementation, thus making them appropriate as cooperative strategies to use with students. These strategies are most often used within a class period, sometimes for only minutes and sometimes for the entire period, but not usually over several periods. Teachers might use several of these strategies intermittently with more traditional teacher-directed lessons to reinforce concepts under study, and all are effective approaches to encourage active engagement of students in the topic examined.

ROUNDROBIN

Roundrobin is an extremely adaptable strategy that can be effective for promoting the expression of ideas and opinions, recalling learned information, and writing creatively. In this strategy, each student has the chance to share a piece of information to contribute to the development of the concept being discussed. The skills of writing and verbalizing ideas and opinions, practicing equal participation and respecting others' contributions are all practiced with this strategy. Figure 4.3. describes a round-robin application for geography.

FIGURE 4.3. ROUNDROBIN ACTIVITY FOR SOCIAL STUDIES: GEOGRAPHY OF THE AMERICAN NORTHEAST

1. The teacher will present a mini-lecture reviewing the significant landforms in the American Northeast. The teacher will ask the class to consider a trip by car that will take them from New York City through Boston, Massachusetts, to Stowe, Vermont, on to Bangor, Maine, and ending at West Point, New York. Students will be given a 30-second think-time, in which there is to be no talking as students individually consider the routes possible for this trip.

2. Students will gather in prearranged groups of four members. The teacher will distribute a blank response map to each group and direct one student from each group to distribute four colored pencils to the group members. The teacher will then direct students to label the identified cities on the blank map, passing the sheet to the person on their right as they each label one of the cities.

3. The teacher will present a large map that is labeled with the four cities and states on the overhead projector. Students can compare their group responses to the teacher's map and edit as needed.

4. Students will gather in groups. Students will draw the route to be taken on the map, moving from identified cities, one section at a time, passing the map to the person on their right when they have drawn their portion of the trip.

5. Once each group's route has been drawn, the teacher will lead a discussion of the landforms that comprise the American Northeast.

6. Students will gather in groups. Students will draw the landforms that would be encountered on their portion of the trip, passing the map to the person on their right when they have drawn theirs.

7. The teacher will present the map used before, adding an overlay of the appropriate landforms. Students will edit their maps as needed.

The business math teacher can make use of the same strategy in the review of the checkbook. Figure 4.4 outlines this application.

FIGURE 4.4. ROUNDROBIN ACTIVITY FOR BUSINESS MATH: USING A CHECKBOOK

1. The teacher will show an enlarged checkbook, with registry and blank checks. The teacher will ask the students to recall the steps used to write a check to a third party and maintain an accurate financial record of their checking account. Students are to use a 10-second think-time to consider these steps. At this time there is to be no talking as students individually consider possible responses to the question posed.

2. Students will gather in prearranged groups of four. The teacher will direct one student from each group to distribute the contents of the activity package, giving one student the blank check, one the check register, and one the calculator (one student is always serving as the monitor). The teacher will then direct students to write a check to "The Lumber Store," with students each completing only one step and passing all materials to the students on their right when they have finished each step. This procedure will continue until the check-writing process is completed.

3. The teacher will show an enlarged check and corresponding register. Students may compare their responses to the teacher's response and discuss steps taken.

4. Students will reform into groups. Using the response sheet given them, students will describe, in sequential order, the steps used to write a third-party check and maintain the check register. Students will each write only one step of the process, passing the response sheet to the person on their right until all steps are completed.

5. The teacher will lead a discussion of the procedures developed in groups, encouraging students to relate the purpose of each step.

THINK-PAIR-SHARE

Think-Pair-Share is a strategy that can be effective for promoting oral participation during classroom discussions. In this strategy, students have the chance to listen to other students and contribute their thoughts in a small group, then provide a response to the question and listen to responses of students from the entire class. The academic skills of factual recall, application, listening, speaking, and higher-order thinking are all practiced with this strategy. The social skills of audience behavior and constructive redirection also occur. The strategy is useful for a review of research references and for application of the various categories of sources. Figure 4.5 depicts this application for a unit on the research paper in a secondary English class (Griska, 1997).

Figure 4.5. Think-Pair-Share Activity for Writing a Research Paper: References

---

1. Students will be directed to think about the categories of resources that were discussed in class the day before. Think-time will be for 30 seconds.

2. Students will write a list of the categories they brainstormed in Step 1.

3. Students will move into prearranged pairs. Taking turns, students will tell their partners their lists of categories.

4. Partner pairs will be called on by the teacher to offer individual categories until a complete class list has been developed.

5. The teacher will distribute a handout of a resource list containing 12 entries to individuals. Individuals will have 30 seconds to consider the categories under which each of the 12 entries belongs.

6. Students will move into their partner pairs. Pairs will categorize the 12 entries from the list.

7. Partner pairs will be called on by the teacher to identify the appropriate classification for each entry.

Science teachers can apply this strategy in their content areas. Figure 4.6 shows a Think-Pair-Share activity for physics.

FIGURE 4.6. THINK-PAIR-SHARE ACTIVITY FOR PHYSICS: EQUATIONS

---

1. The teacher will present to students data collected from a physics experiment:

Time in Minutes	Temperature
1	87.5 degrees
2	91.0 degrees
3	91.5 degrees
4	94.0 degrees
5	94.5 degrees

2. Each student will individually graph these data points on his or her graph paper and try to draw a line that best fits the data.

3. Students will move into prearranged partner pairs. The pairs will take turns explaining to their partners how they chose a scale and a range for their axes and how they decided on the line they drew along with an equation to fit it.

4. Pairs will be allowed 15 minutes for sharing and discussing. Each member of the partner pairs must be able to explain the other's solution.

5. The teacher will call on individual students to explain their partner's response. Partners may assist each other in the oral explanation to the class. All class members will compare their solutions to the oral explanations given.

6. The teacher will clarify responses and answer student questions.

NUMBERED HEADS TOGETHER

Numbered Heads Together is a strategy that can be effective for motivating students to participate in the review of materials previously explored, for preparing students to encounter new information, and for keeping a steady pace during class discussions. In this strategy, students have the chance to discuss information within a small group, expanding their own knowledge of a topic by listening to their peers. This knowledge is further developed during the larger group sharing time. The skills of factual recall, checking for understanding, listening, praising, and developing convergent thinking are all practiced with this strategy. The example in Figure 4.7 develops a Spanish translation activity (Oberrath, 1996).

FIGURE 4.7. HEADS TOGETHER ACTIVITY FOR SPANISH: TRANSLATING FRIENDLY CONVERSATION

---

1. The teacher will provide an oral review of major conversational phrases discussed yesterday with the entire class.

2. Students will move into preassigned groups of four members. Each group member will be assigned a number from 1 through 4.

3. The teacher will present short conversations by showing them on an overhead transparency and reading them aloud one at a time.

4. Each group will be given 1 minute to translate each conversation, being sure each group member can present the complete conversation aloud.

5. After the minute has passed, the teacher will call time and all group members cease discussion.

6. The teacher will call out one number from 1 through 4, and students with that number assigned to them will show their number cards. The teacher will call on one of the students showing his or her number cards to orally present the conversation to the class.

7. Steps 3 through 6 will be repeated until all conversations have been completed.

In a middle-school life science class, the Heads Together activity (Logsdon, 1996) can be targeted, for example, at the water cycle, as Figure 4.8 illustrates.

**FIGURE 4.8. HEADS TOGETHER ACTIVITY FOR
LIFE SCIENCE: THE WATER CYCLE**

---

1. The teacher will have a diagram of the components of the water cycle written on the class board. Students will be told to make educated guesses as to what is happening as water works in the air, soil, plants, and animals around them. Students will need to use their critical thinking skills and their imagination to decide what information is important and to sort out the sequence of events in the water cycle.

2. Students will be given 1 minute to think of answers on their own.

3. Students will move into preassigned groups of three members. Each group member will be assigned a number from 1 through 3.

4. Each group will be given 5 minutes to share individual members' responses, being sure each group member understands other group members' responses.

5. After the 5 minutes have passed, the teacher will call time and all group members will cease discussion.

6. The teacher will clarify the steps of the water cycle for the whole class.

7. Students will reform their groups for 2 minutes to revisit their initial information considering the steps of the water cycle presented.

8. The teacher will have students cease discussion after 2 minutes.

9. The teacher will call out one number from 1 through 3, and students with that number assigned to them will show their number cards. The teacher will call on one of the students showing the number cards to orally present one component of the water cycle.

10. Step 9 will be repeated until the steps of the water cycle have been completed.

PAIRS CHECK

Pairs Check is a strategy that can be effective for practicing skills previously learned in many content areas. In this strategy, each student has the chance to solve a problem or discuss an issue first with a partner then within a small group before interacting with the entire class. The skills of practicing procedures previously learned; applying learned information to new situations; verbalizing cognitive behaviors; and helping, praising, and sharing with each other are all practiced with this strategy. Figures 4.9 and 4.10 describe this strategy in the content areas of algebra (Waychoff, 1996) and French (Fritchman, 1996).

FIGURE 4.9. PAIRS CHECK ACTIVITY FOR ALGEBRA: ORDERED PAIRS AND LINEAR EQUATIONS

1. The teacher will provide a mini-lecture and demonstration about plotting ordered pairs on a graph, substituting ordered pairs in an equation, and determining whether or not they satisfy the equation.

2. Students will form into prearranged pairs. The teacher will distribute group activity worksheets to each partnership. Students will have 30 seconds to review the sheet.

3. The teacher will direct student pairs to plot the ordered pairs on the graph, then take each ordered pair and substitute it in the equation to determine if it is a solution for that equation. At this time students will be working only with their partners.

4. After completing the activity worksheet, student pairs will turn to their assigned checking pair to discuss their responses. At this time students within each group of four may make changes to their original work.

5. The teacher will lead a review of ordered pairs and linear equations by discussing student responses. At this time, student pairs will compare their responses with the teacher's presented answers.

FIGURE 4.10. DUAL PAIRS CHECK ACTIVITY FOR FRENCH: DIRECT AND INDIRECT OBJECT PRONOUNS

1. The students will listen to a tape recording of French students discussing school work, taking notes on the pronouns used during the conversation. The teacher will use a large wall chart to discuss the use of both direct and indirect object pronouns.

2. Students will form into prearranged pairs. The teacher will distribute activity sheets to each partnership. Students will have 30 seconds to look over the sheet.

3. The teacher will direct student pairs to identify the direct and indirect object pronouns used in each question statement on the sheet with their partner. At this time, students will be working only with their partners.

4. After completing the identification of the object pronouns, student pairs will turn to their assigned checking pair to discuss their responses. At this time students within each group of four may make changes to their original work.

5. When all four within each small group agree on the responses, students will move back into their original partnerships to write answers to the original questions on the activity sheet, using correct direct and indirect object pronouns.

6. After completing the creation of answers to the original questions, student pairs will meet again with their checking pairs. Pairs will exchange papers and edit each other's.

7. The teacher will lead a review of pronouns by discussing student answers.

FOCUS FRIENDS

Focus Friends can be effective for promoting attention to information delivered through teacher lecture, video or film viewing, or assigned reading, and summarizing the information gained via these channels. The skills of focused listening, speaking, summarizing, and higher-level thinking are all practiced with this strategy. In addition, students have the chance to increase their personal attention to essential information given to them, discuss the information gained with a peer, then summarize the information in a written format. *Romeo and Juliet* provides the basis for the ninth-grade Focus Friends activity adapted from Bond (1998) in Figure 4.11.

FIGURE 4.11. FOCUS FRIENDS ACTIVITY FOR ENGLISH LITERATURE: *ROMEO AND JULIET*

1. The teacher will present a short overview of the video of biographical information about William Shakespeare and *Romeo and Juliet*, highlighting the main points and information about notes to take. The teacher will distribute a list of guiding questions for students to consider when viewing the video.

2. Students will gather in prearranged triads to discuss the guiding questions for 3 minutes before watching the video.

3. Students will individually watch the video without discussion within their triad. As students watch the video, they are to think about possible responses to the guiding questions. They are not to write any responses at this time.

4. The teacher will direct the students to move back into their triads. Students will discuss responses to the guiding questions given in Step 1 and write their answers on the question sheet. Students will be allowed 10 minutes to complete this task.

5. The teacher will call time and groups will cease discussion and writing. The teacher will show Stratford-on-Avon, England, on a large wall map to begin the discussion of Shakespeare's life. Students will be called on to provide chronological information gathered from the video to facilitate the teacher-led discussion. Students may edit their triad responses during this discussion.

In another ninth-grade class, a Focus Friends activity on the Civil War, as shown in Figure 4.12, is used.

FIGURE 4.12. FOCUS FRIENDS ACTIVITY FOR SOCIAL STUDIES: CIVIL WAR CAUSES

1. The teacher will present a short overview of the video about the Civil War, highlighting the main points and information about notes to take. The teacher will distribute a list of guiding questions for students to consider when viewing the video.

2. Students will gather in prearranged triads to discuss the guiding questions for 3 minutes before watching the video.

3. Students will individually watch the video without discussion within their triad. As students watch the video, they are to think about possible responses to the guiding questions. They are not to write any responses at this time.

4. Teacher directs students to move back into their triads. Students will discuss responses to the guiding questions given in step 1 and write their answers on the question sheet. Students will be allowed 10 minutes to complete this task.

5. The teacher will call time, and groups will cease discussion and writing. The teacher will show the fractured Union on a large wall map and discuss group responses using the map as a reference. Students may edit their triad responses during this discussion.

GROUP WRITING

Group Writing is a strategy useful for encouraging creative and expository writing and promoting critical thinking and listening in many different curriculum areas. In this technique, each student has the chance to listen to, evaluate, and use ideas from his or her peers. Students benefit from each other's experiences and knowledge in the subject area under study and writing skills in general. The skills of writing, verbalization, and respecting others' contributions are all practiced with this strategy. The same strategy can be used in many content areas, as shown in Figure 4.13 on the Constitution in an American history class (adapted from Peacock, 1997), and Figure 4.14 on the rainforest in an ecology course.

FIGURE 4.13. GROUP WRITING ACTIVITY FOR AMERICAN GOVERNMENT: THE CONSTITUTION

---

1. The teacher will lead a review discussion about the Constitutional Convention and the process of developing the new Constitution. The teacher will direct students to consider a document that could be used to guide the operation of this classroom.

2. The teacher will distribute a list of points to consider in creating this document. Students will be given 5 minutes of individual brainstorming time to consider these points. At this time students may individually write any ideas they have about the topic presented.

3. Students will gather in prearranged groups. The teacher will assign the roles of recorder, researcher, grammar proofreader, and content editor and will distribute materials to each group.

4. In groups, students will take turns sharing ideas they brainstormed in Step 1. At this, point all students are listening without comment until everyone has shared initial thoughts.

5. Students will work together in their groups to combine the given ideas into meaningful written passages using their role assignment and taking turns speaking.

6. When the teacher calls time, the editor from each group will read the written Constitution aloud to the group and provide a 30-second think time to consider progress to this point. Students will then make general suggestions for improvement, referring to the social studies text if needed The groups will work together to make improvements. Steps 4 and 5 will continue until the teacher ends this part of the process.

7. At Step 6 each group's Constitution will have been developed and will be ready for proofreading. The proofreader will peruse the

work for mechanics while the researcher will check any points that need clarification. The editor and recorder assist each of these as needed.

8. Students in each group agree to the completed Constitution by signing their individual names to the written work.

FIGURE 4.14. GROUP WRITING ACTIVITY FOR ECOLOGY: THE RAINFOREST

1. The teacher will show a short videotape to review information explored the day before about the deforestation of rain forests. The teacher will then present information about various groups that are intervening to reduce deforestation.

2. The teacher will distribute a list of points to consider for eliminating deforestation. Students will be given 5 minutes of individual brainstorming time to consider these points. At this time students may individually write any ideas they have about the deforestation of the rainforests.

3. Students will gather in prearranged groups. The teacher will assign the roles of recorder, researcher, grammar proofreader, and content editor, and will distribute materials to the groups to assist them in writing a position paper supporting the elimination of deforestation of the rainforests.

4. In their groups, students will take turns sharing ideas. At this point all students will be listening without comment until everyone will have shared initial thoughts.

5. Students will work together in their groups to combine the ideas given into meaningful written passages using their role assignment and taking turns speaking.

6. When the teacher calls time, the editor from each group will read the written paper aloud to his or her group and provide a 30-second think time to consider progress to this point. Students will then make general suggestions for improvement, referring to the science text if needed. The groups will work together to make improvements. Steps 4 and 5 will continue until the teacher ends this part of the process.

7. At Step 6 each group's position paper will have been developed and be ready for proofreading. The proofreader will peruse the work for mechanics while the researcher will check any points that need clarification. The editor and recorder will assist each of these as needed.

8. Students in each group will agree to the completed paper by signing their individual names to the written work.

READ AND TELL

Read and Tell is a strategy that is effective for assisting students in learning information read from content texts. In this approach, students practice reading for understanding, summarizing factual information, recalling facts, and listening. The skills needed to gain content knowledge from textual material are all employed in this approach. Figure 4.15 utilizes this cooperative learning strategy in Hake's (1998) unit on Golding's *Lord of the Flies*.

FIGURE 4.15. READ AND TELL ACTIVITY FOR *LORD OF THE FLIES*

---

1. The teacher will provide an oral overview of information in Chapter One. Students will be directed to read Chapter One noting character traits of each of the characters introduced.

2. Students will independently read Chapter One.

3. Students will form prearranged partnerships. One student will be assigned the job of recaller, and the partner will receive the job of recorder.

4. Students will be directed to consider the characters introduced in the first chapter of their reading. One partner will identify a character while the other partner will write the character's name. Roles will then switch so that partners will take turns recalling characters and writing.

5. When the teacher calls time, partners will work with the list they've created to describe the character traits associated with each name listed.

6. The teacher will discuss the characters and significant character traits as student pairs refer to their generated information. Students may edit their information during this discussion.

In a middle-school classroom, the same strategy provides a student-active exercise on the food chain, as depicted in Figure 4.16.

FIGURE 4.16. READ AND TELL ACTIVITY FOR LIFE SCIENCE: THE FOOD CHAIN

---

1. The teacher will provide an oral overview of information in their text about grasslands, taiga, tundra, tropical rain forests, freshwater biome, deserts, saltwater biome, and temperature forests.

2. Students will independently read the assigned text section.

3. Students will form preassigned partnerships. One student will be assigned the job of recaller, and the partner will receive the job of recorder.

4. Students will be directed to consider the first section of their reading. As the recaller recalls facts from this section, the recorder will write them down.

5. Student roles will be reversed, and students will proceed to the next section of the text. Students will continue exchanging roles as they move through the text sections.

6. When the teacher calls time, partners will work with notes they have made to write a summary of the text material read.

7. The teacher will discuss the main points that should be included in the summaries, allowing a few minutes for student partners to edit if needed.

CONCLUSION

A great deal of information concerning cooperative learning as an instructional technique is available to interested educators. Experts on this topic include David Johnson, Roger Johnson, Robert Slavin, and Spencer Kagan, among others, all of whom have made significant contributions to teachers' understanding of the research conducted on cooperation and the practical application of cooperation in classrooms. Other researchers such as S. Sharan, Elliot Aronson, and E.G. Cohen complement the contributions of Johnson and Johnson, Slavin, and Kagan in providing specific activities that teachers can adapt for their own instructional purposes. Information published by these and other researchers will provide detailed explanations of the summary points given in this chapter. The bibliography of this text may serve as a starting point for those interested in reading detailed clarification of the fundamental principles of cooperative learning as an instructional tool.

5

EXAMINING
TEACHER
DECISIONS

Jana explained to us in the faculty room about her fantastic day yesterday.

"I turned around after writing the theorem on the board and there they were, hanging on my every word. They were into it. Hands went up all over the room. Before I knew it, I was jotting down examples on the board, answering questions, listening to students clarifying for other students. It was wonderful! I sailed out of that room at the end of first period, and I've been bubbling all day!"

As teachers, we have all experienced spontaneous success stories in the classroom. At times, an accomplished lecturer can capture the attention and imagination of the students by launching into a completely unprepared story, using histrionics and the strength of the tale to produce an excellent lesson. At other times, an accomplished teacher like Jana can realize that a teachable moment has appeared and can guide the students to explore a topic or debate a question enthusiastically. No one denies that such opportunities do appear when teachers least expect them. Those teachers capitalize on the moment because of their background knowledge, teaching skills, and talent and savor such rare experiences.

Collaborative strategies and cooperative learning activities, on the other hand, cannot occur spontaneously. They require knowledge of the strategies, careful planning, and the use of appropriate alternative assessment tools to make them successfully integrated activities in the secondary classroom.

For teachers just learning the basics of collaborative and cooperative learning activities, the characteristics of these approaches can seem daunting. They may hesitate to use such learning strategies, feeling that they lack the background in student-active strategies to implement the configurations successfully. Others may feel that the traditional approach, which has served them for the past 20 years, should not be disturbed by recent approaches. Still others have the preconceived notion that the group work they've been doing for years really is cooperative learning and that they have no need for detailed planning or for alternative assessment. Liz's mentor, a 10th-grade English teacher, told her,

> You're really making too big a deal out of what I've been doing every
> year in this class since I started teaching. At least once every few days,
> I count off by 4s, and have groups of students discuss the chapters
> that have been assigned from the novel we're reading. It works, so
> what's the story? This cooperative learning stuff is nothing new. Just
> ignore those education courses! This is the real world!

Other teachers feel pressed to use collaborative and cooperative learning because professional journals emphasize the student-active classroom. There are some school districts that have had disastrous results and even fostered hatred of collaborative and cooperative learning among teachers and students by demanding that teachers use these student-active strategies to the exclusion of all other approaches.

Teachers should consider using these instructional approaches for an entirely different reason: because collaborative and cooperative learning will further the learning and increase the depth of understanding of their students.

Most teachers know what a mistake it is to implement lessons with too little or absolutely no conscious decision-making as discussed in Chapter 1. Yet, the use of the textbook may promote this very approach. Because the text has an organized body of material appropriate to a course, use of the text can lull the teacher into complacency about the direction in which the text is taking the course. If the text says that the literature course will cover figurative language as it relates to the Elizabethan sonnet next, that becomes the school district's end-all rationale for plowing ahead—often against the better judgment of the teacher in the classroom. It becomes easy to forget that the teachers are the experts with this particular group of students. Instead of allowing the textbook to dictate course content and direction, teachers should consider using their own competence more and assuming the role of expert in the teaching/learning situation. That expertise leads to conscious decision-making about subject content and teaching techniques first—before any lesson plans are made.

ACTIVATING TEACHER DECISION-MAKING

Answering the preplanning questions in Chapter 1 increases the teacher's responsiveness to course-planning ownership. Once teachers identify overall goals, content coverage, time elements, and materials, other questions become relevant for daily planning, for example:

- What is the goal of this lesson?"

- What do I expect my students to know and be able to do when they walk out the door?

After the teacher has these questions answered, then the questions become

- What instructional approaches will best achieve these goals?

- What approaches will help nurture students' disposition to learn?

- In the consideration of approaches, why should I use collaborative or cooperative learning?

- What will be gained through the use of a collaborative or cooperative learning activity that could not be done better in some other way?

- In what ways will collaborative and cooperative strategies increase my students' disposition to learn?

Answering these seven preplanning questions leads to the next step: reflecting on the responses. This conscious reflection helps to bring to bear the teacher's knowledge of the subject area and teaching expertise. Questioning and reflection lead teachers to planning that provides students with the most suitable strategies for learning.

Once the teacher has thought out the goals and objectives clearly and answered the decision-making questions relating to student-active strategies, the next task is to decide which collaborative and cooperative approaches are most suited to the learning at hand. Chapters 1, 2, and 4 outlined many common strategies and the benefits of each. Planning the details of the activities helps to ensure their success.

ENVIRONMENTAL DECISIONS

The physical setup of the room must be analyzed, and decisions must be made about the size of groups, the position of desks or tables, and the amount of movement the activity will require. Will the teacher also be able to move among the groups easily to monitor and provide prompts? If resources are to be available, where will they be located or kept?

What will the time limit be for the activity? In initial attempts at collaborative and cooperative learning, teachers often give students too much time to complete the assigned work, thus creating classroom management problems. One suggestion is to decide on time based on some rule of thumb. For example, teachers might set the time limit of three times the amount of time the activity might take them to do. If the students end up needing more time, the teacher can add minutes. With a predetermined time limit, the students tend to stay on task in a more focused way because they're working toward a clearly set time deadline.

Grouping students is a planning factor for teachers. Instead of grouping students as Liz's mentor advised her to do, grouping should be done in a conscious manner, taking into consideration ability levels, gender, personalities, and purpose for the activity. Teachers who think that they can simply split students into groups by calling off "one, two, three, and four" or saying "you four by the computer" miss the opportunity to utilize grouping for a purpose.

CREATING GUIDES

Creating an environment in which students can complete assignments by working together productively involves the construction of a guide for the activity. Teachers discouraged with their attempts to include collaborative and cooperative strategies say, "I told them exactly what to do, their partner assignments, and how much time they'd have. Then I told them to get started, and pandemonium let loose. I'll never use cooperative learning again!" That same teacher need only sit in an in-service meeting and listen to the speaker give directions for a similar, complicated maneuver to see just how difficult it is to comprehend and be able to follow a series of spoken directions.

Distributing direction guides to each group is the most potentially successful method for presenting clear directions. Groups can then consult the guide immediately if they become lost. The directions could be placed on the board or on the overhead, but students need to take longer to consult a guide if it is displayed in this manner. Many collaborative and cooperative learning activities have a series of steps or assignments which can be explained more carefully on a handout than on one board or overhead display. Because of word processing, the direction guide becomes simple to create for multiple classes. Only the names of the student groups need to be changed. A suggested list of items that could appear in a direction guide is shown in Figure 5.1.

FIGURE 5.1. GUIDELINES FOR THE CONSTRUCTION OF COLLABORATIVE/COOPERATIVE LEARNING GUIDE

- Identify the type of collaborative or cooperative learning structure at the top.

- State "You will be able to do or know _____ at the end of this activity."

- List the group members so that students will know with whom they are to work.

- List the location of each group as they are to gather in the room.

- Give a listing of specific directions for the students to follow.

- For each group, assign a taskmaster whose job is to keep track of time and make sure that all students speak before the first student speaks again.

- State very clearly the requirements for group and individual accountability.

In creating direction guides, we must keep in mind the elements of collaborative or cooperative learning described earlier. If the student-active configuration demands several specific roles, the teacher will need to assign those other roles (Slavin, 1995, p. 47).

Also, students need to know on what behaviors the teacher will be evaluating while the activity progresses. They need to know whether their group's work will be graded and also the procedure that will be followed for assigning individual grades. Evaluations, such as quizzes, essay responses, journal entries, participation in discussion, and/or group evaluations of individuals, need to be carefully delineated before the activity begins.

Teachers recognize that identifying specific expectations can be a motivating factor for secondary students; they can be motivated by high expectations and by their perceptions of teacher competence. When the teacher carefully plans the collaborative or cooperative learning activity and structures a detailed student guide, several signals are immediately received by the students (see Figures 5.2 and 5.3).

FIGURE 5.2. SENDING MESSAGES ABOUT TEACHER COMPETENCE

The direction sheet sends messages about teacher competence:

1. I am organized.
2. I have planned a meaningful activity.
3. I understand my purpose in making this assignment.
4. I have specific expectations to be met by my students.

FIGURE 5.3. CONVEYING THE IMPORTANCE OF STUDENT OUTCOMES

The same simple direction sheet conveys the importance of student outcomes:

1. I will have to demonstrate that I am completing the activity to the best of my ability.
2. I must treat the activity seriously.
3. I must come out of the activity knowing and being able to do more than I knew or did when I started the activity.
4. I am required to complete my share of the work.
5. I will have to use my time efficiently and well.
6. I will have to treat my group members with dignity.
7. I will have to demonstrate, with my group and individually, what I've learned.

Direction sheets can take many forms, but they should include the information listed in Figure 5.1. Figures 5.4, 5.5, and 5.6 are sample student guides.

FIGURE 5.4. CO-OP, CO-OP STUDENT GUIDE
FOR COOPERATIVE LEARNING

Goal: At the end of this activity, you should be able to summarize the content of three of the four environmental science articles critiqued in your group. You should also be able to give arguments for and against an author's stand on two of the articles chosen for presentation to the class.

Note: Your group assignment is indicated by your initials below.

Group A	Group B	Group C
A. G.	L. M. N.	D. N.*
K. S.*	E. M.	S. R.
L. H.	D. P.*	K. L.
V. S.	J. M.	J. E. B.

Groups have been made up so that each person in the group has already read one of the four articles dealing with the environment (distributed and assigned in class yesterday). Each group is to complete the following assignments based on previously reading the four articles.

1. The group needs to check the assignment list for groups. The asterisk (*) for a member of your group means that person is the taskmaster.

2. All members of the group must take notes on all contributed information.

3. No member of the group may speak again until all other members of the group have contributed.

4. Members of the group must work together on the assignments and come to answers that all can accept when appropriate to the particular task.

Procedure:

1. Each member of the group describes his/her article's main idea, its application to a specific environmental issue, and the member's opinion of the strengths and weaknesses of the author's argument, referring to sentences in the article that reinforce that opinion. During this task, other members of the group take notes and may question the speaker regarding content and/or application of the content to a specific environmental issue or to clarify an explanation.

2. The member reporting on the article then offers an alternative approach to addressing his or her particular environmental issue. The alternative approach is to be different from the one proposed by the author of the student's article.

3. Each member follows the same directions outlined in Steps 1 and 2 above.

4. Considering the four articles presented, the group must come to a consensus on the article most applicable and valuable for presentation to the entire class. The procedure for presentation must give equal duties for presentation to each member of the group. For example, one member may summarize the article; a second may give the arguments for and against the author's stand on the issue; a third may present the alternative solution; the fourth may ask questions of the listeners to review information just presented.

**FIGURE 5.5. SUMMATIVE DIRECTIONS FOR
THE CO-OP, CO-OP STUDENT GUIDE**

5. The entire time element is 50 minutes: 30 minutes for Tasks 1, 2, 3, and 4; 5–7 minutes for each group's presentation to the whole class.

6. During the whole class presentation, all members not presenting will be responsible for taking notes and asking clarifying questions related to the presentation.

7. Individual accountability will be assured in one of the following ways: an essay response to the presentations, a class discussion of the presentations and alternatives suggested, or an objective quiz on the content of the articles.

FIGURE 5.6. ROUNDROBIN STUDENT GUIDE
FOR COOPERATIVE LEARNING

Goal: At the end of this activity, you should have identified major people and events leading up to the Civil War. You should have predicted alternate actions that might have changed the direction of public opinion during that time. You will have reviewed the reading of Chapter 8 on "Precursors of the Civil War."

Directions: Look for your initials. Form the following groups in areas of the room designated by posted signs with the letters A, B, C, D, E, and F.

(A)	(B)	(C)	(D)	(E)	(F)
H. M.	C. N.	W. A.*	S. D.	P. B.	G. J.
L. S.	M. K.*	M. M. K.	A. K.	L. M.	B. E.*
D. C.	R. S.	N. D.	D. J.	Z. A.*	M. M.
A. A.*	S. J.	B. D.	E. B.*	R. D.	F. J.

1. Each group's taskmaster is the person with the asterisk after his/her initials.

2. The taskmaster must direct member rotation, contributions, and time limits.

3. Addressing each question, each member will contribute one item of information to the total answer. Each member contributes until the answer is complete—in the judgment of the group.

4. All members of the group must take notes on the building of each answer.

5. Students may refer to their previous class notes or to notes that they took when reading Chapter 8 for the previous night's homework; students should also use their English class notes on *Walden*. No student may use the book to contribute to the answer to each question until all questions have been addressed first without using the book.

6. When all questions have been addressed, the group may petition the teacher for permission to consult Chapter 8 in the book to add information to any of the questions. Have the teacher initial that permission here, indicating the time. _____

7. INDIVIDUAL DECISION-MAKING: Following the Roundrobin activity, a quiz will be given.

Questions for the Roundrobin activity in Figure 5.6 are found in Figure 5.7.

FIGURE 5.7. QUESTIONS FOR THE ROUNDROBIN ACTIVITY

---

1. Describe the public reaction to the Mexican War of 1848. Opinion on the war varied with the region of the country. Explain what the differences were and give reasons for that variety of opinion.

2. Using your English class discussion of *Walden*, describe Thoreau's analogy of the ants. In what way did Thoreau protest the Mexican War?

3. Name the three important figures in government other than presidential candidates during the 1848–1860 time period and explain the contributions of each and the importance of each figure to the time period.

4. As the nation moved closer to the beginning of the Civil War, factions and supporters of differing agendas emerged. List the factions described in your notes on Chapter 8 and the leaders of those factions not named in Question 3.

5. Name three incidents that inflamed the public, moving the nation toward confrontation. For each incident tell what happened, who was involved, and where it occurred.

6. For two of the incidents noted in Question 5, give an alternative action that would have helped to de-escalate the intensity of the impending conflict.

7. Who were the presidential candidates in the 1856 and 1860 presidential campaigns? What were their platforms related to military conflict? What were their campaign promises?

You have 35 minutes to complete Questions 1 through 7.

We will then have a 10-minute debriefing in which all students must be prepared to explain the alternatives they came up with for Question 6 as well as information from the other questions. At that time we will clarify and expand on answers prepared by the groups.

You will then take an individual quiz during the last 10 minutes of class.

Total time: 55 minutes

Teachers can use the checklist in Figure 5.8 to determine if they have considered all planning factors before implementing the student-active strategy.

FIGURE 5.8. CHECKLIST: TEACHER DECISION-MAKING BEFORE COOPERATIVE LEARNING ACTIVITY

_____ I determined the goal of the lesson.

(Write that goal here: When students leave class today, they should know and/or be able to do the following: _____)

_____ I considered several teaching strategies and chose collaborative strategies or cooperative learning for a purpose.

_____ I can defend my reasons for using collaborative strategies or cooperative learning activities instead of using another approach to reach my goal.

_____ I have reviewed the various collaborative/cooperative learning strategies and chosen the strategy most likely to help the students reach the goal listed above.

_____ I have chosen the resources to be used for the activity (text, supplementary reading, lab equipment, video, laser disk, computer software, visuals, etc.).

_____ I have decided on the location of all resources.

_____ I have assessed my students for achievement, leadership capabilities, social needs, and personality and have chosen to place students in groups for a particular reason. Write the reason for grouping here: _____

_____ I have constructed the activity and decided on the steps needed to complete the activity successfully.

_____ I have addressed the elements of collaborative strategies/cooperative learning in this plan.

_____ I have determined the time limit by running through the activity myself and tripling the approximate time needed for to me complete the assignments.

_____ I have created the direction sheet for the activity. This sheet has the goal; the groupings; the resources needed; the steps for completion; the manner of group and individual assessment; individual assignment needs such as taskmaster, recorder, etc.; and time limits for each portion of the activity.

_____ I have determined the manner of assessing individual accountability during and after the activity.

_____ I have constructed the rubrics or checklists that either the groups, the individual students, and/or I will use to evaluate the group's interaction and/or final product.

_____ For written responses, I have constructed any test, quiz, or set of questions to be asked orally.

TEACHER DECISION-MAKING DURING COLLABORATIVE AND COOPERATIVE LEARNING: ATTITUDE

One of the hardest assignments a teacher has to undertake is that of being quiet. Accustomed to the role of dispenser of information, teachers may find it uncomfortable to serve as facilitators of learning. In fact, many teachers aren't sure what to do in the facilitator role and may remove themselves completely from the activity, choosing instead to sit at the teacher's desk, correcting papers or catching up on other classroom duties. Such action communicates quickly to students that the teacher doesn't consider the student-active learning to be an important part of the class. Appearing uninterested in the students' progress encourages a similar attitude on the part of the students. A teacher who does not remain focused on student behavior encourages poor behavior. A teacher who leaves the learning environment encourages students to shut down, too.

Students who have observed such teacher disinterest or distancing firmly believe that any student-active learning is time to lessen focus and relax for awhile.

A teacher's decision making rests on several points during collaborative and cooperative activities. However, the first requirement is that the teacher communicate by word and action that the activity is vital to the mastering of this particular course content and that the teacher is both serious and concerned about student progress and the outcome of the activity.

The first indication of the importance that the teacher places on the task at hand comes when passing out the direction sheet and reviewing all directions with the students before they move to their assigned groups. Allowing students to move to their groups before giving thorough directions creates a classroom management problem because the students then must stop moving and refocus on the teacher again as he or she gives directions for the activity.

Secondly, some groups function better when the teacher is observing from a distance. The teacher who is within three feet of a group might be too close, engendering a sense of intimidation on the part of the students related to their contributions to any of the group's discussion and decision making. By circulating unobtrusively and maintaining a distance of approximately three feet from each group, the teacher can encourage the free flow of discussion and also communicate the message that this activity involves the teacher as well as the students. Students need to understand, however, that they must learn to stay focused and continue to progress when another person, especially a teacher, does move closer to the group. This movement can communicate the teacher's continuing role as the facilitator of the activity. At times, the teacher wants to clarify the direction taken by the group, or clear up a point of confusion that is impeding the group's progress. Short interactions to facilitate the students' learning are integral to the teacher-as-facilitator role. However, the teacher needs to avoid sitting down with the group and taking over or stopping too long to teach as the group listens.

TEACHER DECISION-MAKING DURING STUDENT-ACTIVE LEARNING: FOCUSED OBSERVATION

During the activity, the teacher practices focused observation. This observation takes two forms: the first is active observation of groups in order to determine what subject-area content seems to receive enough attention as the group members work on the task at hand and what does not. Dependent on the individuals assigned to a group and the prior class and homework preparation, students may be able to complete the task in a thorough manner or in a less satisfactory way. The teacher, as expert, listens closely to determine what will need further clarification, emphasis, or expansion during the debriefing. A 5×8 notecard is usually sufficient for the teacher to carry to jot down points to be reviewed, clarified, expanded on, and emphasized later. Taking notes on what students are doing and saying communicates clearly that the teacher is very interested and involved in the activity (see Figure 5.9).

FIGURE 5.9. SAMPLE NOTES TAKEN DURING FOCUSED OBSERVATION

Review vocab: sinecure

Go over meter: anapestic

Clear up allusion to nature.

Review universal theme—Use Group B's example.

The second form of teacher observation to be done during the activity is the analysis of group progress and individual contributions. A successful and easily completed assessment of group performance can be a modification of the same rubric that the teacher expects the members of each group to complete on their group's progress at the end of the activity. Chapter 6 presents such rubrics.

However, to assess individual student accountability during the activity, the teacher might consider using the TALK checklist developed by Mark Donato (1992) and discussed in Chapter 6.

Teacher decision making during the collaborative and cooperative learning activities also includes monitoring groups to ensure that all students are on task. Here are some important considerations in the monitoring process:

- One of the benefits of student-active learning is that, when designed correctly, the activity itself promotes self-control and positive contribution. When one member has trouble with self-control, the influence of the group can encourage a return to productive interaction.

- Taskmasters also have the duty to refocus group members to an extent, but all teachers know that student taskmasters may not be acknowledged by some students, and teacher intervention may become necessary from time to time.

- The group cannot be totally responsible for the continual misbehavior of one of the members. When it becomes obvious that a student is continually disrupting and frustrating the progress of the group, the teacher must assume final responsibility for making an adjustment to permit the group to proceed. It should always be obvious that the teacher is in charge of the class although the students are progressing with tasks in their own groups.

- The teacher is responsible for noting the time remaining for the activity. Each group's taskmaster has that assignment as well, but the groups may be so involved in tasks at hand that the attention to time is neglected.

- The teacher's intermittent and quiet reminders of time accomplish three positive results: First, the teacher communicates the need to stay focused and on task. Second, time reminders help the taskmasters to keep the group members working without appearing to be dictators in the group. Third, attention to time promotes continued teacher analysis of group progress according to the allotted time. By analyzing group progress, the teacher can determine if 2 more minutes—or 5 more minutes—would be helpful, or if the time needs to be shortened. He or she can then indicate that an announcement is to be made and when all are attentive, announce that an extra 5 minutes will be given to complete the activity. Students are grateful for such close attention to their needs when the teacher monitors the time factor in this manner, and it reinforces the teacher's role as instructional leader and facilitator.

TEACHER DECISION-MAKING DURING COLLABORATIVE AND COOPERATIVE LEARNING: SUPPORTIVE GUIDANCE

Teacher decision-making during the collaborative and cooperative learning activities includes an extremely important and often neglected requirement. As mentioned earlier, it is most difficult for teachers to be quiet while students pursue their learning in a student-active environment.

♦ The teacher who moves from group to group, sitting with each group and providing input to the group's discussion effectively stops that discussion. Students immediately assume the "lecture mode" sitting quietly while the teacher contributes to the topic at hand. Effectively, the teacher has taken the stage again. Doing so is a very comfortable mode for most teachers, and it becomes very difficult to keep such interjections to a short contribution.

♦ Student-active learning provides an excellent opportunity for teachers to work with students in a new and satisfying role: as the class leader and as the facilitator who enters discussion when needed with short contributions and who provides a supportive role in discussion and in the group's progress.

TEACHER DECISION-MAKING DURING COLLABORATIVE AND COOPERATIVE LEARNING: REINFORCEMENT

Opportunities for student-active learning have been around for a long time. Yet, observation shows us that lecture and discussion (or individual work) often take precedence over collaboration and cooperative activities.

♦ Because of such a teacher-centered classroom structure, students hesitate to contribute, fearing that their observations or opinions may not be valued. This student reluctance becomes a problem that all teachers must address.

♦ One of the most effective motivators of adolescents is positive reinforcement. It is also one of the strategies used fairly often for whole class, with comments such as "Class, you did really well today."

Teachers work less, however, on individual reinforcers, those that really are more meaningful for students. Cooperative learning activities provide opportunities for many nonverbal reinforcers such as a nodding of the head as a teacher stands close enough to a group to hear the contribution of one of its members. A pleased expression, a thumbs-up, or a smile communicates the teacher's approval of a student's work. The active observer, teacher-as-facilitator role provides the time and opportunity to do just this.

♦ When the teacher sees that a group cannot progress because of an impasse, giving reason for praise can be both individually meaningful and valuable for the group. When the teacher steps toward the stymied group and says, "Remember what Stacy said a minute ago about velocity? Take that thought and look at your problem again." This statement reinforces Stacy's contribution in a meaningful way and also moves the group toward progress again.

♦ Because the teacher then moves away, the critical thinking required for the group to revisit Stacy's contribution occurs instead of the teacher's more lengthy intervention, which might turn into a mini-lecture on velocity, thus effectively destroying the structure of the cooperative learning activity.

TEACHER DECISION-MAKING DURING COLLABORATIVE AND COOPERATIVE LEARNING: SPONGE ACTIVITIES

As the students complete the activity, the need for sponge activities becomes apparent. The teacher can construct a sponge activity which will allow those who finish first to be at work on another meaningful task while those who have not finished can continue until the time allotted is over and the work is completed.

The key words here are "meaningful task." Reflecting on the best ways for students to make productive use of extra time leads teachers to ideas for worthwhile sponge activities. Sponge activities should be related to the goals of the day's lesson. The sponge activity might be designed to move the student ahead or to expand the student's analytical skills by applying the content learned and used in previous activity to a thought-provoking question. Teachers might consider using this question to help in the structuring of sponge activities (see Figure 5.10): What might I assign my students that would expand their knowledge, allow them to apply what they've just learned, promote their consideration of new interpretations, or prepare them to add depth to the debriefing that will follow today's cooperative learning activity?

FIGURE 5.10. SPONGE ACTIVITY POSSIBILITIES TO CONSIDER

Sponging Up Time in Meaningful Ways

1. Students can be assigned to other groups and instructed to "lend" their expertise to each of the other groups as an extra member. By using their own notes, they can help another group progress. *(Note: This activity takes a great deal of confidence and social and academic skills; some students can accomplish it, and others cannot.)*

2. Students in the group need to come up with five questions that could be asked during the debriefing session.

3. Students can complete individual assignments such as journal entries or begin homework that applies today's learning to new samples.

4. Students can consider an expansion question posed by the teacher for inclusion in the debriefing discussion.

5. Students can read related materials.

In all cases, the teacher explains the sponge activity before students begin the collaborative or cooperative learning activity. The teacher should have the directions for the sponge activity written on the board, on the overhead, or at the end of the cooperative learning direction sheet. With the sponge activity instructions in written form, the teacher can easily point to the instructions or quietly move students to the next stage without stopping for a whole-class announcement. Staggered finishing is predictable with many cooperative learning activities so effective teachers plan meaningful ways for students to use extra time.

TEACHER DECISION-MAKING AFTER THE COLLABORATIVE OR COOPERATIVE LEARNING ACTIVITY

Once the activity has ended, another crucial step must follow. The teacher plans a debriefing session in which the students ask questions, answer teacher-guided questions, and benefit from teacher clarification and extension of their own work. At this point, the teacher can make good use of the focused observation notes taken earlier during the activity. Students can contribute examples that the teacher noted during the activity for the benefit of the entire group. Any misunderstandings noted through observations of the group discussions can be addressed at this time.

For an academic debriefing, the teacher may address misconceptions, clarify information, add examples, informally assess student accomplishment of the activity's goals and respond to student questions. For a social debriefing, the teacher may concentrate on leading a discussion that explores group dynamics, questions of cooperation for productive goals, leadership skills, development of empathy, strategies for encouraging all members to feel valued for their contributions, effective listening, and/or engendering tolerance and appreciating differing points of view.

A formal individual assessment, in whatever form the teacher indicated in the student direction guide, follows the debriefing session.

ASSESSING OURSELVES

Overall teacher decision-making can be informally measured by responding to the statements in Figure 5.11.

FIGURE 5.11. TEST YOURSELF: HOW DO YOU MEASURE UP?

How Do I Measure Up?

Yes	No	
___	___	I monitored from 3+ feet away.
___	___	I took notes to use in debriefing.
___	___	I kept interjections to a minimum.
___	___	I avoided sitting down for extended time with any one group.
___	___	I kept track of time.
___	___	I positively reinforced individual students nonverbally.
___	___	I monitored the entire activity.
___	___	I provided a meaningful sponge activity.
___	___	I assessed individual contributions by using a checklist.
___	___	I interceded when the group could not handle a misbehaving student.
___	___	I had follow-up debriefing materials ready if applicable.
___	___	I had individual accountability assessment tools ready.

If you feel some responsibility for a less-than-successful activity and are dissatisfied with the results of the plan containing collaborative or cooperative learning activities, you might consider the following:

♦ Your students may need more practice in collaborative and coopera-tive groups.

♦ Your expectations may need to be adjusted.

♦ You may need to analyze your planning and participation with the checklist in Figure 5.11.

♦ You need to go back to the checklist for preplanning teacher deci-sion-making in Figure 5.8 to determine what might have been left out.

♦ You may want to review the collaborative learning elements ad-dressed in Chapter 1 and the principles of cooperative learning in Chapter 4 to help you reflect on areas that you may want to alter.

ANALYZING TEACHER DECISION-MAKING WITH COLLEAGUES

Many times teachers enjoy the advantage of a comfortable professional friendship with another teacher in the building, either someone in the same de-partment or a teacher from another content area. When such a professional friendship has formed, it is sometimes possible to think in terms of these col-leagues working together to assess each other's collaborative and cooperative learning plans and implementation.

Chapter 2 presented strategies for professional collaboration and approach-es which teachers interested in working with a colleague can take to achieve successful collaborative goals. However, another tool might be useful when teacher collaboration extends to the willingness to observe each other in collab-orative and cooperative learning situations. Using the observer guide given in Figure 5.12, the observer agrees to concentrate on the stipulations of the check-list and give an alternative possibility even though the activity might already be very successful. The observer also adds two applications that have proven suc-cessful in his or her own class. Figure 5.12 is an assessment sheet for peer obser-vations.

CONCLUSION

If teachers employ conscious and reflective decision making in the preplan-ning, implementation, and overall impact of the student-active learning strate-gies, they can more effectively provide their students with well-structured, meaningful strategies that increase the students' disposition to learning and the depth of that learning.

FIGURE 5.12. COLLABORATIVE TEACHER ASSESSMENT

Observer:_____Date_____

	Yes	No	The teacher...
1.	___	___	provided clear directions before the activity.
2.	___	___	provided a student direction guide as well as oral directions.
3.	___	___	provided a direction sheet clearly stating the goals, directions, time, and accountability procedures.
4.	___	___	provided an activity that addresses the elements of collaborative and/or cooperative learning.
5.	___	___	facilitated a quick, orderly move of students to group locations.
6.	___	___	monitored from 3+ feet away unless acting as a supporter in short instances of discussion.
7.	___	___	took notes to use in debriefing.
8.	___	___	avoided sitting down to discuss with groups for extended periods of time.
9.	___	___	kept track of time.
10.	___	___	positively reinforced individual students nonverbally.
11.	___	___	used focused observation during the entire activity.
12.	___	___	provided a meaningful sponge activity.
13.	___	___	assessed individual contributions by using a checklist.
14.	___	___	interceded when a misbehaving student could not be handled by the group.
15.	___	___	had follow-up debriefing materials ready.
16.	___	___	had individual accountability assessment tools ready.
17.	___	___	conducted a debriefing session using notes and adding information; clarifying, asking questions, and responding to student questions; and making use of sponge activity results if applicable.

(Figure continues on next page.)

Alternative approaches might include

1.

2.

Two strategies that I've found useful are

1.

2.

Let's discuss this observation on _____.

6

ASSESSING STUDENT PROCESS, PARTICIPATION, AND PRODUCT

With a look of frustration, Cindy sat down in the library at the SAM meeting.

"Obviously something's wrong," she said. "Last night during parent conferences, two of my parents complained that I have too much cooperative learning in my classes. The first one was really upset. She watched her son doing the whole Shakespearean newspaper at home because his group members never worked. Then a second complaint came up in the sixth-period group. Lauri's father said that she should not have to work in groups anymore. He said he's paying taxes for his daughter to learn information and instead, she ends up teaching it to classmates who are behind. I explained that I give everyone instructions to share work assignments and to make good use of their time, but neither one of the parents was impressed. And I was afraid some of the other parents agreed. Either cooperative learning really doesn't work, or I'm not doing something to make it work. You have to help me!"

INTRODUCTION

This chapter addresses Cindy's frustration and that of many teachers who are not quite comfortable with the level of their students' involvement during collaborative and cooperative learning activities. The focus is on the types of classroom-based process, participation, and product assessments useful to teachers for evaluating students' progress and product in student-active lessons. The formative and summative evaluation instruments presented here are helpful in judging the development of students, their periodic levels of achievement, and the assessment of the instructional process itself.

Resnick and Resnick (1992) caution teachers to realize that every form of evaluation used either to justify curriculum to the public or to evaluate programs may impact the direction of the curriculum. Students should engage in meaningful discussions, solve problems, and develop in-depth thinking. Teachers want to develop a spirit of cooperation and downplay the element of competition, but at the same time, they realize that they need to assess the effect of collaborative and cooperative learning activities on the academic progress and social development of their students. Teachers acknowledge the problems associated with motivating students by assigning grades; but it is also necessary to consider the advice of Resnick and Resnick (1992) who emphasize the following in *Assessing the Thinking Curriculum; New Tools for Educational Reform*:

- *You get what you assess*. If we put debates, discussions, essays, and problem solving into the testing system, children will spend time practicing those activities.

- *You do not get what you do not assess*. If the goals of solving complex problems or writing extended essays are educationally important, those activities need to be sampled directly in an assessment program aimed at encouraging improved instruction (p. 59).

If teachers believe that in-depth learning experiences can materialize from the implementation of collaborative strategies and cooperative learning activities in which students must discuss, explain, defend, and predict, then they must provide assessment opportunities to evaluate that belief. These assessments will provide periodic evaluations of student progress and achievement and also reinforce the importance of the activity in the minds of their students. It is imperative that students understand just what such activities are designed to do for their cognitive and affective development and that they begin to view such learning strategies as integral to the learning process instead of peripheral add-ons. Hunter (1987) indicates that middle-level and high-school students are motivated to a great extent by four strategies: the perceived competence of the teacher, the use of positive reinforcement, the use of students' names, and a teacher's high expectations. Assessing collaborative and cooperative activities sends the message that the teacher anticipates that students will do their best work because the work is important.

TEACHER-MADE ASSESSMENTS

Although all teachers recognize that evaluation is essential to effective teaching and learning, they experience mixed feelings about grading students. Within the same school, on the same grade level, and within the same subject area, clarity as to what should be graded and what those grades should show does not exist. Teachers become frustrated when asked to reduce a student's grasp of content, work ethic, interest in learning, ability to work with other students for productive gain, and classroom behavior to a single letter grade. At times, they find that both students and parents are confused as to what those grades indicate related to what other students are achieving. The subjectivity threatening evaluations of students is a concern; and the psychological effects of grades on some students' willingness to hang on for one more quarter color teacher attitudes about grading.

However, Callahan, Clark, and Kellough (1992) note,

> Evaluation and grading are not synonymous. Evaluation implies the collection of information from many sources, including measurement techniques and observation. These data are then the basis for value judgments for such purposes as diagnosing learning problems, recommending vocational alternatives, and grading. Grades are only one aspect of evaluation and are intended to communicate educational progress to both parents and students. (p. 492)

Cindy is not alone in expressing her frustration that students do not respond to her expectations or that parents complain. Teachers should analyze their own behavior and also reflect on their students' accountability for meaningful learning. Some questions posed by Callahan, Clark, and Kellogh (1992) might help individual teachers and schools to reflect on collaborative and cooperative teaching practices and student learning:

♦ What should be the criteria for marking—comparison with a group, self-development, or both?

♦ What kinds of experiences are involved—academic achievement, attitudes, study patterns, personal habits, or social behavior?

♦ What consideration should be given to the psychological effect of grades on students?

♦ What tool will be used—letter or number system, pass/fail, a written description, several grades (one for achievement, one for social skills, and one for study habits), or a combination of these (p. 492)?

It is important to consider moving from what the standardized achievement tests or the textbook-constructed assessments tell teachers about their students to tools that can provide a more complete picture of student achievement. If teachers wish to use a more situation-specific classroom approach to assessment, they may consider turning their attention to the construction of other assessment tools. Using the decision-making process described in Chapters 1 and 5, teachers can use the list of goals that they hope to have their students achieve and reflect on some guiding questions that may help to define the types of assessment instruments needed.

♦ What curriculum goals are addressed adequately by existing tools?

♦ What curriculum goals are not assessed adequately by existing tools?

♦ Are the goals cognitive, affective, psychomotor or one/two/all three?

♦ In what precise ways can the teacher evaluate each of these goals?

♦ Through what ways can a student best show mastery of the goals?

♦ Is a student self-assessment tool of value in addressing mastery of such goals?

♦ Is a group assessment tool of value in addressing mastery of the goals?

♦ Which goals necessitate the student performance of a task to be observed by the teacher?

♦ Which types of assessment (oral response, group response, individual written response, demonstration, pictorial or graphic representation, or another mode of expression) best serve as tools to evaluate student mastery of each goal?

♦ What directions will the students need to prepare for the assessment of their mastery of each goal?

♦ What procedure will be followed during assessment?

♦ Will this goal need progressive assessments to determine development?

♦ Will this goal require summative assessment in the form of a percentage or letter grade?

INITIAL ASSESSMENTS

One of the first teacher-made assessments occurs when the teacher meets his or her assigned classes at the beginning of the course. Although inventories, such as the Learning Styles Inventory (Dunn, Dunn, & Price, 1986) can provide valuable insight into a student's learning preferences, a teacher can also gain knowledge related to learning styles, prior experiences, and related interests by constructing and conducting an initial survey. Such a survey might contain the statements in Figure 6.1.

The survey questions can provide a lot of informal information about students: their favorite learning environment, their preferred way to show what they've learned, the other students they might work well with, and finally, something about themselves that the teacher might not otherwise learn. For example, the student might answer the last question by saying, "Please don't ask me to read in front of everyone. I have a stuttering problem." The student who has a hearing impairment not recognized as a "special need" may use this question to divulge what he or she wouldn't say in front of the other students. The teacher who has made this informal assessment may be able to capitalize on a student's prior experiences, work-related problem solving, and personal learning preferences when planning collaborative and cooperative structures.

From this informal survey, the teacher can also prepare group configurations for cooperative learning activities. Clark and Starr (1991) suggest the construction of a sociogram based on students' answers to questions such as "Name three students that you'd like to work with all the time" and "Name two students you'd like to work with occasionally." Although the teacher needs to create groups for many purposes, a sociogram is an informal assessment of possible groups based on student preferences. It can also give a clear picture of those students who are judged as very popular or leaders in the class as well as the students who might be termed isolates.

Clark and Starr suggest that the teacher construct a key that shows a symbol indicating gender and accompanied by the student's name. For the teacher to show that the choice of working with another student is a mutual one made by both students, a connecting symbol might by a two-way arrow. To show that a student has chosen another student as a possible partner but that the student chosen hasn't listed the corresponding student, Clark and Starr suggest a one-way arrow. In the following sample, shown in Figure 6.2, girls are represented with circles and boys with rectangles.

FIGURE 6.1. TEACHER-MADE INITIAL SURVEY OF STUDENTS IN SCIENCE CLASS

Name: _____

The science project I liked best prior to this class was _____.

My favorite school subject is _____.

When I have free time, I like to _____.

When I do something well, I like _____ to know about it.

(Circle *all* that apply.) I prefer to show what I know by speaking, by writing, by making a diagram or project, by doing a lab, other _____.

(Circle *all* that apply.) I work at a part-time job during the week, on weekends, at home, in someone else's home, on a farm, at a business, not at all, other _____. If a business, which one is it?

_____

(Circle *one*.) 1–5, 6–10, 11–15, 16–20+ hours per week spent on part-time job.

(Circle *all* that apply.) When I have something difficult to learn, I like to work alone, study with another student, work with the teacher one-on-one, study with my parents, other _____.

(Circle *all* that apply.) When I have something difficult to learn, I prefer total quiet, music playing, talking about it, outlining the chapter, drawing diagrams to help me remember, highlighting in different colors, reading in bright light, working in dim light, making flash cards, eating while I concentrate, sitting at a desk, lying on the floor, relaxing on the couch or on my bed, tape-recording the information and playing it back, walking around while I review the information, doing a project that makes me use the information.

If you are new to this school, tell me where you went to school last. _____

If you do know some of the other students in this class, answer the following:

Name three people that you'd like to work with all the time: _____, _____, and _____.

Name two people that you'd like to work with occasionally: _____ and _____.

What haven't I asked you that you'd like me to know about you?

_____

FIGURE 6.2. SAMPLE SOCIOGRAM

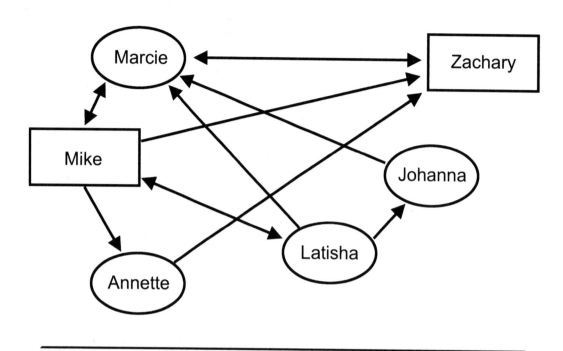

In addition to the survey and the sociogram, the teacher can determine the possible cohesiveness of group configurations by direct observation during the first few days of class. Anecdotal notes made during activities or after class can provide a valuable reference for the formation of groups. Usually teachers make such notes for students who show some characteristic out of the range of what the teacher considers normal behavior for the age group. It is not necessary to take notes on those students who are behaving and contributing as expected. Because only the outlying behaviors are noted, such an anecdotal informal assessment is possible for the teacher with large classes. A chart made for the class with a space for notes on each student functions as the anecdotal record. Only those students whose characteristics might inhibit or enhance learning and cooperation are described; room for all students is necessary, though, so that the anecdotal table may be used all year. Figure 6.3 provides an anecdotal record example.

Clark and Starr (1991) suggest that the teacher might wish to consider a number of indicators when observing students. Picking five or fewer students per day to systematically observe for the following will help the teacher to gather information for an overall picture of the class.

FIGURE 6.3. ANECDOTAL NOTES FOR PERIOD 3

Student	Date	Notes
Anderson, Marcie	9-5	Assisting others spontaneously
Cezneros, Mike		
Gramley, Zachary	9-14	Refusal to move to another seat
Mores, Latisha		
Wong, Annette	9-10 9-18	Having trouble with journaling Irritated at request to do essay response

Some indicators suggested are the following:

♦ Does the student seem to know what to do?

♦ Does the student seem to have the necessary background and skills?

♦ Is the student uncomfortable?

♦ Is the student easily distracted?

♦ Does the student need help or encouragement (p. 62)?

To reinforce his or her expectations of preparation for a collaborative or co-operative learning exercise, a teacher might institute an introductory quiz to evaluate the student's preparation for class by covering in a general way the chapter that was to have been read or the problems done. This may be done by a series of objective questions on the material assigned or by a journal entry in response to the homework. It might also take the form of a short essay question, general in nature, but necessitating that the students have done the assigned work in order to respond. See also the response journal section of this chapter.

Adolescents are quick to point out that some of their group members have not read the material assigned and to complain that these other students are benefiting by someone else's work. Incorporating individual accountability in the form of some response *before* the collaborative or cooperative learning activity begins assures that each student will receive credit for the preliminary work if, in fact, he or she has done it.

FORMATIVE ASSESSMENTS DURING COLLABORATIVE AND COOPERATIVE LEARNING

Teachers can encourage students to do their best work in a student-active exercise if they monitor students as they work. A good way to monitor student performance during the activity is by using a checklist such as that created by Mark Donato (1992). The teacher can carry Donato's checklist on a clipboard. The same clipboard can hold the index card for the teacher's notes. The checklist contains each student's name and a grid so that an evaluation can be done for as many collaborative and cooperative learning exercises as the teacher wishes to use during the grading period. Donato calls his evaluation sheet the *TALK Checklist*; he lists T as the symbol for student *talk*. The A indicates *accuracy* of the student's contribution; the L represents the manner in which the student *listens*, and the K is the symbol for the student's behavior toward others in the group. Donato describes the K as *kindness*.

For the teacher to use the checklist well, the students must know the possible categories (T, A, L, and K) and that the teacher will pick one of the categories to evaluate. The students will not know the specific category chosen on a particular day, but they will know that they can earn 2, 1, or 0 points for their participation. Teachers can attach any number of points to the systematic checklist and then use the checklist easily by simply recording a +, a check, or a – in the grid block for each student on that particular day. Figure 6.4 shows a sample checklist based on Donato's assessment tool.

FIGURE 6.4. CHECKLIST FOR STUDENT PARTICIPATION DURING COLLABORATIVE AND COOPERATIVE LEARNING

Name	Date 9/18	Date 9/22	Date 9/25	Date
Category	*K*	*L*	*T*	
Coles, Ann	+	–	–	
Daniels, Jake	+	–	–	
Gankes, Rich	+	–	+	

Allowing students to self-evaluate gives them the opportunity to compare what they've done during the activity to their own perception of their performance in past activities. Along with self-evaluation, the students can evaluate the progress of their collaborative or cooperative learning group. Such evaluations cause the student to exercise critical thinking, to compare and contrast his or her own performance to that of others, and also to assess the performance of the group. Figure 6.5 is a rubric useful for formative self-evaluation.

FIGURE 6.5. SELF-EVALUATION RUBRIC

Rate yourself according to the criteria below:

Criteria	*Need/s Improvement*	*Average*	*Above Average*	*Excellent*
My listening skills				
My ability to follow directions				
The accuracy of my contributions to the group				
My attitude toward my group members				
My ability to concentrate				
My notetaking				
My overall performance				

Compared to my work in the previous collaborative/cooperative learning exercise, my work today is

Not as good   The same   Better   Much better

When this rubric is printed on one sheet both front and back, four self-evaluation rubrics can be inserted into the student's notebook or portfolio with the use of a single sheet of paper.

If a teacher wants students to engage in more detailed self-evaluation, an individual participation rating form can be used to chart the progression of a student's participation in collaborative and cooperative activities. Figure 6.6 is a participation-rating form adapted from Bechtel (1997).

FIGURE 6.6. SELF-EVALUATION OF PARTICIPATION

Value 1. I respond to others' ideas.   *Points*

10%   0   2.5   5   7.5   10   _____
      (never)   (sometimes respond)   (mostly respond)

      2. I show respect for others' ideas.

10%   0   2.5   5   7.5   10   _____
      (never)   (sometimes   (always
                           respectful)   respectful)

      3. Participation: I…

50%   0   2.5   5   7.5   10   _____
      (never   (sometimes   (always
      participate)   participate)   participate)

      4. Relevance: My remarks are…

10%   0   2.5   5   7.5   10   _____
      (never   (sometimes   (always
      relevant)   relevant)   relevant)

      5. My answers are reasonable and correct.

20%   0   2.5   5   7.5   10   _____
(never)   (50% of the time)   (always)

Grading Scale
80–100   A
60–79   B
40–59   C
20–39   D
0–19   F

With this form, the students evaluate themselves on a more specific scale, thus exercising analytical thought processes. The teacher can also slightly change the rating from the form in Figure 6.6 in order to allow each member of the group to evaluate every other member.

Each student in the group can also give his or her assessment of the group's work during the cooperative learning exercise. Each person can also rate the current group's progress compared to the group in which the student previously worked. Figure 6.7 shows a group-evaluation rubric.

FIGURE 6.7. COMPARATIVE GROUP-EVALUATION RUBRIC

Student's Name _____

Other Group Members Include _____ , _____ ,

    and _____ .

Criteria	Needs Improvement	Good	Excellent
I think that the group…			
made good use of time.	_____	_____	_____
took turns giving information.	_____	_____	_____
made only productive comments to each other.	_____	_____	_____
listened well to each other.	_____	_____	_____
finished the assigned work well.	_____	_____	_____

Compared to my previous group (give names here), _____ ,
_____ , _____ , today's group accomplished the task

    poorly _____ the same _____ better _____ much better _____

Comments (optional):

Figure 6.8 is another approach to a group assessment (Susol, 1997).

FIGURE 6.8. GROUP ASSESSMENT BY STUDENT GROUP MEMBERS

Group Assessment—My View

Members of the Group_____

Date_____

The group...   never   sometimes always

1. gave equal time to all members. |_____|_____|_____|

2. learned from one another. |_____|_____|_____|

3. followed the procedures. |_____|_____|_____|

4. acted kindly in their criticism
   of the work. |_____|_____|_____|

5. avoided placing blame and
   making excuses. |_____|_____|_____|

Teachers might use the same form as an evaluative exercise in consensus if they instruct the group members to discuss the criteria and come up with an assessment of each category that all members of the group can accept (see Figure 6.9). With this rubric, requesting that each student sign his or her name at the bottom of the form before submitting it to the teacher can also be useful. Often no signature is requested when students are evaluating each other or the group as a whole. However, affixing the signature to the consensus rubric adds a serious tone and importance to the process of group evaluation. It signals that the teacher expects thoughtful discussion and group decisions on the rubric categories.

Teachers can collect the forms, or students can keep the formative self-evaluations and group evaluations in their portfolios for periodic review by the teacher. In either case, such formative assessments by students can provide valuable information through which the teacher can assess individual progress and also evaluate the process by which he or she is selecting group composition from one collaborative or cooperative learning activity to the next.

When the teacher wants a less structured assessment, he or she may assign a short journal response in which the student reflects on the cooperative learning activity, his or her own participation, the effectiveness of the group, and the value of the assignment.

Figure 6.9. Rubric for Group Evaluation by Consensus

Our group members are   _____ _____

                             _____ _____

We have evaluated our work and come to agreement on the following:

Criteria	Needs Improvement	Good	Excellent
The group...			
1. made good use of time.	_____	_____	_____
2. took turns giving information.	_____	_____	_____
3. made only productive comments to each other.	_____	_____	_____
4. listened well to each other.	_____	_____	_____
5. finished the assigned work well.	_____	_____	_____

Our signatures below indicate that each of us has agreed with the above evaluation.

Student: _____ Student: _____

Student: _____ Student: _____

Comments:

Summative Evaluations After a Collaborative or Cooperative Learning Activity

Several assessment tools can be used to evaluate the goals of the student-active learning activity. In some cases, the students know ahead of time exactly the type of assessment to be done after completion of the activity. In other instances, the teacher gives the students a range of possible assessments that the teacher may use to evaluate their competence. After a Jigsaw activity in which students take sections of a chapter, they must identify the important concepts in that section, create a series of crucial questions, and list criteria for acceptable answers to those questions. For example, the teacher may stipulate that

Individual accountability will be ensured in one or more of the following ways: teacher monitoring of Jigsaw activity work; an essay response based on questions formulated during the activity; a class discussion of the questions and responses generated; an objective quiz on the content of the questions formulated and responses generated. (Bevevino & Snodgrass, 1998, p. 67)

At all times, students need to expect an assessment to occur with or following the teacher's debriefing.

When students demonstrate what they've learned by giving a group presentation, how can the teacher ensure that each member assumes responsibility for the presentation? One way to do so is to include directions in the collaborative or cooperative learning directions guide outlining the tasks to be presented to the whole class at the end of the activity. If the group comprises four members, the teacher can stipulate that the group must decide who will summarize the section assigned, who will ask the crucial questions that the group has created to address the concepts presented in the section, who will give the acceptable answers to those questions, and who will list important information on the board as the others speak.

Assuring listening accountability can be a problem when students do presentations for the class. The teacher can insist that the audience take notes or follow the presentation with a series of reinforcing questions addressed to the audience. If the teacher chooses to do the latter, the four members of the presenting group can judge the correctness of the responses. Additionally, the teacher can assign the audience the task of completing peer evaluations on each group and deciding a group grade for each presentation. The use of the group grade done by the student listeners is particularly valuable if all groups have seen the rubric and understand that their classmates will be evaluating them during the post-activity presentation. Figure 6.10 shows an example of a peer evaluation form.

The teacher may choose to average the points given to each group for a group grade by averaging the totals given by the student evaluators, adding that average to the teacher's own evaluation total for the group and dividing that sum by 2 to arrive at a composite assessment by both students and teacher. Figure 6.11 is an example of a student evaluator's totals and the teacher evaluation combined as one collaborative grade.

FIGURE 6.10. PEER EVALUATION OF GROUP PRESENTATION

Group Number: _____

Criteria	Needs Work	Acceptable	Good	Excellent	Total
1. Everyone did his/her share.	0	1	2	3	_____
2. Everyone was prepared to present.	0	1	2	3	_____
3. Everyone was audible.	0	1	2	3	_____
4. The questions were useful for review.	0	1	2	3	_____
5. The group gave information useful for review.	0	1	2	3	_____

Total points given out of a possible 15 points: _____

Optional Comments:

FIGURE 6.11. STUDENT AND TEACHER COLLABORATIVE EVALUATION OF GROUP PRESENTATION

---

1. Add all student evaluation totals for Group 1   = 352 points
2. Divide the sum by the number of student evaluators
    $352 \div 25$ = 14.08 points
3. Add the student evaluators' average score and the teacher's evaluation for Group 1 (12 points)
    $14.08 + 12$ = 26.08 points
4. Divide 26.08 by 2 to arrive at the collaborative grade
    $26.08 \div 2$ = 13.04

The teacher may use the peer evaluations in yet another way: for debriefing discussion on the format of group presentations and the extent to which the groups presented their information well in this instance. Some guiding questions for debriefing follow:

♦ In general, what did you note as the strongest qualities of any of the presentations?

- ◆ What are specific examples of the ways in which each of these positive qualities was exhibited?

- ◆ As you watched and listened to the groups, what occurred to you about the way the presentations were organized?

- ◆ Thinking of individual presenters, what is one good point about any one student's presentation? Thinking of the six groups presenting, which group gave the best presentation? What made it so good?

- ◆ If your group were to present again, what might you want to do the same as you did today?

- ◆ If your group were to present again, what improvements might you suggest that the group members consider?

- ◆ What advice can we list for each other so that the next presentations are as good or even better than these group presentations?

These peer evaluations can lead to further discussion of additional concepts and information that need to be reinforced, clarified, or emphasized.

With some collaborative and cooperative learning activities, the teacher wishes the group to designate one representative to present its findings. If this is done, the rubric in Figure 6.12 might be used by the teacher and/or the students to evaluate the presentation.

FIGURE 6.12. DESIGNATED PRESENTER EVALUATION RUBRIC

Criteria	Work on This	Good	Excellent
	(1)	(2)	(3)
1. Getting attention of audience	1	2	3
2. Eye contact	1	2	3
3. Easily heard	1	2	3
4. Use of visuals	1	2	3
5. Enthusiasm	1	2	3
6. Questioning to encourage audience to respond	1	2	3

Total points out of 18 possible points   _____

The teacher may wish to close a student-active learning exercise with a whole-class discussion in which he or she asks guiding questions, choosing at random the student who must answer. In this way, the students know that they are accountable for all material and may be called upon during any stage of the discussion to respond. Some teachers ensure randomness during this question-answer session by drawing names from a box and calling on students by previously assigned numbers in groups, such as Student 1 from Group A. It is important that students realize that they may be called on more than once.

When the closing evaluation is to be done as an essay response, the teacher should be very specific in instructing the students. For example, the essay question might stipulate that the students give information that they have learned in the following manner: two items of information from each of the four sections of the chapter. They should also select two more items from any section for a total of 10 points.

ADDITIONAL ASSESSMENT TOOLS FOR USE WITH COLLABORATIVE AND COOPERATIVE ACTIVITIES

Performance assessments, response journals, and portfolios provide additional evaluation tools for teachers to use in connection with student-active learning experiences.

PERFORMANCE ASSESSMENT

In formative performance assessment, the teacher observes and judges what a student can do in a certain setting instead of relying on a chapter test, an achievement stanine report, or another more indirect assessment of student competence (Resnick & Resnick, 1992). In one example of formative performance assessment, Retzlaff (1998) uses the following rubric to judge her students as they participate in activities that she created for a middle-school unit on magnetism and electricity. Using the rubric, she evaluates each student by indicating a 3 as excellent, a 2 as fair, and a 1 as needs work. For each student, this rubric also provides an easy average if the teacher wishes to record a point total as part of the unit grade. Figure 6.13 is an example of a formative performance rubric.

FIGURE 6.13. FORMATIVE PERFORMANCE RUBRIC FOR A MIDDLE SCHOOL SCIENCE UNIT

Student Performance—Magnetism and Electricity

(Student Identified by Number)

The student is . . .	1	2	3	4	5	6	7
participating in group discussions, trying to communicate ideas. The discussion is task related.	3	1	3				
demonstrating the point of the lesson that is being used in the activity.	2	1	1				
asking relevant questions and offering explanations and predictions. The student is enthusiastically engaging in activities.	2	1	1				
Average	2.3	1	1.6				

Summative performance assessments can combine the questions on content usually covered in a pencil and paper test with oral explanation in which the student has the opportunity to clarify, explain, and/or expand on the processes and skills taught. In science classes, for example, the performance assessment can utilize the models, specimens, and equipment previously used by the student to complete class activities and labs. Although criticized as being time consuming and unwieldy to implement, performance assessments can be very valuable in judging the depth of a student's knowledge. Designing a rubric to be used during a summative oral presentation assessment guides the student in preparing for the examination and gives the teacher well-defined parameters for evaluating the student responses. For an eighth-grade science class that has completed a unit on electricity and magnetism, Retzlaff (1998) has designed the following rubric for use with videotaped performance assessment. This rubric contains space for notes during the assessment and categories for content knowledge, critical thinking processes, and conceptual grasp (see Figure 6.14).

**FIGURE 6.14. SUMMATIVE PERFORMANCE ASSESSMENT
OF ORAL PRESENTATION RUBRIC**

Performance Rubric: Science

	Content Knowledge	*Critical Thinking Processes*	*Conceptual Grasp*
Static Electricity			
Current Electricity			
Magnetism			
Electromagnetism			

Content knowledge: *Definitions, examples, explanation*

Critical thinking processes: *Can perform procedural skills, uses logical explanations, shows plausible relationships*

Conceptual grasp: *Firm understanding of the idea, can make comparisons and connections*

RESPONSE JOURNALS

A useful assessment tool is the response journal. Here the student responds periodically to teacher-initiated questions that bring together various concepts or ask the student to make connections between what has been studied previously and the implications that the student predicts will be part of the new work in class. Such entries are understood to be informal pieces of writing, not to be corrected for grammar and spelling, but to be evaluated only for accuracy, or plausibility of predictions, or logical thought processes as students relate what they've learned to the question at hand. Teachers can complete periodic evaluations with a simple code such as that suggested by Zaremba and Schultz (1993). The evaluation is made on a three-part basis: the student can earn a check-plus ($\sqrt{+}$), a check ($\sqrt{}$), or a check-minus ($\sqrt{-}$). The check-plus designates that the entry is "insightful and thoroughly done" (p. 66); a check indicates that the student has completed the assignment at a level acceptable to the teacher; a check-minus is called for when the entry is incomplete either because of insufficient understanding of the concepts underlying the response assignment or too little time spent on the assignment. Each time the teacher collects the response journal from the student, a check sheet, such as that displayed in Figure 6.15, can be used. The student can keep the check sheet stapled to the inside cover of the response journal.

FIGURE 6.15. SUMMATIVE RESPONSE JOURNAL CHECK SHEET

Response Journal Check Sheet for _____

                           (Student's Name)

Criteria:

     check-plus ($\sqrt{+}$) = excellent response, insightful and thoroughly answered

     check ($\sqrt{}$) = good response, addressing the question adequately

     check-minus ($\sqrt{-}$) = insufficient argument, information, or examples; too little time spent on the response

Response Journal Collection Date: $\sqrt{-}$ $\sqrt{}$ $\sqrt{+}$

comments on Entry #:

Response Journal Collection Date: $\sqrt{-}$ $\sqrt{}$ $\sqrt{+}$

comments on Entry #:

Response Journal Collection Date: $\sqrt{-}$ $\sqrt{}$ $\sqrt{+}$

comments on Entry #:

NOTE

If the teacher collects the response journals twice each quarter and chooses at random one of the responses included in the journal each time, then the teacher can assign points for the journal entries to be averaged in the quarter grade.

Teachers can employ response journals to prepare students for small-group discussion or whole-class review. Used regularly, the response journal can help students keep up with the development of course material, encourage clarity and depth of thought processes, and highlight problems in student analysis.

PORTFOLIO ASSESSMENT

The portfolio process is another form of performance assessment. As with all assessment tools, teachers may want to begin by analyzing the reason for its use. In what ways will students benefit by the inclusion of portfolio assessment in the classroom?

This type of evaluative tool is characterized by a variety of content and also by its collaborative nature. To build the portfolio, the student works with the teacher to create and then select examples of his or her best work. The use of the portfolio encourages a deeper self-reflection on the course and the content studied. A portfolio in which students include their response journal samples or their assessment of collaborative and cooperative activities done in class can provide illumination for the teacher and also can help the students to understand what they have learned and the manner in which they have learned it. As the students pick work samples for inclusion in their portfolios, they also use evaluative problem-solving skills.

However, the portfolio process works best when teachers voluntarily agree to adopt this form of student assessment. Teachers need to decide the projects for portfolio assessment dependent on their own estimate of curriculum requirements and emphasis. Because portfolios should be evaluated on a formative as well as a summative basis, teachers need to read formative inclusions as *works in progress*, looking for and encouraging development and positive change.

One of the pleasant surprises of portfolio implementation is that students may begin informal dialogue in the peer assessment process. When Larry implemented portfolios in his ninth-grade English class last semester, he was ready for students to follow his list of samples to be included and for them to also participate in peer evaluations of their writing. He didn't expect the side comments written on the students' own drafts. They began to engage in informal dialogues with their partners, showing that they were really reflecting on the quality of their work. After Brady finished a peer critique of Eric's character sketch, Eric wrote on the margin of his peer critique form, "Until you said that I made up a neat villain, I didn't think it was very good. Now that I look at my bad guy, he does look really bad! That's good, right?" In her 10th-grade biology class, Maureen read over the response journal entries written by her students on their opinion of the parent portfolio review form that she had used the previous week. A student had written, "I can't remember my mom reading over my school work since middle school. When I asked her to complete the form, she sat down and read everything in my folder. Now she asks me about biology. I've even explained some stuff to her!" The dialogues generated by portfolio implementation can extend beyond the teacher's expectations.

Last, the teacher should realize that he or she has to reevaluate and reshape portfolio requirements and projects as the year progresses. Reading students' response journals on the requirements and projects and asking for parent observations on student work provide data for the teacher to use in such reevaluation. Figure 6.16 demonstrates all contributors to portfolio assessment.

FIGURE 6.16. PORTFOLIO ASSESSMENT: WHO EVALUATES?

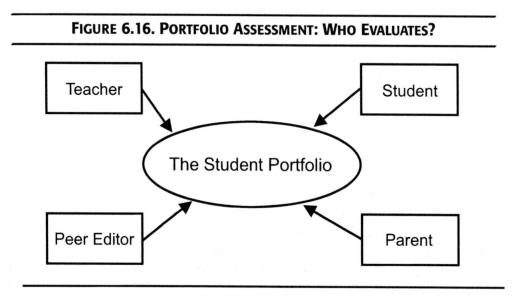

A student's working portfolio should contain the teacher's specific course goals and additional objectives which the teacher wishes the student to attain as well as the student's own list of goals. It should contain formative peer assessments. One example of a formative peer assessment is the "Peer Editing Guide" created by Susol (1997), shown in Figure 6.17.

Formative parent assessments are a valuable part of the continuing portfolio assessment process. DiIulio's "Parent Portfolio Evaluation: Quarter I" (in DiIulio, 1998) is designed to encourage parent-student and parent-teacher collaboration on a quarterly basis (see Figure 6.18).

The student may be instructed to arrange the contents of his or her portfolio according to the three divisions of course goals, teacher objectives, and student goals, or the arrangement may be left up to the student. Yancey (1992) suggests that

> including some sort of summary sheet can help the students set their own course of learning and invite teacher assistance in doing so. On

---

FIGURE 6.17. FORMATIVE PEER ASSESSMENT: PEER EDITING GUIDE

Group Members:_____ _____ Date: _____

_____ _____

Name of the author who will be served by this critique: _____

Answer the questions below in complete sentences. Be Kind—Be Useful!

1. What are two things that stand out in this piece as being particularly good or interesting?

   a.

   b.

2. Point out at least two things that seem unclear or that could be improved upon. Remember, this is your *opinion* so you must *justify* your statements about this work. Give your reasons for the suggestions.

   a.

   reason:

   b.

   reason:

3. Suggest at least three goals for revision that may assist the author in improving the quality of the text.

   a.

   b.

   c.

4. Share any additional positive reactions, comments, or recommendations here.

**Figure 6.18. Formative Parent Assessment
of Portfolio Progress**

Parent Portfolio Evaluation

Quarter 1

Dear Parent or Guardian,

As part of your child's portfolio assessment, I am requiring that a parent evaluation be included of the material submitted. This is an attempt to enable you to view your child's written assignments and monitor the progress made throughout the school year. Your input is important and I will appreciate your comments. Thank you.

Mrs. DiIlulio

Student Name:_____

Parent/Guardian Name:_____

Please comment on the following:

1. Does the student portfolio meet the criteria as explained on the student requirement sheet?

2. Did you discuss the selections for inclusion in the portfolio with your son or daughter?

3. What improvements did he or she make on the selections in the working portfolio before finishing them for the summative quarterly portfolio?

4. Were you able to make any suggestions for improvement? (neatness, presentation, other?)

5. Other comments:

_____   _____
            Signature   Date

---

these summary sheets, the students can note their perceptions of certain portfolio pieces and their relative status; for instance, "ready for presentational portfolio" or "flawed brilliance, [never] to be tackled again." (p. 109)

DiIulio (1998) created portfolio requirements for her ninth-grade English students; these requirements are shown in Figure 6.19.

FIGURE 6.19. SUMMATIVE PORTFOLIO REQUIREMENTS AND TEACHER EVALUATION

Portfolio Assessment Rubric: Quarter 2

Requirement	*Points*
1. All deficiencies from last quarter's portfolio are corrected. Those that do not need corrections receive free points.	10 ____

Include on RIGHT side of portfolio:

2. Table of contents (revised) with list of articles typed on left and page numbers of only the first page of an article to the right.	10 ____
3. Five new selections (total of eight including last quarter).	25 ____

Period 1 and 7: one selection must be the *To Kill a Mockingbird* essay.

Period 2 and 3: one selection must be the *Romeo and Juliet* essay.

Period 4 and 8: one selection must be the poetry pamphlet.

Include on LEFT side of folder:

Parent evaluation (completed and signed)	5 ____
Personal evaluation	5 ____
Peer evaluation	5 ____
Teacher evaluation form	5 ____
All previous evaluation forms	5 ____
(last graded teacher evaluation to be signed by parent)	5 ____

TOTAL AESTHETIC VALUE (includes neatness, revi-   25   _____
    sions, content, grammar, spelling, creativity)

TOTAL   100   _____

DiIulio also incorporates peer evaluation and parent evaluation as part of the formative portfolio process. Peers give students feedback when they receive their quarterly portfolio assessment evaluation as shown in Figure 6.20.

**FIGURE 6.20. SECOND QUARTER PORTFOLIO
ASSESSMENT: PEER EVALUATION**

Name of student: _____

Name of student critiquing: _____

1. Are there five new selections for a total of eight selections in this portfolio?
2. What is your favorite item in the portfolio?
3. What area needs the most improvement in your opinion?
4. Is the table of contents consistent with the selections and do the page numbers coordinate?
5. What would you change about the portfolio if it were yours?

All students must complete a self-evaluation as they look critically at their own work. Figure 6.21 illustrates DiIulio's self-evaluation rubric.

**FIGURE 6.21. SECOND QUARTER PORTFOLIO ASSESSMENT:
SUMMATIVE PERSONAL EVALUATION**

Student Name: _____ Date: _____

1. I have met all the requirements for the second quarter portfolio assessment:
2. My greatest weakness in this portfolio is
3. My greatest strength in this portfolio is
4. I made improvements in the second quarter from the first quarter in the following ways:
5. I hope to improve in the following areas for the third quarter portfolio assessment:

> **NOTE**
>
> Adding the requirement that students need to explain their answers in Question 2 and describe the area of needed improvement for Question 3 will increase student critical thinking in the rubric presented in Figure 6.21.

In addition to a working portfolio, the process dictates a final or summative portfolio in which the student compiles the best of his or her work. The student can present this completed portfolio as representative of his or her best effort and competence.

For the student to complete this portfolio well, the teacher should create a list of entries and options for inclusion. Figure 6.22 is a guide for possible inclusions adapted from suggestions by Yancey (1992).

FIGURE 6.22. SUMMATIVE PORTFOLIO INCLUSIONS

Title page

Table of contents

Acknowledgments

Statement of grade; justification for grade chosen

Inclusions of specific project examples (indicate specific types and number of each type)

Reflection on the course and the student's learning process

ADDITIONAL WRITING ASSESSMENTS

Many approaches to writing in the content areas exist. Posamentier and Stepelman (1995) list student journals and student logs, for example, as alternative assessment tools in the area of mathematics. They also suggest that the mathematics teacher consider having students work with content through the expository writing mode. They might write an explanation of a process, for example, the uses of multiplication and addition in the calculation of probability, after they have finished a series of problems and checked them with their partners. The students might be asked to explain a process, such as the way in which an algebraic equation can be simplified, or to explain a theorem.

Students can write their interpretation of a graph presented by the teacher, or they can wrestle with a verbal explanation of their cooperative learning group's correct solution to a problem. A challenging writing assignment is the request that students connect some mathematical concept studied to a current real-world problem or situation as described in the local newspaper.

In addition, students can write explanations for each other of a concept not clearly understood after textbook reading and teacher explanation. Working through the explanation and listening to the expressions of their group members followed by whole-class discussion can be invaluable in nurturing a deeper understanding of the mathematical concept. Posamentier and Stepelman suggest that a concept be explored through writing by asking the students to generalize, for example, to consider "the Pythagorean theorem and see if it can be generalized to a power higher than two (Fermat's last theorem), or whether a consideration of three dimensions might prove enlightening, or whether it can be generalized to triangles other than right triangles (law of cosines)" (1995, p. 11). Such assignments help students to understand how they are learning as well as what they are learning.

How should the mathematics teacher evaluate such writing assignments? First of all, not all writing assignments need to be collected and evaluated individually. Small-group members may share the results of the writing assignment as the teacher circulates, listening for commonalities and problems. The writing assignments can be presented to the entire class for discussion. Periodically, the teacher can collect the mathematics journal or log and choose an entry to evaluate on a more formal basis. Although all teachers can evaluate for grammar and spelling as well as for their content area, the advantage of writing in mathematics classrooms is that it clarifies, extends, and explains concepts and their connections to the real world. Posamentier and Stepelman (1995, p. 11) give possible criteria for teachers to use in evaluating student writing. This evaluative checklist for student logs in mathematics can be a useful addition to mathematics portfolios as well. These criteria are summarized in Figure 6.23.

Science teachers make use of student collaboration to carry out laboratory experiments. The sharing of equipment and duties helps to make science come to life for students who work as partners to carry out a lab assignment. Ultimately the student may be judged individually on his or her lab report and unit test, but teachers can also incorporate evaluation of the process and the writing of the report. One such assessment might combine the elements listed on Figure 6.24. This type of assessment sheet can also be included as an evaluation of student progress in the student portfolio.

FIGURE 6.23. EVALUATING MATHEMATICS WRITING ENTRIES

Evaluation Checklist: Writing Entries

Student Name:

Log Number:

1. The explanation

    _____ is precise, clear, unambiguous

    _____ is imprecise, too brief, or ambiguous

    _____ is so unclear that it is not useful

    _____ contains accurate diagrams

    _____ contains inaccurate or some incorrectly labeled diagrams

    _____ contains no diagrams or diagrams are too small to work with, too

    many inaccuracies

2. Student Knowledge

    _____ is well described, recognizing the differences between necessary

    and sufficient conditions

    _____ is adequately described with differences between necessary and

    sufficient conditions recognized

    _____ is inadequately described with insufficient recognition of the dif-

    ferences between necessary and sufficient conditions

3. Student Grasp of Content

    _____ justifies implications well

    _____ attempts to justify implications

    _____ does not realize that implications need to be justified

    _____ exhibits awareness of what constitutes a proper proof

    _____ is unaware of what constitutes a proper proof

FIGURE 6.24. ASSESSMENT SHEET: LABORATORY WORK AND REPORTS

Student Lab: Work on Conservation of Momentum

Lab Setup

0–5	15	30	_____ 30%
Took too long to start and needed teacher guidance to follow initial directions	Started with little time wasted and followed directions with few problems	Started quickly obtaining equipment and following initial directions well	

Care/Use of Equipment

0–5	15	30	_____ 10%
Careless and/or inappropriate use	Careful use with a few problems	Careful and appropriate use	

Collaboration with Partner

0–5	15	30	_____ 15%
Refused to help	Helped somewhat	Actively collaborated	

Procedure and Data Use

0–5	15	30	_____ 20%
Procedures not followed; data not used correctly	Procedures followed; data used with some problems	Procedures followed correctly; data used appropriately	

Report Organization with Scientific Method

0–5	15	30	_____ 15%
Not organized correctly	Satisfactory	Organized well	

Overall Appearance of Lab Report

0–5	15	30	_____ 10%
Done carelessly and/or hard to read	Done acceptably and readable	Well done and legible	

ROLE-PLAYING GUIDES

Teachers can use the collaborative strategy of role-playing in their classes in order to help students experience the reality of events studied or to help them put into practice the content taught. Students may have a hard time stepping into such an activity. They may fear embarrassment or feel anxious, but guidelines can decrease such problems. For her Spanish class, Ms. Oberrath has set up guidelines for partners to practice destination, time of day, and vocabulary dealing with travel. Figure 6.25 is an adaptation of her guidelines.

FIGURE 6.25. ROLE-PLAYING GUIDELINES
FOR SPANISH TRAVEL UNIT

When you begin to role-play with your partner, take turns playing two roles: one as the traveler and the other as the check-in person at the airport. Include these points:

Debes incluir:

> el destino
>
> la hora de la salida y de la llegada
>
> la puerta corecta
>
> el numero de maletas que puedes tener
>
> de ida solamente o de ida y vuelta
>
> si necesitas pasaporte
>
> otras ideas originales

After role-playing both roles, answer these questions:

1. List what you felt comfortable doing and able to do acceptably:

2. List areas that caused you trouble.

3. For the next travel role-playing practice, what do you suggest that partners do for better practice?

LEARNING STATIONS CHECKLIST

A very useful activity for collaboration in any classroom is the implementation of learning stations set up so students can proceed through a series of learning activities. A simple checklist carried by each student facilitates movement and also ensures that students are aware of their individual accountability at each station. Figure 6.26 illustrates an adaptation of a simple checklist designed by Reynolds (1997) for her ninth-grade learning station activity on short stories.

FIGURE 6.26. CHECKLIST FOR LEARNING STATIONS

Fill out this checklist for each station. At the end of the four stations, attach all assigned work to this checklist. Put the checklist in the wire basket on the window ledge when you have completed four stations to the best of your ability.

Name:

Partner/partners:

Station	Completed
Station #1	
Story pyramid "On the Bridge"	_____
Eight sentences	_____
Station #2	
Character map	_____
Bio poem	_____
Character questions	_____
Station #3	
Draw a character	_____
Descriptive word	_____
Drama activity	
Acting	_____
Viewing	_____
Station #4	
Writing relay activity	_____
Oral reading in partners	_____
Discussion of stories	_____

Please fill out the following AT THE CONCLUSION OF THE STATION ACTIVITIES:

I would like to do stations in the same way again. _____(yes) _____(no)

I would like to suggest changes as listed below for future work in stations:

Sign your name below or explain the reason for not feeling that you did your best.

I attest that these station assignments have been completed to the best of my ability.

_____   _____

            Signature   Date

I did not do my best work because...

A learning station checklist can also function as a self-evaluation for the student to use during the learning stations and for the teacher to consult at the completion of the stations. Quadri (1997) uses a checklist that functions during the learning stations and after the activities have been completed (see Figure 6.27). Students assign point values as they complete the activities; the teacher also adds points for station assignments in Station 1 and Station 6 after correcting the work produced at those stations.

CONCLUSION

Through the use of a variety of assessments, teachers can create a more complete picture of each student's academic and social progress. Such a composite makes diagnosis for improvement more comprehensive. Multiple indicators allow the teacher to assess many strengths and give the students more opportunities to express their competence. Because of the analytical nature of many of these assessment tools, students learn to evaluate their own progress and development, realizing how they learn what they learn.

As Resnick and Resnick (1992, p. 59) have pointed out, "You get what you assess." Creating multiple assessment tools to evaluate collaborative and cooperative learning activities emphasizes the importance of productive cooperation, in-depth analysis, problem solving, and group processes. It nurtures an in-depth approach to the middle school and high school content areas.

FIGURE 6.27. CHECKLIST FOR LEARNING STATIONS USING SELF-EVALUATION AND TEACHER EVALUATION

Name: Self-Awarded Points

Station 1

My partner and I arranged the essay and left it in the
folder at the stations. (Additional points up to 4 will be   _____ (1)
awarded when the teacher corrects the essay.)

Station 2

My partner and I identified all errors on the first try.   _____ (2)

OR   OR

My partner and I identified all the errors.   _____ (1)

Station 3

My partner and I corrected each sentence.   _____ (1)

We had 17 or more right when we used the correction key.   _____ (1)

Station 4

My partner and I watched the video and wrote the uses of
dialect as we heard them.   _____ (1)

We analyzed our own everyday speech and listed phrases
in dialect that we use.   _____ (1)

Station 5

My partner and I corrected each sentence.   _____ (1)

We had 7 or more right when we used the self-correction
key.   _____ (1)

Station 6

I selected a picture and listed 10 descriptive words about
it.   _____ (1)

Then I wrote a descriptive paragraph about the picture
and turned it in. (Additional points up to 4 will be   _____ (1)
awarded after teacher correction.)

Your total of self-evaluated points   _____ out of 12
Teacher evaluation of your work from Stations 1 and 6 _____ out of 8
Total Score for Station Activities   _____ out of 20

REFERENCES

Ackman, S. (1997). *Bacteria and viruses*. Unpublished Unit Plan.

Anderson, H. H. (1939). Domination and integration in the social behavior of kindergarten children in an experimental play situation. *Genetic Psychology Monographs, 2*, 357–385.

Adger, C., Kalyanpur, M., Peterson, D., & Bridger, T. (1995*). Engaging students: Thinking, talking, cooperating*. Thousand Oaks, CA: Corwin Press, Inc.

Aronson, E., Blaney, N., Stephan, C., Sikes, J., & Snapp, M . (1978*). The jigsaw classroom*. Beverly Hills, CA: Sage.

Ashworth, M.,(1992). *The first step on the longer path: Becoming an ESL teacher*. Markham, Ontario: Pippen Publishing Limited.

Beadle, M. E., & Perrico, R. (1990). *Collaboration among speech and writing teachers: Toward recognizing patterns of methodology*. Paper presented at the 76th Annual meeting of the Speech Communication Association (Chicago, IL, November 1–4, 1990).

Bechtel, R. (1997). *Living matter*. Unpublished Unit Plan.

Berry, L. (1991). *Collaborative learning: A program for improving the retention of minority students*. (ERIC Document Reproduction No. ED384 323)

Bevevino, M., Dengel, J., & Adams, K. (1999). Constructivist theory in the classroom: Internalizing concepts through inquiry learning. *The Clearing House, 72*, (5) 22–27.

Bevevino, M., & Snodgrass, D. (1998). Revisiting coooperative learning…and making it work: Success with cooperative learning on the secondary level. *NASSP Bulletin, 82*, (597) 64–69.

Bond, C. (1998). *Romeo and Juliet*. Unpublished Unit Plan.

Borko, H., Flory, M., & Cumbo, K. (1993). *Teachers' ideas and practices about assessment and instruction: A case study of the effects of alternative assessment in instruction, student learning and accountability practices*. National Center for Research on Evaluation, Standards, and Student Testing (CRESST), Graduate School of Education, University of California, Los Angeles, CA.

Brazelton, T . (1992). *Touchpoints: Your child's emotional and behavioral development*. New York: Addison Wesley Publishing Co.

Bruffee, K. (1987, March–April). The art of collaborative learning, *Changes*, 42–47.

Bruffee, K. (1995). Sharing our toys: Cooperative learning versus collaborative learning, *Changes*, 12–18.

Callahan, J.F., Clark, L.H., & Kellough, R.D. (1992). *Teaching in the middle and secondary schools (4th ed.)*. New York: Macmillan Publishing Co.

Clark, L. H., & Starr, I. S. (1991). *Secondary and middle school teaching methods (6th ed.)* New York: Macmillan Publishing Co.

Cohen, E. (1997). *Designing group work: Strategies for the heterogeneous classroom*. New York: Teachers College Press.

Cooper, J. M. (Ed.). (1990). *Classroom teaching skills*. Lexington, MA: D.C. Heath and Company.

Cooper, J., & Mueck, R. (1990). Student involvement in learning: Cooperative learning and college instruction. *Journal on Excellence in College Teaching, 1,* 68–76.

Davidson, N. (1994). Cooperative and collaborative learning. In J. S. Thousand, R. A. Villa, and A. I. Nevin (Eds.), *Creativity and collaborative learning: A practical guide to empowering students and teachers* (pp. 13–29). Baltimore, MD: Brookes Publishing Co.

DeJong, C. & Hawley, J. (1995). Making cooperative learning groups work. *Middle School Journal*, March, 45–48.

Deutsch, M. (1949). An experimental study of the effects of co-operation and competition upon group process. *Human Relations, 2,* 199–231.

Deutsch, M., & Krauss, R.M. (1965). *Theories in social psychology*. New York: Basic Books.

Dewey, J. (1963). *Democracy in education*. New York: Collier Publishers, Inc.

DiIulio, P. B. (1998). *A Study to determine the improvement in secondary student writing through the use of a quarterly portfolio assessment*. Unpublished Master's Degree Thesis. Edinboro University of PA.

Dishon, D., & O'Leary, P. (1994). *Cooperative learning: Developing minds: A resource book for teaching thinking*. Holmes Beach, FL: Learning Publications.

Donato, M. (1992). TALK checklist. In J. L. Shrum and E. W. Glisen, *Teacher's handbook: Contextualized language instruction*. Boston, MA: Heinle and Heinle, 1994.

Dunn, R. S., Dunn, K. J., & Price, G. E. (1986). *Learning style inventory manual*. Lawrence, KS: Price Systems.

Ellis, S., & Whalen, S. (1990). *Cooperative learning: Getting started*. New York: Scholastic Professional Books, Scholastic Inc.

Flexer, R. J., & Gerstner, E. A. (1993). *Dilemmas and issues for teachers developing performance assessments in mathematics*. Paper presented at the Annual Meeting of the American Educational Research Association, Atlanta, GA.

Foyle, H., & Lyman, F. (1989). The responsive classroom discussion. In A. S. Anderson (Ed.), *Mainstreaming Digest*. College Park: University of Maryland College of Education.

Frederiksen, J. R., & Collins, A. (1989, Dec.). A systems approach to educational testing. *Educational Researcher, 18* (9), 27–32.

Fritchman, M. (1996). *French unit plan: The house*. Unpublished Unit Plan.

Gifford, B. R., & O'Connor, M. C. (Eds.). (1992). *Changing assessments: Alternative views of aptitude, achievement, and instruction*. Norwell, MA: Kluwer Academic.

Golub, J., and the Committee on Classroom Practices.(1988). *Focus on collaborative learning: Classroom practices in teaching English, 1988*. Urbana, IL: National.

Goodman, K., Goodman, Y., & Hood, W. (Eds.). (1989). *The whole language evaluation book*. Portsmouth, NH: Heinemann Educational Books.

Griska, A. (1997). *Writing a research paper*. Unpublished Unit Plan.

Guskey, T. R., & Huberman, M. (Eds.). (1995). *Professional development in education: New paradigms and practices*. New York: Teachers College Press.

Hake, S. (1998). *Lord of the flies*. Unpublished Unit Plan.

Hamayan, E. V., & Damico, J. S. (1990). *Limiting bias in the assessment of bilingual students*. Austin, TX: Pro-Ed.

Harris, L. A., & Lalik, R. M. (1987). Teachers' use of informal reading inventories: An example of school constraints. *The Reading Teacher, 40*, 624–630.

Hendren, L., Keely, B., Mason, C., Sullivan, L., & Weissenberg, T. (1993). Earthquake safety guide: The product of an interdisciplinary thematic unit. In R.

D. Kellough, N. C. Kellough, and D. L. Hough, *Middle school teaching: Methods and resources.* New York: Macmillan Publishing Co.

Henson, K. T. (1993). *Methods and srategies for teaching in secondary and middle schools, (2nd. ed.).* New York: Longman.

Hiebert, E. H., & Davinroy, K. (1993, April). *Dilemmas and issues in implementing classroom–based assessment for literacy. A case study of the effects of alternative assessment in instruction, student learning and accountability practices.* Paper presented at the Annual Meeting of the American Educational Research Association (Atlanta, GA, April 12–16, 1993).

Hilke, E. (1990). *Cooperative learning.* Decatur, IL: Phi Delta Kappa.

Huhtala, J. (1994). *Group investigation: Structuring an inquiry-based curriculum.* Paper presented at the Annual Meeting of the American Educational Research Association (New Orleans, April, 1994).

Humphrey, D., Crain, M., & Bergfield, N . (1991). In R. D. Kellough, N. C. Kellough, & D. L. Hough, *Middle school teaching: Methods and resources.* New York: Macmillan Publishing Co.

Hunter, M. (1987). *Motivation theory for teachers.* El Segundo, CA: TIP Publications.

Ingvarson, L. (1990). *Enhancing professional skill and accountability in the assessment of student learning.* Paper presented at the Annual Meeting of the American Educational Research Association (Boston, MA, April 16–20, 1990).

Johnson, D.W., & Johnson, R.T. (1994). Instructional goal structures: Cooperative, competitive, or individualistic. *Review of Educational Research, 44,* 213–235.

Johnson, D.W., & Johnson, R.T. (1999). *Learning together and alone: Cooperative, competitive, and individualistic learning.* New York: Allyn & Bacon.

Johnson, D. W., Johnson, R. T., Holubec, E. J. (1986). *Circles of learning. Cooperation in the classroom.* Edina, MN: Interaction Books.

Johnson, D.W., Johnson, R.T., & Holubec, E.J. (1993). *Cooperation in the Classroom.* Edina, MN: Interaction Books.

Johnson, D. W., Johnson, R. T., & Smith, K. A. (1991*). Active learning: Cooperation in the college classroom.* Edina, MN: Interaction Books.

Johnston, P. (1989*). Theoretical consistencies in reading, writing, literature and teaching.* Paper presented at the Annual Convention of the National Council of Teachers of English.

Joyce, B., & Weil, M. (1980). *Models of teaching.* Englewood Cliffs, NJ: Prentice-Hall.

Kagan, S . (1992). The structural approach to cooperative learning. *Educational Leadership, 47* (4), 12–15.

Kagan, S. (1996). Avoiding the group-grades trap. *Learning.* Jan/Feb, pp 56–58.

Kellough, R. D., Kellough, N. C, & Hough, D. L. (1993). *Middle school teaching: Methods and resources.* New York: Macmillan.

Kinney, J. H. (1991). *A comparison of cooperative learning strategies to traditional learning strategies used on the same group of multicultural ninth grade biology students during the same school year. A research paper regarding a grant for the Alexandria City School Board aimed at improving existing Programs in this school division.*

Linn, R. L., Baker, E. L., & Dunbar, S. B. (1991). Complex, performance-based assessment: Expectations and validation criteria. *Educational Researcher, 20,* 15–21.

Logsdon, K. (1996). *Ecosystems.* Unpublished Unit Plan.

Lunsford, A. (1991). Collaboration, control, and the idea of a writing center. *The Writing Center Journal, 12* (1), 3–10.

Mailer, J.B. (1929). *Cooperation and competition.* New York: Teachers College, Columbia University.

Mayer, A. (1903). Ubereinzel und gesamtleistung des schul kindes. *Archiv fur die Gesamte Psychologie, 1,* 276–416.

Milk, R., Mercado, C., & Sapiens, A. (1992). *Rethinking the education of teachers of language minority children: Developing reflective teachers for changing schools.* Washington, DC: National Clearinghouse for Bilingual Education.

Milner, J. O., & Milner, L.F. (1999). *Bridging English (2nd ed.).* Upper Saddle River, NJ: Merrill.

Monroe, R. (1993). *Writing and thinking with computers: A practical and progressive approach.* Urbana, IL: National Council of Teachers of English.

Nauman, D. (1997). *The short story.* Unpublished Unit Plan.

Newcomb, A. F., Brady, J. E., & Hartup, W. W. (1997). Friendship and incentive condition as determinants of children's task-oriented social behavior. *Child Development, 50,* 878–881.

Oberrath. W. (1996). *Geography and travel.* Unpublished Unit Plan.

Parrenas, C., & Parrenas, F. (1993). Learning, multicultural functioning, and student achievement. In L. M. Malave (Ed.), *Annual Conference Journal*. Proceedings of the National Association for Bilingual Education Conferences (pp. 181–189). Washington, DC: ERIC Document Reproduction No. ED337 540.

Peacock, J. (1997). *Foundations of the American republic*. Unpublished Unit Plan.

Piaget, J. (1980). *Experiments in contradiction*. Chicago: University of Chicago Press.

Posamentier, A. S., & Stepelman, J. (1995). *Teaching secondary school mathematics: Techniques and enrichment units (4th ed.)*. Englewood Cliffs, NJ: Merrill.

Quadri, L. (1997). *The day no pigs would die*. Unpublished Unit Plan.

Quintero, E. P., & Rummel, M. K. (1998). *American voices: Webs of diversity*. Upper Saddle River, NJ: Merrill.

Reed. A . (1994*). Reaching adolescents: The young adult book and the school*. New York: Merrill.

Resnick, L. B., & Resnick, D. L. (1992). Assessing the thinking curriculum: New tools for educational reform. In B. R. Gifford & M. C. O'Connor (Eds.), *Future assessments: Changing views of aptitude, achievement, and instruction* (pp. 37–75). Norwell, MA: Kluwer Academic.

Retzlaff, K. L. (1998). Performance assessment rubric. *A study to determine to what extent student achievement in a unit on electricity and magnetism is affected by a constructivist approach to lessons as compared to a traditional approach.* Unpublished Master's Degree Thesis, Edinboro University of PA.

Reynolds, S. (1997). *The short story*. Unpublished Unit Plan.

Schipke, R. C. (1991). Using Computer journals to teach critical thinking skills and the writing process. In W. Wresch (Ed.), *The English classroom in the computer age: Thirty lesson plans* (pp. 84–94). Urbana, IL: National Council of Teachers of English.

Sharan, S. (1990). *Cooperative learning: Theory and research*. New York: Praeger.

Sharan, S., Ackerman, Z., & Hertz-Lazarowitz, R. (1980). Academic achievement of elementary school children in small groups vs. whole class instruction. *Journal of Experimental Education, 48*, 125–129.

Sharan, Y., & Sharan, S. (1992). *Expanding cooperative learning through group investigation*. New York: Teachers College Press.

Shepard, L. A., & Bliem, C. L. (1993, Apr.). *Parent opinions about standardized tests, teacher's information and performance assessments.* Paper presented at the Annual Meeting of the American Educational Research Assoication (Atlanta, GA, April).

Shrum, J. L., & Glisan, E. W. (1994). *Teacher's handbook: Contextualized language instruction.* Boston, MA: Heinle and Heinle.

Simmons-O'Neill, E. (1990). *Evaluating sources: Strategies for faculty-librarian-student collaboration.* Paper presented at the Annual Meeting of the Conference on College Composition and Communication. (Chicago, IL, March 22–24).

Slavin, R. E. (1994). Synthesis of research on cooperative learning. *Educational Leadership, 48* (5), 71–82.

Slavin, R. E. (1995). *Cooperative learning (2nd ed.).* New York: Allyn & Bacon.

Slavin, R. E., & Tanner, A.M. (1979). Effects of cooperative reward structures and individual accountability on productivity and learning. *Journal of Educational Research, 72,* 294–298.

Stendler, C., Damrin, D., & Haines, A.C. (1951). Studies in cooperation and competition: The effects of working for group and individual rewards on the social climate of children's groups. *Journal of Genetic Psychology, 79,* 173–197.

Susol, V. (1997). *Descriptive writing and poetry.* Unpublished Unit Plan.

Taylor, P. (Ed.) (1985). *Literature for all students: A sourcebook for teachers.* Los Angeles: Center for Academic Inter-institutional Programs, University of California.

Thelen, H. (1967). *Classroom grouping for teachability.* New York: Wiley.

Thelen, H. (1981). *The classroom society.* London: Croom Helm.

Triplett, N. (1898). The dynamogenic factors in pacemaking and competition. *American Journal of Psychology, 9,* 507–533.

Trowbridge, L. W., & Bybee, R. W. (1990). *Becoming a secondary school science teacher, (5th ed.).* Columbus, OH: Merrill Publishing Company.

Ubbelohde, M. D. (1991). Computer activities with minimal hardware: Debate, continuous story, and mystery sentence. In W. Wresch (Ed.), *The English classroom in the computer age: Thirty lesson plans* (pp. 62–65). Urbana, IL: National Council of Teachers of English.

Vygotsky, L. S. (1978). Mind in society: The development of higher psychological processes. M. Cole, V. John–Steiner, S. Scribner, & E. Sauberman (Eds.). Cambridge, MA: Harvard University Press.

Waychoff, J. (1996). *Linear Equations*. Unpublished Unit Plan.

Well, M. C. (1992). *Improving students' expertise and attitudes during the postwriting stage of the writing process through collaborative revision.* A Practicum Report, Nova University.

Wresch, W. (Ed.). (1991). *The English classroom in the computer age: Thirty lesson plans.* Urbana, IL: National Council of Teachers of English.

Wright. W. (1991). International group work: Using a computer conference to invigorate the writing of your students. In W. Wresch (Ed.), *The English classroom in the computer age: Thirty lesson plans* (pp. 100–103). Urbana, IL: National Council of Teachers of English.

Yancey, K. B. (Ed.). (1992). *Portfolios in the writing classroom: An introduction.* Urbana, IL: National Council of Teachers of English.

Zaremba, S. B., & Schultz, M. T. (1993). *An analysis of traditional classroom assessment techniques and a discussion of alternative methods of assessment.* Paper presented to the 7th Annual Conference on Undergraduate Teaching of Psychology: Ideas and Innovations, (Ellenville, NY, Mar. 24–26).

INDEX